KU-263-583

CHURCHILL

THE GREATEST BRITON UNMASKED

CHURCHILL

THE GREATEST BRITON UNMASKED

NIGEL KNIGHT

David and Charles

941.082
CHU

For Sally, Vic, Joy, Ernie and Iris

A DAVID & CHARLES BOOK
Copyright © David & Charles Limited 2008

David & Charles is an F+W Publications Inc. company
4700 East Galbraith Road
Cincinnati, OH 45236

First published in the UK in 2008

Text copyright © Nigel Knight 2008
Photography © see picture credits (page 380)

Nigel Knight has asserted his right to be identified as author of this work
in accordance with the Copyright, Designs and Patents Act, 1988.

All rights reserved. No part of this publication may be reproduced, stored in
a retrieval system, or transmitted, in any form or by any means, electronic or
mechanical, by photocopying, recording or otherwise, without prior permission
in writing from the publisher.

A catalogue record for this book is available from the British Library.

ISBN-13: 978-0-7153-2855-2 hardback
ISBN-10: 0-7153-2855-7 hardback

Printed in Finland by WS Bookwell,
for David & Charles
Brunel House, Newton Abbot, Devon

Commissioning Editor: Neil Baber
Editorial Manager: Emily Pitcher
Editor: Verity Muir
Art Editor: Martin Smith
Designer: Joanna Ley
Project Editor: Beverley Jollands
Production Controller: Kelly Smith

Visit our website at www.davidandcharles.co.uk

David & Charles books are available from all good bookshops; alternatively you
can contact our Orderline on 0870 9908222 or write to us at FREEPOST EX2 110,
D&C Direct, Newton Abbot, TQ12 4ZZ (no stamp required UK only); US customers
call 800-289-0963 and Canadian customers call 800-840-5220.

CONTENTS

INTRODUCTION

Churchill was aristocratic, high-handed, self-centred, energetic, impatient, inconsistent, prone to rhetoric, had great presence and was most stubborn. He was 'brilliant but unsound'.[1] This being so, why is he considered by so many to be the 'Greatest Briton'? His reputation stems from his warnings about German rearmament in the 1930s and his opposition to the British policy of appeasement – a policy that failed to prevent war: this made him appear a great visionary, able to see what others could not. It also rests on his most memorable speeches and, as Prime Minister in World War II, on his identification with victory. All this was helped considerably by the fact that he wrote some of the history of the period himself.

Churchill's early development holds the key to understanding his later actions. He adored his temperamental bully of a father, Lord Randolph, who constantly chastised him. He was dispatched to a preparatory school at the age of seven and suffered at the hands of its sadistic headmaster. These experiences could easily have broken him, but instead he became rebellious and obstinate. At 13 he entered Harrow School; in his academic work he was good at English and little else, but he loved the Cadets and became a good fencer. He instructed the headmaster in how to do his job and was birched repeatedly, but the propensity to instruct those more expert than himself was a trait that would remain with him. Churchill followed his father's political career with enthusiasm and inherited his inconsistencies – which would have dire consequences in his own career. He entered the military academy, Sandhurst, at his third attempt, but gained entry only to the cavalry rather than the intellectually more demanding infantry. At Sandhurst he learned the need for quick decisions and spirited fighting, qualities that he would exhibit much later in his approach to mechanized warfare. He also learned to enjoy himself and to spend money he didn't have.

In 1895 Churchill endured the deaths of both his father and his childhood nurse, to whom he had been very attached as his American mother, Jennie, had ignored him. These experiences hardened his character and convinced him that his life would not be a long one. Ruthlessly exploiting the former position of his father and the current one of his mother in order to further his own career, he established high-ranking political contacts, was inducted into New York society and saw his first military action in Cuba. Here, to his delight, he was shot at for the first time – on his 21st birthday – and acquired a penchant for fine cigars and a daily siesta, which enabled him to work long into the night.

Churchill's military service would be marked by impetuosity and glory-seeking. He acted as both a war correspondent and a military officer suppressing Afghan tribesmen on the North-West Frontier, where he took foolhardy risks but also displayed great bravery. His bumptiousness became increasingly unpopular with the military hierarchy, and when he sought to join Lord Kitchener's expedition to the Sudan his overtures were resisted – but he insisted and went anyway. He wrote accounts of these military actions, indicating what his superiors should have done, that were concerned less with the facts and more with his own interpretation of events. Then he fought a by-election at Oldham on the back of his exploits, which he lost.

By the turn of the century the Boer War had begun in South Africa, and Churchill was anxious to be in the thick of it – as a newspaper reporter, a status that did not prevent him from actively engaging in the shooting war. He was captured and made a risky escape, thanks rather more to luck than to judgment. He was hailed as a hero, became an officer in the South African forces and used his newfound fame to enter Parliament as member for Oldham in 1900. He immediately set off for a lecture tour in North America, where he met President McKinley. In Parliament he alienated his Conservative colleagues by taking up the issue that had prematurely terminated his father's political career while Chancellor of the Exchequer – military expenditure.

All the qualities Churchill exhibited in his early career would be very apparent when he was granted high political office. The first infamous episode was the Gallipoli campaign during World War I, where he sought to break the stalemate on the Western Front with a disastrous assault on Turkey, the most inconsequential member of the Central Powers. The principal characteristics of this adventure recurred several times in World War II, most notably in the campaigns in Norway, North Africa, the Balkans and Italy – Italy being the 'soft underbelly of Europe' in Churchill's words, or the 'tough old gut' as US Lieutenant-General Mark Clark more accurately called it.[2] Churchill was also obsessed with undertaking a military campaign in Sumatra, to the detriment of the war effort. These were 'dispersionist' campaigns, attacking the enemy at its periphery. A direct and decisive assault was always avoided; instead military efforts were undertaken against objectives of little direct strategic importance. The strategy assumed that the enemy would not offer appreciable resistance if attacked in this way – an assumption clearly refuted by the actual resistance met by all these campaigns.

It was the defeat of Germany and Austria–Hungary on the Western Front in World War I that caused the Ottoman Empire to collapse, not the other way around. Similarly, in World War II the defeats of German forces in Norway, North Africa, the Balkans and Italy were not of vital importance to the defeat of Germany, whereas defeating Germany by a direct assault led to the collapse of German forces in those countries. The outcome of World War II in Europe was decided principally by the Soviets on the Eastern Front and by the Western Allies conducting a Second Front in France, not by Churchill's peripheral campaigns, for which Gallipoli, the most infamous, had set the paradigm.

In World War II Churchill mounted a disastrous raid on the French coast at Dieppe, yet procrastinated over mounting the Second Front in France. This increasingly marginalized him, and Britain, from the USA and USSR. More importantly it postponed the conclusion of the war by about a year, during which approximately ten million lives were lost.[3]

Churchill had an obsession with battleships, vastly overemphasizing their importance and committing a disproportionate amount of British resources to the destruction of the enemy's fleet. Conversely, he underestimated the importance of the Royal Air Force, undermining it before and during the Battle of Britain, and putting insufficient emphasis on the bombing campaign, when this was the only effective way in which Britain alone could attack Germany.

His failures were not confined to the two World Wars. He helped to create the modern state of Iraq, whose problems would continue into the 21st century. He also helped bring about the division of Ireland, which would cause violence for decades. His economic policies, as President of the Board of Trade prior to World War I and as Chancellor of the Exchequer after it, led directly to unemployment, causing the General Strike in 1926 and making the economy more susceptible to the Depression of the 1930s. He introduced expenditure cuts for the British armed forces just at the time when the Nazi movement was growing in Germany, the Fascists were coming to power in Italy and Japan was emerging as a threat. Out of office in the 1930s, he assiduously campaigned for rearmament and opposed the policy of the governments of the day. Yet those governments would rearm sufficiently – as far as public opinion would permit – to defend Britain and ultimately be victorious in World War II. Most importantly, the appeasement policy of Prime Minister Neville Chamberlain, which Churchill so vehemently opposed, ensured that Hitler was identified as having sole responsibility for instigating World War II.

After the war, Churchill failed adequately to lead the Conservative Party in opposition and subsequently became a lacklustre Prime Minister in 1951. He pursued a forlorn and fruitless ambition to act as honest broker between the USA and the USSR to establish a just peace – for which he wanted to be remembered.

This book will identify his principal contributions to political policy and military strategy throughout his long career, addressing each in a themed chapter, and will argue that Churchill's brilliant but unsound judgment resulted in detrimental consequences for Britain and for the world.

1
GALLIPOLI:
CHURCHILL'S FIRST DEFEAT

Churchill was First Lord of the Admiralty when, during World War I, he masterminded the Gallipoli campaign in Turkey, the heart of the Ottoman Empire. However, the Ottoman Empire was the least consequential of the Central Powers; World War I was to be decided by defeating Germany and Austria–Hungary on the Western Front, not by knocking Turkey out of the war. Once Germany and Austria–Hungary had gone, Turkey would collapse of its own accord. Nevertheless, the Gallipoli campaign would set the pattern for Churchill's strategy in World War II, with dire results.

CHURCHILL BECOMES FIRST LORD OF THE ADMIRALTY

It was on Monday, 25 October 1911 that the Prime Minister, Herbert Asquith, replaced Reginald McKenna with Churchill as First Lord of the Admiralty. In fact, Churchill and McKenna swapped jobs: Churchill had been Home Secretary for 20 months, and McKenna took on the Home Office – with surprising reluctance, as it was of superior ranking and status to the Admiralty. So although Churchill relished his new job, it was something of a demotion. Churchill had been appointed to his first government job in 1905, as Under-Secretary of State for the Colonies. In 1908 he became President of the Board of Trade, spending two years there before going to the Home Office. Now, just before his 37th birthday, he was still very young for a government minister.

His appointment as First Lord was not greeted with unalloyed pleasure. *The Spectator* wrote, 'We cannot detect in his career any principles or even any constant outlook upon public affairs; his ear is always to the ground; he is the true demagogue ...'[1] This was the problem of being a turncoat politician, of having left the Conservative Party – his father's party – to join the Liberals in the governments of Sir Henry Campbell-Bannerman and now Herbert Asquith.

Churchill proved most inconsistent in his views on military expenditure. In 1909, while President of the Board of Trade, he had argued for restraint in naval construction, despite the growing threat from Germany. Along with the Chancellor of the Exchequer, David Lloyd George, he argued for the construction of only four new battleships, while the First Sea Lord, Admiral Jackie Fisher – generally regarded as second only to Horatio Nelson in British naval history – wanted eight, and mounted a public campaign with the mantra, 'We want eight, we won't wait.' A compromise of six was proposed, but Churchill still wouldn't agree. On 24 February, Prime Minister Asquith suggested that four be laid down in 1909–10, with four more, if necessary, no later than 1 April 1910. This led the cynics to point out that 'they had asked for four, fought against six, and had got eight!'[2]

Churchill's desire for restraint in 1909 contrasted starkly with his attitude on becoming First Lord, when he immediately ordered 20 new destroyers to be authorized by the 1911 Navy Estimates. He courted Fisher, now retired as First Sea Lord, and would reappoint him at the outset of World War I. Fisher was at first extremely enthusiastic about Churchill's appointment as First Lord, despite their dispute over the eight battleships, but they would fall out again over Churchill's decision to promote three admirals who were favourites of King George V.[3]

As a former junior cavalry officer with no experience of naval matters, Churchill was viewed with disdain by many senior naval officers, particularly the sea lords, who objected to him using his position to hand down orders to them rather than employing their expertise. Churchill replaced the First Sea Lord, Sir Arthur Wilson, with Admiral Sir Francis Bridgeman. However, the new man would have a real falling out with Churchill. He complained of Churchill's constant interference with technical decisions and undermining of naval traditions, and threatened to go to the Prime Minister and the King. Churchill consequently replaced him with Prince Louis of Battenberg. Indeed, Churchill fired four sea lords in the space of a year, which caused adverse comment both in the press and in the House of Commons.[4]

Churchill appointed Rear-Admiral David Beatty as his private naval secretary. This would prove controversial, and the two men would eventually fall out. Beatty, at 40, was the navy's youngest flag officer, and some thought him over-promoted. In April 1913 Churchill appointed

Beatty to command the battle-cruiser squadron of the Grand Fleet. This would itself be a dubious decision: at the Battle of Jutland in 1916 great losses were endured, at which Beatty purportedly commented, 'There seems to be something wrong with our bloody ships today,' as they exploded and sank.[5]

More positively, Churchill commissioned the five *Queen Elizabeth* class 'super Dreadnought' battleships, of the new 'all big gun' design, while taking risks with the protracted development of their 380mm (15in) guns. These ships would play an important role at Jutland and again in World War II. He also presided over the introduction of oil-fired boilers to British warships. When Sir Percy Scott, an expert on naval gunnery, suggested introducing a new centralized 'director firing' system to replace the turret-based gunlayers then in use, Churchill ordered a competition between the old and new systems. Scott's system won and was duly introduced into British warships.[6]

WORLD WAR I BEGINS

During the early stages of World War I, Churchill's concentration on the navy would momentarily wear off. The former Conservative Prime Minister, Arthur Balfour, commented in September 1914, 'Winston for the moment, unfortunately, is much more anxious to rival Napoleon than Nelson, and thinks more of the Army than the Navy.'[7] Churchill made forays to the front and consulted with General Sir John French, then in command of the British Army in Flanders. This did nothing for his relationship with the Secretary of State for War, Field Marshal Lord Horatio Kitchener, or indeed French, who commented that Churchill's judgment was highly erratic.[8]

Another disturbing factor was Churchill's ominously growing list of failures. He initiated a foray into Antwerp, organizing the defence of the port himself with disastrous consequences, an operation that was also compromised by the use of untrained troops. He admitted in Cabinet on 15 October 1914 that the navy could not prevent German submarine operations in the English Channel. He failed to prevent the cruiser *Emden* from wreaking havoc in the Indian Ocean, or German surface raiders from doing the same off East Africa. HMS *Audacious* was sunk by a mine on 27 October 1914, and the navy was defeated at the Battle of the Coronel

Islands on 4 November. The debit side of the balance sheet was becoming very apparent, but there was little to compensate on the credit side.

It was at this point that Churchill decided to change his First Sea Lord – again – exhibiting the disturbing propensity to blame others for his own failures that would be apparent throughout his career. Prince Louis of Battenberg was accused of having pro-German ties; given that he was of German extraction (as was King George V), this was an easy charge to make.[9] He was replaced by an older man who had little support from anyone apart from Churchill. The older man was none other than Jackie Fisher, so it is easy to question the wisdom of those who opposed his appointment. However, recalled out of retirement at 74, Fisher was past his best, and the motive for his appointment was highly dubious: Churchill hoped that the great man could rouse himself and pull Churchill's chestnuts out of the fire, yet Fisher would also be someone to hide behind – a scapegoat for his failures. Churchill also wanted to manipulate the 'old and weak' Fisher, as he admitted to Asquith's daughter in May 1915. So he wanted it both ways: to draw on Fisher's immense ability while Fisher took the flak for whatever went wrong, and yet to ensure that his, Churchill's, wishes were ultimately implemented.[10]

The initial result of Fisher's appointment was unalloyed success. The navy soon won a great battle in the South Atlantic, off the Falkland Islands, and a skirmish off the Dogger Bank. Fisher's complaint that there was no attempt to follow up the Falklands victory was kept quiet. But relations between the two men quickly soured because of Churchill's interference in purely operational matters. He stopped Fisher's plan to send out the Grand Fleet after the German High Seas Fleet had undertaken a naval bombardment off Hartlepool, and also blocked his plans first to mine the Elbe and Heligoland, then to mount an attack on Prussia's Baltic coast. Already Fisher was minded to go, and would go soon.[11]

GALLIPOLI TAKES SHAPE

World War I was settling into stalemate along the Western Front, and Churchill frantically searched for any strategy that could overcome this inertia and try to win the war pretty much at a stroke; he eventually came up with Gallipoli. A more patient and rational response would have been to address the problems on the Western Front and attempt to gain advantage there. Churchill's involvement in the creation of the tank was a very real attempt to do precisely this. But the technology of the period was too impoverished to make the tank an effective instrument of war. Twenty years later it would be different, but the technology of World War I favoured defence almost exclusively.

It was the machine gun, artillery and barbed wire that made defensive tactics superior to offensive ones. This was because artillery and machine guns were largely immobile: they worked efficiently from the gun line and the trenches respectively, and barbed wire was a very effective barrier against an infantry advance – a problem the tank was intended to solve. During an offensive operation, troops moved ever further from their railhead and so became increasingly difficult to supply, while the defending army was pushed back nearer to its own railhead and thus could be supplied more readily. The failure fully to appreciate these realities meant that Churchill did not foresee that the Gallipoli campaign would necessarily bog down into stalemate just like the Western Front – the very situation it was intended to avoid.

Before Churchill settled upon Gallipoli, among a myriad of possible operations he decided that the Dutch island of Ameland should act as a springboard for the defeat of Germany. This was despite the fact that its occupation would violate Dutch neutrality and in the limiting case risk pushing Holland into the war on the side of the Central Powers (Germany, Austria–Hungary and the Ottoman Empire). His response to these objections was merely to select another island, Borkum, even though it was defended with modern fortifications, the seas around it were mined and it was easily defensible with U-boats and torpedo boats. Alternatively, he came up with another island: Sylt.[12] The notion that warships could defeat fortified emplacements on land would be a hallmark of his naval strategy, directly contrary to Nelson's dictum that ships cannot destroy forts.

According to Churchill, Germany would be defeated as the result of the Borkum occupation because the minute military power of Denmark would give up its neutrality and join the Allies, and with the Baltic in Allied hands the Russians would be able to land forces close to Berlin. The occupation of Borkum would prevent any raid on, or invasion of, Britain – such as had been suggested in Erskine Childers' famous 1903 novel *The Riddle of the Sands* – and would initiate a naval battle that would determine the outcome of the war. The whole strategy was predicated on the occupation of an island, and in Churchill's mind this objective could be readily accomplished. His chief of staff, Admiral Henry Oliver, commented: 'Churchill would often look in on his way to bed to tell me how he would capture Borkum or Sylt. If I did not interrupt or ask questions he would capture Borkum in twenty minutes.'[13]

It was out of this chaotic thinking that the whole Gallipoli campaign arose. It was the beginning of Churchill's 'peripheralist' or 'dispersionist' strategic thinking: to mount raids dispersed around the enemy's periphery, rather than concentrating forces in a decisive *Schwerpunkt* ('focal point') action against the heart of the enemy. He believed that Turkey was a 'prop' supporting the war effort of the Central Powers, and that by knocking this away those powers would collapse. (In World War II he would again see Turkey as pivotal and encourage it to enter the war on the Allied side to aid Russia.) Balfour, for one, saw the obvious: he pointed out that Germany was quite indifferent to the fate of its allies when their loss was of no strategic importance to its own fortunes.[14] However, the Gallipoli proposal gained credence in the government because David Lloyd George, as Chancellor of the Exchequer, and Sir Maurice Hankey, the Secretary of the Committee of Imperial Defence (CID), both had the idea of a Balkan Front to ease pressure in Flanders. Also, Kitchener (Secretary of State for War) considered that a naval attack on the Dardanelles area of Turkey would relieve pressure on the Russians. Churchill presented his plan precisely in Kitchener's terms, though he elaborated it out of all proportion to Kitchener's original intent,[15] and others in the government, such as Lloyd George and even Balfour, were at times similarly seduced.[16]

Churchill now saw the Dardanelles as fundamental to winning the war, and when the War Council met, it agreed to his plan. The stalemate on the Western Front was palpable, and with both Kitchener and Churchill seeing the Dardanelles as a useful operation the balance of argument was tipped and the council pressed for it. However, Fisher, who had supported the plan, now openly opposed it, to the point of walking out of the meeting, only to be stopped by Kitchener.

Churchill wanted to occupy the Gallipoli Peninsula; much more ambitiously, he perceived that the naval operation might precipitate a revolution in the Turkish capital of Constantinople, and he wanted the army to be ready to occupy it. Indeed, he had managed to persuade himself of the most optimistic outcome – that the 'fall of [the] first fort' might precipitate revolution by itself.[17] However, whereas a plan for naval bombardment alone could have been enacted and terminated at any point, a military landing and occupation would be a very obvious failure if it had to be withdrawn.

According to Churchill, the desired outcome could be accomplished with just one army division, the 29th, though its precise function was rather vague in his mind: it was to be used variously to mop up the forts, or perhaps to mount some undefined local operations or, in the most optimistic case, to occupy Constantinople itself. Thus, the naval operation plus the deployment of the 29th Division was, in one go, to precipitate the defeat of Turkey in the war.[18]

However, Churchill would press ahead with the naval operations before the deployment of the 29th, and as luck would have it, he said that if a disaster happened to occur due to an insufficiency of troops, which – given this action – there was, he would disclaim responsibility for the whole affair. This would be an important get-out clause later on. There would always, of course, be debate over where the threshold for an 'insufficiency' actually was.[19]

THE GALLIPOLI ASSAULT BEGINS

The assault was initiated on 19 February 1915. The initial long-range bombardment gave way to a close-range engagement and, as a result, the Turks abandoned the outer forts. This enabled minesweepers to penetrate 10km (6 miles) into the Dardenelles. Churchill was so buoyed up by this that he drew up a draft armistice for the Turks to sign. But the Turkish inner forts, often out of the ships' line of sight, were difficult for the naval bombardment to silence. Further minesweeping operations were severely hampered by Turkish shore fire, and the minesweepers had to be withdrawn. Churchill chivvied the naval commander, Vice-Admiral Sackville Carden, to make better progress, a characteristic he would display in World War II with dire results.

As things became desperate Churchill became ever more rash: he wanted to send older battleships to force a way through the Turkish defences, on the grounds that it didn't matter if they were sunk. This notion was not new to him: in October 1914 he had come up with the idea of sending such ships into Germany's River Elbe.[20] He telegrammed Carden on 3 January 1915:

> Do you consider the forcing of the Dardanelles by ship a practicable operation. It is assumed older Battleships fitted with mine bumpers would be preceded by Colliers or other merchant craft as bumpers and sweepers. Importance of results would justify severe loss. Let me know your views.[21]

Carden replied two days later, 'I do not consider Dardanelles can be rushed.'[22] Carden wanted a more patient and conscientious strategy, to which Churchill, together with the First Sea Lord and the Cabinet War Council, would assent. He telegrammed Carden on 15 January, 'We entirely agree with your plan of methodical piecemeal reduction of forts as the Germans did at Antwerp.'[23] However, on 4 March Carden received another telegram from the Admiralty asking for ambitious results to be accomplished in short order. Churchill pressed even harder, assuming that this would be the turning point of the war; on 11 March he wrote:

> The results to be gained are however great enough to justify loss of ships and men if success cannot be obtained without. The turning of the corner at Chanak may decide the whole operation and produce consequences of a decisive character upon the war . . .'[24]

In the same telegram he urged Carden to 'overwhelm the forts at the Narrows at decisive range by the fire of the largest number of guns . . .' then added, 'We do not wish to hurry you.'[25]

Commodore Roger Keyes was chief of staff to Carden. He, like Churchill, believed in a more assertive attempt to force the straits. Keyes volunteered for, and was given responsibility for, the minesweeping operation. On the night of 13 March he led six trawlers and the cruiser HMS *Amethyst* to clear the Kephez minefield. Four of the six trawlers were badly damaged, as was the *Amethyst*.

The strain was now telling on Carden, and his doctors diagnosed an approaching nervous breakdown. He was replaced with Vice-Admiral Sir

John de Roebeck, who immediately ordered an advance of the Allied fleet through the straits, directly in line with Churchill's wishes. Once again, Keyes was chosen to lead the minesweeping force. This operation occurred on 18 March, with eighteen British and three French battleships.[26] The French ship *Bouvet* was the first to hit a mine and capsize; then the British ships *Irresistible* and *Ocean* were sunk. Three more ships were severely damaged before the fleet retreated, with over 700 dead in all.

Rather than the Turkish forts constituting the primary problem, as Churchill had thought, it was the mines that caused the most serious impediment to the progress of the operation. So it was not insufficiency in troop numbers but insufficiency in the minesweeping operations that was the problem.

Churchill had argued that losing the older battleships would risk fewer lives than an all-out military campaign on land. But he failed to appreciate either the consequences of the mines or the fact that a military campaign was necessary if the fortifications were to be silenced and the Turks defeated.[27] Vice-Admiral de Roebeck telegrammed him on 27 March: 'The utmost that can be expected of ships is to dominate the forts to such an extent that gun crews cannot fight the guns.'[28] De Roebeck continued that the German experience at Antwerp was misleading, and that if ships approached the forts at decisive range they would come under the enfilade fire of more than one fortified artillery emplacement.

Thus a full-scale opposed landing had now to be initiated, as Churchill admitted much later in a telegram to de Roebeck on 13 May: 'We think the moment for an independent Naval attempt to force the Narrows has passed and will not arise again under present conditions.'[29] Senior Greek army officers told Kitchener that a force of 150,000 men would be required to accomplish the task. Kitchener decided to deploy precisely half that number, and in March appointed General Sir Ian Hamilton to take charge. These, plus troops from Australia and New Zealand – the 'ANZACS' – and from the French Colonial Force, were assembled on the Greek island of Lemnos. Meanwhile, the Turkish commander, Otto Liman von Sanders, deployed his 84,000 troops of the Turkish Fifth Army along the expected assault beaches. The assault was initiated on 25 April 1915 and two beachheads were established at Helles and Gaba Tepe, with a third at Sulva Bay much later, on 6 August.

IMMEDIATE TROUBLE

When the War Council met on 14 May the situation was already becoming grave, and the council agreed with Churchill that more reinforcements should be sent. Fisher's concern at Churchill's interference in the operational conduct of the navy was growing to crisis proportions, and he resigned. He would tell the future Prime Minister, Andrew Bonar Law, that Churchill was 'a bigger danger than the Germans by a long way'.[30] Field Marshal Sir Henry Wilson, reflecting on Churchill's performance during World War I, said, 'His judgment is always at fault, and he is hopeless when in power.'[31]

Churchill seemed relatively unperturbed by the growing difficulties, but others begged to differ. King George V felt that Fisher's resignation would have a disastrous effect on public opinion, and Bonar Law intimated that the Conservatives should instigate a debate on the matter in the House of Commons. It was this, together with the concern over insufficient munitions for the Western Front, that weakened the government sufficiently for it to be drawn into coalition with the Conservatives in May, and so Bonar Law became part of the government. These events, undermining Asquith's position as they did, would have profound ramifications for British politics to this very day.[32]

The fact that Churchill's position was now untenable was apparent to all but him. He pleaded with the Prime Minister that he should remain in office to do his duty and complete the Gallipoli operation, but very soon there would be few who believed there was a Gallipoli operation left to be completed. When Churchill intimated that only he could bring victory at Gallipoli, Lloyd George commented, 'He is on his way to a lunatic asylum.'[33]

It is often said in politics that your real enemies are not your political opponents but those in your own party. But Churchill, who had begun his political career in the Conservative Party and was now in the Liberal Party, had enemies in both, and the two parties were now in coalition. The fact that he was kept in the Cabinet at all is astonishing given the debacle; the fact that he was appointed Chancellor of the Duchy of Lancaster indicated that Asquith wanted him as a lightning conductor, yet in a post where he was incapable of doing harm. The latter function was assented to by most in both parties. Asquith appointed Balfour as First Lord of the Admiralty, and Churchill's close association with Balfour caused him to feel that he might still have some sway with the navy. He used his position in the Cabinet to fire off letters dictating the military conduct of Gallipoli, particularly to Conservative politicians, despite the fact that he no longer had any authority over the navy, let alone the army.[34]

By the end of August some 40,000 Allied servicemen had been lost and the peninsula had still to be gained. Hamilton requested an additional 95,000 men, and Churchill wanted him to have them, but the futility of the operation was now plain to see. Gallipoli had become a battle that paralleled the situation in Flanders: not a quick decisive victory but a protracted defensive battle of attrition, constrained by the technology of warfare. The one decisive difference between Gallipoli and Flanders was that Gallipoli was of no strategic importance. Lloyd George and Bonar Law (who was by then Secretary of State for the Colonies) argued that continuation of the campaign was 'insane', and Bonar Law threatened resignation over the issue.[35]

Hamilton was replaced on 14 October by General Sir Charles Munro, who recommended withdrawal. Kitchener travelled to the peninsula a fortnight later and concurred. So 105,000 men were evacuated, starting on 7 December at Sulva Bay; the operation was completed on 9 January at Helles. In all, approximately 480,000 Allied troops had been engaged in the Gallipoli campaign. The British suffered 205,000 casualties, the ANZACS 33,600 and the French 47,000. Turkish casualties were estimated at approximately 250,000.

THE RECRIMINATIONS TAKE THEIR TOLL

Churchill now needed his escape clause – 'not enough troops'. The fact that he had envisaged the capitulation of Turkey in the face of fewer troops than were actually deployed was a minor detail that he found easy to ignore. The problem was that as he insisted in meddling in naval and military strategy rather than confining himself to political issues, he left himself open to the accusation that he was the culpable party – an accusation that was well corroborated by the evidence.

Churchill's post in the Cabinet as Chancellor of the Duchy of Lancaster was now itself becoming untenable. Few Cabinet members of either party had much, if any, time for him; indeed hostility to his presence was high.

Asquith had been severely weakened by events and had no stomach for keeping him. Churchill variously aspired to become a major-general in the army (four ranks above his actual former rank of major) or to be commander-in-chief in East Africa. Finally, on 11 November, he resigned from the government and went to the Western Front, promoted to lieutenant-colonel (just one rank above major). He was out of office for the first time in a decade.

The Gallipoli disaster fundamentally undermined Kitchener's reputation as a military strategist, despite the fact that he had not been the main culpable party. He would also soon be embroiled in the scandal, which was to engulf the government, over the lack of munitions for the Western Front. He offered to resign as Secretary of State for War, but Asquith had already lost Fisher and could not afford to lose Kitchener as well. Kitchener was now politically damaged, however, so the following spring Asquith decided to send him to Russia on a goodwill mission. On 5 June 1916, Kitchener's ship, HMS *Hampshire*, struck a mine off the Orkney Islands and he was drowned. So the unholy affair of Gallipoli would ultimately cost the nation its two principal service commanders.

THE GRAVE CONSEQUENCES

The importance of Gallipoli was that it devoted resources to a futile campaign that resulted in very considerable additional Allied casualties. Given the logistical problems of supplying it, compared with those of supplying the Western Front, it sapped a disproportionate amount of Allied resources from the one front where victory over the Central Powers was to be achieved. This would have been bad enough had the campaign achieved any measure of success, but its failure was inevitable and the misallocation of resources had the effect of lengthening the war. It is true that the Ottoman Empire endured severe casualties, but the Allied casualties were even greater.

It was said that Gallipoli always haunted Churchill, but this did not prevent him from repeating the error several times in World War II. Indeed, in those episodes where his strategy replicated Gallipoli, it had exactly the same effect. The Norwegian campaign was so limited and quick it lacked significant long-term importance, but it exhibited the very same qualities, as did the campaigns in Greece, Crete and Italy, and to a considerable extent that in North Africa. And Churchill would continue his obsession with Turkey. The Allied assault force endured significant casualties, the objective had, at best, limited strategic importance, and the result was a failure to defeat Nazi Germany decisively. The net result was that Allied forces were subject to attrition in futile campaigns when Britain was desperately short of resources and needed to focus those that were available on strategically important objectives. By bleeding forces in this way, enduring casualties and, with the exceptions of North Africa and Italy, being defeated, these campaigns necessarily extended World War II. Churchill's influence over the USA ensured that this approach was adopted by the joint Anglo-American operations in the European and North African theatres, and consequently that US resources were misallocated in the same way.

Churchill himself identified Gallipoli as the pivotal event that precipitated his political downfall. He did this for two reasons: first, because it was such a cataclysmic event that no attempt at spinning would interpret it otherwise; second, because emphasizing Gallipoli disguised the fact that his political career was, in fact, already in difficulty. So it is entirely false to claim that his rising star was momentarily brought down by one unfortunate event. Far from it: by the time of Gallipoli Churchill had accomplished little apart from that catastrophe.

THE LIBERALS ARE CRIPPLED

The calamity of Gallipoli eroded the government's position in a fundamental way. Although it was the munitions scandal – principally the lack of munitions – that was the proximate cause of the downfall of the Prime Minister, Herbert Asquith, Gallipoli had already brought into question the government's handling of the war. In addition, Churchill was in favour of a coalition government. By May 1915 the Conservatives were drawn into just such a coalition with the Liberals, precisely because of Gallipoli and the munitions scandal. With Conservative help, David Lloyd George succeeded Asquith as Prime Minister the following year. The split this caused in the Liberal Party – between the Asquith Liberals and the Lloyd George Liberals – meant there would never be a Liberal government again once the Conservatives decided to end the coalition in 1922.

The Liberals had given Churchill everything he had in government up to this point. Sir Henry Campbell-Bannerman gave Churchill his first job, and Asquith brought him on, developing his political career as President of the Board of Trade, Home Secretary and First Lord of the Admiralty. Yet Churchill's behaviour undermined Asquith and helped bring an end to his career, that of his government and that of a once great party.

CHURCHILL RETURNS TO GOVERNMENT

In July 1917 Lloyd George appointed Churchill as Minister of Munitions in the coalition government, though Churchill would not sit in the War Cabinet. Lloyd George decided to include him in the government when many – including many Conservatives – saw him as a loose cannon, on the basis that it was better to have him inside the tent pissing out than outside pissing in. Although the Prime Minister would outwardly display support and friendship towards Churchill, privately he thought that Churchill was a vain and egocentric Napoleon. Publicly, he said Churchill was 'a man of dazzling talents', with 'a forceful and a fascinating personality'. Privately, he said that 'reckless impatience has been his besetting curse through life', and that he would 'make a drum out of his mother's skin if he could use it to sound his own praises'.[36] However, Lloyd George correctly judged that he could exercise the necessary restraint over Churchill's wilder ideas.

When, after the end of World War I, Churchill was made Secretary of State for War, he said of the appointment; 'What is the use of being War Secretary if there is no war?' To which Bonar Law, then Lord Privy Seal and later Prime Minister, responded: 'If we thought there was going to be a war we wouldn't appoint you War Secretary.'[37]

2
THE GENERAL STRIKE
AND THE DEPRESSION

Churchill's failures were clearly evident in peacetime in his mismanagement of the economy. He was responsible for contradictory economic policies introduced both before and after World War I, which caused unemployment and led to the 1926 General Strike – the only time in history that Britain was subject to a national strike. The weakening of the economy prior to the Wall Street Crash in 1929 meant that the Depression in Britain during the 1930s was deeper than it would otherwise have been. As we will see, eminent economists were pointing out these problems at the time.

SOCIAL REFORM

Appointed President of the Board of Trade in 1908, Churchill was a leading figure in the Liberal government's wide-ranging programme of social reform. In 1909 he introduced 'Trade Boards', statutory organizations that established minimum wages in staple industries. He also prepared the selective compulsory sickness and unemployment bill – which became the 1911 National Insurance Act – though it would be Lloyd George, the Chancellor of the Exchequer, who would present it to Parliament, as Churchill had by then left the Board of Trade. The act established Britain's first contributory system of insurance against unemployment and illness.

Churchill strongly supported the introduction of the 1908 Coal Mines Regulation Act, which became known as the 'Eight Hours Act' because it limited the time miners were permitted to spend below ground. It was the Home Secretary, Herbert Gladstone, who introduced the bill, but Churchill wound up the debate for its second reading with a rousing speech. In 1911, when Churchill was himself Home Secretary, he introduced a Mines Bill strengthening mining safety regulations.

He assisted the Trades Union Movement by helping to introduce collective bargaining, which increased union bargaining power. In 1908 he also introduced the Standing Court of Arbitration – much later to become the Advisory Conciliation and Arbitration Service (ACAS) – to deal with trades union disputes.

Churchill attempted to introduce a Shops Bill in 1910 to regulate shop workers' hours. This was opposed, and when a revised bill was introduced in 1911 it was decimated in Parliament. However, a bill along similar lines was finally enacted in 1920. As a member of Asquith's government Churchill was also party to the introduction of state pensions in 1908 and, as a member of Lloyd George's government, to the statutory shortening of the working day in 1919.[1]

When Churchill was appointed Chancellor of the Exchequer in 1924 he continued his policy of social reform. Neville Chamberlain, as Secretary of State for Health, was responsible for extending social provision with the introduction of the Widows, Orphans and Old Age Pensions Act. Churchill was keen to collaborate with Chamberlain on the implementation of this scheme, so he announced it himself in the Budget of 1925. Chamberlain wrote on 1 May in his diary:

> Winston's exposition of the Budget was a masterly performance, and though my office and some of my colleagues are indignant at his taking to himself the credit for a scheme which belongs to the Ministry of Health, I did not myself think that I had any reason to complain of what he said. In a sense it is his scheme. We were pledged to something of the kind, but I don't think we should have done it this year if he had not made it part of his Budget scheme, and in my opinion he does deserve special personal credit for his initiative and drive.[2]

Chamberlain's generosity of spirit here is remarkable. Churchill had co-opted Chamberlain's scheme to himself and had run roughshod over the armed services in order to finance it (see chapter 3). It was an extraordinary piece of political opportunism.

However laudable these socially reforming measures may have been, in terms of the economy they created various difficulties. They vitiated the efficiency of the wage-price adjustment mechanism by reducing the downward flexibility of wages and thus output prices; in other words, wages and prices did not respond well to market forces, meaning that resources were not allocated efficiently. Churchill's Trade Boards fixed minimum wages in major industries on a statutory basis and so created a 'floor' for 'nominal' or money wages for low-paid workers.

The National Insurance Act, by creating a modern system of unemployment benefits and insurance against illness, and the introduction of state pensions, gave the workforce greater security. This strengthened its position in relation to employers and so encouraged trades union 'pushfulness' in disputes with management. Churchill's assistance with the introduction of collective bargaining and the other trades union measures further strengthened the position of the unions. Trades union membership had increased massively by the 1920s, and collective bargaining now extended to approximately three-quarters of the labour force.

The level of unemployment benefits was one criterion that determined the wage demands of the unions. If such demands led to increased unemployment the workforce would always have state benefits to fall back on. Unemployment benefit levels also influenced the Trade Boards in their setting of minimum wages.[3] This tended to make nominal wages higher than they would otherwise have been, making labour more expensive and thus reducing the demand for it. This naturally meant higher unemployment. The celebrated Cambridge economist AC Pigou noted in 1927:

> . . . partly through state action and partly through the added strength given to work peoples' organisations engaged in wage bargaining by the development of unemployment insurance, wage rates have, over a wide area, been set at a level which is too high . . . and the very large percentage of unemployment during the whole of the last six years is due to this new factor in our economic life.[4]

Only in the introduction of Labour Exchanges did Churchill facilitate greater efficiency, through the reduction of 'frictional' unemployment (people between jobs), which tended to help the unemployment situation rather than making it worse.[5]

THE GOLD STANDARD

Britain had been on the gold standard until World War I, and a restricted version of the gold standard continued until March 1919, when it was formally abandoned due to a large trade deficit and low gold reserves. However, the Cunliffe Committee, under the chairmanship of the retiring Governor of the Bank of England, Lord Walter Cunliffe, concluded that Britain should return to the full gold standard, and this became government policy. It was Churchill, as Conservative Chancellor of the Exchequer between 1924 and 1929 in Stanley Baldwin's government, who restored the gold standard in 1925. However, its re-introduction was inconsistent with his socially reforming measures, and the resultant policy mix constituted an additional cause of unemployment.

A gold standard requires strict convertibility of paper money into gold, as the money supply is restricted to the stock of gold held by the central bank (in this case the Bank of England). This prohibits the bank from undertaking a discretionary monetary expansion. The gold standard also creates a fixed exchange rate, as currencies are each convertible into a fixed amount of gold and thus are convertible into each other at the ratio of their gold values.

The Cambridge economist John Maynard Keynes – the most important economist of the era – advised Churchill against the re-introduction of the gold standard, as did Reginald McKenna, who had been Chancellor for a while during World War I, and the politician and press baron, Max Aitken, Lord Beaverbrook. At this point Churchill vacillated, but the Governor of the Bank of England, Montagu Norman, the Treasury official Sir Otto Niemeyer, and Lord John Bradbury, head of the successor to the Cunliffe Committee, all argued for re-introduction. Churchill said, 'The Treasury have never, it seems to me, faced the profound significance of what Mr Keynes called the "paradox of unemployment amidst dearth".' However, he now completely accepted the re-introduction of the gold standard, and his letters to Baldwin demonstrate that he was very pleased by the outcome;[6] on 15 December 1924 he wrote:

> The Governor of the Bank will, I hope, have told you this weekend about the imminence of our attempt to re-establish the gold standard, in connection with which he is now going to America. It will be easy to attain the gold standard and indeed almost impossible to avoid taking the decision, but to keep it will require a most strict policy of debt repayment and a high standard of credit. To reach it and have to abandon it would be disastrous.[7]

Baldwin was convinced. However, regarding the issue of it being 'easy to attain the gold standard', as we shall see, for the real economy (employment and output) it was anything but.

In April 1925 Churchill restored the gold standard to the pre-1913 mint parity, which gave an exchange rate of £1 = $4.86. After World War I the government had relaxed wartime price controls and ended rationing; it had also reduced interest rates to encourage economic growth. This had led to inflation.[8] With a flexible exchange rate regime, the nominal exchange rate depreciates to compensate for an inflation, and this is exactly what had happened. In order to return to the old exchange rate and ensure that the economy remained competitive, this inflation had to be reversed. The government had started the process in 1920 by contracting the money supply, thus raising interest rates, and Churchill as Chancellor from 1924 continued it.[9]

However, this action was directly contradicted by the effects of the social legislation that he had enacted and supported before and after World War I. The monetary policy contracted aggregate demand for goods and services as it increased the cost of investment to businesses and the cost to consumers when buying on credit. As aggregate demand contracted, prices tended to fall; 'real wages' (nominal wages divided by prices) tended to rise because nominal wages were downwardly inflexible. This made it more expensive to employ people at a time when aggregate demand for goods and services was falling. Workers were made redundant and unemployment grew. Employers tried to reduce wages to cut costs, and this led to the General Strike in 1926.

The effect of these policies was stark. Unemployment had been falling quite sharply, from more than 12 per cent in 1921 to under 8 per cent when Churchill became Chancellor in 1924. This fall was immediately halted.[10] Unemployment then fluctuated, rising above 14 per cent in 1926 at the time of the General Strike.[11] By the time Churchill was out of office in 1929 it had settled back to about 8 per cent.[12]

KEYNES ATTACKS CHURCHILL

John Maynard Keynes attacked Churchill vociferously at the time of the re-introduction of the gold standard in his seminal essay, 'The Economic Consequences of Mr Churchill'. He wrote that the government's contractionary monetary policy, or 'credit restriction', could accomplish its goal, '*In no other way than by the deliberate intensification of unemployment. The object of credit restriction, in such a case, is to withdraw from employers the financial means to employ labour at the existing level of prices and wages. The policy can only attain its end by intensifying unemployment without limit . . .*' (Emphasis added.)[13]

Churchill and all those who supported the return to the gold standard were fundamentally in error, as they failed to understand that if a government wishes to introduce a contractionary monetary policy to reduce prices and restore international competitiveness, the economy must operate on purely 'classical' (or more precisely 'neo-classical') – free market – principles, with frictionless markets in which wages and prices adjust automatically to market forces. However, if a government introduces social legislation, causing wage and price rigidity, it cannot contract the economy without causing unemployment. This is precisely what Churchill had done. Keynes wrote:

> Deliberately to raise the value of sterling money in England means, therefore, engaging in a struggle with each separate group in turn, with no prospect that the final result will be fair, and no guarantee that the stronger groups will not gain at the expense of the weaker . . . Nor can the classes which are first subjected to a reduction of money wages be guaranteed that this will be compensated later by a corresponding fall in

the cost of living, and will not accrue to the benefit of some other class. Therefore they are bound to resist so long as they can; and it must be war, until those who are economically weakest are beaten to the ground.[14]

When Churchill restored sterling to the gold standard, the exchange rate was naturally restored to its pre-1913 level. But by 1925 the American economy had grown more efficient relative to the British economy, so that sterling was now overvalued at this exchange rate. Consequently, British exports were more expensive and so less competitive on world markets. Imports, on the other hand, were now cheaper on the British domestic market and so penetrated more deeply in what was still largely a free market. This was a major cause of unemployment during this period.[15] As Keynes pointed out, with the return to the gold standard,

> . . . we know as a fact that the value of sterling money abroad has been raised by 10 per cent., whilst its purchasing power over British Labour is unchanged. This alteration in the external value of sterling money has been the deliberate act of the government and the Chancellor of the Exchequer, and the present troubles of our export industries are the inevitable and predictable consequences of it . . . Failing a fall in the value of gold itself, nothing can retrieve their position except a general fall of all internal prices and wages. Thus Mr. Churchill's policy of improving the exchange by 10 per cent. was, sooner or later, a policy of reducing everyone's wages by 2s [shillings] in the £ . . . What faces the government now is the ticklish task of carrying out their own dangerous and unnecessary decision.[16]
>
> . . . British wages, measured in gold, are now [1925] 15 per cent. higher than they were a year ago. The gold-cost of living in England is now so high compared with what it is in Belgium, France, Italy and Germany that the workers in those countries can accept a gold-wage 30 per cent. lower than what our workers receive without suffering at all in the amount of their real wages. What wonder that our export trades are in trouble![17]

Britain's decision to part-finance its role in World War I via the sales of foreign assets resulted in a loss of some £300 million. Together with assets lost through enemy action, Britain saw a decline in its overseas assets of approximately 20 per cent by the end of the war. This, and the consequent reduction in its foreign earnings from interest, profits and dividends from abroad, because of the sale of these assets, meant that the British economy was subsequently even more dependent upon its export markets, and thus the economy was more vulnerable to a slowdown in the world economy. However, there was increasing competition for these markets, particularly from the USA and Germany, making the British position even more precarious. By the 1920s exports were at approximately 80 per cent of their 1913 level, as at times was total British industrial output.

The return to the gold standard meant that there was no impediment to the shipment of gold abroad to finance trade deficits. If there is a balance of trade, a nation buys its imports with its exports and there is no net movement of gold into or out of the country. But if there is a trade deficit, the excess of imports over exports is paid for by exporting gold to the value of the deficit. In 1925, this freedom to move gold in and out of the country resulted in an exodus of finance abroad, as investors recognized that the British economy had been weakened by Churchill's policies. The government raised interest rates massively in an attempt to attract investment back into Britain and so stem the outflow of gold, but to no avail. The policy simply contracted the domestic economy further, as domestic investment became even more expensive because of the high interest rates. Keynes wrote:

> What we need to restore prosperity to-day is an easy credit policy. We want to encourage business men to enter new enterprises, not, as we are doing, to discourage them. Deflation does not reduce wages 'automatically'. It reduces them by causing unemployment. The proper object of dear money is to check an incipient boom. Woe to those whose faith leads them to aggravate a depression![18]

As we have seen, Montagu Norman had been one of the strong advocates of the policy, yet, as Keynes pointed out, he appeared to be reluctant to implement it:

So far as I can judge, the Governor of the Bank of England shrinks from it. But what is he to do, swimming, with his boat burnt, between the devil and the deep sea? At present [1925], it appears, he compromises. He applies the 'sound' policy half-heartedly; he avoids calling things by their right names; and he hopes – this is his best chance – that something will turn up.[19]

THE COAL INDUSTRY

Churchill's policies caused export industries, including the coal industry, to try to cut costs by lowering wages. However, he denied that they were having this effect, as Keynes wrote, 'The Chancellor of the Exchequer has expressed the opinion that the return to the Gold Standard is no more responsible for the condition of affairs in the coal industry than is the Gulf Stream. These statements are of the feather-brained order.'[20]

Competition for coal export markets was intensified after World War I, particularly from the United States, Poland and Germany. The latter influenced the market from 1925 because the Dawes Plan, among other provisions, permitted Germany to export 'free coal' to France and Italy as part payment of reparations under the Versailles settlement. During the war the huge demand for coal had depleted the richest seams, causing productivity to fall. Output per man in Britain had been 247 tons prior to the war, and was 199 tons by the mid-1920s. Keynes wrote:

> If our collieries lower their prices, as they are compelled
> to do, so as to be on as good a competitive level with foreign
> countries as they were a year ago, they have to lower their
> sterling prices by something like 1s. 9d. a ton . . . the Coal
> Industry consumes very few foreign goods. Moreover, the
> Wages Bill makes up a very high proportion of the total
> costs of raising coal. Thus, more than any other industry,
> the Coal Industry has to sell at the foreign value of sterling
> and to buy at the home value of sterling . . . The same
> causes which depress the trade in coal operate to depress
> the trade in the industry which is the biggest user of coal,
> namely iron and steel.[21]

The Eight Hours Act and the new safety legislation meant that the cost of coal production could not be reduced appreciably, and because coal was used either directly or indirectly in the production and distribution of most goods and services this meant the entire economy was now less competitive.

In the face of the proposed wage cuts, the miners threatened to strike. On the day the action was due to start, the Baldwin government announced that it would provide a subsidy for nine months in order to sustain the mine workers' wages, and set up a royal commission to examine the problems faced by the industry under Sir Herbert Samuel, the former High Commissioner of Palestine, later to be leader of the Liberal Party. This was clearly seen as a victory for the Labour movement, and the day became known as 'Red Friday', though in reality it was simply a tactic to defer a strike and enable the government to plan to deal with it.

The Samuel Commission's report was published in March 1926: it supported the mining companies' case for wage reduction and said the government subsidy should be withdrawn. The companies planned to reduce wages by extending the existing seven-hour working day – though they were limited by the Eight Hour Act – and reducing pay rates by between 10 and 25 per cent. If the miners did not accept these conditions from 1 May there would be a lockout.The union opposed them with the refrain, 'Not a penny off the pay, not a second on the day.' Negotiations were opened to settle the dispute, but when printers at the *Daily Mail* went on strike to prevent publication of an editorial vociferously opposed to the unions, Baldwin decided to call them off.

THE GENERAL STRIKE

The General Council of the Trades Union Congress (TUC) met on 1 May 1926 to call a General Strike. This began on 3 May and lasted for nine days. By 4 May there were between 1.5 and 1.75 million people on strike. The government employed the armed forces and volunteer workers to maintain basic services and law and order on the streets. It also created a militia of special constables, called the Organization for the Maintenance of Supplies.

Baldwin gave Churchill the editorship of the *British Gazette*, a government newspaper designed to disseminate government propaganda. Baldwin said this was 'to stop him doing worse things', but he also ensured that he ultimately had censorship over what Churchill published. The TUC also had its own newspaper, the *British Worker*, which Churchill opposed, and he co-opted control of the paper supply, forcing a reduction in the extent of its later issues. Despite his conciliatory tones in the House of Commons,[22] in July he responded to criticisms in the House of bias in his editorship of the *British Gazette* by saying, 'I decline utterly to be impartial as between the fire brigade and the fire.'[23]

With government support for blackleg workers, the TUC capitulated on 12 May. The coal strike continued for a while after the General Strike, and was settled by Churchill's negotiations with unions and management. He was surprisingly conciliatory towards the unions and promoted the settlement with vigour, though as the union members were close to being starved back to work, he could afford to appear conciliatory.

Kingsley Martin, editor of the *New Statesman*, wrote in his book *Father Figures* (1966):

> The General Strike of 1926 was an unmitigated disaster.
> Not merely for Labour but for England . . . Churchill and
> other militants in the cabinet were eager for a strike, knowing
> that they had built a national organization in the six months'
> grace won by the subsidy to the mining industry. Churchill
> himself told me this on the first occasion I met him in
> person . . . I asked Winston what he thought of the Samuel
> Coal Commission . . . When Winston said that the subsidy had
> been granted to enable the Government to smash the unions,
> unless the miners had given way in the meantime, my picture
> of Winston was confirmed.[24]

THE CONSEQUENCES FOR CHURCHILL

In 1929, after the Conservatives were swept from power in the general election, Churchill decided to travel across the United States, giving speeches and relaxing. He stayed with the press magnate William Randolph Hearst on his magnificent estate in California, and met Charlie Chaplin, who became a friend. At the time Chaplin was intending to play Jesus Christ in a film, and Churchill asked him, 'Have you cleared the rights?'

In the economic boom just prior to the Wall Street Crash, Churchill invested heavily on the stock market. When the Crash came and the Depression began he lost much of his personal wealth. He said it was a mystery to him why the Depression had occurred, but that he was sure that with co-operation between the governments of the English-speaking peoples it could be put right. Churchill had also over-extended his family finances by buying a large house, Chartwell in Kent, and needed to impose some stringent home economy measures as a result. He now badly needed to augment his personal income and he would turn to writing to do this.[25]

ECONOMIC RECOVERY AFTER THE ABANDONMENT OF CHURCHILL'S POLICIES

The British economy had been recovering from 1921, before Churchill became Chancellor of the Exchequer. However, as the result of his policies it went into recession for the remainder of the 1920s, furthering its relative decline. Churchill's policy errors thus made Britain much more vulnerable to the effects of the Wall Street Crash in 1929 and the consequent Depression in the 1930s than otherwise would have been the case. He had no excuse for being unaware that his policies were at fault, not least because Keynes and Pigou had pointed it out at the time, though Keynes had not advocated reversing the policy or devaluing the exchange rate.

By 1931 the government had reversed Churchill's policy and abandoned the gold standard. Consequently interest rates were reduced and the sterling exchange rate immediately fell by a quarter, from $4.86 to $3.75. The improved balance of trade initiated economic recovery, with unemployment falling from 1933 onwards. This stimulus was augmented in 1932, when Neville Chamberlain, as Chancellor of the Exchequer, introduced the General Tariff of 10 per cent on imports from outside the British Empire (see chapter 17). Churchill had always been opposed to such a protectionist trade measure. The abandonment of the gold standard was to prove permanent, a reversal of policy that clearly demonstrated Churchill's misjudgment.

The National governments of Ramsay Macdonald, Stanley Baldwin and Neville Chamberlain initiated a rearmament policy in the 1930s, and the consequent fiscal stimulus to the economy helped to reduce unemployment

CARDIFF
CAERDYDD

further. These governments inherited an inefficient wage-price adjustment mechanism caused by the social legislation. As nominal wages were fixed, at least in the short run, by strong unions, an increase in government expenditure for rearmament increased output prices and so reduced real wages. This made it cheaper for employers to take on staff. Unemployment fell from over three million at the peak of the Depression to 1.5 million by 1937, and was back to its 1929 level by 1939. The military mobilization from September 1939 and the concomitant massive increase in government expenditure subsequently eradicated unemployment altogether.

3
DISARMAMENT: WEAKENING BRITAIN'S DEFENCE IN THE 1920S

Churchill is remembered for his assiduous pursuit of rearmament against the threat from Nazi Germany in the 1930s, when he was not in government. However, during the 1920s, as the Nazi movement grew in Germany, the Fascists came to power in Italy and the threat from Japan became ever more palpable, Churchill, then a government minister, chose to argue for cuts in Britain's armed forces.

THE MIDDLE EAST

Lloyd George appointed Churchill as Secretary of State for War and Air in January 1919, and it was while in this post that he began cutting Britain's defence commitment. He started in the Middle East, with dire results.

The Sykes–Picot agreement of 1916, negotiated by the British and French diplomats Sir Mark Sykes and François Georges-Picot, had carved up the Arabian possessions of the defeated Ottoman Empire between British and French interests. This agreement gave Britain effective colonial domain over Mesopotamia, out of which would come modern-day Iraq, a state Churchill would help to create.[1]

It was the high cost of maintaining the Mesopotamian garrison of 105,000 British and Indian troops that prompted Churchill, in August 1919, to warn of the need for drastic cuts. In November he suggested the garrison should be cut massively and focused in a fort near Baghdad, and that mechanized units should be used on land, river and air to police the remainder of the country. In early 1920, with costs still running at £18 million a year, Churchill sought more radical cuts.

There was unrest in the Kurd-dominated part of what would become Iraq during the winter of 1919–20, and British aircraft bombed Arab positions to suppress it. A separate Kurdistan was mooted, but Feisal bin Al Hussein Bin Ali El-Hashemite, who had led the Arab uprising in World

War I with TE Lawrence (Lawrence of Arabia) and who would subsequently become King of Iraq, believed that such separatism would result in Iraqi Kurds joining with the Kurds in Turkey and Persia (modern-day Iran), constituting a potential threat to the creation of the state of Iraq. Resisting separatism would also result in an inbuilt majority of Sunni over Shia Muslims in the Constituent Assembly – which Feisal favoured. As a result the British abandoned the idea of a separate Kurdistan.

Wider Arab resistance to British rule in Mesopotamia resulted in a nationwide uprising in 1920, and Churchill decided to expand the use of aircraft equipped with mustard gas bombs to accomplish colonial control at reduced cost, although officials in London had qualms about this exacerbating the violence.[2] During February 1920 Churchill approached Air Marshal Sir Hugh Trenchard, the Chief of the Air Staff, to ask if he was 'prepared to take Mesopotamia on'. Churchill felt that with the facility of air power the ground troops could be cut to 14,000. Trenchard provided a formal proposal and Churchill announced the intended policy to the House of Commons on 22 March. The Cabinet publicly accepted the Mesopotamian Mandate in the same month. What became known as the Air Force Scheme would be officially scheduled to come into force on 1 October 1922.[3]

By the summer of 1920 there was a full-scale revolt in Mesopotamia. The Arab forces were led by those who had been marginalized under British rule: the Shia mujahideen, who had been civil servants or officers of the Turks during the Ottoman days, plus Arab patriots and the wealthy merchants of Basra who stood to lose out due to British tax policy. They commanded over 130,000 tribesmen, about half of whom were equipped with rifles.[4] The fighting was intense during the first week of July on the Euphrates around Samawa and Rumaitha, but Churchill told the Cabinet on 7 July, 'Our attack was successful . . . The enemy were bombed and machine-gunned with effect by aeroplanes which co-operated with the troops.' Rumaitha was subject to an Arab blockade, and aircraft attacked the Arabs as well as supplying the beleaguered imperial garrison. By mid-September the British had the better of the situation, though serious fighting would continue for some weeks.[5]

The American President, Woodrow Wilson, had been sceptical about the effectiveness of air control, and the 1920 rebellion convinced many that aircraft could never replace the garrison. Lieutenant-General Sir

(James) Aylmer Haldane, General Officer Commanding Mesopotamia, recognized that aircraft provided reconnaissance, swift communication, close support and the pursuit of hostile forces, but argued that air power could not accomplish the task alone. Sir Arnold Wilson, who would be replaced by Sir Percy Cox as Civil Commissioner, went further: he argued that it was precisely the use of air power rather than ground forces that had constituted the principal cause of the uprising, as it was concomitant with a reduction in the garrison strength, which the Arab forces interpreted as a sign of weakness. He also argued that air power had caused great antipathy among the Arabs, worsening the crisis.[6] Despite these concerns, the use of air power was extended to cover Palestine in 1922 and Aden in 1928.[7]

In a memorandum to Churchill in April 1920, Major-General Sir Percy P de B Radcliffe, Director of Military Operations, wrote:

> In view of the scheme for the control of this area
> [Mesopotamia] being taken over by the RAF . . . it would
> seem in every way desirable not to risk an outbreak of trouble
> by the premature withdrawal or reduction of our garrison . . .
> I would urge, therefore, that no arbitrary reduction should
> be ordered contrary to the expressed opinion of the
> commander responsible.[8]

Haldane sent a telegram to Churchill at the War Office on 28 August 1920. This was a chilling portent of what was to come, and what would recur with the British military presence in Iraq in the early 21st century: 'The Muntafiq [an important confederation of tribes] disturbance is developing and a violent Jehad is being preached.' Haldane referred to 'the tide of fanaticism' in Mesopotamia, and continued, 'If the Muntafiq throw in their lot with the insurgents, as seems probable, a new situation will arise. The infection will probably spread to Tigris tribes and the only lines of communication between Basra and Baghdad, by the river, will become precarious.' He made it clear that Churchill's policy of cutbacks in ground forces was wrong and that additional forces were needed to operate along the Tigris and Euphrates: 'The early arrival of such a force might even prevent the spread of disaffection to the extent otherwise probable . . .'[9]

Two days later Haldane sent another telegram to Churchill: 'I am convinced that the rising is anarchical and religious though initiated on political basis, and peace can only come by the sword.'[10] On 7 September 1920, he again telegrammed Churchill: 'Elusiveness of insurgents is main obstacle to decisive action. Their great mobility and knowledge of country enabled them to assemble and disperse quickly and harass communications . . . Campaigning is not unlike that in South Africa in later stages of Boer war . . .' He went on to say that Britain had had superiority of numbers in the Boer war, but did not here. 'My resources as I have frequently pointed out debar me from acting at more than one point at a time. This has led to spread of insurrection elsewhere before it could be tackled . . . my numbers are quite inadequate.'[11] Churchill telegrammed Haldane and Cox on 8 January 1921:

> It is impossible for us to throw upon the British taxpayer the burdens for military expenditure in Mesopotamia which are entailed by your present schemes for holding the country. Unless some better method can be devised and brought into operation within the financial year 1921–22, retirement and contraction to the coastal zone is inevitable and must be accomplished as rapidly as possible.[12]

Churchill was still pursuing further cuts. On 13 January 1921 he minuted the Chief of the Air Staff: 'Would it not be possible to maintain a garrison at Mosul entirely by air and dispense with all the lines of communication?'[13] The question exposed his lack of understanding of the severe limitations of the operational performance of the aircraft of the period. On the same day, Haldane telegrammed Churchill:

> In my opinion, if chaos is to be avoided no reduction in the forces already sanctioned . . . can be made until Arabs, or other forces, have proved themselves able to take the place of our troops both for maintaining internal order and for resisting external aggression . . . As regards the Air Force Scheme . . . as a result of experience during 1920 I do not consider that the Scheme, which would involve a large reduction of troops, could be applied to Mesopotamia without grave risks, until the Royal Air Force have proved that they can maintain law and order in the country.[14]

In his telegram to Haldane and Cox on 8 January 1921 Churchill had said, 'We may be able to set up an Arab Government through whose agency the peaceful development of the country may be assured without undue demands upon Great Britain.' He also referred to 'the selection of an Arab ruler'.[15] But by 7 February he was ready to bolt, and telegrammed Haldane: 'You should advise me of any measures which can be taken to increase the amount of transport at your disposal for the purposes of ensuring a swift evacuation should that be decided on.'[16] On 21 September he wrote, 'The whole object is to get the troops out of the country as quickly as possible.'[17]

TE Lawrence was a severe critic of government policy. Presciently, he had written in *The Sunday Times* on 22 August 1920:

> The people of England have been led in Mesopotamia into a trap from which it will be hard to escape with dignity and honour. They have been tricked into it by a steady withholding of information . . . Things have been far worse than we have been told, our administration more bloody and inefficient than the public knows. It is a disgrace to our imperial record, and may soon be too inflamed for any ordinary cure. We are to-day not far from a disaster . . .
>
> The Cabinet cannot disclaim all responsibility. They receive little more news than the public: they should have insisted on more, and better. They have sent draft after draft of reinforcements, without enquiry . . .
>
> Our government is worse than the old Turkish system. They kept fourteen thousand local conscripts embodied, and killed a yearly average of two hundred Arabs in maintaining peace. We keep ninety thousand men, with aeroplanes, armoured cars, gunboats, and armoured trains. We have killed about ten thousand Arabs in this rising this summer.

THE CREATION OF IRAQ

In February 1921 Lloyd George appointed Churchill as Secretary of State for the Colonies in his coalition government, and at Churchill's invitation TE Lawrence was appointed as a political adviser to the Middle East

Department in the Colonial Office – a post in which he remained only until the following year. In his new capacity Churchill, with Lawrence, the administrator Gertrude Bell and Sir Percy Cox, created the state of Iraq out of Mesopotamia, including in it both the Sunni and Shia Muslim sects, and imposed the Hashemite King Feisal as its ruler. The entrenched schism this created in Iraq would continue to constitute a fundamental problem into the 21st century. With alarming echoes of British policy in the early 21st century, Churchill said in the House of Commons on 14 June 1921:

> . . . Our object and our policy is to set up an Arab Government, and to make it take the responsibility, with our aid and our guidance and with an effective measure of our support, until they are strong enough to stand alone, and so to foster the development of their independence as to permit the steady and speedy diminution of our burden . . . our policy in Mesopotamia is to reduce our commitments and to extricate ourselves from our burdens while at the same time honourably discharging our obligations and building up a strong and effective Arab Government which will always be the friend of Britain and, I will add, the friend of France.[18]

On 25 November 1921 Churchill sent a note to Sir James Masterton Smith, Permanent Under-Secretary for the Colonies, and John Shuckburgh, Assistant Under-Secretary of State at the Colonial Office: 'What is all this talk about [£]9 millions for Mesopotamia next year? There is absolutely no question of anything over 7. Not one farthing more than 7 will be asked for by me . . . Everything has got to be cut down to this level by any means that you like and at any risk or cost.'[19] And on 2 December he wrote, 'I am not prepared to accelerate the date at which the Air Ministry take over. I shall nevertheless require a reduction in expense within the seven million limit.'[20]

The Royal Air Force was not only to control Iraq, but Afghanistan as well. In a memorandum on 24 December Churchill wrote:

> It would be possible to organise in a few months at a moderate expense an air force capable of controlling the political action of the Afghan Government and ensuring the correct demeanour of that Government towards India . . .

We do not wish to occupy Afghanistan, but only to make her behave in a proper manner. We ought not, therefore, to keep any troops or make any arrangements solely for the purpose of a ground invasion or occupation of Afghanistan.[21]

He wrote to Lloyd George on 1 September 1922:

I think we should now put definitely, not only to Feisal but to the Constituent Assembly, the position that unless they beg us to stay and to stay on our own terms in regard to efficient control, we shall actually evacuate before the close of the financial year. I would put this issue in the most brutal way, and if they are not prepared to urge us to stay and to co-operate in every manner I would actually clear out. That at any rate would be a solution. Whether we should clear out of the country altogether or hold on to a portion of the Basra Vilayet is a minor issue requiring a special study.

It is quite possible, however, that face to face with this ultimatum the King, and still more the Constituent Assembly, will implore us to remain. If they do, shall we not be obliged to remain? If we remain, shall we not be answerable for defending their frontier? How are we to do this if the Turk comes in? We have no force whatever that can resist any serious inroad. The War Office, of course, have played for safety throughout and are ready to say 'I told you so' at the first misfortune.

Surveying all the above, I think I must ask you for definite guidance at this stage as to what you wish and what you are prepared to do . . . At present we are paying [£] eight millions a year for the privilege of living on an ungrateful volcano out of which we are in no circumstances to get anything worth having.[22]

In fact, Churchill would shortly be out of office, as Lloyd George's government was to fall before the end of the year, though when he returned in 1924 as Chancellor of the Exchequer he would continue to cut defence expenditure. But he had already helped to initiate a policy that would have dire consequences. The British-appointed monarchy would be overthrown in 1958, and in a coup five years later the secular Arab Socialist Baath Party would take over, entrenching the Sunni elite and subsequently enabling Saddam Hussein to come to power. In the early 21st century, history would repeat itself, this time with American as well as British occupation of Iraq, as Saddam's regime was overthrown and a government consistent with western interests was installed.

REPRISALS IN IRELAND

There was another pressing issue for Churchill to contend with while he was Secretary of State for War: the continuing trouble in Ireland. Once again the policy would prove mistaken and precipitate withdrawal, and once again economy was a motivating factor. As in Mesopotamia, air power would be used to suppress Irish opposition to British rule.[23]

Far more pressing, however, was the need to address policing on the ground. The nationalist organization the Irish Republican Army (IRA) had mounted attacks upon, and in some cases murdered, police officers of the Royal Irish Constabulary (RIC) during and after World War I, resulting in a recruitment problem for the force. At a Cabinet meeting on 11 May 1920, Churchill suggested the creation of a 'Special Emergency Gendarmerie, which would become a branch of the Royal Irish Constabulary'. This was a quick and cheap security measure, but it would soon prove disastrous.

General Sir Nevil Macready, commander-in-chief of the British forces in Ireland, rejected the proposal. However, a couple of months later, Major-General Henry Tudor, the Police Adviser to the Dublin Castle administration, took a different view. He argued that a body was needed that would use the same tactics as the IRA if it was to be defeated. On 12 July 1920, Field Marshal Sir Henry Wilson informed Churchill of Tudor's plan. Lloyd George had agreed to it and Churchill assented.[24]

The force became known as the 'Black and Tans', because the high demand for uniforms resulted in khaki army trousers being supplied together with dark green surplus RIC tunics; the name also commemorated a well-known Limerick pack of foxhounds.[25] They soon gained a reputation for violence and murder. On 30 August 1920 Wilson discussed them with Churchill, and his diary entry reads:

Black & Tans carrying out wild reprisals & deprecating
their policy. I told Winston that I thought this a scandal
& Winston was very angry. He said these Black & Tans
were honorable & gallant officers, etc. etc. & talked
much nonsense.[26]

The next month Wilson argued that Churchill should stop the Black and
Tans, but he refused.[27] On 2 November Wilson noted in his diary, 'I had
a long talk with Winston and for the 100th time I urged him to take over
the Govt of Ireland and not leave it to the Black & Tans & the soldiers.' Yet
Churchill was so committed to the force that the following day he wrote to
Lloyd George, 'I am prepared to support and defend in Parliament a policy
of reprisals . . . [by the Black and Tans and the soldiers].'[28] It wasn't only the
Black and Tans that Churchill supported; just as he had advocated the use
of air power to exercise control in Mesopotamia, he did so now in Ireland.
On 1 July he had written to Trenchard that aircraft should be used to bomb
and strafe 'rebel gatherings'.[29]

As Secretary of State for the Colonies in Lloyd George's coalition
government, the future of Ireland was Churchill's responsibility. He was
one of the negotiators of the Anglo-Irish Treaty of 6 December 1921 with
Michael Collins of Sinn Fein, the political wing of the IRA. This created the
26-county Irish Free State and left six counties part of the United Kingdom
as Northern Ireland. And so ended British rule in the greater part of
Ireland. Churchill wrote, 'We had become allies and associates in a common
cause – the cause of the Irish Treaty and of peace between the two races
and two islands.'[30] In fact this division of Ireland, and continued British
sovereignty over the North, would not end the violence – far from it – and
the political settlement would remain a problem into the 21st century.

CHANCELLOR OF THE EXCHEQUER

In 1922, while Churchill was convalescing from an appendectomy, the
Conservatives pulled out of the coalition government; a general election
was called in which Churchill lost his seat as Liberal MP for Dundee.
He commented, 'I am without office, without a seat . . . and without
an appendix.'[31] After unsuccessful attempts to re-enter Parliament he

finally won the Epping seat two years later and rejoined the Conservative Party. Much later, in 1941, he was to remark on changing parties, 'They say you can rat, but you can't re-rat,' though he had in fact successfully accomplished it.[32] To the surprise of most – including Churchill himself – Stanley Baldwin, the new Prime Minister, appointed him Chancellor of the Exchequer in 1924. (Many years later, when asked to send a letter to Baldwin on his 80th birthday, Churchill demurred, saying, 'I wish Stanley Baldwin no ill, but it would have been much better if he had never lived.')[33]

Churchill wanted to implement deep economies in defence across all the services, but particularly in respect of the air force. His 1925 budget committed the country to a decrease of £10 million per year in the Service Estimates.[34] To accomplish this Churchill wanted to pare down Sir Samuel Hoare's proposal for a 52-squadron air force. Yet on 12 June 1923 the Salisbury Committee had produced an interim report on air defence that recommended a frontline strength of 600 aircraft, and Baldwin had commented that he backed Hoare's proposal for completion by 1928. He had said to the House of Commons: 'British air power must include a home defence force of sufficient strength adequately to protect us against air attack by the strongest Airforce in striking distance of this country.' However, a belief that the Air Ministry was exaggerating the threat as the situation in Europe improved, and the arguments for economy, meant that the proposal's completion date was to be put back to 1935–6.[35]

Churchill also wanted to reject the navy's proposal for new construction. To justify this he invoked the Ten-Year Rule – the assumption that no major war would occur in the next ten years. Of course, it would indeed be the case that Britain would not be involved in a major war during this period, but by invoking the rule Churchill helped to ensure that British and Imperial defences were being run down precisely as Adolf Hitler was beginning his rise to power in Germany. Benito Mussolini was already in power in Italy, and there was a growing threat from Japan when the Anglo-Japanese Alliance ended in 1922 and Japan rearmed. It is ironic that in 1934, at the end of this ten-year period, it would be Ramsay MacDonald's government that would initiate the programme to develop what would become the Hurricane and Spitfire fighter aircraft, which would save Britain in its hour of greatest need (see chapter 8).

Churchill believed that cuts in the proposed increases in the armed forces' estimates were necessary in order to reduce taxation, thereby stimulating trade, and to facilitate increased expenditure on policies for social reform. His position was summed up in a letter to Baldwin on 15 December 1924:

> To accept these armament increases is to sterilise and paralyse the whole policy of the government. There will be nothing for the taxpayer and nothing for social reform. We shall be a Naval Parliament busily preparing our Navy for some great imminent shock. Voila tout! ... The Governor of the Bank will, I hope, have told you this weekend about the imminence of our attempt to re-establish the gold standard ... To reach it and have to abandon it would be disastrous. Therefore I repeat, there is nothing for it, if we accept the armament policy, but to put out of our mind all idea of reduction of taxation and practically all plans of social reform during the whole lifetime of the present Parliament.
>
> I feel sure that such a policy will not only bring the Government into ruin but might well affect the safety of the state. The vast growth of the Navy Votes will be challenged not only by the Socialists and Liberals, who will increasingly make common cause against it, but also by all the formidable body of opinion on our side which was marshalled so effectively by Rothermere in the last year of the Coalition, and did so much to make it unpopular. We should come up to the Election with these enormous Navy Estimates and nothing else to show. Besides this, we should be accused of starting up the whole armament race all over the world and setting the pace towards a new vast war. I cannot conceive any course more certain to result in a Socialist victory ...
>
> I am sure you have no intention of allowing our policy to follow such a foolish course, and I know you will be supported by the Cabinet, by the House of Commons and by the nation itself in a wise and far-reaching restraint. I daresay the Admiralty themselves are to a certain extent trying it on ...[36]

Though written in 1924, the letter perfectly describes the situation ten years later. The financial constraints in 1924 were much less severe than in 1934, when the nation was still in the grip of the Depression. Not only did

Churchill lay the groundwork for the country's dire defence situation of the early 1930s, as Chancellor he also cited the constraints on government that he refused to recognize a decade later. And, as he admitted, his policy was largely brought about by the financial constraints of his own disastrous decision to return to the gold standard (see chapter 2).

However, consistency was not one of Churchill's virtues: having opposed the First Lord of the Admiralty, William Bridgeman, on the Navy Estimates, by 1925 he was supporting a new construction programme. Yet by 1927 he was again opposing Bridgeman. The latter wrote to him on 6 January 1927:

> The only complaint I have to make is the shortness of your memory. Two years ago you realised fully that the effect of embarking on a new construction programme must be to cause a steady increase of Navy Estimates as the cost of that programme rose to its peak. You told the Cabinet so . . . I have before me a memorandum in which you warned the Cabinet that once the programme of new construction is sanctioned there could be no turning back; and that 'as larger and more complicated vessels are built, further considerable addition [to the Estimates] . . . will of course be necessary year by year.'[37]

Churchill gave a long-winded reply on 7 February, but his defence amounted to no more than, 'The programme of new construction we were then discussing was a very different one from that upon which we finally agreed.'[38]

It could be argued that Churchill's policy of constraining defence expenditure preceded Hitler's rise to power, and that the threat of the creation of the Third Reich was not, and could not have been, foreseen. However, the continued threat from Germany *was* foreseen by Maréchal Ferdinand Foch, the French Chief of the General Staff in World War I and *de facto* supreme Allied commander at the end of that war, when British and American forces were put under his command. Of the Versailles Peace Treaty in 1919, Foch said, 'This is not a peace. It is an armistice for 20 years' – a truly prescient statement. By the mid-1920s, economic difficulties and political agitation in Germany meant that the accuracy of Foch's prophecy was becoming even more evident. The basis for European instability was clear to the far-sighted. However, Churchill sought to cut military expenditure in the 1920s, when the economic circumstances were not as bad as they would be in the Depression of the 1930s, by which time he would be out of office. Military cuts were understandable in the Depression, but not so in the economic circumstances of the 1920s, when they would have been less necessary had Churchill not created a recession by his own policies.

THE JAPANESE THREAT

With the ending of the Anglo-Japanese Alliance in 1922, the Admiralty increasingly saw Japan as a threat. By 1924 it was already convinced that Japan would constitute as formidable a foe as Germany had ten years earlier, and was stationing submarines in Hong Kong and rapidly developing the base at Singapore. Yet of this policy Churchill wrote in his 15 December letter to Baldwin about the Navy Estimates: 'For what? A war with Japan! But why should there be a war with Japan? I do not believe there is the slightest chance of it in our lifetime. The Japanese are our allies . . . Japan is at the other end of the world. She cannot menace our vital security in any way.'[39] He also wrote to the Foreign Secretary, Austen Chamberlain, on the same day: 'What I seek is a declaration to the Cabinet by you, ruling out a war with Japan from among the reasonable possibilities to be taken into account in the next 10, 15 or 20 years.'[40] War with Japan would come just less than 17 years later.

It was not until both Germany and Japan were actually rearming for all to see that Churchill perceived the threat. This was not the behaviour of a visionary: he failed to understand what the Admiralty could foresee all too readily. In fact, Japanese rearmament meant it already enjoyed a preponderance of 203mm (8in) gun cruisers by 1924.[41] The Admiralty was right; Churchill was wrong. He believed that the Admiralty should be told 'that they are not expected to be in a position to counter Japan in the Pacific Ocean and they are not to prepare for such a contingency . . . They should be made to recast all their plans and scales and standards on the basis that no naval war against a first class Navy is likely to take place in the next twenty years.'[42] This period would, of course, have included World War II. It seems that Baldwin did not reply to Churchill's letter.

Churchill also questioned the construction of Admiralty facilities in Singapore on financial grounds, an issue that Baldwin insisted needed to be addressed on purely strategic defence grounds.[43] This is ironic, given that Japan would occupy Singapore in 1942 when Churchill was Prime Minister (see chapter 13). He also caused considerable friction when he called for the budget for the cruiser replacement programme to be cut, though his position was undermined by a decision of the United States Congress on 18 December 1924 to finance the construction of eight new cruisers and to modernize six existing ones. The battle lines were now drawn between Churchill and the Admiralty, particularly the First Sea Lord, Admiral of the Fleet Sir David Beatty, who wrote to his wife on 26 January 1925:

> That extraordinary fellow Winston has gone mad.
> Economically mad, and no sacrifice is too great to achieve what in his short sightedness is the panacea for all evils, to take 1/- off the Income Tax. Nobody outside a lunatic asylum expects a shilling off the Income Tax this Budget. But he has made up his mind that it is the only thing he can do to justify his appointment as Chancellor of the Exchequer . . . The result will be a split in the Conservative Party and nothing else. As we, the Admiralty, are the principal spending department, he attacks us with virulence and now proclaims that a Navy is a quite unnecessary luxury.[44]

This illustrates an aspect of Churchill's character that would be significant in World War II – his proclivity for ideas that service professionals saw as bordering on the lunatic – and how he needed to be constrained.

During a CID meeting on 5 February 1925 Baldwin had yet again to deal with Churchill's opposition to the Singapore base. Beatty subsequently told Baldwin that the navy had reached the end of its concessions and, unless Churchill desisted, the Cabinet would have to decide between Churchill and himself, the First Sea Lord, staying in office. This was clearly a calculated gamble by Beatty. But Churchill would have none of it and continued to press home his case. In the end the Cabinet sided with Churchill and his desire for Navy Estimates of £60 million, and the navy was eventually obliged to settle for £60.5 million.[45] However, Churchill's arguments were incoherent and contradictory. In the CID he began with his previously stated position that Japan did not constitute a threat and thus that the Singapore-based fleet and increased naval construction were not required. But then, quite extraordinarily, he began to argue that the Japanese position was so unassailably superior to the British that it was impossible for Britain to out-build Japan, and thus it should not even try! The Cabinet, not a little alarmed at this, agreed to the somewhat exceptional step of instructing the Secretary to the Cabinet, Sir Maurice Hankey, to strike such 'misleading' remarks from the record.[46] This was another quality of Churchill's that would prove significant in World War II – his alarmingly erratic behaviour.

Not content with this, Churchill insisted that the cruiser replacement programme should be scrapped in its Admiralty form, that no cruiser keels should be laid in the construction yards in 1925 and in subsequent years cruiser construction should proceed at a maximum of one a year. In the end the Cabinet came down largely on Churchill's side. However, the Foreign Secretary, Austen Chamberlain, and his half-brother, the future Prime Minister Neville Chamberlain – then Minister of Health – both wanted no more than a limited delay to the cruiser programme, and not the draconian cuts Churchill was forcefully advocating.[47]

The government had long accepted the 'one-power standard': that the Royal Navy should be at least equivalent in size to any other single navy in the world. Baldwin himself had said on 2 May 1924 in the Albert Hall, 'We stand for a One-Power Navy sufficiently equipped with cruisers to protect our trade routes . . .' But Baldwin recognized that Churchill's 'butter rather than guns' position reflected the mood in the country, and that Churchill's emphasis on welfare reform programmes would be popular. He appreciated the need to compromise towards Churchill's position: it was ironic that Churchill failed to recognize this fact just a decade later, when he was out of office and Baldwin was again Prime Minister, and needed to face the same political realities.

However, the problem was now escalating into something much more than a dispute between Churchill and Beatty, or indeed the more important conceptual issue of the policy balance between defence and welfare spending. It was developing into a major political split within the governing party, which could have had significant long-term consequences for the Conservatives, just as the split between Asquith and Lloyd George had finished the Liberals as a party of government.

The Conservative Party was splitting along coalitionist and traditional Tory lines. The coalition had come apart only three years previously and the division between the two strands of political thought in the party remained very significant. Baldwin knew that a perceived victory for Churchill's policy would alienate the traditional Tory faction, and he would in the end ensure that the navy received more in the cruiser replacement programme than Churchill wanted: the navy would have two new cruisers by the autumn of 1925, four in 1926 and a further one in early 1927.[48] But Churchill never let up in his vociferous opposition to the cruiser programme, and harried the navy throughout his remaining years as Chancellor. Although the cruiser programme had been partially rescued, the lack of sufficiently developed defence facilities at Singapore meant that the Japanese attack on Shanghai in 1937 was successful, as was its occupation of Singapore itself in 1942 (see chapter 13).

So the ground was laid. Churchill was undermining defence strategy, had failed to see the threat from Japan – despite the fact that the Admiralty saw it clearly – and opposed the Singapore fleet base that would be lost so catastrophically under his stewardship in 1942. His divisive behaviour was also splitting the Conservative Party. It was his energy and single-mindedness that made him doggedly determined to pursue a given course of action, blinded him to the wider effects this was having and thus constituted the basis for the distrust he engendered in so many, among politicians and the electorate alike. The fundamental problem was his inconsistency of policy, first weakening the national defences at a time of some, but not severe, economic restraint; then advocating their massive expansion in the early 1930s when the nation could hardly afford it, as the next chapter will show.

4
CHURCHILL UNDER BALDWIN: THE WILDERNESS YEARS

When the Conservatives lost the 1929 general election, Churchill was keen for the government to try to remain in power, despite the result: 287 seats for Labour, 261 for the Conservatives and 59 for the Liberals. It was clear that the Liberals would support Labour rather than the Conservatives. Baldwin hesitated, but then correctly resigned the government.

Churchill's period out of office, his 'wilderness years' as he described them, ran from 1929 to 1939. He was a backbench Conservative MP, under the party leadership of Baldwin until 1937 and then Neville Chamberlain. He spent most of this time writing – living, as he put it, 'from mouth to hand'. He wrote newspaper articles, biographical essays and books. The sixth and final volume of *The World Crisis*, about the Eastern Front in World War I, was published in 1931. He wrote four volumes of his *Life of Marlborough*, about his ancestor the first Duke of Marlborough, during the 1930s and also the autobiographical *My Early Life*. His *magnum opus, A History of the English-Speaking Peoples*, was also largely written then, though not completed. His writing style was romantic rather than factual, particularly concerning his great ancestor and his own life; indeed he began writing about the former before he started his research. All this time his political beliefs were moving away from his liberal, socially reforming past towards a much more conservative belief in strong leadership.[1]

The popular belief is that Churchill could see the threat from Hitler in the 1930s whereas the government could not. Why then was it precisely during the period when he was out of office that the MacDonald, Baldwin and Chamberlain governments rearmed sufficiently to enable Britain to resist being overrun by Hitler? In reality, Britain took adequate steps to protect itself and thus ultimately to be on the victorious side in the war, avoiding the conquest and occupation to which so much of Europe became subject. The governments patiently rearmed as quickly as public opinion would permit – this issue is crucial – and as quickly as the economy would permit, an economy Churchill had weakened as Chancellor in the 1920s.

It must be understood that much British public opinion was in favour of appeasement and against Churchill in the 1930s. Just as Franklin D Roosevelt was constrained from acting against Hitler by isolationist sentiment in the USA, British governments were similarly constrained. Baldwin retired, fully seeing the coming conflict and getting out before it began. Chamberlain was genuinely, if naively, a man of peace who successfully bought Britain some additional but vital time for rearmament and in the end conditioned the British public to war. The reputations of both would be sullied subsequently, particularly by comparison with Churchill. Despite this, as chapter 8 will show, it was not Churchill, but rather MacDonald, Baldwin and Chamberlain who were to put in place the necessary organization and materiel, particularly for Fighter Command, which would prove decisive in protecting Britain in its hour of greatest danger, indeed in its 'finest hour'.

THE PROBLEM OF INDIA

The proximate cause of Churchill entering the political wilderness after the general election defeat of 1929 was the issue of India. Baldwin was in favour of granting India dominion status, or self-government within the Empire. This had been recommended by Edward Wood, Baron Irwin (later Lord Halifax), whom Baldwin, when previously in office, had appointed as Viceroy of India. Churchill vehemently opposed it, seeing it as the beginning of the end for British rule, as did the other two most senior members of Baldwin's Shadow Cabinet: the former Foreign Secretary, Austen Chamberlain, and the former Lord Chancellor, Frederick Edwin Smith, Earl of Birkenhead. Churchill referred to dominion status for India as 'a hideous act of self mutilation astounding to every nation in the world'.[2]

Churchill had joined the India Empire Society, which, as its name implied, was a group devoted to the maintenance of India's existing status within the British Empire. However, although conservative in nature, the society's members were not averse to criticizing official Conservative Party policy. Churchill would do this decisively and with considerable effect on his own future career. On 11 December 1930 he gave a speech to the society in which he said that in an independent India the presence of white people would be tolerated 'only upon sufferance', that 'debts and obligations of all kinds will be repudiated' and that 'an army of white janissaries, officered if necessary from Germany, will be hired to secure the armed ascendancy of the Hindu'.[3] He said of Mahatma Gandhi, and his movement:

> The truth is that Gandhi-ism and all it stands for will, sooner or later, have to be grappled with and finally crushed. It is no use trying to satisfy a tiger by feeding him with cat's-meat . . . We have no intention of casting away that most truly bright and precious jewel in the crown of the King, which more than all our other Dominions and Dependencies constitutes the glory and strength of the British Empire. The loss of India would mark and consummate the downfall of the British Empire. That great organism would pass at a stroke out of life into history. From such a catastrophe there could be no recovery.[4]

Much later, during World War II, when he was Prime Minister, he would say to his Cabinet colleague Leo Amery, 'I hate Indians, they are beastly people with a beastly religion.'[5]

In order to assist a diplomatic solution to India's problems, on 25 January 1931 the Viceroy released Gandhi from imprisonment and legalized his political movement, the Congress Party. This was too much for Churchill: he left the Shadow Cabinet, and would not be invited to return to a Cabinet post until the outbreak of war.[6]

The Government of India Act 1935 was the last prior to Indian independence in 1947. Direct elections were introduced for the first time and the franchise was increased from 7 to 35 million. The act granted autonomy to Indian provinces, and provincial assemblies were to incorporate additional elected Indian representatives, who were enabled to lead majority governments. However, governors retained discretionary powers over the summoning of legislatures and assent to bills.

Churchill's son Randolph decided to stand as an anti-India Bill Conservative against the official Conservative candidate in the Wavertree by-election. On 19 January 1935 Churchill said that this was 'upon his own responsibility'. Six days later Churchill spoke against the India Home Rule Bill on a visit to Bristol, and on 11 February he made the final opposition speech to the second reading of the bill in the House of Commons. Seven days after that he began his involvement in the bill's committee stage, where he eventually accepted it and helped to improve it.[7]

Churchill's intemperate attitude towards India and its independence movement was most ill judged; in 1931 he said Gandhi was 'a seditious Middle Temple lawyer posing as a fakir' and striding 'half naked up the steps of the vice regal palace'.[8] But Gandhi was immeasurably more than that even in 1931. The recurrent theme for both Churchill and the Indian Empire Society – that the Indians were not capable of self-government and that British withdrawal would lead to internecine conflict and much bloodshed – proved to be inaccurate. The creation of Pakistan and later Bangladesh certainly did create bloodshed, and there are continuing problems in Kashmir to this day. Yet as 60 years of Indian independence have proved, of all the decolonized British imperial possessions, India has been the most capable of democratic self-governance.

CHURCHILL IS LEFT OUT

On 17 November 1935 Nancy Astor, the first woman MP, said to Baldwin, 'Don't put Winston in the Government – it will mean war at home and abroad.'[9] Baldwin had previously decided not to invite Churchill back into the Shadow Cabinet or to participate in Ramsay MacDonald's National government. Now he decided not to include him in his own 1935–7 ministry. This was not only because of Churchill's stance on India, but also because of adverse party reaction to his outbursts in defence debates and his later stance over the abdication issue. Baldwin also had concerns over his own succession. In consequence the party whips opposed Churchill's inclusion and so did senior Conservative figures such as Neville Chamberlain, though his brother Austen was in favour.

Another reason Churchill remained out of favour with the Conservatives was that from early 1936 he was associated with a group called 'The Focus', a broad coalition of political interests with one uniting aim: to oppose the Nazis. Many of its members were pacifists or socialists, and it was naturally attractive to many Jewish people. For the Tories, pacifism and socialism were anathema, and there was some anti-Semitism as well. The Focus supported the League of Nations, which was traditionally supported by the left and was thus not particularly popular with the Tories. And Churchill did not help his own cause when, having been opposed to Bolshevism for many years, he declared: 'Russia can for the present be looked upon as an asset to the cause of peace.'[10] The people he consorted with didn't help either. His close associates at this time included the Tory MPs Robert Boothby and Brendan Bracken. Boothby was a bisexual who had a long affair with Harold Macmillan's wife and was rumoured to be the father of her youngest son. Bracken was an Irishman with a shadowy past, and few barring Churchill seemed to trust his judgment.

Baldwin wrote to Viscount JCC Davidson MP, who had been Chairman of the party from 1926–30, in the autumn of 1935: 'As for Winston, I feel we should not give him a post at this stage. Anything he undertakes he puts his heart and soul into it. If there is going to be a war – and no one can say there is not – we must keep him fresh to be our war Prime Minister.' Also, to his Parliamentary Private Secretary, Sir Thomas Dugdale (later Lord Crathorne), Baldwin commented: 'One of my biggest problems was whether to include Winston in the Cabinet. We may not get through this business without war. If we do have a war, Winston must be Prime Minister. If he is in now we shan't be able to engage in that war as a united nation.'[11] Baldwin's belief in Churchill's energy, focus and dynamism was prescient in its application to the coming war. However, it has always been questioned to what extent Baldwin actually believed this at the time, and to what extent it was the consequence of 'spin' later on. What is clear is that Baldwin, in retirement, openly favoured Churchill to replace Chamberlain in May 1940. Churchill would be 65 years old when he became Prime Minister, yet it was common for politicians to serve beyond that age, and Churchill was surprisingly vigorous both then and for some time afterwards.

When the possibility of a new Ministry of Defence was contemplated, and after it was rejected, Baldwin was minded to create a small department to co-ordinate defence matters; Austen Chamberlain thought Churchill should be put in charge. But Baldwin commented that if it was given to Churchill, 'it would alarm those Liberal and central elements who had taken his exclusion as a pledge against militarism'.[12] Also, it was indicated that the job might become that of Deputy Prime Minister; if Churchill had it, this would mean he was likely to succeed Baldwin as Prime Minister on the latter's retirement. This Baldwin felt would be divisive, so he did not favour it.

After Baldwin became Prime Minister, Churchill offered reconciliation in July 1935, but already in June Baldwin had decided not to include him in his new government. Instead he asked Churchill to join the Air Defence Research Sub-Committee of the CID. Baldwin thought his technical interests and capacity for hard work could be put to good use there.[13]

THE RACE TO REARM

The total defence budget had been £116 million in 1926–7. Ramsay MacDonald's Labour government would reduce it to £110 million in 1930–1, first because the Labour Party believed in cutting defence expenditure and second because of the October 1929 Wall Street Crash and the consequent Depression. In fact, Churchill had himself originally proposed a defence budget of £110 million for 1926–7, until others in government and the defence chiefs stopped it.[14] The cuts continued under the National government, and defence spending hit its nadir of £102.7 million in 1932–3, precisely because the Depression was at its worst. But in 1932 the government abandoned the Ten-Year Rule, and Churchill fretted about the defence budget because it had fallen so far below even his economies as Chancellor. Relieved of the responsibility of the Chancellorship and the discipline of being in office, he could now afford to be frightened about the likely defence implications; he no longer had to worry about displacing social policy through greater defence spending. By 1933 he would be advocating rapid rearmament.[15]

The issue had turned full circle – again. As President of the Board of Trade in the run-up to World War I, Churchill advocated restraint in rearmament; as First Lord, he rearmed; in the 1920s as Chancellor he was disarming; and now, in the 1930s, he was arguing for rearmament yet again. In his defence one could use Harold Macmillan's expression when a change of policy was needed: that it was caused by 'events, dear boy, events'. Churchill believed that the international situation required rearmament from 1911 as it would in the 1930s, but there was no major threat in the 1920s and so contraction in the armed forces could be accepted. But this was obvious – it was not the contribution of a visionary who could see what others could not. The French military commander Ferdinand Foch saw the coming threat remarkably early, but Churchill did not. If large armed forces were to offer a deterrent, he should have been advocating their enlargement instead of weakening them while in office in the 1920s.

AIR POWER

Churchill would insist that it was he, rather than the party leadership, who could see the coming threat, particularly from the air. Yet Baldwin said to the House of Commons on 10 November 1932: 'The bomber will always get through. The only defence is in offence, which means you have to kill more women and children more quickly than the enemy if you want to save yourselves.'[16] This was a remarkably prescient statement at a time when bombers were biplanes with open cockpits and fixed landing gear. It would be fully corroborated in World War II, when air defence could not prevent the effects of the Blitz, and the Allied offensive aerial campaign against Germany would have devastating effect. It is true that the battle between bombers and defending fighters waxed and waned throughout the war, with first one then the other enjoying the advantage, but overall the bomber won out, in both the Allied campaign against Germany and the Luftwaffe campaign against Britain. Even though Fighter Command retained air superiority in the Battle of Britain, this did not prevent the Luftwaffe from wreaking havoc with British cities: only victory over Germany would end it.

Churchill wrote that he made public his concerns about the RAF's deficiencies, as well as German rearmament, as early as March and November 1933.[17] But of course, he had contributed to those deficiencies by opposing the 52-squadron proposal in 1924. It may be argued that even if he had not, the aircraft commissioned in the 1920s would have been technologically obsolete by the late 1930s, but if a large air force were to constitute a deterrent – as Churchill would argue in the 1930s (I shall argue in the following pages that against Hitler it would not) – then having had a larger force in the 1920s would have offered a greater deterrent than simply expanding it from 1933. If Churchill had had the foresight of Foch this is precisely the stance he would have taken.[18]

In fact, state-of-the-art production aircraft in 1933 were also technologically obsolete by 1939, yet in *The Second World War* Churchill referred to 'the time lost [in air force rearmament] by the Cabinet from 1932 to 1934'.[19] He wrote: 'It would have been possible in 1933, or even in 1934, for Britain to have created an air power which would have imposed the necessary restraints upon Hitler's ambition, or would perhaps have enabled the military leaders of Germany to control his violent acts.'[20] This was wrong: production aircraft technology from 1932 to 1934 was quite inadequate for the task; the canvas-skinned biplane fighters and short-range bombers of the period, with limited armament, open cockpits and fixed landing gear, could not have constituted a threat to German ambitions.

A technological revolution occurred in the late 1920s and early 1930s, in Britain and elsewhere, that would produce stressed-skin all-metal cantilever production monoplanes with retractable landing gear, using leaded fuel. It was this that resulted in the development of the aircraft that would win the Battle of Britain. But production military aircraft based on such technology were not available anywhere in the world prior to 1934 (the Messerschmitt Bf 109 first flew in 1935, the same year as the Hawker Hurricane). If the RAF had been re-equipped in 1932–4, it would have received aircraft that were entirely outclassed and obsolete by 1939, or indeed by 1938. However, if Churchill believed that the RAF should have been re-equipped *from* 1934, this is exactly what happened anyway.

Churchill's claim that a few more biplanes in the RAF would have caused German generals to constrain Hitler is laughable. If any German generals had tried to constrain Hitler they would have suffered the fate of so many of Hitler's internal opponents: they would have been dismissed or shot. It was very naive of Churchill to have written such a thing in the first volume of *The Second World War*, published in 1948 when the full extent of Hitler's ruthlessness was well known.

He also wrote in that volume, 'If we had taken steps betimes to create an air force half as strong again, or twice as strong, as any that Germany could produce in breach of her treaty, we should have kept control of the future.'[21] In reality 'we' did have control of the future: the Battle of Britain was successful and the USA and USSR ensured total German defeat. If Churchill was suggesting that such an air force would have constituted a deterrent to Hitler's ambitions in the early 1930s, then he had been culpable in not vouchsafing that as Chancellor in the 1920s. But it seems that even in 1948 Churchill still did not understand Hitler, who had been hell-bent on his plans come what may, and was influenced by Allied policy as to timing and detail, but not with regard to his ultimate goal. It is curious that Churchill, whose all-seeing eye was supposed to be so aware of the threat, would write in November 1935: 'We cannot tell whether Hitler will be the man who will once again let loose upon the world another war in which civilization will irretrievably succumb, or whether he will go down in history as the man who restored honour and peace of mind to the Great Germanic nation . . .'[22]

On 3 February 1935, Sir John Simon, the Foreign Secretary, and Pierre Laval, the French Foreign Minister, released a joint statement that, among other things, called for a negotiated arms agreement to replace the Treaty of Versailles. Their proposal included a clause ensuring air support for the victims of aggression, and the creation of pacts with nations including those in Central and Eastern Europe. This was largely a recognition of the reality that Hitler was flouting the Versailles Treaty and was a move to shore up alliances to contain him. But its corollary was a fresh look at defence domestically. On 4 March a white paper was published entitled 'Statement Relating to Defence'.[23] It concluded that increased defence expenditure was necessary on all three defence services. The white paper was MacDonald's last significant political contribution before Baldwin replaced him as Prime Minister on 7 June.[24]

So MacDonald, the man who was so strongly associated with the striving for peace, before Chamberlain and to some extent Baldwin took on that mantle, recognized that the threat from Hitler required this turnaround in defence expenditure. This marked the beginning of what would become the Hurricane and Spitfire, the 'heavenly twins' that would constitute the backbone of Britain's defence in its hour of greatest need. Churchill had persistently carped from the sidelines for such a requirement, but it was the MacDonald National government, including Baldwin's Conservative Party, that had actually done it, at a time of huge strain on the national finances and when there was no public appetite for rearmament and another war.

Ironically, it would be Neville Chamberlain, the very man who would become so identified with appeasement, who had direct responsibility for the rearmament process from 1934 while Chancellor of the Exchequer, particularly regarding the air force.[25] The new aircraft resulting from this rearmament programme would be the only state-of-the-art aircraft in service by 1939 capable of defending the realm.

Chamberlain was influenced by the theories of Basil Liddell-Hart: that the army should be relatively small, but mechanized, while Britain's principal defence requirement was for a robust navy and air force. This was consistent with existing British practice: for generations the navy had been the principal instrument of exercising hegemonic power, and Britain had no history of establishing a large permanent standing army.[26] Thus Chamberlain's policy emphasized the air force and navy, precisely the areas Churchill had sought to cut as Chancellor a decade earlier. So defence, not just appeasement, was central to Chamberlain's policy accomplishments.[27]

On 9 February 1936 Chamberlain wrote to his sister:

> I have had to do most work on the programme, which has been materially modified as a result, and I am pretty satisfied now that, if we can keep out of war for a few years, we shall have an air force of such striking power that no one will care to run risks with it. I cannot believe that the next war, if it ever comes, will be like the last one, and I believe our resources will be more profitably employed in the air, and on the sea, than in building up great armies.[28]

This is prophetic of course, as the RAF would play a decisive role in what would indeed be a fundamentally different kind of war, one where Fighter Command would save Britain. Chamberlain, as Prime Minister from the following year, would see to it that war was postponed just long enough for defence preparations to be adequate.

THE NAVY AND 'WEIGHT OF SHOT'

The British Government concluded the Anglo-German Naval Agreement in 1935, without French involvement, which permitted the Germans to develop their navy well beyond Versailles limits.[29] Churchill railed against this agreement, and implied that it was directly facilitating the German arms build-up. But Hitler had already flouted the Treaty of Versailles with the construction of the battle-cruisers *Scharnhorst* and *Gneisenau*, as Churchill himself admitted.[30] So with or without such an agreement, Hitler was going to build anyway. Churchill's implication that a more draconian agreement would have inhibited Hitler from rearming is simply not the case; it is clear that Hitler had every intention of rearming and was fully prepared to violate any agreement or treaty that stood in his way. Churchill said that the failure to include the French in the agreement divided Hitler's enemies and was consequently a help to him.[31] He was perhaps right, but it is extremely unlikely that Hitler would have been stopped had the French been included, as he was pursuing his plans come what may.

Churchill referred to the laying down of the battleships *Bismarck* and her sister ship *Tirpitz* at this time, and that Germany was not bound by the Washington Naval Treaty. Consequently these ships displaced over 45,000 tons, when the British, French and Americans, who were subject to the treaty, were restricted to 35,000 tons. He wrote that, when launched, they were 'certainly the strongest vessels afloat in the world'.[32] He also referred to the need to develop British battleships in the 1930s with modern 406mm (16in) guns as opposed to the 356mm (14in) gun battleships Britain was then building under the treaty, because the weight of shot of a nine-gun broadside from a 406mm (16in) gun battleship was far greater than that of the nine-gun broadside from a 356mm (14in) gun battleship.[33] These are decidedly odd statements to have made in a book published in 1948, when all the principal facts were known. Churchill fails to point out that only *Bismarck* and *Tirpitz* were built beyond those treaty limits, and they each had eight 380mm (15in) guns, compared to the ten 356mm (14in) guns of the *King George V* class built for the Royal Navy under the treaty, or indeed the pair of nine 406mm (16in) gun battleships, *Nelson* and *Rodney*, which were already in service. So the German Navy was not as well equipped compared with the Royal Navy as Churchill had implied. *Bismarck*, like all the battleships of the period, proved to be vulnerable to air power and was sunk without having inflicted decisive damage on Britain's defences, apart from sinking *Hood* – which had eight 380mm (15in) guns like *Bismarck*, and was equally vulnerable. Precisely because of this vulnerability, *Tirpitz* would be holed up in Norway doing little, until it was dispatched by the Royal Air Force (see chapter 9).

In 1948 there was no evidence to support this 'weight of shot' argument. The Japanese had built a pair of 457mm (18in) gun battleships that were dispatched by the Americans without having offered any significant threat to the Allied war effort. All this was known to Churchill, yet he insisted on perpetuating the myth that he had been right about this matter all along, and that Baldwin had been remiss in not initiating the laying down of new 406mm (16in) gun battleships.

THE IRRELEVANCE OF ITALY

In Paris in December 1935, Sir Samuel Hoare, the new Foreign Secretary in Baldwin's government, met the French Foreign Minister Pierre Laval and concluded a pact to address the Abyssinian crisis, largely to the benefit of Mussolini. This was done to try to drive a wedge between Hitler and Mussolini, as the conflict in Abyssinia was tending to bring them together. Public opinion was appalled at the outcome, and Hoare was forced to resign. Sir Robert Vansittart, the Permanent Secretary at the Foreign Office, was compromised because he had been in full agreement with the policy, and Chamberlain would manage to sideline him in 1938.[34] Laval would subsequently collaborate with Vichy, and endure the opprobrium of his nation after the war.[35]

Churchill wrote of how the association between Germany and Italy, along with Britain losing air parity with Germany, 'enabled Hitler to advance along his predetermined deadly course.'[36] In fact, Mussolini proved a dubious asset to Hitler throughout their association, and in 1943 after the Italian capitulation Hitler had to re-install him in a puppet German regime. It was quite clear that Hitler had embarked upon 'his predetermined deadly course' irrespective of Mussolini or Italy, so the Hoare–Laval pact was irrelevant.

BALDWIN'S COMPROMISE

On 28 July 1936 Churchill was the principal advocate for a deputation in Parliament on the subject of rearmament, though Austen Chamberlain and James Gascoyne-Cecil, 4th Marquess of Salisbury, were in principle leading it for the Commons and the Lords respectively. Churchill made much of it being his baby, while Baldwin was increasingly ill and the Chancellor, Neville Chamberlain, was on holiday.[37] But the fact was that both Chancellor and Prime Minister, despite their health problems and holidays, were all too well aware of the threat and were addressing it. However, Baldwin understood the political realities in a way that Churchill did not.

Austen Chamberlain, together with Admiral of the Fleet Sir Roger Keyes (now an MP), Leo Amery (who would be in Churchill's wartime Cabinet) and Salisbury, as well as Churchill, were all calling for British rearmament.

Chamberlain was the chairman of two Conservative Parliamentary delegations in late 1936, which remonstrated with Baldwin about the rearmament programme. Chamberlain was more respected at this time than Churchill, and became an icon to young Conservatives, but all these men were out of office during this period. All were thus disgruntled, on the sidelines and without responsibility, which made it far easier for them to complain.

On 29 July Baldwin said: 'I am not going to get this country into a war with anybody for the League of Nations or anybody else or for anything else.' This was to obviate a hostile response from the opposition in Parliament and, most particularly, from the electorate. He was also reported as saying, 'If there is any fighting in Europe, I should like to see the Bolshies and Nazis doing it.'[38] Politically, one can see the merit in this: letting the two enemies fight each other would keep Britain out of the conflict and eliminate the human, economic and political costs for Britain and for Baldwin. It is obvious from his statement that Baldwin already recognized the Soviet Union as well as Nazi Germany as constituting a fundamental threat to Britain's interests, yet it would be Churchill who would be credited with identifying the threat from the 'Bolshies' in his Fulton, Missouri, speech a decade later in 1946 (see chapter 18). Baldwin was nevertheless wrong: had the twin enemies fought it out, the USSR would have eventually prevailed, with the entire continent coming under its power – not at all a satisfactory outcome for Britain.

Baldwin identified his position more precisely:

> I put before the whole House my own views with an appalling frankness. From 1933, I and my friends were all very worried about what was happening in Europe ... You will remember at the time there was probably a stronger pacifist feeling running through the country than at any time since the War [World War I]. I am speaking of 1933 and 1934. You will remember the election at Fulham in the autumn of 1933, when a seat which the National Government held was lost by about 7,000 votes on no issue but the pacifist ... That was the feeling in the country in 1933. My position as a leader of a great party was not altogether a comfortable one. I asked myself what chance was there ... within the next year or two

of that feeling being so changed that the country would give a mandate for rearmament? Supposing I had gone to the country and said that Germany was rearming and we must rearm, does anybody think that this pacific democracy would have rallied to the cry at that moment? I cannot think of anything that would have made the loss of the election from my point of view more certain.[39]

In response to this Churchill wrote: 'It carried naked truth about his motives into indecency. That a Prime Minister should avow that he had not done his duty in regard to national safety because he was afraid of losing the election was an incident without parallel in our Parliamentary history.'[40] However, in June 1935 the League of Nations Union undertook a 'peace ballot', which showed that almost 10.5 million people in Britain wanted greater disarmament, that 10 million wanted no more than economic sanctions employed against any aggressor, and that such sanctions should be implemented only upon a League of Nations decision.[41]

Baldwin was absolutely right and fully justified, and Churchill was wrong to criticize him. If rearmament had been a primary policy in the 1935 election, and Baldwin had lost that election in consequence, the rearmament programme that he actually put into effect during his final two-year stint as Prime Minister from 1935 to 1937 would not have taken place. Instead, a Labour government with Liberal support would have taken power, and both these parties were opposed to rearmament at the time. Thus, by 1939 the rearmament situation would have been worse than it actually proved to be, not better. Churchill wrote, 'It is much better for parties or politicians to be turned out of office than to imperil the life of the nation.'[42] But if any party seeking election in 1935 had proposed rearmament as their primary policy, or even a major one, they would have suffered precisely this fate at the hands of the electorate; no party could have acted in this way. If they had, the life of the nation *would* have been imperilled. Churchill went on, 'There is no record in our history of any Government asking Parliament and the people for the necessary measures of defence and being refused.'[43] Yet this is precisely what would have happened had the government at the 1935 election asked for the level of rearmament Churchill wanted; indeed he effectively admitted as much when he referred to opposition from Labour and the Liberals to the modest air rearmament programme of 1934.[44] This was the same electoral constraint to which Roosevelt was subject in the United States. The best that could be done was what Baldwin actually did: to enunciate publicly the need to avoid war in order to get elected, then to introduce a cautious rearmament programme that did not appreciably alienate the electorate. This policy worked, as it enabled Britain to remain free from Nazi invasion and subjugation.

In fact, Neville Chamberlain, the man who would become ineluctably linked with appeasement rather than rearmament, had wanted to fight the 1935 election principally on the issue of defence. Even though Baldwin demurred, the stance the government did take resulted in the opposition Labour and Liberal parties denouncing rearmament during the election and raising the issues of 'war-mongering' and the creation of an 'arms race'.[45] How much worse this opposition would have been, and how much more likely the defeat of the Conservative Party, had Churchill been its leader saying what he said while in the wilderness. There would not have been rearmament, but a Labour–Liberal government committed to pacifism: Britain would have been defeated in the Battle of Britain, invaded and occupied by Germany, and world history would have been entirely different.

ACTIVE INTERFERENCE

Churchill suggested that early substantial rearmament by Britain would have galvanized the League of Nations into collective defence, and that to constrain Hitler, 'The only way was to concentrate all air power in the hands of the League, which must be united and become a reality.'[46] There seems little evidence that the League ever had the gumption to act in this way; it proved a very ineffectual organization and it is hard to see why unilateral British rearmament – rearmament greater than actually took place – would have made any material difference in this regard. Churchill's contention that such rearmament would have *prevented* World War II (as chapter 5 will argue in detail) is patently false.

In 1936 Churchill characterized government policy towards rearmament thus: 'The Government adhered to their policy of moderation, half-measures, and keeping things quiet.'[47] As for 'moderation', and 'half-measures', by the time the war started rearmament was in fact just sufficient for the defence of the realm; as for 'keeping things quiet', this was necessary to avoid alienating the public or Parliament. He went on: 'It was astonishing to me that they did not seek to utilise all the growing harmonies that now existed in the nation. By this means they would have strengthened themselves and have gained the power to strengthen the country.'[48] But in reality the harmonies in 1936 were still for peace, not for war, as the public and Parliamentary support for appeasement made clear. In *The Second World War* Churchill wrote:

> Once Hitler's Germany had been allowed to rearm without active interference by the Allies and former associated Powers, a second World War was almost certain. The longer a decisive trial of strength was put off, the worse would be our chances, at first of stopping Hitler without serious fighting, and as a second stage of being victorious after a terrible ordeal.'[49]

But what was 'active interference by the Allies' to consist of? Churchill gives no credible answer. Britain did not have the resources to defeat Hitler while he was rearming. Had Churchill not compromised the armed forces in the 1920s, Germany could have been threatened or attacked as soon as Hitler came to power: then and only then could his ambitions have been thwarted by Britain. 'Serious fighting' was always going to occur given that this opportunity had been missed. The 'decisive trial' was put off precisely because there was not yet the public will to devote the necessary resources to fight it and win it; the 'terrible ordeal' was therefore inevitable. Churchill indicated that had all of Germany's ostensible opponents ganged up against it early on, they might have defeated it.[50] And so they might, but what could the British government have done to achieve this? Britain would have appeared as a bellicose warmonger, chivvying others to fight a war that few had an appetite for, either in Europe or in Britain.

When, on 7 March 1936, Hitler announced that he was to reoccupy the Rhineland, Churchill said that the French were minded to mobilize but needed the engagement of Britain. He argued that it was the lack of British support then that constituted the problem. But he then contradicted himself, saying, 'Nothing however can relieve the French Government of their prime responsibility,'[51] indicating that it was the responsibility of the French to mobilize irrespective of British intentions.

Had both nations mobilized in response to this act, what then? Would Hitler have backed down? Possibly, but what would the allies have done next: attacked Germany, or waited for it to rearm further? Surely they would not have attacked Germany if it had not annexed the Rhineland, so they would have had to wait while Germany rearmed further, and that would have defeated the object. If they *had* attacked Germany and occupied the Rhineland, would this have been responded to positively by other nations in the League? Britain and France would have been open to condemnation as aggressors, and other nations would have opposed this Anglo-French action. If the Anglo-French alliance had then resisted international opposition, would they have restored the Rhineland to the requirements of Versailles? If this was all the Anglo-French did, assuming they could, Hitler would have continued the rearmament process in parts of Germany other than the Rhineland and tried again later. If the Anglo-French action had not stopped at occupation of the Rhineland, and they had invaded the rest of Germany, and assuming they were not effectively resisted by Hitler's forces, they would surely have incurred the opposition of virtually all other nations. The really important point is that there is no credible evidence that such a policy could have been accomplished with the resources available in 1936, or that there was public appetite for such a policy. Churchill wrote:

> When Hitler met his Generals after the successful re-occupation of the Rhineland, he was able to confront them with the falsity of their fears and prove to them how superior his judgement or "intuition" was to that of ordinary military men. The generals bowed. As good Germans they were glad to see their country gaining ground so rapidly in Europe and its former adversaries so divided and tame. Undoubtedly Hitler's prestige and authority in the supreme circle of German power was sufficiently enhanced by this episode to encourage and enable him to march forward to greater tests.[52]

Yet in 1940, with General Erich von Manstein's plan working so successfully to defeat France, it would be Hitler who was timidly holding back his generals, and so Churchill's claim that the German General Staff were timid appears false (see chapter 7).

Churchill intimated that any backing down by Hitler over the annexation of the Rhineland, precipitated by robust Anglo-French opposition, would perhaps have resulted in his generals usurping him and ending his rule.[53] This seems a forlorn hope, particularly given that the much greater defeats and reversals later on in the war did not achieve this objective. Even when defeat for Germany was certain, the 20 July 1944 plot had only a small number of active conspirators, and was put down very forcibly. It seems unlikely that in 1936, on the basis of such a comparatively minor reversal, Hitler's generals would have ganged up against him and succeeded in replacing him. Indeed, Churchill's proposal was particularly feeble, as a robust Anglo-French resistance to Germany was reliant for its success entirely on the assumption of a German General Staff uprising against Hitler. The examples he gave of Hitler's ostensible near-overthrow in the immediate pre-war years were similarly unfounded, as chapter 5 will show.

THE ABDICATION CRISIS

Although rearmament was the principal issue over which Churchill and Baldwin clashed, the abdication of King Edward VIII was another issue that would further alienate Churchill from the Conservative Party and pretty much seal his fate in the wilderness. His wife Clementine insisted that he was perhaps the only one left who believed in the divine right of kings.[54]

Baldwin believed there would be strong public opposition to the King's decision to marry the twice-divorced American, Wallis Simpson, and that this would reflect adversely upon himself and his government. In fact, when the British press first publicized the affair in the week before the abdication, there was much public support for the King's desire to marry the woman he loved.[55]

Baldwin lured the King into accepting the will of the Cabinet. He also convinced him that the Empire should be consulted on the matter and that this should influence the outcome. The Cabinet, and indeed Parliament, strongly opposed the marriage, but Baldwin told the King that the governments of the Dominions were unanimously opposed when in fact they were split on the issue.

Churchill made a political mistake in supporting Edward VIII in his wish to marry Wallis Simpson, as it cost him further support in his party and in Parliament in general. But it is hard not to have sympathy with Churchill on a personal level. He was an emotional person, and he wanted the King to marry the woman he loved. He called the King a 'poor little lamb'.[56] It was Churchill who proposed the notion of a morganatic marriage, whereby the King could marry Mrs Simpson but she would not become queen. This was rejected by Baldwin, who wished to stop the marriage come what may.

However, Churchill was rather more disingenuous regarding the pledge that Baldwin had asked of his colleagues: that none should try to form a government if the Cabinet was obliged to resign over the King's decision to marry. He initially agreed, but it then became clear that he might try to form a government if other Cabinet colleagues were to fall out over the issue. A King's party, to support the King in his marital decision, was advocated by some, and would have been formed from disaffected politicians. Churchill dallied with the possibility of participating in such a party, despite being asked by Baldwin not to. The King consulted Churchill personally on the marriage issue, despite the fact that he did not enjoy any official position, and this fuelled the idea of a conspiracy. But Churchill would soon tire of Edward and his 'court of dagos'. He would come to judge the new King George VI his superior and would be overcome by the splendour of his coronation.[57]

The abdication crisis cost Churchill dear: he was not only socially and politically ostracized, but his attempt to create a rearmament movement called 'Arms and the Covenant' foundered in consequence. Yet he subsequently reversed his position over the abdication: during the war he told Baldwin that Wallis Simpson becoming Queen was 'an eventuality almost too horrible to contemplate'.[58] He was principled when he supported the King, less so in his mischievous intent to exploit disaffection in the Baldwin line and his dalliance with a King's party. But regarding Wallis Simpson he was inconsistent; either the King should have been free to marry her, or her being Queen was unacceptable.[59]

Baldwin had long prepared for his retirement; having steered the nation through the abdication crisis, he felt it was a high to go out on. After his misjudgment in 1924, when he called and promptly lost a general election having only just become Prime Minister, Baldwin was acutely aware of the significance of public opinion in politics. He could see the world situation deteriorating and wanted to get out while still enjoying significant support from the electorate. Reflecting on Baldwin's attitude towards Churchill, one wonders how keen he was to lumber Churchill with the responsibility of a war he fully recognized would be so difficult to win. This was not a unique view: Halifax, who was pessimistic about the outcome of the war, would decline the possibility of succeeding Chamberlain as Prime Minister for fear of leading Britain into defeat and possible German occupation. Baldwin's failure of judgment was that, although he remained popular on his retirement in May 1937, he would shortly be identified as one of the guilty men who supposedly failed to do enough to stop Hitler earlier. With Neville Chamberlain's death in 1940, Baldwin, by default, became the principal target for the nation's opprobrium. He would die a rather sorry figure in 1947 at the age of 80.

THE ISSUE OF BLAME

The critical issue is that delayed rearmament ensured that Hitler received the blame for the coming war. The early rearmament Churchill wanted would have looked like an arms race between rival imperial powers, and Germany would not have been identified as the sole aggressor. If rearmament had been faster, and Churchill's bellicose foreign policy stance had been adopted, what reaction would this have created in Berlin? Would Hitler have been cowed into a negotiated settlement of his concerns, or have failed to pursue any part of his aggressive policy? Certainly not. He would have simply accelerated the process of German rearmament to out-build the British. The relative armaments position would not have been closed and reversed, as Churchill wanted, and Hitler would have accelerated his programme of annexation and aggression. So, though Churchill referred to World War II as an avoidable war, in reality it was an inevitable war, and if he had had his way it would have been inevitable sooner.

5
CHURCHILL UNDER CHAMBERLAIN: APPEASEMENT

For just over two years, from May 1937 to September 1939, Churchill was out of office, a backbench Conservative MP under the Prime Minister and party leader, Neville Chamberlain. The beginning of this period would see him at his lowest ebb; the end of it would see him on the cusp of immortality.

Churchill said of himself at this time that he was 'a very old man': he would be 63 in November 1937. He almost sold the family home, Chartwell: the children had grown up – as he put it, 'the kittens had become cats' – and his finances, ever precarious, were another good reason for selling, until a wealthy friend of his crony and fellow Conservative MP Brendan Bracken came to his financial aid. But soon his old hobbyhorse, the threat of the rise of Nazi Germany and the need for rearmament, would galvanize him again.[1]

Churchill's principal claim about World War II was that it was an unnecessary war: it could have been prevented, and it was appeasement and late rearmament that had helped bring it about. He argued that Hitler could have been stopped if Chamberlain had initiated a grand alliance (or what he later referred to as a triple alliance) between France, Britain and the Soviet Union, which could have guaranteed the sovereignty of Czechoslovakia against the German threat. This would have required earlier rearmament, as Britain would have needed to be ready to fight in 1938; nevertheless Churchill would still be advocating the policy *in* 1938, despite the lack of sufficient rearmament. This policy, he argued, would have stayed Hitler's hand, as he would have faced a war on two fronts, and it would thus have prevented his territorial acquisitions. This in turn, Churchill suggested, would have precipitated a coup against Hitler by the German military High Command. The new German leadership would then have responded rationally to the robust stance of the alliance and refrained from precipitating the war.

THE MUNICH AGREEMENT

The four-power Munich Agreement was signed at the Munich Conference
on 29 September 1938 between Germany, Britain, France and Italy,
in settlement of the Sudetenland crisis. Ethnic Germans constituted
a substantial proportion of the population of the Sudeten region of
Czechoslovakia, which also contained the armament production facilities
of the Skoda factories and much of Czechoslovakia's border defences.
Czechoslovakia was not invited to the conference.

Hitler had been cajoled into holding the conference by Mussolini,
because Italy was unprepared for a general European war and Mussolini
wanted to constrain German power. The signatories to the agreement
were Hitler, Chamberlain, Mussolini and Edouard Deladier for France.
On 30 September the Czechoslovakian government reluctantly accepted
its terms, giving Hitler control of the Sudetenland from 10 October. It
also gave Hitler effective control over the rest of Czechoslovakia, provided
he exercised no further territorial ambitions. Hitler and Chamberlain also
signed a resolution to address all future Anglo-German disputes through
peaceful negotiations. It was this resolution that Chamberlain waved
triumphantly at Heston Airport on his return to England, while making
his 'Peace for our time' speech. For Churchill, the Munich Agreement
was a disaster. It simply led to Germany's decision to annex the whole of
Czechoslovakia and subsequently Poland.

In February 1938, Anthony Eden had resigned as Foreign Secretary
over the 'appeasement' policy. Yet afterwards Churchill was a signatory
to a round-robin letter supporting Chamberlain's policy. He told David
Margesson, the Chief Whip, 'he felt sure that the Prime Minister's point
of view on the present foreign situation and his own were not divergent'.[2]
Seven months later the Munich Agreement was signed.

Air Chief Marshal Sir Hugh Dowding, Air Officer Commanding-in-
Chief Fighter Command, recognized that it was necessary to perfect the
defensive systems the RAF was putting in place in the late 1930s, and
that this required time. Thus, he advised Chamberlain that the policy of
appeasement was necessary in order to prepare Fighter Command for the
coming war, and supported Chamberlain's decision to go to Munich to
sign the peace agreement.[3] Churchill's claim, which he would make again
after the war, was that it would have been better to have gone to war earlier

and that Munich was a fiasco. The country would have been hopelessly ill prepared had the government followed this advice. Churchill denounced the Munich Agreement in the Commons on 5 October 1938:

> We have sustained a total and unmitigated defeat . . . You will find that in a period of time which may be measured by years, but may be measured by months, Czechoslovakia will be engulfed in the Nazi régime . . . We are in the presence of a disaster of the first magnitude . . . we have sustained a defeat without a war, the consequences of which will travel far with us along our road . . . we have passed an awful milestone in our history, when the whole equilibrium of Europe has been deranged, and that the terrible words have for the time being been pronounced against the Western democracies: 'Thou art weighed in the balance and found wanting.' And do not suppose that this is the end. This is only the beginning of the reckoning. This is only the first sip, the first foretaste of a bitter cup which will be proffered to us year by year unless by a supreme recovery of moral health and martial vigour, we arise again and take our stand for freedom as in the olden time.[4]

When Chamberlain and his Parliamentary Private Secretary, the future Prime Minister Alec Douglas Home, went to Munich, they agreed that Russia had territorial ambitions and Germany could constitute a check on it.[5] How prescient they were to see the threat from the USSR, long before Churchill would denounce the Soviets in his 1946 speech in Fulton, Missouri.

When Chamberlain became Prime Minister, the British public still had no appetite for war or rearmament; appeasement was not so much Chamberlain's policy as that of the British people. Many still had visceral memories of the trench warfare of World War I, just two decades earlier, and there was a very strong belief among the public that a repetition should be avoided at (almost) any price. Thus Chamberlain and his foreign policy were much lauded by the public at the time: how fickle they would prove. Churchill was considered a warmonger and people treated him with suspicion and sometimes hostility, yet later he would be remembered as the greatest Briton. Chamberlain did not include Churchill in his Cabinet until the declaration of war. His judgment was astute, as he appreciated that Churchill's inclusion would have inflamed relations with Hitler and Mussolini and thus brought war closer. And this was precisely the point: Churchill would have precipitated war before Britain was ready and incurred some of the blame. Chamberlain understood this at the time. Once the war had started, Chamberlain could include him.

REARMAMENT

Churchill claimed, both in the late 1930s and subsequently in *The Second World War*, that Chamberlain was particularly culpable for what he saw as the lamentable state of British rearmament. By 1938–9, he wrote,

> No one could deny that we were hideously unprepared for war . . . Great Britain had allowed herself to be far surpassed by the strength of the German Air Force. All our vulnerable points were unprotected. Barely a hundred anti-aircraft guns could be found for the defence of the largest city and centre of population in the world.[6]

But Britain was not unprepared for war. Chamberlain's preparations were sufficient to win the Battle of Britain and so for the country to remain unconquered, which is all that, standing alone and with limited resources, Britain could realistically have achieved. Chamberlain devised the first two white papers in defence during the 1936–8 period, and was ultimately responsible for the final one. In 1936 defence expenditure was £188 million; this rose to £280 million the following year when Chamberlain succeeded Baldwin as Prime Minister, and to £700 million in 1939. Indeed Chamberlain's estimate in the 1937 white paper was £1,500 million.[7] The one poorly developed element of home defence by the start of the war, as Churchill indicated, was the anti-aircraft artillery batteries, or 'ack-ack guns'. However, the problem was not lack of numbers, as he intimated, but lack of accuracy: no optical or radar-based system of guidance then existed that could accurately shoot down enemy aircraft. When Churchill was Prime Minister he would tell the units to keep firing even though it was known that they were hitting virtually nothing, simply to keep up civilian morale.

Britain was subject to the London Treaty until the end of 1936, so the starting point for naval rearmament was modest: it possessed 15 capital ships, of which only three had been constructed after World War I, and 50 cruisers, whereas in 1914 it had had 69 capital ships and 108 cruisers. Much of the responsibility for the number of ships in 1914 was Churchill's as First Lord of the Admiralty; much of the responsibility for the number two decades later was also Churchill's, as Chancellor in the 1920s.[8]

Chamberlain's proposals were flexible: the planned 1,500-plane strength of the home air force in 1935 was to be raised to 1,750 by March 1939 with the most advanced aircraft; this was subsequently raised in 1938 to 2,370 for introduction by March 1940, then to 8,000 in 1939. For the army, four new battalions were to be created plus general modernization. In early 1938, six regular divisions were planned, two of which were armoured, plus 13 territorials, and two more in Palestine, making 19 in all. By April 1938 this had been increased to 32. Artillery production capacity increased five times between 1935 and 1939. For the navy, planning in 1936 was for an additional 20 cruisers, and replacement of destroyers. By 1938, 24 cruisers and 40 destroyers had been laid down, together with seven battleships and five aircraft carriers. New naval tonnage under construction would exceed the previous peak of 1912–14. So Churchill's efforts as First Lord prior to World War I would be exceeded, without him, prior to World War II.[9]

However, the transformation in technology, particularly of aircraft design, created fundamental obstacles. The handcrafted system of building aircraft from wood and fabric was being replaced by the machine-tool method of constructing all-metal cantilever monoplanes. The use of mass production technology was essential in all aspects of military materiel production, but Britain had lagged behind the USA and Germany in this transition since early in the century. Britain had a substantial supply of comparatively cheap labour, which militated against the use of modern capital-intensive production methods. It also had a highly stratified society, which demanded differentiated goods for the various markets determined by social class; that meant small production runs, which also militated against mass production techniques. This was a structural problem for industry as a whole that would attenuate military production significantly. It would not be addressed entirely adequately under either Chamberlain or Churchill, or indeed for decades after the war.

In late 1937 Chamberlain appointed the industrial adviser to the Bank of England as effective chairman of all Britain's main aircraft producers. In early 1938 he created a supply board under the Air Council, with substantial financial powers to intervene. Also in 1938 he created the Prime Minister's panel of advisory industrialists, to supervise rearmament, ascertain problems and propose solutions. Missions were dispatched to the USA to secure additional sources of supply. It was not until the summer of 1938 that substantial benefits began to flow from these measures, but that in itself ensured that Britain was seen as responding to Hitler's rearmament programme and not fuelling it in an arms race.[10]

DEFENSIVE POLICY

In Chamberlain's government, economic probity was to be accomplished principally through balanced budgets and maintaining Britain's international trade. But most significantly the government believed that Britain's military and political role should be defensive. After Munich, Chamberlain's speeches emphasized this defensive policy, and that the ultimate aim was agreed or multilateral disarmament.[11] The last point is crucial, because it was this that ensured that Hitler received the blame for the war: quite clearly Britain was reluctantly responding to German rearmament and aggression; Britain practised appeasement but Germany practised war. There could be no legitimate German claims that the Versailles settlement was improper, that the Sudetenland needed to be returned, that war when it finally came was simply the result of a mutual arms race between rival imperial powers, with each equally to blame.

Had Churchill been Prime Minister at this time he would have engaged in precisely such an arms race with Germany. This would have conveyed the impression that Britain was attempting to regain supremacy over Germany for imperial purposes. Britain had begun its imperial expansion in the 18th century, and engaged in the Napoleonic Wars precisely to prevent a European hegemonic power threatening its imperial interests. Churchill, an old imperialist, would have appeared to be doing precisely the same in the 1930s, and Britain would have appeared as much to blame as Germany for the war. Instead, posterity has recognized that Hitler and the Nazis, and only they, were guilty of precipitating the war in Europe.

Chamberlain had listed the government's objectives to the House of Commons in May 1938:

> (1) the security of the United Kingdom . . . The resources of man-power, productive capacity, and endurance of this country, and unless these can be maintained not only in peace but in the early stages of war, our defeat is certain; (2) trade routes; (3) defence of British territories overseas; not as vital as the defence of our own country, because as long as we are undefeated at home, although we sustained losses overseas, we might have an opportunity of making them good thereafter; (4) co-operation, and the defence of the territories of any Allies.

These were not the beliefs of an appeaser uninterested in defence, but of a man who understood the centrality of defence quite clearly. Early on as Prime Minister he wrote: 'I believe the double policy of rearmament and better relations with Germany and Italy will carry us safely through the danger period, if only the Foreign Office will play up.'[12] His belief in better relations was forlorn, but it played a vital role in buying time, and it was his naive, genuine character that helped so much to ensure that Britain was blameless in the coming war.

POLAND AND CZECHOSLOVAKIA

By 1938 moves were already afoot by the government to establish an agreement with the Soviet Union, thus augmenting Britain's existing relationship with the French. Churchill exhorted Chamberlain to form this 'grand alliance', which he saw primarily as a Franco-British-Russian triple alliance developed from the Franco-Russian pact.[13] However, as early as 9 May 1938 Churchill said that Britain should not go 'cap in hand' to the Soviet Premier, Joseph Stalin. He also suggested that the alliance should include Poland, Romania and Bulgaria, as well as Czechoslovakia. But Poland had its own territorial desires over Czechoslovakia, as would become clear when Czechoslovakia fell to the Germans, and Romania and Bulgaria were never likely to take the risk of siding with either the USSR or Germany. Churchill did not advocate an unconditional guarantee for Czechoslovakia, and he adhered to a view, shared by others at the time, that the Czechoslovakian President, Edvard Beneš, should negotiate with Konran Henlein, head of the Czechoslovakian Sudetenland, even though it was quite clear that he was Hitler's stooge.[14] On 20 March 1938 Chamberlain wrote to his sister:

> As a matter of fact, the plan of the 'Grand Alliance', as Winston calls it, had occurred to me long before he mentioned it . . . I talked about it to Halifax, and we submitted it to the chiefs of staff and the F.O. experts. It is a very attractive idea; indeed, there is almost everything to be said for it until you come to examine its practicability. From that moment its attraction vanishes. You have only to look at the map to see that nothing that France or we could do could possibly save Czechoslovakia from being overrun by the Germans, if they wanted to do it. The Austrian frontier is practically open; the great Skoda munitions works are within easy bombing distance of the German aerodromes, the railways all pass through German territory, Russia is 100 miles away. Therefore we could not help Czechoslovakia – she would simply be a pretext for going to war with Germany. That we could not think of unless we had a reasonable prospect of being able to beat her to her knees in a reasonable time, and of that I see no sign. I have therefore abandoned any idea of giving guarantees to Czechoslovakia, or the French in connection with her obligations to that country.[15]

Churchill later argued that guaranteeing Czechoslovakia would have been strategically more advantageous than guaranteeing Poland a year later. He stated that the Czechoslovakian Bohemian mountains offered a better defensive line than the flat Polish frontier.[16] This was of course true, but as Chamberlain pointed out, Britain could not help the Czechs defend it. Churchill said that the Czech Skoda works produced nearly as much military materiel between August 1938 and September 1939 as all of Britain's armament works, and that the Czechs had 21 frontline divisions, plus 15 or 16 secondary ones. He also said that Generaloberst Franz

Halder, head of the Army General Staff, and Generaloberst Alfred Jodl were later to admit that the Germans had only five frontline divisions plus eight secondary divisions in the west at the time of Munich.[17] The suggestion, therefore, is that with robust Allied backing the Czechs could have – what? Repelled a German attack or defeated Germany? The former may have been possible, but then the Germans would have rearmed further and tried again. The latter seems particularly fanciful, for there would have been little appetite in the League of Nations or outside it to annex and occupy Germany and to execute regime change, given the circumstances of 1938.

Churchill again misses the fundamental point: it was never the case that numbers alone would determine the outcome. In 1940 German armed forces were numerically inferior to the Allies and much of their equipment was no better, but their *Blitzkrieg* tactics, honed in the Spanish Civil War, proved decisive against France, the Low Countries and the British Expeditionary Force (BEF). This was Hitler's ace, and it could have been played in 1938 against a grand alliance backing Czechoslovakia as it would be played two years later against France. It seems fanciful to suggest that the Czechs could have withstood the German *Blitzkrieg*, particularly as Germany would not have attacked until it had amassed sufficient forces. Given subsequent experience, it seems equally fanciful that the French could have provided the Czechs with effective military assistance when they would not be able to defend themselves in 1940, even with the help of Belgium and the BEF.

As for a pact with Stalin, the most likely result would have been that the USSR would itself have ended up taking power over Czechoslovakia and whatever other territory it could digest. But even if the USSR had been keen to defend Czechoslovakia in 1938, the Soviet military had been denuded of able officers by the Stalinist purges and lacked equipment and trained men. It was thus unlikely to offer much resistance against an invading German army, as its appalling military failures in the first few months after Operation Barbarossa (the German invasion of the USSR in 1941) would make clear. Thus quite a bit of the fighting would have had to be left to Britain and France. But how would Britain have successfully deployed forces in Central Europe in 1938 when it could only just defend itself in 1939? Clearly, Churchill knew that Britain lacked the necessary forces to defend Czechoslovakia when he advocated the pact. If Britain had merely declared war on Germany over Czechoslovakia as it did in defence of Poland in 1939, such a declaration would not have appreciably helped either the Czechs defend themselves, or the Soviets against Germany. Churchill claimed that the prospect, not of the defence of Czechoslovakia but of a Europe-wide war, would have 'deterred or delayed Hitler's next assault'.[18] But it is clear from Hitler's attitude to Britain's guarantee of Poland in 1939 that he was neither deterred nor much delayed in his efforts by the threat of a Europe-wide war.

Chamberlain understood that Britain could not readily defeat Germany, that delay was necessary in the hope of finding peace, and crucially that delay was also necessary to bring Britain's armed forces up to a level necessary for its effective defence. When he finally committed Britain to war, it was on the *pretext* of Poland, not in any belief that Britain could defend it any more than it could have defended Czechoslovakia. Churchill wanted the threat of a European war on the pretext of Czechoslovakia, and this is what happened later in respect of Poland. Had Churchill had his way, Britain could not possibly have won such a war. Its only hope would have been to attempt to employ the USA's resources, but as isolationist sentiment would ensure that the USA was not engaged until after 7 December 1941, this would have meant that Britain would have been fighting an extra year before significant help from the USA was forthcoming.

Having urged a defence of Czechoslovakia, Churchill then said on 26 July 1938, in response to German demands, that the Czechs 'owe it to the Western Powers that every concession compatible with the sovereignty and integrity of their State shall be made and made promptly'. Then he told the Czechs they should fight.[19]

Churchill said that in the period between Hitler's aggression towards Czechoslovakia and towards Poland, 'Hitler's power and prestige had almost doubled!'[20] It is not clear what indices he was using to measure this, particularly as Czechoslovakia was not actually annexed until 15 March 1939 and Poland only a short time later in September. However, had Churchill been right that the threat of a European war at the time of Czechoslovakia would have delayed or deterred Hitler from fighting, Hitler would then have built up his armed forces quickly during the period of delay and *this* would have given him power and prestige – it would not have deterred him at all. Churchill argued that the Germans continued to rearm between 1938 and 1939 and that they were only strong enough to conduct a general war by 1939. But as we have seen, *Britain* rearmed during this period; and if Britain had rearmed more quickly, as Churchill wanted, Germany would have as well.

AN ALLIANCE WITH THE SOVIET UNION

Churchill's whole policy hinged on engaging the Soviets in a grand alliance. Since the collapse of Communism in the 1980s, and the opening up of Russian archives to western academics, some research has shown that Soviet foreign policy was ill defined and Stalin may have been open to the creation of such an alliance.[21] But this misses the essential point: the reason that British efforts to establish such an alliance failed was that Stalin had no vested interest in it. Rather, Stalin got into bed with Hitler, and the two carved up Eastern Europe between them. The result was the Treaty of Non-aggression between Germany and the Soviet Union, better known as the Molotov–Ribbentrop Pact. It was named after the Soviet and German Foreign Ministers of the period: Vyacheslav Molotov and Joachim von Ribbentrop, and was signed in Moscow on 24 August 1939. Thus Stalin increased his controlling influence through territory acquisition in Central and Eastern Europe, at virtually no cost to himself – at least for a while.

Nevertheless, Churchill remained under the illusion that Stalin wished to defend the integrity and sovereignty of Czechoslovakia and would participate in a grand alliance to accomplish it. It was titillated by a message to Churchill from the Soviet Ambassador, Ivan Maisky, on 2 September 1938, saying that he wanted a private meeting. This duly took place at Chartwell, and Churchill reported it to Halifax in a subsequent letter. It indicated that Russian support for Czechoslovakia was in some sense contingent upon French support for the Czechs, and that Russia sought more general support through the League, that consultation was needed between France, Czechoslovakia and Russia, and that a joint declaration should be made by France, Russia and Britain.[22] This was all music to Churchill's ears, and it gave him a clear sense, then and after the war, that his grand alliance proposal had been realistic and that he was being privately consulted to help promote it. The reality was hopelessly different; it was simply naive of Churchill to have been seduced by Maisky in 1938, but more so to continue after the war to believe that there was some merit in the case. The only reason Stalin would have wanted to fight Germany for Czechoslovakia was to annex the place himself – which is precisely what he did later on.

Churchill referred to the personal ties between the Czech President, Edvard Beneš, and Stalin, and a debt that he claimed the latter owed the former. He insisted that this was not well understood by Chamberlain's government and intimated that it might have formed the basis of a Russian desire to defend Czechoslovakia, thus constituting the basis of an effective grand alliance.[23] It is true that in March 1945 Beneš would go to Moscow and that he was re-installed as President of Czechoslovakia. However, in June 1948, a Soviet-type political system was introduced and Beneš resigned. He died three months later, a broken man. Whatever debt Stalin felt towards Beneš, it did not prevent him from imposing his hegemony over Czechoslovakia. Stalin had no desire to keep Central Europe free; rather he wanted, and indeed would achieve, control over all of Central and Eastern Europe.

On 16 April 1939 the Soviet Union made a formal offer to create a united front with Britain and France, plus Poland, which would guarantee those Central and Eastern European states that were subject to potential German aggression.[24] The British and French governments knew full well that these states feared Soviet military assistance almost more than German aggression, because once the Soviets had moved their forces in to render them ostensible assistance, they were likely to remain as occupiers. Quite understandably, this made the British and French hesitate. The British government gave a guarded response to the Soviet offer and presented counter-proposals: Churchill interpreted this as a failure to grasp the offer while it was on the table, and would continue to hold this view after the war, even when in full knowledge of subsequent events. This was an almost unbelievable judgment, which he justified by saying:

> Allies in war are inclined to defer a great deal to each other's wishes; the flail of battle beats upon the front, and all kinds of expedients are welcomed which, in peace, would be abhorrent. It would not be easy in a Grand Alliance, such as might have been developed, for one ally to enter the territory of another unless invited.[25]

However, this is just the point: under such an alliance the Soviet forces *would* have been invited by Czechoslovakia and the other states to enter their territory. The problem would have been that when invited to leave at the end of the conflict, they would have declined.

It is most telling that the Soviets were conducting contemporaneous talks with Germany while they approached Britain concerning the triple alliance. Maksim Litvinov, who as Soviet Foreign Commissar had discussed the possibility of a triple alliance with the British Ambassador on 15 April, leading to the offer of such an alliance the following day, was replaced by Molotov, for Litvinov was a Jew and thus unsuitable for the Soviets' relationship with Nazi Germany.[26] Yet for Churchill, still the penny failed to drop: that the Litvinov approach was vacuous, and had Britain signed a triple alliance with the Soviets, it would have been worth no more than the paper Chamberlain signed at Munich. To the extent that Stalin had negotiated with Britain and France at all, it had only been to see if this was a better way of achieving his own objectives, never about achieving Britain's. Churchill wrote: 'The alliance is solely for the purpose of resisting further acts of aggression and of protecting the victims of aggression.'[27] But Stalin's purpose was precisely the subjugation of Central and Eastern Europe to his will; this is why the Molotov–Ribbentrop Pact was signed by the Soviets.

On 22 May 1939, in Berlin, the German and Italian Foreign Ministers, von Ribbentrop and Count Galeazzo Ciano, signed the 'Pact of Steel' between Italy and Germany.[28] Churchill now insisted that, by the time of the Molotov–Ribbentrop Pact, the other side had done a better job of forming alliances than Britain had. But Mussolini, like Stalin, wanted territorial acquisition, as he had already demonstrated in Abyssinia, and for him, too, a pact with Germany seemed an effective way to get it. It is true, of course, that in the end Britain was reliant upon the Soviet Union for its defence because the Soviets did most of the fighting in Europe: the western Allies killed 200,000 Germans; the Soviet Union killed 3.5 million. But that was only after Germany had attacked the Soviet Union, giving the latter a vested interest in an alliance with the western powers. More importantly, it was the USA that acted as guarantor that the Soviets would not march right across Europe and annex everything, including Britain.

Not only would an alliance with the Soviets not have come about, but, as the coming Battle of France would illustrate, France would not have participated effectively in a grand alliance as it was politically too weak, as were its senior military brass. Clearly, there was nothing Britain could do to change this. It seems that the Munich Agreement, or at least a tacit acceptance of the demise of Czechoslovakia, was inevitable, as there was nothing that Britain could realistically do to prevent it. And finally, it was not possible for Britain to have rearmed more quickly and for this reason it was not ready to fight in 1938.

ARREST HITLER!

Churchill insisted that there was opposition to Hitler's plans in the *Oberkommando der Wehrmacht* (OKW), the German High Command, and he principally cited General Beck in this regard.[29] Generaloberst Ludwig Beck would be one of the conspirators in the 20 July 1944 plot to assassinate Hitler, when he would be dispatched by a bullet to the head. When Beck opposed Hitler after the *Anschluss* (the annexation of Austria in 1938) he resigned his position and Hitler merely replaced him; had he offered more opposition he would have been shot earlier. Hitler had had Ernst Röhm and the private Nazi army, the *Sturmabteilung* (known as the 'Brown Shirts') annihilated as far back as 1935; if he was able to do this and get away with it, the German High Command, or individuals in it, were not going to stop him the way Churchill suggested. In 1938, before the true extent of Hitler's atrocities was apparent, Beck and others would not have taken the appalling risks they were to take in 1944.

Churchill referred to a plot to arrest Hitler in 1938, which Generaloberst Halder mentioned after the war. The conspirators were mainly those who would be engaged in the 20 July 1944 plot. Churchill insisted that the plan, to arrest not only Hitler, but also Hermann Göring and Joseph Goebbels, would have gone ahead had it not been for Chamberlain's visit to Berchtesgaden to negotiate peace with Hitler.[30] But there were many plots against Hitler, and one to 'arrest' him appears particularly feeble. Only assassination could have been effective, of which there were some 17 attempts during the Third Reich, and realistically only a suicide attack would have worked – something that no one ever attempted.

On 26 September 1938 there was a deputation to Hitler that included General Hermann von Hanneken, Generaloberst Wilhelm Ritter von Leeb and Oberst Karl Bodenschatz. Hitler would not see them, but they subsequently wrote a paper that they submitted to the Chancellery. It complained generally about almost everything. In *The Second World War* Churchill set great store by the contents of the paper and the argument contained in it that the German position was weak in 1938.[31] But these were the views of a few inconsequential officers, not the High Command as a whole, and Hitler proved to be more right than wrong in his military judgments in the early stages of the war. Churchill seemed to think that this general bitching by some minor members of the High Command amounted to a nascent opposition that could conceivably have been fanned up. In fact von Hanneken ended up in charge of forces in Denmark and von Leeb saw effective service in France and against the Soviet Union, so both men served Hitler effectively. Only Bodenschatz would be involved in the unsuccessful attempt on Hitler's life on 20 July 1944, and then as one of the less important conspirators. For Churchill to have relied upon these people was a most forlorn hope. Curiously, although the German resistance movement was potentially the most significant in Europe, Churchill never helped it when he was Prime Minister, despite helping just about every other resistance movement.

Großadmiral Erich Raeder, head of the Kriegsmarine (the German Navy), met Hitler on 27 September with news that the British fleet was being mobilized, and he appealed to Hitler to moderate his plans. According to Churchill, Hitler wavered at this point.[32] To Churchill this indicated that Raeder's influence, and that of others in the High Command, was significant, and that they could halt Hitler's plans provided there was a sufficiently robust military response from Britain. But Hitler was influenced, to the extent that he was influenced at all, only on timing and precise tactics; he was not going to be influenced by anyone in the High Command or anywhere else regarding his overall objectives. Hitler was hell-bent on his plans and the High Command was not going to be able to stand in his way. Indeed Churchill happily concurred with this view, having tried to contradict it, when he wrote:

> All these generals were patriotic men. They longed to see
> the Fatherland regain its position in the world. They were
> devoting themselves night and day to every process that could
> strengthen the German forces. They therefore felt smitten in
> their hearts at having been found so much below the level of

the event, and in many cases their dislike and their distrust of Hitler were overpowered by admiration for his commanding gifts and miraculous luck. Surely here was a star to follow, surely here was a guide to obey. Thus did Hitler finally become the undisputed master of Germany, and the path was clear for the great design.[33]

STAND BY PRAGUE

Churchill invoked Generalfeldmarschall Wilhelm Keitel, and his response to a question at the Nuremberg trials after the war. Colonel Eger, who represented Czechoslovakia at the trials, asked Keitel: 'Would the Reich have attacked Czechoslovakia in 1938 if the Western Powers had stood by Prague?' Keitel answered: 'Certainly not. We were not strong enough militarily. The object of Munich [the Agreement] was to get Russia out of Europe, to gain time, and to complete German armaments.'[34] It is not clear if Hitler knew this. Keitel was very much a flunky. But the important point is that Britain was not ready to fight in 1938 either, and if Britain had rearmed earlier, Germany would have accelerated its rearmament programme in response. Churchill mentioned that Germany spent £1,500 million on war materiel in 1938–9 and Britain only £304 million. He also said that German tank production rose dramatically in 1940 to facilitate the successful invasion of France. He used this to justify his claim that the Allies were in a better position to defeat Germany in 1938 than in 1939 or 1940.[35] But this only underscores the point that Germany had the capacity to accelerate its rearmament programme when it wanted to. A robust response by the Allies in 1938 might have stayed Hitler's hand momentarily, but only to accelerate rearmament and to attack later on. Hitler could, and did, pick a time of his own choosing to attack.

It is true that, without Skoda and the Sudeten and Austrian annexations, Germany's ability to accelerate its rate of armaments production would have been more limited. But even if Hitler had backed down in 1938 in the face of a robust response from Britain, there would simply have been a longer interval before Germany had rearmed sufficiently. War would have been delayed – which is what Munich did anyway – but not prevented altogether, as Churchill insisted. With regard to

Hitler's attitude to Russia, the point of the Molotov–Ribbentrop Pact was to engage Russia in the conquest of Europe, which Stalin was eager to do, before Germany was strong enough to try to conquer Russia as well.

THE FRENCH POSITION

Churchill insisted that France could have defeated Germany alone in 1935 or 1936 (though there was then no international appetite to do so) and that it was capable of this even in 1938.[36] But once again, his assumptions were based simply on numbers, not tactics. In any case, this was a French problem, not a British one; no bellicose stance in Whitehall would have appreciably changed the situation in France. Chamberlain's appeasement was consistent with French policy but, had Churchill been Prime Minister in 1938, French policy would not have been readily open to fundamental change – the French politicians simply didn't want it. There would just have been friction between the French Government and Churchill's.

Churchill argued that France could have crossed the Rhine or occupied the Ruhr in 1938.[37] But this was not realistic even if France had acted in consort with Britain. If the French had attempted to occupy the Ruhr alone, what on earth would they have done? They would either have eventually withdrawn, only delaying the German onslaught, or stayed and seen Germany shift its rearmament programme out of the Ruhr. Either way, Germany would eventually have counterattacked. If this was an unrealistic policy for France and Britain together, it was quite unrealistic for France acting alone.

Chamberlain understood the situation well. On 20 March 1938 he wrote to his sister:

> . . . with Franco winning in Spain by the aid of German guns and Italian planes, with a French government in which one cannot have the slightest confidence and which I suspect to be in closish touch with our Opposition, with the Russians stealthily and cunningly pulling all the strings behind the scenes to get us involved in war with Germany (our Secret Service doesn't spend all its time looking out of the window), and finally with a Germany flushed with triumph, and all too

conscious of her power, the prospect looked black indeed. In face of such problems, to be badgered and pressed to come out and give a clear, decided, bold, and unmistakable lead, show 'ordinary courage', and all the rest of the twaddle, is calculated to vex the man who has to take the responsibility for the consequences.[38]

This is not a man unable to see the reality, and who would subsequently go to Munich without any understanding of the situation. On the contrary, this is a man beleaguered by the responsibility of trying to defend his country when he perceived threats all around him. He had no confidence in the French, yet Churchill would be prepared to commit everything to France in 1940, when it had already been decisively defeated (see chapter 7). Chamberlain would say of Hitler that he was 'abnormal', and his advisers were 'evil'; that Hitler's 'hysteria' was such that he was not likely to live long. When Chamberlain set off for his meeting with Hitler at Berchtesgaden he said he was 'going to fight with a wild beast'.[39]

GERMANY RECEIVES ALL THE BLAME FOR WAR

The Irish politician Eamon de Valera wrote to Chamberlain as he left for Munich:

> I believe you will be successful. Should you not be so, you will be blamed for having gone at all. To stop half way – to stop short of taking any action which held out even the slightest chance of success, in view of what is involved, would be wrong.[40]

One could respond to de Valera, as Churchill might have, that such action had not the slightest chance of success anyway; but the point is profound: what Chamberlain did was to make it crystal clear to posterity that he pursued peace even when there was only the slightest chance of success, or indeed not even that. Had Churchill been Prime Minister, no attempt would have been made to so do, and historians would have argued ever since whether this 'avoidable war' as Churchill put it, might have been avoided, not by rearmament, but by some form of agreement giving back the Sudetenland. Chamberlain's actions proved that this was impossible, that Hitler was bent on war come what may, that the war was 'unavoidable' because, and only because, Hitler was determined to initiate it. On 11 September 1938 Chamberlain wrote to his sister:

> I fully realise that, if eventually things go wrong and the aggression takes place, there will be many, including Winston, who will say that the British government must bear the responsibility, and that if only they had had the courage to tell Hitler now that, if he used force, we should at once declare war, that would have stopped him. By that time it will be impossible to prove the contrary, but I am satisfied that we should be wrong to allow the most vital decision that any country could take, the decision as to peace or war, to pass out of our hands into the ruler of another country, and a lunatic at that. I have been fortified in this view by reading a very interesting book on the foreign policy of Canning . . . Over and over again Canning lays it down that you should never menace unless you are in a position to carry out your threats, and although, if we have to fight I should hope we should be able to give a good account of ourselves, we are certainly not in a position in which our military advisers would feel happy in undertaking to begin hostilities if we were not forced to do so.[41]

Chamberlain's reference to Hitler as a 'lunatic' clearly demonstrates that he was under no illusions and did not have a realistic expectation of a benign outcome. His actions would at best delay war. His reference to Canning is decisive: clearly Britain was in no position to carry out threats against Germany, but had Churchill been in power he would have made precisely such threats. But most significant is that Britain's military advisers were not happy to undertake hostilities. No doubt Churchill would retort that had Britain rearmed earlier, the advisers *would* have been happy with undertaking military action and that Canning's dictum would be satisfied. The problem with this argument is that during Churchill's five years as wartime Prime Minister, the military advisers never were happy to undertake hostilities

– not without the infinite resources of the USA to provide the necessary manpower and materiel. Ironically, the only really decisive victory Britain achieved while Churchill was Prime Minister and before the Americans entered the war was the Battle of Britain, and the system of defence that facilitated this was brought into existence by MacDonald, Baldwin and Chamberlain, not Churchill (see chapter 8). So even when the brake of appeasement on rearmament was removed, Churchill was never able to threaten and carry out those threats without the USA and the USSR. Yet Britain was not to have their active support in the 1930s.

Churchill admitted that in the last year before the war, Britain's fighter strength grew dramatically, and intimated that it was while he was in government that the real acceleration occurred.[42] This is true, but as First Lord he had no responsibility for it, and by the time he became Prime Minister he was overseeing the completion of an existing programme to rearm Fighter Command in time for the Battle of Britain. He wrote:

> Look back and see what we had successively accepted or thrown away: a Germany disarmed by solemn treaty; a Germany rearmed in violation of a solemn treaty; air superiority or even air parity cast away; the Rhineland forcibly occupied and the Siegfried Line built or building; the Berlin-Rome Axis established; Austria devoured and digested by the Reich; Czechoslovakia deserted and ruined by the Munich Pact; its fortress line in German hands; its mighty arsenal of Skoda henceforth making munitions for the German armies; President Roosevelt's effort to stabilize or bring to a head the European situation by the intervention of the United States waved aside with one hand, and Soviet Russia's undoubted willingness to join the Western Powers and go all lengths to save Czechoslovakia ignored on the other; the services of thirty-five Czech divisions against the still unripened German army cast away when Great Britain could herself supply only two to strengthen the front in France; all gone with the wind.[43]

Let us take these issues in turn. Germany was hell-bent on rearmament whatever Britain did; no treaty would contain it, only invasion, annexation, occupation, and regime change would have prevented it, and Britain could not have done that in the mid-1930s, even under Churchill. However fast Britain grew its air power, the Germans – with their greater resources – were always going to exceed it. The Rhineland, Austria and Czechoslovakia would have been occupied sooner or later whatever Britain did, short of the occupation of Germany and regime change. The Siegfried Line was irrelevant: no fixed fortified line would constitute an effective barrier; this would be a war of mobility. The Maginot Line exhibited this fact perfectly: it was a vast and complex series of fixed fortifications constructed during the inter-war years to protect France's eastern border against any possible threat from Germany, but in fact it offered no resistance at all (see chapter 7). The Berlin–Rome Axis meant nothing; the Italians were more a liability for Hitler than an asset. Skoda and the Czech divisions were not going to be employed on Britain's side – it was never practical for Britain to offer Czechoslovakia effective military assistance. The USA would not intervene directly at this time: 'splendid isolation' prevented Roosevelt from doing that, and nothing less by the Americans would have stopped Hitler. Indeed, in July 1939 the Senate would rebuff the President's attempt to amend the law on neutrality in order to facilitate armaments exports, let alone direct intervention.[44] Churchill's assertion that Russia would 'go all lengths to save Czechoslovakia' is patent nonsense. We know full well what Stalin's intentions were. In 1948 Czechoslovakia became a Soviet puppet state, a dictatorship controlled from Moscow. This is what Stalin wanted and what he achieved, and this remained the case at Churchill's death.

Conscription was introduced on 27 April 1939, the government having pledged against it when the Secretary of State for War, Leslie Hore-Belisha, strongly advocated it. Churchill, as ever, argued that this was too late, but once again it was a response to Hitler, not something that could in any way be interpreted as causing the war.[45]

The Anglo-German Naval Agreement, Churchill insisted, helped German policy.[46] But this very step once again underscored Britain's desire for peace and showed what little regard Hitler had for such pieces of paper. The German–Polish Non-Aggression Pact was largely undermined by the Anglo-Polish Guarantee, and Hitler used the latter effectively to revoke the former. The Polish Guarantee had been augmented with a guarantee to Greece and to Romania, and an alliance with Turkey.[47] In 1939 the Americans denounced their trade treaty with Japan, but Congress rejected any fortifying of the American base at Guam in the Pacific.[48]

Finally, when the House of Commons effectively demanded that Chamberlain guarantee Poland – something with which Churchill concurred – and when Germany invaded Poland on 1 September, the 'unavoidable' war occurred. At 11.15am on 3 September 1939 Chamberlain broadcast via the BBC:

> You can imagine what a bitter blow it is to me that all my long struggle to win peace has failed. Yet I cannot believe that there is anything more, or anything different, that I could have done, and that would have been more successful . . . We have a clear conscience, we have done all that any country could do to establish peace . . .[49]

Clearly he could have done things differently, yet had he done so, war would still have come – and this is as certain as certain can be. War could have come earlier, perhaps a little later, but it was inevitable because Hitler wanted it. Chamberlain's last sentence is most poignant, for what he had done was not simply to ensure his own conscience was clear, but more importantly that Britain's was. No other olive branch could be extended; the dove of all doves had exhausted all possible ways of achieving peace. But even now there were still secret communications with both Hitler and Göring via a neutral intermediary seeking a settlement over Poland and a subsequent Anglo-German agreement.[50] This laid Chamberlain open to the accusation of treachery, but at the same time underscored his continuing desire to achieve peace at almost any price. The important point is that appeasement and delayed rearmament ensured that Hitler received the entire blame for the war. Thus Chamberlain sacrificed his own political career and reputation, and indeed his life, to ensure that Britain was entirely innocent.

After the declaration of war, Chamberlain recalled Churchill to the Admiralty as First Lord, the post he had first held between 1911 and 1915. So after ten years in the political wilderness, Churchill was finally back in office.

6
NORWAY:
GALLIPOLI ALL OVER AGAIN

'Winston is back' is how the Admiralty signalled the fleet as Churchill returned to government as First Lord of the Admiralty in September 1939. This was a particularly emotional moment for a particularly emotional man. Much was the same, including many of the ships, but the people were new to him. Churchill noted that it was 'like suddenly resuming a previous incarnation'. Despite being only two months short of his 65th birthday, he threw himself into his duties with great energy. He quipped that there wasn't enough to do because there was only Germany to fight, and endeared himself to many when he insisted, 'My doctor has ordered me to take nothing non-alcoholic between breakfast and dinner.' Yet his First Sea Lord, Admiral Sir Dudley Pound, would need to perform the function that, when Churchill became Prime Minister, all the chiefs of staff would do – restrain him. Churchill responded with a panoply of emotional weapons, as Admiral John Godfrey noted. He would use 'persuasion, real or simulated anger, mockery, vituperation, tantrums, ridicule, derision, abuse and tears'. Occasionally, he would get his way.[1] He also continued to exhibit familiar tendencies: he interfered with operational issues and exhorted his forces to undertake premature attacks.

In his new job, Churchill's first adventure was a repeat of Gallipoli, this time in Norway. It proved to be one of the least strategically important campaigns, and German servicemen would refer to the occupation of the Scandinavian countries as the 'whipped cream front'. Like Gallipoli, the Norwegian campaign was undertaken to avoid a direct confrontation with German forces on the strategically important battlefields of Western and Central Europe – something Hitler relished but Churchill forever shied away from.

There had been some German interest in Norway prior to the war. A senior German naval officer, Vizeadmiral Wolfgang Wegener, had published *The Naval Strategy of the World War* in 1929. In it he argued that in the event of war, Germany should occupy Norway to facilitate access to the

Atlantic for German naval forces.[2] The potential benefits were not
limited to the navy: a German occupation of Norway would also ease
the importation of iron ore from Sweden. Germany imported some
ten million tons at the beginning of the war, of which nine million were
brought in via the northern Swedish port of Luleå. This port became
icebound and impassable in the winter, but the Norwegian port of
Narvik remained navigable and was used instead. Thus the notion of
the importance of Norway to Germany was established. At first, Admiral
Pound managed to prevent Churchill from sending the fleet to the Baltic,
where it would certainly have been defeated. However, throughout the war
Churchill would continue to desire, to use General Sir Hastings Ismay's
term, 'an Arctic Gallipoli'.[3]

Finland had been attacked by the Soviet Union early in the war, while
the Molotov–Ribbentrop Pact was in force, and the Finns had initially
rebuffed the Soviet forces. Churchill saw Norway as a possible conduit
through which the Finns could be supported against the Soviets.[4] This was
a remarkably risky strategy, as it made war between Britain and the Soviet
Union likely. Britain would be saved from Churchill's folly by the failure
of the Norwegian operation and by the fact that the Soviets would soon
find themselves on Britain's side after Operation Barbarossa – the German
invasion of the Soviet Union in 1941. The Finns would eventually succumb
to the Soviets, but then Stalin would have more pressing issues to deal
with. But now Churchill increasingly saw Norway as vital to the German
war machine. On 29 September 1939 he wrote a memorandum for the War
Cabinet in which he outlined his concerns:

> At the end of November the Gulf of Bothnia normally freezes,
> so that Swedish iron ore can be sent to Germany only through
> Oxelosund in the Baltic, or from Narvik at the north of
> Norway. Oxelosund can export only about one-fifth of the
> weight of ore Germany requires from Sweden. In winter
> normally the main trade is from Narvik, whence ships can
> pass down the west coast of Norway, and make the whole
> voyage to Germany without leaving territorial waters until
> inside the Skagerrak.
>
> It must be understood that an adequate supply of Swedish
> iron ore is vital to Germany, and the interception or

prevention of these Narvik supplies during the winter months, i.e., from October to the end of April, will greatly reduce her power of resistance. For the first three weeks of the war no iron-ore ships left Narvik owing to the reluctance of crews to sail and other causes outside our control. Should this satisfactory state of affairs continue, no special action would be demanded from the Admiralty. Furthermore, negotiations are proceeding with the Swedish Government which in themselves may effectively reduce the supplies of Scandinavian ore to Germany.

Should however the supplies from Narvik to Germany start moving again, more drastic action will be needed.

. . . Our relations with Sweden require careful consideration. Germany acts upon Sweden by threats. Our sea power gives us also powerful weapons, which, if need be, we must use to ration Sweden. Nevertheless, it should be proposed . . . to assist the Swedes so far as possible to dispose of their ore in exchange for our coal; and, should this not suffice, to indemnify them, partly at least, by other means. This is the next step.[5]

Churchill's position then began to harden on Norway. On 16 December he wrote in a memorandum to the War Cabinet:

The effectual stoppage of the Norwegian ore supplies to Germany ranks as a major offensive operation of war. No other measure is open to us for many months to come which gives so good a chance of abridging the waste and destruction of the conflict, or of perhaps preventing the vast slaughters which will attend the grapple of the main armies.

. . . If the advantage is held to outweigh the obvious and serious objections, the whole process of stoppage must be enforced. The ore from Luleå [in the Baltic] is already stopped by the winter ice, which must not be [allowed to be] broken by the Soviet ice-breaker, should the attempt be made. The ore from Narvik must be stopped by laying successively a series of small minefields in Norwegian territorial waters at the two or three suitable points on the coast, which will force the ships carrying ore to Germany to quit territorial waters and come on to the high seas, where, if German, they will be taken as prize, or, if neutral, subjected to our contraband control. The ore from Oxelosund, the main ice-free port in the Baltic, must also be prevented from leaving by methods which will be neither diplomatic nor military. All these three ports must be dealt with in various appropriate ways as soon as possible.

. . . To every blow struck in war there is a counter. If you fire at the enemy he will fire back. It is most necessary therefore to face squarely the counter-measures which may be taken by Germany, or constrained by her from Norway or Sweden. As to Norway, there are three pairs of events which are linked together. First, the Germans, conducting war in a cruel and lawless manner, have violated the territorial waters of Norway, sinking without warning or succour a number of British and neutral vessels. To that our response is to lay the minefields mentioned above. It is suggested that Norway, by way of protest, may cancel the valuable agreement we have made with her for chartering her tankers and other shipping. But then she would lose the extremely profitable bargain she has made with us, and this shipping would become valueless to her in view of our contraband control. Her ships would be idle, and her owners impoverished. It would not be in Norwegian interests for her Government to take this step; and interest is a powerful factor. Thirdly, Norway could retaliate by refusing to export to us the aluminium and other war materials which are important to the Air Ministry and the Ministry of Supply. But here again her interests would suffer.[6]

Churchill's proposal to deny Germany access to Narvik by mining the harbour was initially opposed by the Cabinet, as they did not wish to violate Norway's neutrality, though it was instigated later when the Germans attacked Norway.

GERMANY ATTACKS NORWAY

While allowing for possible Norwegian retaliation, Churchill failed to address the German response. The fact that the British were considering measures against Germany via Norway had been picked up by German intelligence, and as early as the end of September 1939, Admiral Wilhelm Canaris, head of the *Abwehr* (military intelligence), communicated this fact to the supreme commander of the Kriegsmarine, Großadmiral Erich Reader, who passed it on to Hitler.[7] The Royal Navy's action against the *Graf Spee*'s supply ship, *Altmark*, in Norwegian waters the following February (see chapter 9) would inflame Hitler and spur on his plans.[8] Großadmiral Raeder wrote in *Struggle for the Sea* that German forces had 'to get in ahead of the British'.[9] So Churchill's desire to mine Narvik harbour and his petulance over the *Altmark* precipitated the very German action against Norway that he had intended to prevent.

Denmark's fate was sealed in the process, as logistics required its occupation as well. Hitler had a non-aggression pact with Denmark, which had enjoyed neutral status during World War I and was hoping for the same in this one. However, Churchill's Norwegian decision had condemned Denmark to years of German occupation. In *Struggle for the Sea* Raeder wrote:

> Up to February, 1940, Naval Operations Command had not concerned itself with an occupation of Denmark, which was regarded as neither militarily necessary not politically desirable . . . however, in view of the great distance from Germany to Norway the Luftwaffe insisted that it must have the use of air-fields in Jutland for its operations, and with this Denmark was involved.[10]

On 14 December 1939 Hitler ordered the OKW, the military High Command, to undertake a study of the military implications of a German invasion. On 16 and 18 December he had meetings with Major Vidkun Quisling, who had been Norwegian Minister for War and was the country's leading National Socialist: his name subsequently became synonymous with 'traitor'.[11] Generaloberst Nikolaus von Falkenhorst was appointed leader of the expedition on 21 February

1940, and on 1 March Hitler ordered that the invasion plans, which were codenamed *Weserübung*, should proceed.

Oslo was to be subject to assault from both land and sea, Stavanger was to be captured by paratroopers and the nearby airbase at Sola was to be assaulted from the air. The ports of Narvik, Trondheim and Bergen were to be subject to naval assault with troop landings. Falkenhorst's expectation was that Norway would be overcome rapidly with little bloodshed, and indeed German forces were ordered not to fire unless Norwegian forces proved hostile.[12]

To facilitate the attack on Norway, Denmark was to be occupied via two motorized brigades securing vital bridges, while Copenhagen was secured through a naval landing of troops with air support. The northern airfields, vital to the Norwegian expedition, were to be secured by paratroopers. As in Norway, it was anticipated that occupation would meet with little effective opposition. On 2 April 1940 Hitler ordered an attack for the 9th.[13] Although British army units were being readied in Scotland for a possible seaborne landing in Norway, no action was to be taken until the German intentions became clear. Raeder was nervous about the British naval potential and wanted German naval forces to return to German ports immediately after the assault to avoid, if at all possible, any engagement with the Royal Navy.[14]

During early April 1940 Chamberlain appointed Churchill to preside over the Military Co-ordination Committee, the joint committee of service ministers and chiefs of staff that was responsible for determining the direction of the war. Thus Churchill had a high degree of executive responsibility in determining the Norway campaign.[15]

On 7 April the Home Fleet left Scapa Flow to instigate the mining of Norwegian waters the following day, in Operation Wilfred.[16] The Norwegian Admiral Carsten Tank-Nielsen readied his forces for a German attack. He dispatched a pair of minelayers to block the approaches to Narvik, stationed torpedo boats and smaller patrol vessels in the approaches, ensured that coastal forts were alerted and that coastal lighting was switched off in Bergen as well as Narvik, and liaised with both the army and the air force. As planned, German forces entered Denmark, and seaborne and airborne units landed in Norway on 9 April at Oslo, Stavanger, Bergen, Narvik and Trondheim. Poor weather gave the German forces cover, frustrating the Royal Navy's attempts to interdict them.

BRITAIN ATTACKS NORWAY

An Allied seaborne assault on Trondheim to force the Trondheim Straits – Operation Hammer – was mooted to oppose the Germans, but postponed due to the presence of the battle-cruisers *Scharnhorst* and *Gneisenau*.[17] A British naval attack on Bergen was substituted, but the First Sea Lord was fearful of the German battle-cruisers, and Churchill concurred with him that an attack should be avoided.[18] He summed up his ambitious plans for the Norway operation to the Military Co-ordination Committee:

> The object of operations at Narvik is to capture the town and obtain possession of the railway to the Swedish frontier. We should then be in a position to put a force, if necessary, into the Gallivare ore-fields, the possession of which is the main objective of the whole of the operations in Scandinavia . . . The object of operations in the Trondheim area is to capture Trondheim, and thereby obtain a base for further operations in Central Norway, and in Sweden if necessary.[19]

Hammer has all the hallmarks of a Churchillian operation. He himself recounted its similarities with the Dardanelles and insisted that the straits at Trondheim could be forced in just the same way he had believed was possible at Gallipoli nearly a quarter of a century earlier. But the chiefs of staff, having at first supported the idea, then opposed it, though Sir Roger Keyes, who had supported forcing the Dardanelles all those years before, was, like Churchill, in favour.[20]

Instead, a more limited response to Hitler's invasion, Operation Sickle, was initiated, with small Allied troop landings either side of Trondheim on 14 and 17 April, from the north at Namsos and from the south at Andalsnes, to undertake a pincer movement. A frontal assault on Trondheim was now deemed unnecessary, releasing naval forces. The new plan was not appreciably less risky than its predecessor, and the pincer movement was vitiated by the fact that the southern force had to dig in to withstand a German counterattack and thus was not ready to move north for some time.[21] The Allied forces had no anti-aircraft artillery and were consequently bombed at will by the Luftwaffe, particularly at Namsos. The northern force moved south from Namsos under Major-General Carton de

Wiart and was promptly stopped in its tracks by strong German opposition. The half-hearted Allied response was unable to withstand the German aerial onslaught: withdrawal followed from Andalsnes on 1 May and two days later from Namsos.[22] The evacuation was almost complete by 4 May, save the most precarious of holds on Narvik.[23]

Churchill insisted in *The Second World War* that he knew that the Germans could reinforce their position and stop the British advance, and had warned the chiefs accordingly.[24] So he knew all along that the expedition was certain to fail, and that it was the failings of the chiefs that were responsible for the fiasco, even though he had previously asked for enhanced powers as chair of the Military Co-ordination Committee, which Chamberlain had granted him on 1 May.[25] No doubt Churchill could have blamed the late provision of his enhanced powers, effectively making him Minister of Defence, but even without them he was in a very strong position to direct the Norwegian campaign. As John Colville (Assistant Private Secretary to Chamberlain and then to Churchill) said at the time, 'The country believes that Winston is the man of action who is winning the war and little realises how ineffective, and indeed harmful, much of his energy is proving itself to be.'[26]

The portent of failure was apparent from Churchill's own lips. At a meeting of the French and British Supreme War Council in Paris on 22 April 1940, with Chamberlain and the French Prime Minister Paul Reynaud present, the minutes read, 'Mr. Churchill said that the task of landing troops and stores on the Norwegian coast in the face of enemy aircraft and submarines was fraught with immense difficulty and dangers . . .'[27] In a meeting of the Council four days later, this time in Downing Street with Chamberlain present and the French represented by their senior generals, Churchill explained that the situation in Norway was grave and that he had decided against a direct attack on Trondheim. He said: 'Even if Trondheim was captured by a direct assault, we would not be able in the face of air attack to maintain the forces which would be necessary to keep it in our hands.'[28]

Once the advantage had been lost to Hitler, Churchill decided to attack Narvik, and British forces were amassed at Harstad in the Lofoten Islands for that purpose. Churchill put Admiral of the Fleet the Lord Cork and Orrery (William Boyle) in overall charge of the assault, with Major-General Pierse Mackesy commanding land forces. These forces were then kept idle for a month until the heavy snow had receded, and the assault finally occurred on 28 May 1940, by which time Churchill had been Prime Minister for 18 days.[29]

Lord Cork had been given no brief by Churchill; General Mackesy had not been consulted by Cork, who hadn't seen the written orders that the Chief of the Imperial General Staff (CIGS), General Sir Edmund Ironside, had given Mackesy, nor indeed had the Military Co-ordination Committee. The 24th Guards Brigade, responsible for the Narvik landings, lacked artillery, engineers or adequate landing craft or other transport; they also lacked the necessary equipment to conduct warfare in arctic conditions. To compound the confusion, Churchill, for whom Narvik had been so important, had suddenly changed his mind on 13 April – the day upon which the Kriegsmarine suffered the loss of seven destroyers in Norwegian waters – and accepted what others had been saying: that assaults were needed in other areas. At 2.00am the following day Churchill saw Ironside and told him, 'We should go for Trondheim.' Ironside was livid, and told Churchill that this would weaken their Narvik forces decisively. But this was not the worst of it: in all Churchill changed his mind four times over Trondheim.[30]

British forces occupied Narvik until 8 June 1940 when, since they could not be supported, they were withdrawn. An *ad hoc* mix of some 6,000 Germans had defeated, over a six-week period, around 24,000 Allied servicemen.[31] Churchill's hope that hanging on to Narvik would constitute a base from which further advances against the Third Reich could be made was clearly forlorn. He had thought that, given the terrain, forces could be brought in by sea more easily than the Germans could reinforce by land.[32] However, the restrictions of the terrain also meant that the beachhead was of little value to the Allies, as it would have been difficult for Allied forces to proceed inland.

NORWAY IS LOST

Churchill said in the House of Commons: 'When I last spoke, I expressed opinion that Hitler's invasion of Norway was a major political and strategic mistake. I have been rebuked for over-confidence but I remain impenitent.'[33] Norway's King Haakon VII and his government had retreated as the German troops advanced. After about two months of sporadic fighting, and the subsequent British withdrawal from Norway, the King and his government were taken by the British cruiser HMS *Devonshire* to England on 8 June to set up a government in exile.[34] Denmark's King Christian X had ordered a ceasefire at approximately 6.00am on 9 April, after the deaths of a total of 16 Danes. However, the Danish commander-in-chief continued to oppose the Germans until 6.45am, when the King dispatched his personal adjutant to ensure compliance with the order. The King and his government remained in Denmark during the occupation.

In *The Second World War* Churchill expressed his opinion that the Norwegian operation had crippled the Kriegsmarine and so prevented an invasion of Britain.[35] When examining the Allied and German losses, it is not so obvious that this was the case. The Royal Navy lost an aircraft carrier, HMS *Glorious*, in decidedly less than glorious circumstances. It also lost two cruisers, whereas the Germans lost three; the RN lost nine destroyers, the Germans ten; the RN six submarines, the Germans eight. The RN suffered serious damage to six cruisers and eight destroyers, whereas the Germans suffered serious damage to three battle-cruisers (if the *Lützow* is included as a battle-cruiser, not a pocket battleship) and two cruisers. The balance sheet doesn't appear appreciably in Britain's favour, but Churchill's point was that this left few effective operational surface ships in the Kriegsmarine, particularly because the damaged German battle-cruisers were the *Scharnhorst* and the *Gneisenau*, the scourge of the Royal Navy, as well as the *Lützow*. Temporarily, the Kriegsmarine cupboard did seem to be pretty bare.[36] However, it would later recover, and the decision to invade Britain in Operation Sea Lion was to be determined rather by air superiority: it was RAF Fighter Command that would prevent the German invasion, rather than temporary deficiencies in the Kriegsmarine. In any case, Churchill's belief that the Norwegian operation had crippled the Kriegsmarine was merely a feeble excuse thought up to try to justify Britain's expulsion from Norway.

Churchill insisted that he had asked Chamberlain to take the chair of the joint committee from 15 April 1940 in the midst of the Norwegian crisis, and that by this time it was too late to save Norway.[37] Churchill made plain that the German plans were well developed – they had been working on them since October – implying that once again the British government had been negligent.[38] The implication is, of course, that it was Chamberlain rather than Churchill who was responsible for the fiasco. However, Churchill had been First Lord since September, and thus had had ample opportunity to consider the Norwegian issue. When debating the matter in the House of Commons, Chamberlain graciously said that Churchill had not been in charge and therefore was not responsible. In reality, of course, Churchill was.[39]

The reason for Churchill asking Chamberlain to take control of the committee becomes clearer from a letter he wrote to Chamberlain on 24 April 1940:

> I am very grateful to you for having at my request taken over the day to day management of the Military Coordination Cte.
>
> I think I ought however to let you know that I shall not be willing to receive the responsibility back from you without the necessary powers. At present no-one has the power. There are six Chiefs of the Staff, three Ministers, two C-in-Cs and General Ismay who all have a voice in Norwegian operations, apart from Narvik. But no-one is now responsible for the creation and direction of military policy except yourself. If you feel able to bear this burden, you may count upon my unswerving loyalty as First Lord of the Admiralty. If you do not feel you can bear it, with all your other duties, you will have to delegate your powers to a Deputy who can concert and direct the general movement of our war action, and who will enjoy your support and that of the War Cabinet, unless very good reason is shown to the contrary.[40]

So from Churchill's perspective the problem was insufficient executive authority: had that been enhanced, he would never have given up this responsibility in the first place. He was fortunate that it hadn't been, because it would have been much more difficult to deflect the blame for the fiasco. In fact Churchill had already caused strains in the committee by insisting on using his own tactical ideas as the basis of planning and bullying people to accept them.[41] The entire Norwegian campaign had endured disastrous organization, planning and execution, and, more than anyone, Churchill had been in charge.

Churchill would insist, when he had to recount these unhappy matters to the House of Commons (he would acquire great experience of performing this function), that it was the neutrality of Norway that constituted the problem, as it inhibited British action: 'It is not the slightest use blaming the allies for not being able to give substantial help and protection to neutral countries, if they are held at arm's length by the neutral countries until those countries are actually attacked.'[42] However, even when they didn't hold Britain at arms length and were not neutral, as was the case with France, the result would be defeat. Blaming the neutral countries for Britain's lack of strategic facility served to deflect attention from Churchill's own decisions. He also complained in the House, 'The reason for this serious disadvantage of our not having the initiative is one which cannot speedily be removed, and it's our failure in the last five years to maintain air parity with Germany.' Concerning this lack of rearmament for the air force he continued, 'It was not only the government who objected, but both the Opposition parties.'[43] So Churchill's failure in Norway was, as usual, someone else's – indeed pretty much everybody else's – fault.

The House of Commons debate that followed the Norwegian debacle did more than any other single event to seal the fate of Neville Chamberlain. His position was now untenable. In it, Churchill argued passionately in favour of the whole campaign: he could do little else given that it had been his idea. The fiasco has largely been airbrushed out of history, despite the fact that it was clear that Churchill undertook political and military direction and had learned nothing from the experience of Gallipoli. It is deeply ironic that the immediate cause of Churchill succeeding Chamberlain as Prime Minister was a catastrophic event for which he himself had been culpable.

FUTILITY OF THE NORWAY OPERATION

It is often argued that Hitler's occupation of Norway meant that substantial numbers of his forces were diverted from other theatres. This is true, but Churchill did not initiate the campaign for this reason. It is also said that German occupation of Norway threatened Allied supply lines to the USSR. This is also true, but it is not why Churchill planned in 1939 to occupy Norway: the Molotov–Ribbentrop Pact had been signed in August 1939 and was the pretext for Germany's invasion of Poland the following month. Churchill could not then have expected that the USSR would subsequently be an ally of Britain.

As we have seen, Hitler was also subject to the illusion that Norway was potentially crucial to Britain's plans. If a British invasion of Norway had been successful, if its borders had been secured and Norwegians had come forward to join the conflict in larger numbers than they actually did, how could British occupation of Norway have been sustained, and how could any further action have been taken against Germany from Norway? Even a limited occupation of Norway would have consumed a huge proportion of Britain's resources, considerably depleting its national defence and so opening it up more readily to the proposed German invasion. Ferrying resources across the North Sea would have meant they were open to attack by U-boats as well as surface warships and Luftwaffe air attack. We know how devastating the German attacks were on the Royal Navy and the Royal Air Force during the subsequent Dunkirk retreat (see chapter 7).

In the Battle of Britain, RAF Fighter Command would perform a crucial function, changing world history, but that was with the benefit of a world-beating home radar network and excellent 'sector control' organizational system. To cover the communication lines to Norway, Fighter Command would have been obliged to conduct standing patrols, just as they were to do over France and while covering the Dunkirk retreat, where they were subject to substantial attrition. Supplying Norway would thus have been unsustainable.

Even if these seemingly insurmountable difficulties had not obtained, could an assault against Germany have been undertaken from Norway? A seaborne operation would have been required, leading to an opposed landing on the German coast. But supplying Norway and then launching an opposed landing would have posed greater logistical problems than one launched directly from Britain, as many of the necessary resources would first have to be shipped from Britain to Norway. The Germans would thus have been given two bites at the cherry: they could attack men and materiel as they were shipped to Norway, and again when they made their landing on German soil. The short communication links enjoyed by the Germans would have meant that the Luftwaffe and the Kriegsmarine's U-boats would have had plenty of opportunity to attack Allied forces.

Thus it seems extremely doubtful that such an opposed landing would have been successful, let alone that Germany could have been defeated by it.

Perhaps Norway could have been used simply as a platform for mounting aerial attacks on Germany by the RAF. Yet, logistically, it would seem far better to have conducted raids from bases in England, as was actually done, rather than trying to supply men and materiel to Norway and conducting raids from there. Bases in Norway would have enabled raids to reach targets in eastern Germany that were out of range from England with the twin-engine bombers then in RAF service. But because of the logistical impediments, it seems more sensible to have awaited the introduction of the four-engine heavies to undertake this work from English bases. Thus, the RAF would not have gained an appreciable strategic advantage by being based in Norway, and it would have been more than outweighed by the vast resources needed to secure and defend Norway.

In reality, Churchill's Norwegian strategy fell into the 'peripheralist' or 'dispersionist' category: it was just another pinprick around the edge of Hitler's fiefdom, and beyond that had not been properly thought through. Had it progressed, as with so many of his plans, resources that were extremely limited would have been grossly misallocated, and this attrition of resources would have extended the war, not shortened it – this is the essential point.

NORWAY YET AGAIN

Churchill wanted to occupy Norway again in 1941 – in Operation Jupiter – when the Soviet Union was in the war on the Allied side. However, the military chiefs persuaded him that it was not possible. General Sir Alan Brooke, then Commander-in-Chief Home Forces but Chief of the Imperial General Staff from 30 November 1941, noted in his diary on 3 October:

> At midnight received [a] special messenger from the War Office with orders to carry out [an] examination for [an] attack on Trondheim and preparation of [a] plan of attack. The whole to be in by next Friday! Also that I was to dine tonight at Chequers and spend [the] night there to discuss [the] plans. I motored back to London in the morning and

spent most of the afternoon studying details of the plan. At 6pm picked up [Sir John] Dill [Chief of the Imperial General Staff] at the WO [War Office] and drove down to Chequers discussing details with him on the way. Dudley Pound [Head of the Royal Navy], Portal [Head of the RAF] and Attlee [Labour Party Leader] formed the party. We sat up till 2.15am discussing the problem and I did my best to put the PM off attempting the plan. Air support cannot be adequately supplied and we shall fall into the same pitfall as we did before.[44]

The following day he wrote, 'Resumed discussion at 11am and went on till 1pm, I think [the] PM was beginning to weaken on the plan.' He added retrospectively:

How little did I know him [Churchill] at that time, to imagine that he was weakening on this plan. From then onwards we were to be continually in trouble riding him off mad plans to go back to Norway. Why he wanted to go back and what he was going to do there, even if he did succeed in capturing Trondheim, we never found out. The only reason he ever gave was that Hitler had unrolled the map of Europe starting with Norway, and he would start rolling it up again from Norway. It should be remembered that the plan for the capture of Norway had already been examined by the Chiefs of Staff Committee, and had been turned down as impracticable owing to insufficient air support for the operation.

Now at Chequers, I, in my capacity as C-in-C Home Forces, had just received orders from him to prepare a detailed plan for the capture of Trondheim, ready to the last button. A commander for the expedition was to be appointed by me and the plan was to be sufficiently ready only to require the order to start. I was given one week to prepare the plan. I said that if I was to do so I must have the C-in-C Home Fleet, AOC Fighter Command, AOC Bomber Command, Minister for Transportation and several others at my disposal for repeated conferences during the week. I was told that they were all to be made available. It was an unpleasant assignment, I had been told by Dill of the results of the Chiefs of Staff inspection of the problem, and I felt convinced that I should arrive at similar conclusions. It was going to entail a great deal of wasted work on the part of many busy people.[45]

On 12 October, as he noted in his diary, Brooke was obliged to explain to Churchill the plan he had drawn up with senior members of all of the armed services: Admiral Sir John Tovey, Air Chief Marshal Sir William Sholto Douglas and General Sir Bernard Paget:

All Chiefs of Staff, Tovey, Sholto [Douglas], Paget and I attended. [The] PM [was] very dissatisfied with our appreciation! Told me that he was expecting a detailed plan for the operation and instead of that I had submitted a masterly treatise on all the difficulties! He then proceeded to cross question me for nearly 2 hours on various items of the appreciation, trying to make out that I had unnecessarily increased the difficulties! However I was quite satisfied that there was only one conclusion to arrive at.

I repeatedly tried to bring him back to the main reason – the lack of air support. He avoided this issue and selected arguments such as: 'You state that you will be confronted by frosts and thaws which will render mobility difficult. How can you account for such a statement?' I replied that this was a relatively trivial matter and that the statement came from the 'Climate Book'. He at once sent for this book, from which it at once became evident that this extract had been copied straight out of the book. His next attack was: 'You state that it will take you some 24 hours to cover the ground between A and B. How can you account for so long being taken, explain to me exactly how every one of those 24 hours will be occupied'! As this time had been allowed for overcoming enemy resistance on the road, removal of road blocks and probable reparation to demolition of bridges and culverts, it was not an easy matter to paint a detailed picture of every hour of those 24. This led to a series of more questions, interspersed with sarcasm and criticism. A very unpleasant grilling to stand up to in a full room, but excellent training for what I had to stand up to on many occasions in later years![46]

Churchill was by no means finished. Next he sought to accomplish the Norwegian adventure with the Canadians, and asked to see Lieutenant-General Andrew McNaughton. Brooke noted in his diary for 16 October:

McNaughton arrived one morning to inform me that he had been invited to Chequers for the following weekend and to discuss something about Norway! I told him all the back history and the fact that the operation had already been examined twice for Churchill and turned down each time as impracticable. I warned him that he might well now try to have an attack done by Canadian troops. He assured me that he would not dream of accepting such a task for his troops, and I asked him anyhow to come and see me on Monday after his visit to let me know the results of his talk.

On the following Monday a limp looking McNaughton walked into my room and literally poured himself into my armchair! I asked him how he had got on. He informed me that he had had a ghastly weekend, he had been kept up all hours of the morning until he did not know which way he was facing. Winston's control of the English language and his qualifications as a barrister had left him dumbfounded. When I pressed him as to what he had agreed to, he began to beat about the bush and would not be very precise. Finally, however, I extracted from him that [he] had agreed to examine the Trondheim operation. When he saw the effect on me he hurriedly added that he had since sent a telegram to [Prime Minister] Mackenzie King asking him on no account to agree to the employment of the Canadian forces in any operations in Norway! This was one way of shelving the responsibility of refusing, but as far as I was concerned, it made little difference. I knew that the Canadians would not now be used in this wild venture.

This ended Winston's third attempt to have his own way! It did not mean that he relinquished the idea – far from it – he was always hankering after it, and the sight of a Norwegian map alone was enough to start him off again.[47]

He started off again in the summer of the following year. This time he attempted to couch it in terms of securing supplies to Russia, as he wrote in a letter to President Roosevelt on 28 May: 'I have also told the staffs to study a landing in the north of Norway, the occupation of which seems necessary to ensure the flow of our supplies next year to Russia. I have told Molotov [Soviet Foreign Minister] we would have something ready for him about this to discuss . . .'[48]

Brooke noted in his diary on 5 June 1942: 'We then turned to examine the PM's pet attack on Northern Norway which appears even more impossible, except possibly for limited operations to secure Petsamo in combination with the Russians.'[49] By the following month it was back to the Canadians again. Brooke noted on 9 July:

> At this Morning's COS [chiefs of staff meeting] we had invited Andy McNaughton so as to give him the task of examining the possibility of capturing North Norway with the Canadian Corps! This was according to the PM's orders, it having been suggested by Attlee that with his more flexible and fertile brain he would find a way out where the Chiefs of Staff had failed![50]

On 15 September Churchill returned to the subject of Norway yet again; this time he wanted the north of the country captured in January 1943.[51] McNaughton was dispatched to Moscow to discuss the operation with the Russians. Mercifully this never came about, yet Churchill never fully let go. Instead he instigated British commando raids on Norwegian fish factories that were supplying the Third Reich. This resulted in the deaths of a handful of German servicemen and the recruitment to the war effort of a handful of young Norwegians, who returned with the withdrawing commandos. The Germans implemented such severe reprisals against Norwegian citizens that the Norwegian underground movement told London that the benefits of the raids were not worth the costs. The Norwegian government in exile in London was also furious that it had not been told of the raids.

FINALLY THE DEBACLE ENDS

Eventually, mercifully, Churchill's obsession petered out. When the Second Front finally came, there was no attempt to invade Norway; the military brass understood that defeating Germany itself would lead the German occupation of Norway and Denmark to collapse, which is precisely what happened. This strategy had the additional virtue that the civilian population of the Scandinavian countries escaped being fought over by Allied and Axis forces. Churchill then ordered Britain's most successful military officer, General Sir Bernard Montgomery, into the area to prevent the Soviets from occupying Scandinavia, but to expect such an occupation was a little unreal. He opined in *The Second World War*:

> Of course it may be said that all Norwegian enterprises, however locally successful, to which we might have committed ourselves would have been swept away by the results of the fearful battle in France which was now so near. Within a month the main Allied armies were to be shattered or driven into the sea. Everything we had would have been drawn into the struggle for life. It was therefore lucky for us that we were not able to build up a substantial army and air force round Trondheim. The veils of the future are lifted one by one, and mortals must act from day to day. On the knowledge we had in the middle of April, I remain of the opinion that, having gone so far, we ought to have persisted in carrying out 'Operation Hammer', and the threefold attack on Trondheim on which all had been agreed; but I accept my full share of responsibility for not enforcing this upon our expert advisors when they became so decidedly adverse to it and presented us with serious objections.[52]

It is curious that Churchill intimates here that Allied forces would have had to be withdrawn from Norway anyway in order to fight in France; Hitler split his forces most effectively to secure German occupation of Norway and Denmark as well as France and the Low Countries, and he secured materiel supplies from Sweden in the process. It is most significant that Churchill believed that the service chiefs should have been overridden and a full-scale Gallipoli-type operation undertaken – the forcing of the Trondheim Straits so that British forces could occupy Norway. This would have led to a far heavier defeat and denuded Britain's ability to fight in France or indeed to defend itself. It is also curious that after the war he still believed that he was right in April 1940 to support 'Hammer', when forces would have had to be withdrawn subsequently, and any gains forsaken, in order to undertake the battle in France.

Churchill said of Norway, 'We can now see that we were well out of it.'[53] So all the vital objectives he had identified in the Norwegian campaign he subsequently brushed aside. How important could these objectives have been if they could all be dismissed so easily? He wrote in *The Second World War*: 'Considering the prominent part I played in these events . . . it is a marvel I survived and maintained my position in public esteem and Parliamentary confidence.'[54]

7
DUNKIRK:
CHURCHILL'S DEFEAT

By May 1940 it was crystal clear that Chamberlain's position as Prime Minister was an impediment to unity in the Conservative Party and in Parliament. Churchill's cronies – Leo Amery, Alfred Duff Cooper and Robert Boothby – all helped to undermine Chamberlain.[1] It is ironic that Churchill was chosen to replace him, as he had been little else but an impediment to unity, which is why both Baldwin and Chamberlain had kept him out of their Cabinets, as had MacDonald and his National government before them.

It was in the House of Commons on 7 May, when Churchill was defending the Norway debacle, that Leo Amery interjected while Chamberlain was speaking and quoted Oliver Cromwell's famous statement to the Long Parliament: 'You have sat too long here for any good you have been doing. Depart, I say, and let us have done with you. In the name of God, go!'[2] On the morning of 10 May Chamberlain held a meeting at 10 Downing Street to determine his successor. Present were David Margesson (the Conservative Chief Whip), Lord Halifax (the Foreign Secretary) and Churchill. Chamberlain, along with King George VI, wanted Halifax to succeed him, and Margesson made the formal proposal. Churchill was asked if he saw any reason why the Prime Minister should not be a member of the House of Lords (the last one had been the 3rd Marquess of Salisbury, who had retired in 1902). For Churchill this was a trap: if he answered 'Yes' he was openly favouring himself to succeed Chamberlain and might thus prejudice his chances; if he said 'No' he was effectively endorsing Halifax. He said nothing. After a long silence, Halifax himself mumbled that it would be inappropriate for the Prime Minister to be in the Lords.[3]

So the choice was between someone who did not wish to do the job and someone who did. It is often argued that this moment was decisive in British history, for if Halifax – the appeaser – had been chosen, the nation would almost certainly have been defeated. But Halifax simply did not want the job, and as the Commons had forced Chamberlain's resignation because he was an appeaser it is hard to see how its members would have accepted as his replacement a man who was even less capable of robust action against Nazi Germany. Even if Halifax had agreed and the Commons had given him a period of grace, unless he had undergone a remarkable transformation it is almost impossible to believe that they would not quite soon have insisted that he be replaced. It is equally hard to believe that there were no politicians in Parliament, other than Churchill, who were keen to continue the fight. On the contrary, there was no shortage: this is precisely why they were so motivated to get rid of Chamberlain.

The choice of Churchill to succeed as Prime Minister was, in the end, supported by Baldwin but certainly not by Chamberlain. Churchill's virtues were seen as his stance on appeasement in the 1930s, his focus and capacity for hard work, his oratory, and the fact that he had been a senior member of the government before, during and after World War I, and thus carried that experience. But, ominously, that experience included Gallipoli and now Norway.

Churchill became Prime Minister on 10 May 1940. He made himself Minister of Defence and initially Leader of the House of Commons as well. Chamberlain retained the leadership of the Conservative Party in order to preserve party unity, though it was clear by then that he was an even greater impediment to such unity than Churchill. Chamberlain's final illness caused his resignation as party leader on 9 October, and Churchill – who, three years earlier, had seconded the proposal for Chamberlain to lead the party – succeeded him. Chamberlain died on 9 November.[4]

On taking office, Churchill commented to Major-General Sir Hastings Ismay of the British public, 'Poor people. They trust me, and I can give them nothing but disaster for quite a long time.'[5] During his first two months as Prime Minister, Holland and Belgium capitulated, France was overrun, German forces advanced to the English Channel, Paris was abandoned and France capitulated, Italy entered the war and attacked both Kenya and the Sudan, Japan intensified its assault on China, and Germany amassed men and materiel across the entire sweep of territory between Norway and Finisterre. And, of course, there was Dunkirk. Yet even this was not the end of the disasters; it wasn't even the beginning of the end, only the end of the beginning.

THE BRITISH EXPEDITIONARY FORCE GOES TO WAR

Churchill's failure to see the threat from Japan has already been discussed in chapter 3, but all the other events, from a British point of view, hinged on the handling of the British Expeditionary Force (BEF) in France and Belgium. Once he was Prime Minister, Churchill had ultimate political responsibility for the BEF.

The BEF, commanded by General John Vereker (Lord Gort), had been sent to the Franco-Belgian border in the early stages of the war. When in May 1940 the decisive German assault began, it was comprised of three corps, encompassing ten infantry divisions, and a tank brigade. It was just one-tenth of the total Allied force. Churchill himself described it as 'B.E.F. a fine Army. Only 10 Divisions. Without proper armoured Divisions.' He continued that it was 'well equipped, but placed in a hopeless strategic situation'.[6] One wonders why he did not immediately do something about it: it is not as though he was unaware of the realities. Major-General Edward (Louis) Spears, who had supported Churchill in his rearmament campaign in the 1930s and would be his representative to the French Prime Minister in the summer of 1940, had written to him on 26 September 1939, just after his reappointment as First Lord of the Admiralty:

> I am very worried indeed about the feeling in France. There is clearly a sense of exasperation in the countryside at the fact that France and France alone appears to be bearing the main brunt of the fighting and will have to continue to do so . . . that really after all they have been duped and are fighting for England . . . The line taken, natural enough perhaps, is England first, France afterwards. But where are these 'pooled resources' that they were told about? People well placed to know tell me that if we were to broadcast to the world that the total resources of the French and British Empires were really pooled, and that steps were being taken to carry this into effect, it would have an excellent effect.[7]

In September 1939 the RAF had sent the Advanced Air Striking Force (AASF) to France; it was comprised of light bombers: the hopelessly vulnerable single-engine Fairey Battles, and the lightly armed twin-engine Bristol Blenheims. The Air Component of the BEF was also sent; it too was comprised of Blenheims, plus Westland Lysanders to undertake reconnaissance and photographic sorties, and a few Hurricane fighters. Things were not helped when these fighters were augmented with obsolete Gloster Gladiator biplanes.

During the inter-war years the British military strategists Major-General John Fuller and Captain Sir Basil Liddell Hart had developed the concept of close co-operation between armoured vehicles and aircraft.[8] It was the Germans who would adopt this and call it *Blitzkrieg* ('lightning war'). It would prove to be decisive in conquering Poland in September 1939 and in Norway, Denmark, Holland, Belgium and France in the spring of 1940. Ironically, during World War I, the principal task of the Royal Flying Corps (RFC) had been close support for the British armies in France and Flanders. However, by the outset of World War II, what had by then become the Royal Air Force (RAF) had abandoned this strategy.

If France could have been prevented from falling, stiffened by effective stewardship and substantial reinforcements of the BEF as well as political support from Britain, then the Low Countries could have been defended and Mussolini would have been circumspect about Italy entering the war. But the reality was very different: the BEF would be withdrawn pell-mell, France and the Low Countries would fall in a trice, and Mussolini would enter the war to get his snout in the trough while there was still something to be had.

On 10 May 1940 Hitler initiated the invasion of Holland, Belgium and France. The 'Phoney War' was over. Generalleutnant Erich von Manstein had been the architect of the battle plan, heavily modifying the original version codenamed *Fall Gelb* ('Case Yellow'). The original plan required a main thrust into Belgium, but von Manstein believed the Allies would anticipate this, as it had been the strategy of the Schlieffen Plan of World War I, devised in 1905 by the former German Army Chief of Staff, Feldmarschall Alfred Graf von Schlieffen. So von Manstein argued that German forces should make only a diversionary feint into Belgium to draw Allied forces there, while the main German thrust should come through the Ardennes at Sedan. Since the Allies assumed the Ardennes Forest to be impenetrable by mechanized forces, the fixed fortifications of the Maginot Line, intended to protect France's eastern border, did not

Churchill as a government minister, speaking in Manchester in April 1908. His last book, The History of the English Speaking Peoples *concluded its chronicle at about this time, when Britain was still great – before Churchill had any serious influence.*

Churchill (centre) with David Lloyd George (centre-right) inspecting a naval dockyard in 1912. In 1909 Churchill had called for restraint in warship construction, by 1911 as First Lord of the Admiralty he argued for expansion. Of the Gallipoli campaign in 1915, Lloyd George commented of Churchill: 'He is on his way to a lunatic asylum.'

Admiral Jackie Fisher – generally regarded as second only to Horatio Nelson in British naval history. Fisher's concern at Churchill's interference in the operational conduct of the Navy during World War I caused him to resign as First Sea Lord. He told the future Prime Minister, Andrew Bonar Law that Churchill was 'a bigger danger than the Germans by a long way'.

Churchill and TE Lawrence – 'Lawrence of Arabia' amongst the experts attending the Cairo conference on the Middle East – primarily for settling the terms of the British Mandate of Mesopotamia (Iraq) – in March 1921 (Churchill front row middle; Lawrence 2nd row, fourth from right). Lawrence, though a colleague of Churchill, was a critic of government policy in Iraq in the early 1920s when Churchill was Secretary of State for War and subsequently Secretary of State for the Colonies.

Churchill at Buckingham Palace in 1924 to receive the seals of office of Chancellor of the Exchequer. The First Sea Lord, Admiral Sir David Beatty, wrote of Churchill's 1925 Budget: 'That extraordinary fellow Winston has gone mad. Economically mad.'

Churchill (centre) on Budget day in 1928 walking to the House of Commons with his daughter Diana, his Parliamentary Private Secretary Robert Boothby MP (left), and his long-serving bodyguard Walter Thompson (centre-right, in plain clothes). His policy of returning to the Gold Standard was inconsistent with his socially reforming policies.

The most eminent economist of his day, John Maynard Keynes had warned Churchill of the adverse consequences of his economic policies – to no avail.

Churchill, when Chancellor, with the Prime Minister Stanley Baldwin (centre) and the Foreign Secretary Austen Chamberlain (left) in January 1925. Austen and his brother Neville opposed the extent of Churchill's cuts in the Navy, and Baldwin didn't like Churchill's proposed cuts in the Royal Air Force.

Churchill and the Prime Minister, Stanley Baldwin (right) in August 1925, en route to the House of Commons to debate the coal miners' strike. Much later, Kingsley Martin, editor of the New Statesman, wrote that Churchill's attitude was 'to smash the unions'.

Churchill with the Prime Minister, Neville Chamberlain (right) in 1939. It was Chamberlain's peace overtures which ensured that Hitler received the entire blame for causing World War II. Both Chamberlain and Stanley Baldwin prevented the bellicose Churchill from precipitating Britain into war before she was ready.

Churchill and his crony Brendan Bracken MP (left) attending Parliament in June 1930.

Although Churchill often receives the credit for seeing the threat from Germany when others could not, the prescient French Field Marshall, Ferdinand Foch saw World War II looming long before Churchill did.

Early in World War II, the Prime Minister Neville Chamberlain with his War Cabinet: (back row, from left to right) Sir Kingsley Wood, Secretary of State for Air, subsequently Lord Privy Seal; Churchill, First Lord of the Admiralty; Leslie Hore-Belisha, Secretary of State for War; Lord Hankey, Minister Without Portfolio; (front row, left to right) Lord Halifax, the Foreign Secretary; Sir John Simon, Chancellor of the Exchequer; Neville Chamberlain; Sir Samuel Hoare, Lord Privy Seal before replacing Kingsley Wood at the Air Ministry; and Lord Chatfield, Minister for Coordination of Defence.

General Sir Claude Auchinleck ('the Auk') commanded British forces in North Africa in World War II. Churchill pressured him to undertake offensive operations prematurely; withdrew forces from his command at a crucial juncture; then sacked him despite his victory in the first battle of El Alamein.

Air Chief Marshall Sir Hugh Dowding, the 'architect of victory' in the Battle of Britain. Churchill wanted to fritter away his fighters in the Battle of France, then tried to pressure him into a premature, rash attack in the Battle of Britain. Dowding was sacked at the moment of victory.

Churchill's scientific advisor Lord Cherwell (Frederick Lindemann) was another crony. He often got the science wrong: overestimating the effect of area bombing, treating the Dams of the Ruhr valley as being of little consequence and arguing that Barnes Wallis's earthquake bombs were unsound.

extend that far north, and the area was only lightly defended. Von Manstein was promoted to full general as a result of the success of the plan.

The Heer (the German Army) deployed 136 divisions and 2,700 tanks, and the Luftwaffe 2,500 aircraft. The French, Belgians, Dutch and British had 125 divisions, 3,600 tanks and 1,500 aircraft in defence. Belgium, a small country, supplied ten of these divisions, and Holland, also small, supplied 22. Britain, as has been said, supplied just ten divisions, plus three to perform supporting functions only, not for combat. The 1st Armoured Division was added after the German attack.[9]

THE SITUATION BECOMES DESPERATE

General Maurice Gamelin, commander-in-chief of all French forces, had his headquarters in the Château of Vincennes, where there were no radio or telephone communications: orders were dispatched on the hour by motorcycle, and one observer commented that it was like a submarine without a periscope. Gamelin kept issuing halt orders, only to find that the halt lines had already been overrun by German forces by the time those orders had been received. It was a set of circumstances guaranteed to yield German victory. At 6.45am on 10 May (the day Churchill became Prime Minister) Gamelin made the fatal mistake of committing the bulk of his forces, including his strategic reserves, to Belgium and the defence of Holland – his Plan D. This was precisely what the Germans had intended.

By 14 May, General Heinz Guderian and his armoured force had crossed the River Meuse, despite AASF Fairey Battle and Bristol Blenheim light bombers mounting desperate attacks to stop them. Guderian's forces punched an 80km (50-mile) hole in the Allied front. By midday on 20 May Amiens had been captured, despite desperate fighting by the French and the 12th and 23rd Divisions of the BEF. German forces were at Abbeville, at the mouth of the River Seine, by that evening. On the following day there was a brief counterattack by Gort at Arras, which demonstrated what could be done with determination, particularly as it was against one of the Germans' greatest generals, Generaloberst Erwin Rommel. The counterattack held up the advance of his 7th Panzer Division and SS units, but it was not pressed home with sufficient forces, either British or French, and failed.[10] Thus, the day after that the Germans crossed the River Scheldt and were heading north to encircle the Allied forces. Gort would make up his mind to race for the coast – a hopelessly risky venture.

At 7.30am on 15 May Paul Reynaud, the French Prime Minister, telephoned Churchill to report that the Germans had broken through at Sedan. He said: 'We are beaten. We have lost the battle.'[11] Churchill replied: 'Surely it can't have happened so soon?' He then said:

> All experience shows that the offensive will come to an end after a while. I remember the 21st March 1918. After five or six days they have to halt for supplies, and the opportunity for counter-attack is presented. I learned all this at the time from the lips of Marshal Foch himself.[12]

Ferdinand Foch had been an excellent commander-in-chief of the French Army in World War I, but technology had changed in the interim and Churchill understood little of these changes. In *The Second World War* he wrote:

> What was the Maginot line for? It should have economised troops upon a large sector of the frontier, not only offering many sally-ports for local counter-strokes, but also enabling large forces to be held in reserve; and this is the only way these things can be done. But now there was no reserve.[13]

And of the reserve issue itself:

> I was dumbfounded. What were we to think of the great French Army and its highest chief? It had never occurred to me that any commanders . . . would have left themselves unprovided with a mass of manoeuvre . . .[14]

He could only conclude, 'I admit this was one of the greatest surprises I have had in my life.'[15] He went to Paris on 16 May to meet Reynaud and Gamelin and was told of the situation, but incredibly he failed to inform the BEF. The latter would discover it only by accident, and then not from Churchill, but from the French. On 17 May General Alphonse Georges, in command of the North-East Front, inquired whether the British 23rd Division could fill a gap in the line. This division had been deployed in France, not as a combat force, but to perform practical functions behind the lines, so Lieutenant-Colonel (Viscount) Robert Bridgeman, in command of the BEF's Rear GHQ, was surprised at the request. He immediately smelt a rat and undertook some clandestine enquiries. Only then did the true extent of the catastrophe become apparent to the BEF. Georges and Gamelin were both sacked on that very day.[16]

CHURCHILL DENUDES FIGHTER COMMAND

Reynaud, in a desperate plea, asked for an additional ten squadrons, and Churchill personally promised to supply them. This was a catastrophic mistake when defeat was certain anyway, a venture that risked the loss of Fighter Command's frontline strength and the subsequent loss of the Battle of Britain. As it was, Fighter Command would lose half its strength in the French campaign. It was Air Chief Marshal Sir Hugh Dowding, Air Officer Commanding-in-Chief RAF Fighter Command, who fought to stop Churchill from taking this action, with Neville Chamberlain also opposed to it.[17]

Dowding was summoned to the War Cabinet Room at 10 Downing Street on 15 May. Those present were Churchill, Sir Archibald Sinclair (Air Minister), Sir Cyril Newhall (Chief of the Air Staff) and Lord Beaverbrook (Minister of Aircraft Production). Churchill said that he had already promised the French the additional fighter squadrons, but Dowding stated that because of the existing commitment, fighter losses were already exceeding the rate of replacement. Dowding wrote to the Under-Secretary of State at the Air Ministry the following day – it was a seminal letter:

> Sir,
> I have the honour to refer to the very serious calls which have recently been made upon the Home defence Fighter Units in an attempt to stem the German Invasion of the Continent.
>
> 2. I hope and believe that our armies may yet be victorious in France and Belgium, but we have to face the possibility that they may be defeated.

3. In this case I presume that there is no one who will deny that England should fight on, even though the remainder of the Continent of Europe is dominated by the Germans.

4. For this purpose it is necessary to retain some minimum fighter strength in this country and I must request that the Air Council will inform me what they consider this minimum strength to be, in order that I may make my dispositions accordingly.

5. I would remind the Air Council that the last estimate which they made as to the force necessary to defend this country was 52 squadrons, and my strength has now been reduced to the equivalent of 36 squadrons.

6. Once a decision has been reached as to the limit on which the Air Council and the Cabinet are prepared to stake the existence of the country, it should be made clear to the allied Commanders on the Continent that not a single aeroplane from Fighter Command beyond the limit will be sent across the Channel, no matter how desperate the situation may become.

7. It will, of course, be remembered that the estimate of 52 squadrons was based on the assumption that the attack would come from the eastwards except in so far as the defences might be outflanked in flight. We have now to face the possibility that attacks may come from Spain or even from the North coast of France. The result is that our line is very much extended at the same time as our resources are reduced.

8. I must point out that within the last few days the equivalent of 10 squadrons have been sent to France, that the Hurricane squadrons remaining in this country are seriously depleted, and that the more squadrons which are sent to France the higher will be the wastage and the more insistent the demands for reinforcements.

9. I must therefore request that as a matter of paramount urgency the Air Ministry will consider and decide what level of strength is to be left to the Fighter Command for the defence of this country, and will assure me that when the level has

been reached, not one fighter will be sent across the Channel however urgent and insistent the appeals for help may be.

10. I believe that, if an adequate fighter force is kept in this country, if the fleet remains in being, and if Home Forces are suitably organized to resist invasion, we should be able to carry on the war single-handed for some time, if not indefinitely. But, if the Home Defence Force is drained away in desperate attempts to remedy the situation in France, defeat in France will involve the final, complete and irremediable defeat of this country.[18]

In his meeting with Reynaud on the 16th, Churchill pointed out that Britain had only 39 fighter squadrons for national defence, yet Dowding had stated that there were 36. The minutes read: 'Churchill said . . . that the French had asked for ten fighter squadrons. The British had given . . . another four as the result of this morning's decision. This meant that six more were now asked for.'[19] The War Cabinet in London had sanctioned the four additional squadrons, but Churchill then contacted the Cabinet and suggested that Fighter Command should send another six Hurricane squadrons to France in accordance with the French request. The Cabinet agreed to a compromise: the six Hurricane squadrons would be sent to bases in northern France, so they could fly home at night! Thus, they were neither available for the frontline defence of France nor were they part of Dowding's national defence force.

Churchill then told his Cabinet that Dowding had informed him that only 25 squadrons were needed for national defence, and thus that sending a further six to France would not compromise national security.[20] He perpetuated this notion in *The Second World War*, writing: 'Dowding . . . declared to me that with twenty-five squadrons of fighters he could defend the Island against the whole might of the German Air Force . . .'[21] Of this, Dowding said:

What can one say about Churchill's statement other than that it was totally untrue . . . I never discussed such a point with him. I'd never had any opportunity to discuss with him anything about any such matter until the Cabinet meeting of 15 May, and then the point I made was only about the

Hurricane wastage in the squadrons that were being sent to France. We had no other meeting at that time, and the subject that he claimed we'd discussed never came up.[22]

In fact Dowding had made it crystal clear in his letter that the original estimate was that 52 squadrons would be needed, and that home defence requirements had increased since that estimate had been made. It is hardly credible that he would have told Churchill that less than half that figure was now the minimum. Yet Churchill was prepared to denude the home defence forces far beyond the point of risking 'final, complete and irremediable defeat'.

This was not the end of it, however. Churchill and Reynaud had another meeting on 22 May at Vincennes, outside Paris. The minutes read: 'It was agreed that . . . the Metropolitan British Air Forces would be wholly employed in the battle . . . the fighter squadrons, which, since they operated from bases in England, could hardly remain on the scene for more than 20 minutes, would act in relays or successive waves of attack.'[23] The very thing Dowding had most feared had now been agreed to by Churchill.

In fact, during the seven-week duration of the Battle of France, from mid-May to June 1940, the RAF lost more aircraft than in the entirety of the subsequent Battle of Britain. An enormous amount of ground equipment was abandoned as well. This vindicated Dowding's strategy more than any other single fact, and indicated how catastrophic Churchill's policy would have been had he been allowed to get away with it.[24]

While Churchill was promoting the use of Fighter Command's frontline strength in France, he was already vacillating about sending more army divisions. In a letter to Major-General Ismay for the chiefs of staff on 18 May, he wrote: 'The Chiefs of Staff must consider whether it would not be well to send only half of the so-called Armoured Division to France. One must always be prepared for the fact that the French may be offered very advantageous terms of peace, and the whole weight be thrown on us.'[25] This inconsistency in regard to the army and the RAF was most worrying: Churchill seemed more willing to sacrifice the RAF, which would constitute Britain's first line of defence in the coming Battle of Britain, than to sacrifice the army, which would not. The lack of wholehearted support for the French itself constituted a reason for defeat:

half believing that the French would capitulate made it a self-fulfilling prophecy that they would. Dowding recognized that defeat was inevitable in France and that committing more forces would be a disaster. Gort also came to this decision, though very late in the day. There needed to be either full support for the French or complete withdrawal – a halfway house was a disaster.

FRANCE COLLAPSES

On 19 May General Maxime Weygand replaced General Gamelin as commander-in-chief of all French forces, but it was all too late. Weygand planned a pincer movement whereby the BEF plus French forces would attack southwards towards Cambrai, while other French forces attacked northwards from the Somme. This was in fact little different from Gamelin's plan, known as Instruction No 12. Churchill and General Sir Edmund Ironside, the CIGS, opposed the notion of a withdrawal of the BEF and supported the Weygand plan.[26]

It was midnight on 18 May when Gort was visited by the French General Gaston Billotte, a subordinate of Weygand who would command the French forces striking south. Gort was not impressed by Billotte's proposals to halt the German advance and it was at this moment that he began to think of a withdrawal. In a dispatch he wrote: 'The picture was now [night of the 19th] no longer that of a line bent or temporarily broken, but of a besieged fortress.'[27]

While supporting the Weygand plan for attack, Churchill was already half expecting a withdrawal. The minutes of the War Cabinet meeting of 20 May record: 'The Prime Minister thought that as a precautionary measure the Admiralty should assemble a large number of small vessels in readiness to proceed to ports and inlets on the French coast.'[28] But by preparing for withdrawal, the plan for attack was already being undermined. On the following day Churchill telegraphed Reynaud: 'Many congratulations upon appointing Weygand, in whom we have entire confidence here . . . I feel more confident than I did at the beginning of the battle . . .'[29] But his level of confidence in both Weygand and the battle was clearly contradicted by his consideration of withdrawal.

On 24 May Reynaud telegraphed London:

... you had instructed General Gort to continue to carry out
the Weygand plan. General Weygand now informs me that,
according to a telegram from General Blanchard, the British
Army had carried out, on its own initiative, a retreat of twenty-
five miles towards the ports at a time when our troops moving
up from the south are gaining ground towards the north,
where they were to meet their allies.[30]

On the following day, with the northward attack from the Somme failing
to materialize and the situation in Belgium perilous, Gort made his
fateful decision. Any intention of supporting the Weygand plan was now
abandoned and he decided finally on a dash to the coast. The following day
plans were drawn up accordingly.[31]

THE DUNKIRK EVACUATION BEGINS

German Panzers were already at Gravelines, only 16km (10 miles) from
Dunkirk, by 22 May. It was Churchill who authorized the Dunkirk
evacuation. Vice-Admiral Bertram Ramsay, based in Dover, formulated
Operation Dynamo to facilitate it, in consort with Gort and Dowding.
Churchill had in fact already sacked Ramsay as Fifth Sea Lord some time
before, over a wrangle concerning the Fleet Air Arm. Now he would rely on
him for the evacuation.[32]

The Dunkirk docks were being bombed heavily by the Luftwaffe, so
there was only limited scope for large British vessels to use these facilities.
The beaches had a shallow slope, so large vessels could not approach
them directly and smaller boats were required to pick up men from the
beaches and transfer them to larger vessels offshore. Any boat capable
of the trip was requisitioned: fishing boats, pleasure craft, sailing boats,
yachts, tugs. Many of these had not been to sea before and some were
flat-bottomed riverboats, unsuitable for the crossing. Engineer units built
jetties out of trucks to enable the troops to embark, and vast lines of them
patiently waited.

Dowding and Air Vice-Marshal Keith Park, Air Officer Commanding,
No 11 Group Fighter Command – located in the south-east of England
– covered the Dunkirk evacuation, and managed to gain air superiority

over the Luftwaffe. Churchill would 'spin' this, glossing over the fact that Fighter Command lost more aircraft in the Battle of France than in the decisive Battle of Britain. He wrote in *The Second World War*:

> By intense effort Fighter Command maintained successive patrols over the scene, and fought the enemy at long odds. Hour after hour they bit into the German fighter and bomber squadrons, taking a heavy toll, scattering them and driving them away. Day after day this went on, till the glorious victory of the Royal Air Force was gained. Wherever German aircraft were encountered, sometimes in forties and fifties, they were instantly attacked, often by single squadrons or less, and shot down in scores, which presently added up into hundreds.[33]

Despite the fact that the RAF was providing air cover, that the distance to the English south coast was short, and that the German supply lines were by that time pretty long, the attrition of British warships was so substantial that the senior admirals withdrew the new class destroyers until it became clear that they were vital to complete the evacuation in time, and Ramsay was permitted to re-deploy them.

Churchill had a strong affinity with the French and he wanted, quite understandably, to withdraw the French forces from Dunkirk along with the British troops. This could also have bolstered the number of Allied forces available to attack Germany in subsequent campaigns. But it didn't stop the French forces being lumbered with conducting much of the rearguard action, effectively defending the British as they withdrew. The outcome of the evacuation was thus determined by the valiant fighting of those French, and indeed British, troops on the Dunkirk perimeter.

On 24 May Churchill wrote to Ismay:

> Apparently the Germans can go anywhere and do anything, and their tanks can act in twos and threes all over our rear, and even when they are located they are not attacked. Also our tanks recoil before their field guns, but our field guns do not like to take on their tanks. If their motorised artillery, far from its base, can block us, why cannot we, with the artillery of a great army, block them?[34]

This passage amply demonstrates Churchill's lack of grasp of the realities of *Blitzkrieg* warfare. German tanks could go where they pleased because the swiftness of their attack had pushed the Allies off balance and precipitated a rout – just as it was intended to do. The issue of the field guns is easy to answer: the German Krupp 88mm was originally an anti-aircraft gun, but developed as an anti-tank gun it could destroy a British tank even at long range. The British had no such field gun in their inventory. For a Prime Minister who was so 'hands-on' in military affairs, and the man who was credited with the original idea for the tank, it is surprising, to say the least, that he understood so little of these matters.

The following day Churchill wrote to General Ironside, the CIGS: 'I must know at earliest why Gort gave up Arras, and what actually he is doing with the rest of his army.' On the same day he wrote to the Secretary of State for War and the CIGS:

> Pray find out who was the officer responsible for sending the
> order to evacuate Calais yesterday, and by whom this very
> lukewarm telegram I saw this morning was drafted, in which
> mention is made of 'for the sake of Allied solidarity'. This is
> not the way to encourage men to fight to the end. Are you sure
> there is no streak of defeatist opinion in the General Staff?[35]

This is clearly a Prime Minister who was following little of events as they rapidly unfolded. It would have required a very much quicker grasp of the situation to have reversed it. Regarding the streak of defeatism, it was clear to the General Staff that the position was already lost; it was some time before Churchill realized this.

On 27 May, Ironside was replaced as CIGS by General Sir John Dill, who had been Vice-Chief since 23 April. In *The Second World War*, Churchill insisted that this was something he 'greatly desired', but then added ominously that it was 'appropriate for the time being'.[36] In fact he would later sack Dill. This was characteristic of Churchill: he was reluctant to overrule his chiefs of staff, but he would sack them.

Churchill would find excuses for the British failure. The minutes of a meeting with Reynaud in Paris on 31 May record that 'Mr. Churchill said . . . the Belgian desertion . . . had forced the British to cover the whole left flank'.[37] In reality it was the magnitude and swiftness of the onslaught, combined with a supreme strategy, that accomplished success for the Germans. A small nation such as Belgium could hardly be blamed, nor could its defeat be termed 'desertion'. Victory would have required Churchill to provide vastly more British Empire ground forces.

From 27 May to 4 June, 693 vessels, including 39 destroyers, 36 minesweepers and the 'little ships', returned 338,226 troops to Britain. Of these, about 140,000 were French. The forces abandoned 2,472 guns, 84,427 vehicles and 657,000 tons of ammunition in France. The Royal Navy lost six destroyers and 24 smaller warships. More than 70 'little ships' were lost too. However, the cost to the RAF, the one service upon which the entire defence of Britain would now depend, was crippling. In the Battle of France nearly 1,000 aircraft were destroyed, 320 pilots were killed or reported missing, and 115 pilots became prisoners of war. At Dunkirk alone, 100 aircraft were shot down.[38]

CHURCHILL INTERFERES

Although Churchill was quite out of touch with events as they unfolded, he insisted on interfering with military strategy at a most critical moment, as General Alan Brooke became all too well aware. Brooke, who would later succeed Dill as CIGS, but was then in France, performed an invaluable role as a field commander. As Churchill himself recorded in *The Second World War*, when the Belgians capitulated on 28 May, Brooke and II Corps 'fought a magnificent battle' to fill the gap.[39] However, Brooke's view of Churchill was less flattering; he noted in his diary on 14 June that he was '. . . called up by Dill who was at 10 Downing Street and put [the] PM onto me. I had a difficult discussion with him as regards the evacuation of the 2 bdes [brigades] of 52nd Div[ision]. He considered they might be used to assist the French, or to fill the gap between X Army and army on its right [some 30 miles].' Brooke then went on to give a more detailed account of the exchange, starting from his initial conversation with Dill:

> I gave him an account of the dispositions [of the forces] . . . which I had agreed with him on my previous talk. He replied: 'The Prime Minister does not want you to do that.' And I think I answered: 'What the hell does he want?' At any rate Dill's

next reply was: 'He wants to speak to you': and he handed the receiver over to him! . . . He [Churchill] asked me what I was doing with the 52nd Division, and after I had informed him, he told me that that was not what he wanted. I had been sent to France to make the French feel that we were supporting them. I replied that it was impossible to make a corpse feel, and that the French army was, to all intents and purposes, dead, and certainly incapable of registering what we had done for it . . . At last, when I was in an exhausted condition, he [Churchill] said: 'All right, I agree with you.'[40]

It is interesting to compare this with Churchill's own account of the event in *The Second World War*: 'On the night of June 14, as I was thought to be obdurate, he [General Brooke] rang me up on a telephone line which by luck and effort was open, and pressed this view [up]on me. I could hear quite well, and after ten minutes I was convinced that he was right and we must go. Orders were given accordingly.'[41] Of this, Brooke noted:

In the first place he states that I rang him up, this was hardly likely as I did not know him and had never spoken to him. All my communications were direct with the CIGS. His statement did not, however, disclose the fact that he was interfering with a commander in the field, and that without sufficient knowledge of conditions prevailing on that front at that time, he was endeavouring to carry out his wishes against that commander's better judgement.[42]

HITLER'S LARGESSE SAVES THE BEF

On 28 May Churchill said to the House of Commons of the evacuation, 'The enemy was hurled back by the British and French Troops. He was so roughly handled that he did not dare molest their departure.'[43] In fact the only reason that Operation Dynamo resulted in much of the BEF's manpower returning home (albeit without its heavy equipment) was because of Hitler's 'halt order' and his decision to shift much of his air power to Paris rather than Dunkirk. Without the Führer's generosity and a millpond-calm English Channel, pretty much the entire BEF would have been killed or captured in France. Then there would have been no scope for spinning Dunkirk into some sort of success – in reality it was clearly nothing of the kind.

There has always been speculation as to why Hitler issued the halt order. It is clear that General (Karl Rudolf) Gerd von Rundstedt (promoted to Generalfeldmarschall on 19 July), one of the principal instigators of the plan, had argued that General Guderian had advanced too far ahead of the infantry. It is also clear that German forces were outrunning their supply lines. Despite the mechanization of the German Army, much of the force still relied on horse-drawn carts, and the mechanized elements needed to wait while these antiquated transports caught up. It is also the case that as the BEF ran for the coast, the Germans saw it as a busted flush, and felt that they could now concentrate on rolling up the rest of France.

It seems clear that Hitler was exceptionally nervous about the whole operation: it was his first big test against any major power, and he lacked confidence. It was Rommel who appreciated that, more than anything, it was essential to keep moving swiftly; the essence of *Blitzkrieg* was to keep the enemy off balance. The German materiel, apart from the Krupp 88mm anti-tank gun, was for the most part no better than that of the Allies, particularly in respect of armoured vehicles and aircraft. It was how they were used that was critical: swift armoured assaults with close air support constituted the decisively effective tactic. However, Hitler concurred with von Rundstedt and on 24 May the halt order was given. Part of the Luftwaffe was then employed to polish off the Allied forces at Dunkirk, while the rest, plus much of the army, looked south to Paris and the fall of France.

THE CONSEQUENCES

Churchill said to the House of Commons on 4 June: 'We must be very careful not to assign to this deliverance the attributes of a victory. Wars are not won by evacuations.' How true. He also referred to it as 'the miracle of Dunkirk': this was even more accurate, as it intimated that it was divine intervention, rather than Churchill's carefully laid plans, that had resulted in the return of so many men. He told the House that the Germans had attacked 'like a sharp scythe'.[44] His own subsequent dispersionist strategy in the Mediterranean would be very different, as we shall see, yet clearly he saw how effective the sharp scythe had been. He also admitted: 'When a week ago today I asked the House to fix this afternoon as the occasion for a statement, I feared it would be my hard lot to announce the greatest military disaster in our long history.'[45] In reality, it was a disaster of just such magnitude, though it would subsequently be eclipsed by the defeat in Singapore (see chapter 13).

In *The Second World War* Churchill wrote, 'Gort's decision, in which we speedily concurred, to abandon the Weygand plan and march to the sea was executed by him and his staff with masterly skill, *and will ever be regarded as a brilliant episode in British military annals.*'[46] (Emphasis added.) This last remark strains credulity to the utmost. It was an almighty relief that Hitler had held back his forces and enabled the BEF to escape. Despite this, the situation was dire: Hitler now controlled the continent of Europe and Britain was alone, without the necessary resources to win.

The BEF should have stood and fought or not been there in the first place: to run was catastrophic. Had it fought, and done so decisively, it would perhaps have halted the German advance sufficiently to permit the French to regroup, to restore morale, and thus to halt the German onslaught permanently. If a French victory over the Germans with BEF help was not realistic, that was because the BEF needed to be bigger from the start: Britain would have needed to put all its eggs into the BEF basket, and so risk all on defending France. If this was not to be the policy, the BEF should not have been sent to France in the first place. These were all ultimately political issues and so were Churchill's responsibilities (Chamberlain had clearly been culpable as well in this regard). None of this was properly understood by Churchill: he had insufficient grasp of what was occurring, of how to deal with it, and more importantly how he could have prevented the catastrophe in the first place. Despite all his interest in the military and his meddling, he simply did not understand what a modern military force and tactics could do. The catastrophe of Dunkirk was thus presented to him as a *fait accompli*; all he did was to provide the spin.

Despite winning the Victoria Cross in World War I, Gort was not the appropriate general for the task. He was subsequently appointed Inspector-General of the Forces, then Governor of Gibraltar in May 1941. He had been CIGS until the start of the war, and in November 1941 Churchill considered (and then decided against) re-installing him in this post. Though both Brooke and Bernard Montgomery ('Monty') thought Gort had been over-promoted, Churchill then decided he wanted Gort to replace General Sir Claude Auchinleck in the Middle East Command during March 1942, though Brooke opposed this and stopped it. In the end, in May 1942 Churchill made Gort Governor of Malta, where he organized the defences, and finally High Commissioner of Palestine in October 1944. He died in March 1946.[47]

Prior to the Dunkirk episode Churchill had asked Chamberlain and other ministers to consider the prospect of Britain fighting on alone. Based on their recommendations, he drafted a reference to be put before the military chiefs for consideration. It concluded: 'To sum up, our conclusion is that *prima facie* Germany has most of the cards; but the real test is whether the morale of our fighting personnel and civil population will counterbalance the numerical and material advantages which Germany enjoys. We believe it will.'[48] This was a parlous state for Britain to be in, where only morale could compensate for military deficiencies.

After the Dunkirk evacuation, one division, the 51st (Highland) Infantry Division, remained at Saint-Valéry-en-Caux; it surrendered in June together with elements of the French Tenth Army. A second expeditionary force, commanded by Brooke, was then evacuated from Cherbourg and Saint-Malo from 14–25 June, in Operation Ariel. At this time evacuations were also being conducted from Saint-Nazaire, Brest and Nantes in the Bay of Biscay. During the evacuation from Saint-Nazaire, on 17 June the liner RMS *Lancastria* was bombed and sunk. It is estimated that there were between 4,000 and 9,000 Allied troops and nationals on board, of whom approximately 2,500 survived. Churchill covered this up.[49]

Churchill admitted the real consequences of Dunkirk in *The Second World War,* when he wrote that Germany had acquired 'immense quantities of equipment of all kinds . . . from France and the Low Countries . . . The Germans had therefore plenty of modern weapons . . . We, for our part, having lost so much at Dunkirk, [were] having to build up our home army against invasion . . .'[50]

With the British back in their island, Churchill famously said, 'We shall fight them on the beaches, we shall fight them on the landing grounds, we shall fight them in the fields and in the streets, we shall fight them in the hills . . .' Apparently he then muttered to a colleague, 'And we'll fight them with the butt ends of broken beer bottles because that's bloody well all we've got!'[51] Anthony Eden discovered that there were no tanks or anti-tank guns in the south-east of England to halt Operation Sea Lion, the planned German invasion of England. Not only were the ground forces denuded but, vitally, so was the RAF. Churchill had commented at a meeting with the French in Paris on 31 May, 'Of the 39 squadrons allotted to the Air Defence of Great Britain, 10 had been sent to France, originally for a few days only; but as matters had turned out there was now very little of these 10 squadrons left. Great Britain was, therefore, left with only 29 Squadrons . . .'[52] Yet the Air Council had stated that 52 squadrons were needed for the defence of the realm. So not only did the Dunkirk adventure end in catastrophe, but Churchill had fundamentally undermined RAF Fighter Command, now the only thing standing between Britain and occupation and total defeat.

8
THE BATTLE OF BRITAIN: DOWDING'S VICTORY

After the fiasco of Dunkirk came the Battle of Britain. Hitler and the German High Command assumed that the defeat of France would lead Britain to capitulate. When it had not done so by 2 July 1940, Hitler ordered his armed forces to initiate plans to mount an opposed landing on the south-east coast of England and to occupy Britain. To this effect he gave a directive on 16 July that such an invasion, Operation Sea Lion, should be executed. A necessary precursor of this operation was for the Luftwaffe to gain air superiority over southern England: this would be the Battle of Britain. Already, on 18 June, Churchill had said to the House of Commons:

> What General Weygand called the Battle of France is over, I expect that the Battle of Britain is about to begin. Upon this battle depends the survival of Christian civilisation. Upon it depends our own British life and the long continuity of our institutions and our Empire . . . Let us therefore brace ourselves to our duties, and so bear ourselves that, if the British Empire and its Commonwealth last for a thousand years, men will still say, 'This was their finest hour'.[1]

He rather over-egged it with 'Christian civilization', as it would be the United States that would be the guarantor of this, but in respect of the rest he was correct, and it proved to be a remarkable victory. However, Churchill would play no part in the direction of the battle itself.[2]

DOWDING – THE ARCHITECT OF DELIVERANCE

Air Chief Marshal Sir Hugh Caswell Tremenheere 'Stuffy' Dowding, GCB GCVO CMG, later 1st Baron of Bentley Priory, was Air Officer Commanding-in-Chief (AOC-in-C) of Fighter Command, Royal Air Force, during the Battle of Britain. As an air marshal, and already a knight of the realm, he had been appointed to this post on 14 July 1936, during Stanley Baldwin's government. He was promoted to air chief marshal on 1 January 1937 and would remain in the post until 25 November 1940. He has justly been compared with Sir Francis Drake and Admiral Horatio Nelson for his historic part in the nation's defence.[3]

Dowding's role in the Battle of Britain was fundamental, and began long before the battle itself. By 1930 he had been appointed Air Member of the Air Council for Supply and Research (later Research and Development), where he promoted the development of advanced technology and the need for adequate funding. He was engaged in the design competition that resulted in the Hurricane and Spitfire fighter aircraft, and he was involved in the development of radar.[4]

It was Dowding, more than anyone else, who had been responsible for the total organization of Britain's air defences by the time of the Battle of Britain, and it was he who saved Britain from invasion and defeat. The Luftwaffe had more aircraft than the RAF, but Dowding had set up the 'sector' control system, with special sector airfields and their information centres, and, crucially, advance warning from radar plus visual observers to guide defending fighters on to attacking Luftwaffe formations. The system was already functioning by the outbreak of war, having been put in place before Churchill returned to government.

Dowding's protégé, Air Vice-Marshal Keith Park, was AOC No 11 Group, covering the crucial area south of the Thames to the Kent coast. This was where the brunt of the fighting was to occur and thus where the bulk of Fighter Command's resources were deployed. It was Dowding and Park who were thus principally responsible for ensuring victory.

THE AIRCRAFT

Also fundamental to victory in the Battle of Britain were two fighter aeroplanes, the designs of which were initiated during Ramsay MacDonald's National government; they first flew during Stanley Baldwin's government, and were commissioned into service during Neville Chamberlain's government. It was in 1934, the last full year of Ramsay Macdonald's government, that the Air Ministry announced that it wanted a new fighter. Both the Hawker and the Supermarine aircraft companies offered designs. Hawker's chief designer, Sydney Camm (who was knighted in 1953), produced the Hurricane, while Supermarine's chief designer, Reginald Mitchell, produced the Spitfire. The Air Ministry specification F.36/34 for the new fighter would be written around the Hawker Hurricane, which was ordered by the Macdonald government in February 1935 and first flew on 6 November the same year. The Supermarine Spitfire first flew on 5 March 1936. The 'heavenly twins' were born.[5]

Both aircraft were single-seat, single-engine, stressed-skin, low-wing cantilever monoplanes, though the Hurricane had a fabric-covered aft fuselage. The Hurricane was reasonably well armed, had a good performance, and was very sturdy and highly manoeuvrable. The Spitfire, which had the same armament and was also highly manoeuvrable, had a slightly better performance but was more complicated and expensive to build than the Hurricane. Consequently more Hurricanes would be deployed than Spitfires, and thus the less glamorous Hurricane would do much of the fighting.

On 3 June 1936, Baldwin's government ordered 600 Hurricanes and 310 Spitfires to equip RAF Fighter Command. The first Hurricane rolled off the production line in October 1937, and the first Spitfire at about the same time – early in Chamberlain's government.[6] The Spitfire entered service with No 19 Squadron of the RAF, based at Duxford, on 4 August 1938. Nine months earlier, the Hurricane had entered service with No 111 Squadron at Northolt. By the outbreak of war, 497 of the original order of 600 Hurricanes had been delivered to the RAF, equipping 18 frontline squadrons, and 306 Spitfires had been delivered, equipping nine squadrons. These frontline, state-of-the-art fighters had been delivered courtesy of the MacDonald, Baldwin and Chamberlain governments. Churchill was not responsible for their instigation, development, manufacture or deployment until just prior to the Battle of Britain: virtually everything of importance had occurred during his 'wilderness years'. Many of the planes were lost in the Battle of France, a consequence of his policy of propping up the French when defeat was already apparent. He had dangerously denuded Fighter Command and there was now a frantic effort to build up numbers to ensure the minimum necessary to defeat the Luftwaffe.

By the time of the Battle of Britain, Fighter Command had 60 squadrons and some 700 operational aircraft, of which 400 were Hurricanes and 200 Spitfires. The rest were Boulton Paul Defiants, Bristol Blenheims and Gloster Gladiators.[7] The Defiant was a single-engine stressed-skin low-wing cantilever monoplane, but designed to a World War I layout, with an air gunner located behind the pilot equipped with the aircraft's main armament of four Browning .303 machine guns in a powered turret. This layout was deficient by comparison with single-seat fighters with fixed forward-firing armament, as the latter were lighter and more manoeuvrable, as well as being more heavily armed. Consequently, many of the Defiants were relegated to defending the north of Britain, where no serious attack was expected. The twin-engine Blenheim was originally designed as a civil transport, but when introduced in the 1930s it was found to be significantly faster than the then frontline RAF fighters. A light bomber version was developed, as was a night fighter variant with an under-fuselage pack of four machine guns. However, the new single-engine fighters would completely outclass it. The Gladiators were biplanes and thus obsolete.

The task Germany faced to gain air superiority required a form of warfare for which the Luftwaffe had neither trained nor was appropriately equipped. The Luftwaffe was structured to provide the army with tactical support, not to undertake an independent strategic role. Thus it was never equipped with long-range four-engine heavy bombers, as the RAF and the United States Army Air Force would be, though with bases in northern France it could be argued that the Luftwaffe's twin-engine medium-range bombers were all that was necessary. However, the backbone of the Luftwaffe fleet, the Heinkel He 111 and Dornier Do 17, had limited bomb-carrying capacities and very limited defensive armament, particularly for the more vulnerable daylight raids. The Junkers Ju 87 'Stuka' was an effective dive-bomber, but easy meat for the British fighters. Of the Luftwaffe fighters, the Messerschmitt Bf 109, like the Hurricane and Spitfire, was a single-seat single-engine stressed-skin low-wing cantilever monoplane. It had a high performance and was well armed, but with limited range – it could spend only a few minutes over London – it could not effectively support the bombers over Britain. The Messerschmitt Bf 110 had twin engines and a longer range but lacked sufficient manoeuvrability to avoid successful attack by the British single-engine, single-seat fighters. The Junkers Ju 88 had excellent performance and armament, but being twin-engine like the 110, lacked manoeuvrability.

During the war Churchill referred to the superiority of the best of the British aircraft and the British pilots.[8] However, in *The Second World War* he expressed a different opinion: 'In the quality of the fighter aircraft there was little to choose. The Germans were faster, with a better rate of climb; ours more manoeuvrable, better armed.'[9] In fact this was not true: the Spitfire and the Messerschmitt Bf 109 were well matched in speed, the Hurricane was a little slower, and all were very manoeuvrable. Regarding armament, the Bf 109 with its 20mm cannon firing through the propeller spinner and twin 20mm cannon (or twin machine guns) in the inner wings, plus twin 7.92mm machine guns in the nose, was somewhat superior to the two British fighters with their eight .303 calibre (7.7mm) machine guns in the wings.

By the summer of 1940 the Luftwaffe possessed air bases in Norway and the Low Countries as well as in France, with some 2,500 operational aircraft deployed. These included 1,000 Heinkel He 111s, Dornier Do 17s and Junkers Ju 88s; 270 Stukas; 800 Messerschmitt Bf 109s and 280 Bf 110s. Fighter Command deployed 870 operational aircraft, including 750 Hurricanes and Spitfires (32 squadrons of the former and 19 squadrons of the latter), plus second-line aircraft – 30 Defiants and 90 Blenheims.[10]

RADAR

Victory was also dependent upon radar. This was initiated during MacDonald's government and developed during Baldwin's; the system was put in place during Chamberlain's government. Like the aircraft, it was deployed and functioning by the time Churchill had returned to government.

On 25 February 1935, while Ramsay MacDonald was Prime Minister, Robert Watson-Watt (a distant relative of James Watt, pioneer of the steam engine) demonstrated his developments in what was originally known as 'radio direction finding' (RDF), and later as 'radio detection and ranging', or 'radar' for short.[11]

On 14 February 1935, Churchill, his scientific adviser Professor Frederick Lindemann and Austen Chamberlain asked Prime Minister Ramsay MacDonald to set up a committee for air defence. When Baldwin succeeded MacDonald, he asked Churchill to join the Air Defence Research Sub-Committee of the Committee of Imperial Defence (CID). Baldwin had been interested in the development of radar, and thought that Churchill's technical interests and capacity for hard work could be put to good use here. Churchill made it a condition that Lindemann should join the technical sub-committee.[12]

In *The Second World War*, Churchill gave the impression that he had played a vital role during his wilderness years in the development and application of radar to national defence.[13] Of course the vital role was played by scientists, and political direction and finance was given, not by Churchill, but by the Baldwin and Chamberlain governments. The radar system was in place by the time Churchill returned to office as First Lord of the Admiralty in September 1939. He himself admitted:

> The plans for the air defence of Great Britain had as early as the autumn of 1937 been rewritten round the assumption that the promises made by our scientists for the still unproven Radar would be kept. The first five stations of the coastal Radar chain, the five guarding the Thames estuary, had watched Mr. Chamberlain's aeroplane go and come on its peace missions of September 1938.[14]

The dig at Chamberlain's Munich peace mission is an adolescent touch. The point that Churchill was making so eloquently is that the crucial facility of radar was commissioned and would become operational while he had no executive authority, despite his involvement in the research committee. He continued:

> Eighteen stations from Dundee to Portsmouth began in the spring of 1939 a twenty-four-hour watch, not to be interrupted in the next six years. These stations were the watchdogs of the air-raid warning service; they spared us alike grave losses in war production and intolerable burdens on our Civil Defence workers. They spared the anti-aircraft gun crews

needless and tiring hours at action stations. They saved us from the exhaustion of man and machine that would have doomed our matchless but slender fighter force had it been compelled to maintain standing patrols. They could not give the accuracy required for night-time interception, but they enabled the day fighters to await their prey at the most favourable altitudes and aspects for attack. In their decisive contribution to victory in the day battles they were supported and supplemented by other stations of new technical design, which gave warning – all too brief, but invaluable – of the approach of the low fliers.[15]

Churchill's own words convey what he was to inherit intact. The reference to Fighter Command not having to undertake standing patrols with this system is most telling: if he had had his way and committed ever more fighters to France, without the benefit of the British radar system, the outcome would have been catastrophic.

In May 1940, Churchill appointed as Minister for Aircraft Production the newspaper proprietor Lord Beaverbrook. He was intent on increasing production significantly, but civil servants found him difficult to work with and his publicity campaign, 'Saucepans into Spitfires', attracted a lot of saucepans, but few that could be used to make Spitfires. It was the Chamberlain government, principally the Secretary of State for Air, Lord Swinton (1935–8), and Air Chief Marshal Sir Wilfrid Freeman, who had had the vision prior to the war to create 'shadow factories', built and left empty to facilitate the increased production needed when war came.[16]

THE GERMANS ATTACK

On 1 August 1940 Hitler ordered the Luftwaffe and its head, Reichsmarschall Hermann Göring, to gain air superiority over southern England. The initial assault, *Adler Tag* ('Eagle Day'), was originally slated for 10 August but was delayed until the 13th because of bad weather. The battle on that day resulted in the downing of 45 Luftwaffe aircraft, of which 39 were destroyed by RAF fighters. Fighter Command would lose 13 planes and 7 pilots.[17] Churchill said of the expected ratio of German to

British losses: 'We hope to improve upon the rate of 3 or 4 to one, which was realised at Dunkirk.'[18] But this was an impossibly ambitious target. During the eight days from *Adler Tag* the Luftwaffe lost 317 aircraft against Fighter Command's losses of 148, a rate of better than two to one.[19] While it did not meet Churchill's exaggerated expectations, this was good from the RAF's perspective, but the Luftwaffe could afford it.

Having recklessly gambled with Fighter Command's strength in France, Churchill was not yet finished playing fast and loose with Britain's fighter defence. He now made a characteristic blunder: he tried to push Dowding into making a premature, rash, and all-out attack on the Luftwaffe, something Dowding knew had to be resisted at all costs. As the historian and journalist Max Hastings has commented:

> Dowding . . . understood what Winston Churchill did not:
> that his job was not to destroy the Luftwaffe, an almost
> impossible task, but simply to keep his force flying and
> fighting. If Dowding had thrown everything into the Battle,
> as the Prime Minister instinctively wanted, the RAF could not
> have supported its rate of attrition against the much bigger
> German air force.[20]

In fact, Hastings is slightly wrong: Fighter Command had to do more than simply keep 'flying and fighting', it had to maintain air superiority – a considerable feat, which it accomplished successfully. Simply flying and fighting would not have prevented an invasion; the air forces of German-occupied European countries had been flying and fighting before and during invasion, but this had not prevented their countries' defeat. If the RAF maintained air superiority, any invading German force could realistically expect to be defeated, and it was this accomplishment that made the Battle of Britain decisive. But Hastings is right to say that if Churchill had had his way the Battle of Britain would have been lost. Fighter Command would have been subject to attrition to the point where it could no longer have maintained air superiority, and the German invasion would have gone ahead.

The Luftwaffe's initial strategy was to attack radar installations, to attack No 11 Group's airfields – including its important 'sector' stations – and also to attack aircraft production facilities. This had considerable effect in disrupting Fighter Command's ability to function, even though production was increasingly augmented by the shadow factories. Some of these were disguised so their function was not obvious from the air, but the airfields could not be disguised and patching them up became increasingly difficult. Fortunately the Luftwaffe did not fully appreciate the vital significance of radar, and attacks on the antenna installations were not pressed home with continued vigour.

The apogee of the battle came on 15 August 1940, with the Luftwaffe flying 1,786 sorties and Fighter Command flying 974, over a vast area of Britain and the English Channel.[21] The losses were exaggerated on both sides, but after the war it became clear that the Luftwaffe had lost 79 aircraft: the greatest loss of Luftwaffe aircraft on a single day during the entire battle. Fighter Command's losses were 31, a loss rate of two and a half to one.[22] However, the fighting continued to be intense, and during the final week of August and the first week of September the Luftwaffe deployed over 1,000 aircraft each day in the battle. During that period Fighter Command was losing more pilots than the training programme could replace, with 231 dead or wounded. The fighter losses were also becoming very high, with 295 Hurricanes and Spitfires destroyed and 171 damaged, and of course the airfields were being plastered regularly.[23] Dowding's stewardship of the Battle of Britain was remarkable, but he recognized that this attrition was becoming critical. Churchill urged him to reduce the quality of pilot training in order to increase the supply of pilots. Dowding recognized that some corners had to be cut, but this measure would clearly be damaging. Churchill thought that simply throwing men into the fight was the route to victory – a defective view to which he would continue to subscribe in his Mediterranean campaigns.[24]

Though the war weighed heavily upon Churchill at this crucial time, he rarely showed it. His day began at around 8.00am with a mix of government red boxes and a breakfast of beef, cutlets or grouse and sometimes white wine. He was once presented with a salmon for breakfast and protested: 'No! No! I will have meat. Carnivores will win this war.' (This was at a time when food was rationed for ordinary folk.) Much of the morning was spent working in bed, and after a lunch to match his breakfast, replete with champagne, there would be a siesta for about an hour and a half. His day of meetings and dictation to secretaries was fuelled by countless weak whiskies, brandy and eight cigars. (Beside his bed stood an ice bucket from the Savoy, which acted as an ashtray.) He said to his wife: 'Always remember, Clemmie, that I have taken more out of alcohol than alcohol has taken out of me.'[25] Dinner would be the most lavish meal of the day. Churchill himself commented, 'I always manage somehow to adjust to any new level of luxury without whimper or complaint.'[26]

After dinner he would work long into the night, with perhaps a feature film for entertainment. Throughout the war he watched films such as the Walt Disney cartoons *Bambi* and *Dumbo* (ironically, he shared his fondness for Disney with Hitler), and he very much liked wartime morale boosters, such as *One of Our Aircraft is Missing*, *The Battle of Midway* and *In Which We Serve*, the last of which was based on the story of Lord Louis Mountbatten (whom Churchill would appoint to high office) and the loss of his destroyer. But his favourite film was *Lady Hamilton*, starring Vivien Leigh and Laurence Olivier. It concerned the love affair between Horatio Nelson and Emma Hamilton, and Churchill watched it 17 times.[27]

Not every day was spent indoors. Throughout the Battle of Britain Churchill travelled the country, visiting fighter bases, bomb-damaged areas and invasion defences, and watched dogfights on the roof of the annexe to 10 Downing Street. One leisure pursuit was feeding his goldfish. When Clement Attlee, Labour Party leader and later Deputy Prime Minister to Churchill, was asked what the old man was actually doing to win the war, he replied, 'Talk about it.' It was above all Churchill's rhetoric that constituted his principle contribution to victory.[28]

THE LUFTWAFFE CHANGES TACTICS

On the night of 24 August 1940, Luftwaffe bombers failed to identify their prescribed target – the oil refineries of Thameshaven – and mistakenly bombed the City of London. Churchill and Air Marshal Charles 'Peter' Portal, then AOC-in-C Bomber Command, ordered the bombing of Berlin and other major German cities on the following night. The Berlin raid was mounted with what were then the most advanced British bombers, all twin-engine: Vickers Wellingtons, Armstrong Whitworth Whitleys and Handley Page Hampdens. The damage they inflicted was comparatively minor, but Hermann Göring had stated that Berlin would not be attacked and had insisted that the RAF was being 'eliminated'. Crucially, this raid would precipitate a fundamental change in Luftwaffe strategy: now, British cities would be attacked rather than Fighter Command's airfields.[29]

Not everyone in the Luftwaffe believed that Fighter Command had been sufficiently degraded and that the new strategy would be effective. But Hitler supported Göring, and on 4 September he made a statement in the Reichstag: 'Just now . . . Mr Churchill is demonstrating his new brainchild, the night air raid . . . When they declare that they will increase their attacks on our cities, then we will raze their cities to the ground. We will stop the handiwork of these night air pirates, so help us God!'[30]

The first mass attack on London occurred during the afternoon of 7 September 1940. The raid was mounted with more than 300 bombers: Junkers Ju 88s, Heinkel He 111s and Dornier Do 17s. The fighter escort comprised 600 Bf 109s and 110s. This new strategy – the 'area' bombing of British cities – became known in Britain as the 'Blitz'. It relieved Fighter Command's airfields, and to some extent the aircraft production facilities, and proved to be a crucial mistake by the Germans, fundamentally changing the course of the war in Britain's favour.[31]

Although Dowding's approach to the Luftwaffe attacks was to prove victorious, he was criticized at the time by Air Vice-Marshal William Sholto Douglas, Assistant Chief of the Air Staff, and by one of his own subordinates, Air Vice-Marshal Trafford Leigh-Mallory, AOC of No 12 Group Fighter Command, which covered East Anglia. Douglas believed that fighters should be sent out to attack incoming German planes over the Channel. Leigh-Mallory was an exponent of the 'big wing' policy, arguing that large numbers of fighters should be assembled for attack even if the time this took meant the German planes were on their return journeys.[32]

Dowding and Park rejected both strategies. First, they argued that the only effective way of interdicting German planes was with fighters in radar-controlled areas, and that this necessarily meant that only small numbers of fighters could be scrambled in time. Second, given the chronic shortage of pilots, if British fighters were shot down it was more likely the pilots would survive if this occurred over southern England than over the Channel. Third, because the Luftwaffe's strategy during the early stages of the battle had included attacks on RAF airfields, Fighter Command could not afford to concentrate its attacks on German planes on the return leg of their missions, after they had bombed their targets. But the critics would ultimately bring down Dowding and Park, and Churchill would not prevent it.

The change of Luftwaffe strategy provided relief for No 11 Group, located south of the Thames, and revealed London as a target, the Luftwaffe would be in range of No 12 Group, north of the Thames, giving Leigh-Mallory an opportunity to show what his 'big wing' could do.

On 15 September the Luftwaffe mounted its most concentrated attack on London, a raid that Göring stated would eliminate the RAF. The day was a turning point in the Battle of Britain. Although the Luftwaffe deployed an escort of almost five fighters per bomber, a quarter of their bomber force was destroyed. It would be called 'the Greatest Day' and it occurred on a Sunday, as had the Battle of Waterloo.[33] On this day, as chance would have it, Churchill was in No 11 Group's headquarters at Uxbridge. The group had 25 squadrons to deploy to protect the south-east of England (the same number that Churchill falsely claimed Dowding had told him could protect the entire country). At first it was not apparent how significant this raid was, but Park would be obliged to commit all of his forces. When Churchill asked about reserves, Park said there were none.[34]

The Luftwaffe's change of strategy had enabled Fighter Command to repair its airfields and deploy more aircraft. Tactically the Hurricanes were now directed to concentrate on attacking the bombers, while the faster Spitfires took on the Messerschmitt fighters. According to the official RAF history, Fighter Command claimed at the time that 185 Luftwaffe planes were shot down (though in *The Second World War* Churchill claimed he was told the figure was 183) for the loss of fewer than 40 of Fighter Command's aircraft. However, each side exaggerated the other's losses, and after the war the official RAF history claimed that the true figure for German losses was only 60 planes, while the RAF lost 26. (Churchill claimed the post-war figure was 56 German planes destroyed.)[35] However, the pivotal issue was the effect this had on German strategy. Given that Luftwaffe losses constituted a quarter of their bombers. Göring and Hitler realized that air superiority could not be gained over southern England. This resulted in what would be interpreted by some as the 'narrow margin' of victory for the RAF. On 17 September Hitler postponed Operation Sea Lion while his interest was attracted to the east – the attack upon the Soviet Union, codenamed Barbarossa. On 12 October Sea Lion was rescheduled for the spring of 1941. But in July 1941 Hitler further postponed it until the spring of 1942, when he assumed the Soviet Union would be defeated. On 13 February 1942 Sea Lion was abandoned permanently.[36]

By the end of October 1940 the Luftwaffe had lost 1,594 aircraft, while Fighter Command had lost 917.[37] British fighter production remained relatively constant throughout the Battle of Britain, despite the German attacks on production facilities. Indeed, the Luftwaffe's attrition of the RAF's forces was sufficiently slow to ensure that Fighter Command had a larger force of fighters at the end of the battle than at the beginning, whereas German fighter production actually fell during this period. Dowding recognized the crucial need to provide an adequate flow of trained fighter pilots, and despite its problems the British training programme was superior to that of the Germans.

The Blitz continued, however, though night attacks were favoured to reduce German losses. It would be an increasingly technological war, fought by the scientists, though Churchill's stewardship would create problems with the bomber offensive (see chapter 16). But the threat of invasion had gone, and Britain could subsequently function as an unsinkable aircraft carrier from which the Second Front could be launched.

Dowding set up the crucial night-fighter force to tackle the Blitz night attacks. Initially, although his organization was excellent, it had only limited success, but night fighters would subsequently play a profound role in national defence with the use of onboard radar systems to execute interceptions. However, Dowding's critics would seize on this early lack of success, as well as the bickering over the tactics of the day fighters.

CHURCHILL ACCEPTS THAT DOWDING SHOULD BE SACKED

In July 1940, Sir Archibald Sinclair, Secretary of State for Air, told Churchill that Dowding's critics in the RAF wanted him to go by November, when his contract of employment would expire. Churchill wrote to Sinclair on 10 July:

> I was very much taken aback the other night when you told me
> you had been considering removing Sir Hugh Dowding . . .
> Personally, I think he is one of the very best men you have got,
> and I say this after having been in contact with him for about
> two years. I have greatly admired the whole of his work in the
> Fighter Command, and especially in resisting the clamour for
> numerous air raid warnings, and the immense pressure to

dissipate the Fighter strength during the great French battle. In fact he has my full confidence . . . I hope you will consider whether it is not in the public interest that his appointment should be indefinitely prolonged while the war lasts. This would not of course exclude his being moved to a higher position, if that were thought necessary. I am however much averse from making changes and putting in new men who will have to learn the work all over again, except when there is some proved failure or inadequacy.[39]

Having expected Dowding to be given an indefinite extension to his contract as the result of this letter, Churchill took up the issue again with Sinclair a month later, on 10 August:

I certainly understood from our conversation a month ago that you were going to give Dowding an indefinite war-time extension, and were going to do it at once. I cannot understand how any contrary impression could have arisen in your mind about my wishes. Let me however remove it at once, and urge you to take the step I have so long desired. It is certainly wrong to keep an officer in the position of Commander-in-Chief, conducting hazardous operations from day to day, when he is dangling at the end of an expiring appointment. Such a situation is not fair to anyone, least of all to the nation. I can never be a party to it.[40]

But despite the outstanding victory Dowding achieved over this period, Churchill accepted the arguments of his critics, and in November Charles Portal, by then Chief of the Air Staff, was obliged to replace him with Sholto Douglas, who had been promoted to air marshal. Dowding's concern for his airmen – his 'chicks' as he called them – and his personal belief in spiritualism counted against him. Sholto Douglas, with his agreeable social skills, was considered a more appropriate man. So at the moment of victory Dowding was ignominiously sacked, and his career was over. He was never offered an operational command again and never promoted to marshal of the Royal Air Force, though later he was raised to the peerage. As Dowding's opponents were keen to get him out of the way,

Churchill required him, against his will, to take up a post in the United States. When Churchill ordered the ringing of church bells to declare the Battle of Britain won, Dowding was not even in the country to hear them.

Leigh-Mallory replaced Keith Park, who was given a position responsible for flying training, though later he was given command in Malta where he fought a mini-Battle of Britain. Subsequently he was given a command in South-east Asia. The two architects of victory, Dowding and Park, had gone. Air Vice-Marshal Donald Bennett, who would pioneer the pathfinder squadrons in Bomber Command, wrote in *Pathfinder*:

> I had a visit from Air Chief Marshal Sir Hugh Dowding, who had been relieved of Fighter Command after the Battle of Britain was over. As the Commander-in-Chief of Fighter Command he had, of course, saved us and thereby, I believe, the civilized world . . . Britain behaved as it always seems to in such circumstances – it promptly turned round and started criticizing the man who had been responsible for our salvation. Petty jealousies amongst senior Air Force officers are unhappily all too frequent, and on this occasion I believe that such jealousies were responsible for one of the most deplorable examples of lack of appreciation for a great Englishman which we have ever displayed. Old 'Stuffy' Dowding had not only been the C-in-C. in the whole of the Battle of Britain proper, but he had also been responsible for the introduction of the 8-gun fighter and many of the developments which made that victory possible.[41]

Despite trying to defend Dowding, Churchill allowed the chain of command to have its way. The 'petty jealousies amongst senior Air Force officers' destroyed the career of the man 'responsible for our salvation'.

Having denuded Fighter Command's strength in a vain attempt to prop up France, Churchill had tried to cajole Dowding into undertaking an all-out attack in the Battle of Britain. The fact that victory occurred is a tribute to those, especially Dowding, who stood up to Churchill.[42] In the end Churchill accepted that Dowding had been correct; in *The Second World War* he wrote: 'We must regard the generalship here shown as an example of genius in the art of war'.[43]

9
THE WAR AT SEA: CHURCHILL'S BATTLESHIP FETISH

In 1943 Hitler decided to abandon his surface fleet because of their vulnerability from air and submarine attack.[1] He said, 'Large ships are a thing of the past. I would prefer to have the steel and nickel contained in these ships rather than send them into action again'.[2] When Großadmiral Karl Dönitz replaced Erich Raeder as commander-in-chief of the Kriegsmarine in that year, his principal strategy was to concentrate on using the U-boat fleet, although he did persuade Hitler to retain a few capital ships. These included Germany's one aircraft carrier, the *Graf Zeppelin*, although construction of this ship was never completed.[3] Dönitz's decision to keep surface ships may seem surprising considering he had previously been responsible for the U-boat fleet, but the very presence of the German ships would pin down the Royal Navy. Churchill played right into his hands.[4] German surface ships were to play no important role in the war except for encouraging Churchill to devote a disproportionate amount of British resources to their destruction.

Unlike Hitler, Churchill could not see that battleships would be hopelessly vulnerable to both submarine and air attack, whereas the submarine and the aircraft carrier would prove to be the most potent weapons in the sea war. The battleship would gradually be displaced as the navy's 'capital ship'. When Churchill returned as First Lord of the Admiralty in 1939, the Royal Navy was still the largest navy in the world and had 15 battleships and battle-cruisers. By 1960 Britain had dispensed with its last battleship – HMS *Vanguard*.

SCAPA FLOW

When Churchill visited Scapa Flow, his bodyguard asked him whether a U-boat might not follow a Royal Navy surface vessel into the harbour before the defensive boom closed. Churchill replied, 'I hope they will not be able to do so. According to the powers-that-be, who give me information on this subject, the possibility of U-boats entering is very remote'.[5] A few weeks later, on 13 October 1939, Kapitänleutnant Günther Prien sneaked in with his U-boat, *U-47*, and sank the battleship HMS *Royal Oak*. The deaths amounted to 786 officers and men, including Rear-Admiral Henry Blagrove of the Second Battle Squadron. Churchill responded to the sinking by saying, 'It might well have been politically fatal to any Minister who had been responsible for the pre-war precautions. Being a newcomer I was immune from such reproaches . . .'[6] However, although he had undertaken some additional defensive provision, he was wise after the event. Scapa Flow would remain dangerously vulnerable for some time. In January 1940, Churchill wrote to the Scapa Flow authorities:

> Two and a half months have passed since the *Royal Oak* was torpedoed. What, in fact, has been done since? How many blockships sunk? How many nets made? How many men have been in work for how many days? . . . Up to the present I share the Commander-in-Chief's anxieties about the slow progress of this indispensible work.[7]

THE *GRAF SPEE*

When the 'pocket battleship' the *Deutschland* ran amok in the Atlantic at the beginning of the war, Churchill wrote: 'The mere presence of this powerful ship upon our main trade route had however imposed, as was intended, a serious strain upon our escorts and hunting groups in the North Atlantic.'[8]

Germany had built three *Panzerschiffe* ('armoured ships') of the *Deutschland* class, which the British took to calling pocket battleships. They were really battle-cruisers, but with welded hulls, diesel engines and a main armament of six 280mm (11in) guns arranged in two triple-gun turrets – one forward, one aft. This facilitated a smaller displacement (originally only 10,600 tons at standard load) than conventional ships with riveted hulls, steam turbine power and three or four twin-gun turrets. In addition to the *Deutschland* (later renamed the *Lützow* as Hitler did not want to lose a ship named after the Fatherland) there was the *Admiral Scheer* and the *Admiral Graf Spee*.

In the Battle of the River Plate in December 1939, the *Graf Spee* was engaged by three British and New Zealand cruisers under the command of Commodore Henry Harwood. During his stint as First Lord of the Admiralty Churchill keenly followed the battle, and the First Sea Lord, Admiral Sir Dudley Pound, had to intervene to prevent him from determining the dispositions of Commodore Harwood's ships.[9] Churchill, not for the last time, would misinterpret the strategic threat posed by such surface raiders.

Kapitän zur See Hans Langsdorff, in command of the *Graf Spee*, at first thought that his opponents were one light cruiser and two destroyers; he did not believe that the Allied ships would take on the *Spee*, given that they were completely outgunned. When it became clear that they were going to, Langsdorff closed the range, and both sides engaged each other almost simultaneously. HMS *Exeter* was crippled, *Ajax* was badly damaged and the New Zealand ship *Achilles* was also damaged. A fourth cruiser, the *Cumberland*, joined the hunt late on. A battle-damaged *Spee* retreated to Montevideo harbour in neutral Uruguay for repairs.[10] Then Churchill got cold feet. He wrote to Chamberlain on 17 December, 'We should prefer that she [the *Graf Spee*] should be interned, as this will be less creditable to the German Navy than being sunk in action. Moreover, a battle of this kind is full of hazard, and needless bloodshed must never be sought.'[11] Of course Churchill was assuming that the Germans would have obeyed an internment order.

Then, believing the false information that the aircraft carrier HMS *Ark Royal* and the battle-cruiser HMS *Renown* were awaiting him, when in fact they were over 3,000km (2,000 miles) away, Langsdorff scuttled *Graf Spee* outside the harbour, afterwards committing suicide.[12] Churchill believed this was a wonderful victory. However, if Captain Langsdorff had obeyed his order that, 'Enemy forces, even if inferior, are only to be engaged if it should further the principal task [of destroying commercial shipping]', the outcome could have been very different. Instead of engaging at close range, Langsdorff could have used the superior range and firepower of his guns to escape and perhaps have sent the Allied ships to the bottom.[13] The inherent vulnerability of surface ships was not at all apparent in this battle: all Churchill saw was one German surface raider neutralized by the heroic action of smaller Allied vessels. Harwood was promoted to rear-admiral and knighted; however, he did not trouble the record books with any subsequent action of distinction during the war.

Churchill next developed an obsession with the *Graf Spee*'s supply ship *Altmark*. It is true that this ship had Allied seamen on board as prisoners of war, but Churchill devoted a disproportionate amount of British resources to its capture when it was unarmed and of no strategic or tactical importance. It was in Norwegian waters when it was captured by British forces, violating Norwegian neutrality, and the incident helped to precipitate Hitler's occupation of Norway, the very thing Churchill had sought to avoid (see chapter 6).[14]

Had Churchill been farsighted, the inherent vulnerability of surface ships should have been apparent to him. There was visceral evidence of this very early in his premiership, with the mauling the Royal Navy took in the retreat from Dunkirk. The autopsy on that fiasco illustrated that the RN was suffering unacceptable losses: the ships' anti-aircraft artillery did not provide adequate protection against air attack and, even combined with Fighter Command, British forces could not fend off the merciless German assault. It is unlikely that they could have done so even with improved anti-aircraft artillery. This stark evidence could and should have taught Churchill a clear and decisive lesson, as it had for Hitler, but it did nothing of the kind.

THE FRENCH FLEET

When France fell, Prime Minister Paul Reynaud asked Churchill if he could be released from their prior agreement that neither country would sign a peace treaty independently with Germany. Churchill agreed, on condition that the French fleet should sail for British ports. Because of internal political problems Reynaud felt obliged to resign and was replaced by the ageing Maréchal Philippe Pétain, who promptly signed an armistice with Germany. Under its terms Germany gained direct control of much of France, but the southern part was to be governed by Pétain from the town of Vichy. Churchill feared that this puppet government would be forced to hand over French capital ships to Germany.

The French Navy was largely scattered, with some ships already in British ports. But the principal element, the Atlantic Squadron, was based at Mers-el-Kebir and nearby Oran, in Algeria. Under the command of Admiral Marcel-Bruno Gensoul, it consisted of the battleships *Provence* and *Bretagne*, the battle-cruisers *Dunquerque* and *Strasbourg*, thirteen destroyers, four submarines and a seaplane carrier.

Vice-Admiral Sir Andrew Cunningham was in command of Mediterranean forces and sent the Royal Navy's battle-group Force H, under Vice-Admiral Sir James Somerville, to the region. It consisted of two battleships, HMS *Resolution* and HMS *Valiant*, the battle-cruiser HMS *Hood*, the aircraft carrier HMS *Ark Royal*, plus two cruisers and eleven destroyers. The British offered the following alternatives to the French fleet: they could join the British fleet; they could sail to a British port with crews to be repatriated to Vichy-controlled France; they could sail to Martinique or the USA for the ships to be decommissioned; or they could scuttle the ships.[15]

On 3 July 1940, Admiral Sir Dudley Pound, the First Sea Lord, told Somerville that he could accept the 'demilitarization of the French ships' as a legitimate alternative. Gensoul had in fact already offered this, but the War Cabinet objected that it looked as though the British were displaying weakness, so the British fleet was ordered to attack. *Bretagne* was sunk and *Provence* was damaged, as was *Dunquerque* and one of the destroyers, while *Strasbourg* got away. The total French dead or missing amounted to 1,300, plus 350 wounded.[16]

Somerville said it was 'a filthy job'. After the war Cunningham wrote to Admiral Lord Fraser, then First Sea Lord, stating that '90 per cent of senior naval officers, including myself, thought Oran a ghastly error and still do'.[17] In *The Second World War* Churchill recounted this unhappy episode in a remote, objective way. He mentioned those involved and provided some detail of the events, but he did not mention that he was the responsible party.

The threat these ships had presented was ostensibly that if they fell into German hands they would provide support for a German invasion of Britain.[18] If the Luftwaffe had defeated the RAF by continuing to target radar stations and airfields rather than bombing cities, a German invasion force might indeed have made use of such ships. However, Operation Sea Lion was abandoned because the Luftwaffe failed to achieve air superiority over southern England and because, with Britain neutralized as an effective offensive power, Hitler turned his interest to his real objective, the Soviet Union. It was the maintenance of air superiority by the RAF over southern England that was critical for Britain's defence, not denying the Germans French ships.

TARANTO

The British air attack against the Italian Navy, at its principal port of Taranto on Italy's south coast, demonstrated conclusively how vulnerable armoured warships were to air attack. Churchill, however, did not learn its lessons, regarding either the threat of air power against British warships, or the limited threat that such enemy warships presented to Britain.

The Italian Navy had a substantial fleet in the Mediterranean, including six battleships. Four of these, the *Caio Duilio*, the *Cesare*, the *Conte di Cavour* and the *Andrea Dorea*, had a main armament of ten 305mm (12in) guns; the other two, the *Littorio* and the *Vittorio Veneto*, were equipped with nine 380mm (15in) guns.[19] They were superior to all the Royal Navy's ships in the Mediterranean, under Admiral Cunningham, save aircraft carriers. However, the Italians' reluctance to take effective offensive naval action meant that invariably much of the fleet was in port; indeed, all of it would be on the occasion of the raid.

The plan was to employ two aircraft carriers, HMS *Illustrious* and HMS *Eagle*, in what was codenamed Operation Judgment. Originally it was to have taken place on 21 October 1940, Trafalgar Day. However, the *Illustrious* suffered an accidental fire that destroyed two of its planes, and the operation was postponed to 11–12 November. Obsolete Fairey Swordfish biplanes were used, equipped with torpedoes, all operating from the *Illustrious*.[20]

The port possessed no radar, but a Swordfish arrived early and triggered the Italian defences while it waited for the others to turn up. The anti-aircraft artillery greeting the Swordfish proved to be exciting but somewhat ineffective. These slow British aircraft, of which just two were lost, scored five torpedo hits on three of the battleships: *Littorio*, *Caio Duilio* and *Conte di Cavour*. Two of these would be repaired and serviceable by May 1941, but one would be put permanently out of action. The remaining ships were redeployed in Naples, which, being further north, increased the fleet's radius of operation and thus reduced its effectiveness. But the real effect was to eliminate any intention the Italians might have had of using the fleet as an effective offensive force. In spring 1941 the Royal Navy would defeat it again in the Battle of Cape Matapan.[21]

Cunningham said: 'Taranto, and the night of November 11th and 12th, 1940, should be remembered for ever as having shown once and for all that in the Fleet Air Arm the Navy has its most devastating weapon.'[22] This perceptive enunciation of air power was not understood by Churchill. The Japanese, however, would learn from the episode, basing their plans for attacking the American Pacific Fleet at Pearl Harbor in Hawaii on its principles of lightweight torpedoes dropped by aircraft from low level so they could be used in the shallow waters of a harbour.

THE *BISMARCK*

Just as with the *Graf Spee*, Churchill saw the German battleship *Bismarck*, under Admiral Günther Lutjens and the captaincy of Kapitän zur See Ernst Lindemann, as constituting a fundamental threat to Britain's supply lines. The pride of the Kiegsmarine, launched in 1939, *Bismarck* displaced in excess of 50,000 tons fully laden, of which two-fifths was armour, yet its maximum speed was still 30 knots. Its main armament consisted of eight 380mm (15in) guns arranged in four twin-gun turrets, two forward, two aft.

As the new battleships HMS *King George V* and its sister ship HMS *Prince of Wales* were being completed in November 1939, Churchill wrote: '. . . the arrival of the *Bismarck* on the oceans before these two ships were completed would be disastrous in the highest degree, as it can neither be caught nor killed.'[23] In August 1940, in a letter to the Air Minister asking for heavy air raids to disrupt the fitting out of *Bismarck*, he wrote: 'Even a few months delay in *Bismarck* will affect the whole balance of sea-power to a serious degree.'[24] Finally, Churchill signalled to the fleet, 'The *Bismarck* must be sunk at all costs.'[25] Admiral Sir John Tovey, Commander-in-Chief of the Home Fleet, ordered HMS *Hood* and HMS *Prince of Wales* to sail from Scapa Flow with six destroyers on 22 May 1941.

Fully laden, *Hood* displaced over 49,000 tons and had a design speed of 32 knots, but it was in need of an overhaul by 1941 and could only attain 28.8 knots. It had been launched in 1918 and its main armament, like that of *Bismarck*, consisted of eight 380mm (15in) guns arranged in four twin-gun turrets, two forward, two aft. The *Prince of Wales* was a modern battleship, which fully laden displaced over 44,000 tons and had a main armament of ten 356mm (14in) guns arranged in three turrets: two quadruple-gun turrets, one forward, one aft, and a twin-gun turret forward. It had originally been intended to carry three quads, or twelve guns in all, but design problems reduced this. Its guns were also restricted by a pre-war treaty limiting main armament to 356mm (14in) guns – something that did not trouble Hitler. The fourth ship to engage in this episode was the German heavy cruiser the *Prinz Eugen*, equipped with a main armament of eight 203mm (8in) guns arranged in four twin-gun turrets, two forward, two aft.

Two days after sailing, the *Hood* was sunk and the *Prince of Wales* crippled by the *Bismarck* and the *Prinz Eugen*. This disastrous encounter demonstrated the futility of such engagements between surface vessels. It had also been a mistake to use *Hood* in this role. It was an upgraded battle-cruiser and was very long from stem to stern. Its deck armour had been strengthened while under construction – a consequence of the lessons learned at the Battle of Jutland in 1916 – but the structure was inadequate for the additional load this imposed. *Hood* thus had a structural weakness amidships. Vice-Admiral Lancelot Holland, who was aboard *Hood*, and the vessel's captain, Ralph Kerr, understood this and sought to close the range on *Bismarck* to minimize the period when the deck amidships would be vulnerable to the falling shot from *Bismarck*'s elevated guns. But this was to no avail: *Bismarck*'s shells struck *Hood* and detonated one of its magazines; its back broke and it went down like a stone. Out of a complement of 1,418 officers and men, only three survived; neither Holland nor Kerr were among them.

The battleship *Prince of Wales*, under Captain John Leach, was crippled and had to make smoke and withdraw – despite Churchill rashly wanting him to press home the attack.[26] It was the precise gunnery of the *Bismarck* and its attendant cruiser *Prinz Eugen* that proved decisive against the British ships. But there were also British tactical errors. For example, because the *Bismarck*'s radar had failed (due to a previous encounter with British warships), *Prinz Eugen* was in the van, but as both ships had a similar profile the *Hood* opened up on the cruiser, assuming that *Bismarck* would be leading. The *Prince of Wales* realized this mistake and Holland corrected it after a short while.

After this fiasco, obsolete Fairey Swordfish biplanes equipped with torpedoes, led by Lieutenant-Commander Eugene Esmonde and operating from the aircraft carrier HMS *Victorious*, attacked the *Bismarck* without success. The task of dealing with the ship then fell to the battle-group Force H under Vice-Admiral Sir James Somerville. It comprised the aircraft-carrier HMS *Ark Royal*, the battle-cruiser HMS *Renown* and the cruiser HMS *Sheffield*, plus six destroyers.[27] On the evening of 26 May, in very poor weather, the *Ark Royal* launched its Swordfish aircraft. They mistook the *Sheffield* for the *Bismarck* and attacked. Mercifully no hits were scored, largely because the magnetic detonators on the torpedoes malfunctioned. This turned out to be a bit of luck, as on return to the *Ark Royal* contact detonators were fitted to the next wave of torpedoes. At approximately 9.00pm the same day the Swordfish attacked again and a torpedo jammed *Bismarck*'s rudder. The crew were unable to free the rudder and at one stage toyed with using explosive charges to remove it altogether. Using differential engine speeds to try to manoeuvre proved unsuccessful, and *Bismarck* was stuck travelling in a large circle. It was subject to ineffectual torpedo attacks during the night by the destroyers *Cossack, Sikh, Mouri, Zulu* and the Polish destroyer *Piorun*. However, on the following morning, 27 May, the battleships HMS *Rodney* and HMS *King George V* were able to close on the *Bismarck* because of its steering difficulties and cripple the ship.

Rodney was an old battleship that could make only 21 knots but, like its sister ship *Nelson* – the flagship of the Royal Navy – it carried a main armament of nine 406mm (16in) guns arranged in three triple-gun turrets. However, *Bismarck* still did not sink. The cruiser *Dorsetshire* then attacked with three torpedoes. The precise reason for the sinking of the *Bismarck* has long been contentious, with some of its survivors insisting that it was scuttled.[28]

It is ironic that it was the obsolete, carrier-launched Fairey Swordfish torpedo aircraft of the Royal Navy's Fleet Air Arm that rendered the *Bismarck* fatally vulnerable to a surface attack by jamming its steering gear. Yet still Churchill did not understand the vulnerability of even the mightiest of armoured warships to air attack.

PRINCE OF WALES AND REPULSE

Without appreciating the lesson of either the Taranto episode or the *Bismarck* one, Churchill sent the battle-group Force Z to the Far East to interdict Japanese convoys as they landed troops in Malaya. The force comprised the repaired *Prince of Wales*, the battle-cruiser HMS *Repulse* (equipped with a main armament of six 380mm (15in) guns arranged in three twin-gun turrets, two forward, one aft), and four destroyers: *Electra*, *Express*, *Vampire* and *Tenedos*. Churchill believed that the *Prince of Wales* and *Repulse* would threaten Japan as *Bismarck* had threatened Britain. But just three days after Pearl Harbor, on 10 December 1941, the same, predictable result occurred, and air power alone dispatched *Prince of Wales* and *Repulse*, with 840 officers and men killed or missing, and the Japanese aircraft filming the action for posterity. Churchill was obliged to withdraw the Royal Navy from the region until 1945, when the Americans led the assault on Japan.[29]

Air cover had not been available for the British task force because the prescribed aircraft carrier, HMS *Indomitable*, was not serviceable, and the RAF was not optimistic about providing cover with its Australian Brewster Buffalo fighters. These were of limited capability, and the Japanese were already threatening their bases. Just four of them arrived in time to witness *Prince of Wales* disappearing beneath the waves.[30]

Yet Churchill must already have been fully aware of the prospective problem. On 10 January 1941, nearly a year before the loss of the two capital ships, he had been worried about a German air attack upon the then new Royal Navy aircraft carrier HMS *Illustrious* in the Mediterranean, and would chronicle the event in *The Second World War*:

> . . . in three attacks she was hit six times with big bombs. Heavily damaged and on fire, with eighty-three killed and sixty seriously wounded, she successfully fought back, thanks to her armoured deck, and her aircraft destroyed at least five assailants. That night, under increasing air attack, and with disabled steering gear, Captain Boyd brought the *Illustrious* into Malta.[31]

He had then written to Major-General Sir Hastings Ismay and the Chiefs of Staff Committee on 13 January, concerning among other subjects the attack on *Illustrious* and its cruiser escorts:

> The effective arrival of German aviation in Sicily may be the beginning of evil developments in the Central Mediterranean. The successful dive-bombing attacks upon *Illustrious* and the

two cruisers show the need for having these ships fitted with aerial-mine throwers. I do not know why *Illustrious* could not have had a couple. The improved naval pattern of aerial mine should be pressed on with to the utmost. The need for high-speed aircraft to catch dive-bombers out at sea seems very great. Surely we ought to try to put half a dozen Grummans on *Formidable* before she goes into the Mediterranean.[32]

The use of aerial mines for anti-aircraft defence proved to be rather fanciful, but Churchill's concern for anti-aircraft defence and the possible use of American-built Grumman fighters on the other aircraft carrier mentioned, HMS *Formidable*, demonstrates that he was aware of the potential threat to capital ships from the air. Also, the fact that American battleships galore were sunk by air power at Pearl Harbor on 7 December 1941, just three days before the loss of *Prince of Wales* and *Repulse*, would, it might be thought, have taught Churchill a vital lesson and stayed his hand.

Of course it was the British admiral in charge, Sir Tom Phillips, who took the actual decision to go ahead with the operation despite these difficulties; he was to pay with his life. Churchill was keen to emphasize this in *The Second World War*: 'In reply to certain questions of the Chiefs of Staff about why no fighter aircraft were sent from Singapore . . . it was confirmed that Admiral Phillips did not signal his change of plan on the 9th, as he was keeping radio silence . . .'[33] However, with his overview of the war, attendant interest in the navy and hands-on approach, Churchill should have realized the risk. A newspaper headline at the time read, 'Premier accused for loss of Warships.' The article itself read:

> Blunt criticism of the Premier as an advocate and arbiter of strategy, and the assertion that the sending of the *Prince of Wales* and *Repulse* to the Far East without adequate protection was a political decision, was made in the House of Lords yesterday by Lord Chatfield, former Minister for Co-ordination of Defence. The Prime Minister had said on Tuesday, he pointed out – 'That the two ships were sent out as spearpoints.' Battleships are not spearpoints, they are not forwards in the game, they are full-backs,' said Lord Chatfield. 'Repeated avoidable disasters make a reasonable man wonder

whether the strategic machine that guides these decisions is
all that it should be' . . . In a Commons debate last night,
Commander Southby said – 'he could not believe that expert
naval officers failed to advise that the *Prince of Wales* and
Repulse should be accompanied by an aircraft carrier. I have
heard it stated,' he alleged, 'that orders given for an aircraft
carrier were countermanded by the Prime Minister himself.'[34]

The Taranto, *Bismarck* and Pearl Harbor episodes constituted an
overwhelmingly significant set of lessons: that armoured ships were
inherently vulnerable to air attack. As Churchill himself would comment,
'Japan was supreme and we everywhere were weak and naked.'[35]

SCHARNHORST AND *GNEISENAU*

On 29 January 1942 in the House of Commons, Churchill won a vote
of confidence over his handling of the war by 464 votes to 1. A few days
later, the German battle-cruisers *Scharnhorst* and *Gneisenau* and the cruiser
Prinz Eugen (of *Bismarck* fame) made a successful dash through the English
Channel. The two battle-cruisers were equipped with nine 280mm (11in)
guns mounted in three triple-gun turrets, two forward and one aft, and
displaced 38,900 tons at full load.

Churchill fretted greatly about these ships. He had written to Sir
Charles Portal on 17 April 1941: 'The German battle-cruisers are two of
the most important vessels in the war, as we have nothing that can both
catch and kill them'.[36] They were subjected to repeated Allied air attacks
while in the French port of Brest, and the damage incurred meant they
were unserviceable until late 1941. The Germans then decided that their
surface fleet should be concentrated in the Norwegian theatre, and so on
11–13 February 1942 the two battle-cruisers and *Prinz Eugen*, with a flotilla
of destroyers and motor torpedo boats – S-boats (*Schnell* or 'fast' boats),
though the British always referred to them as E-boats – and with air cover
provided by the Luftwaffe, made their daring dash through the English
Channel to reach Germany.

The Channel run, officially known as Operation Cerberus, caught the
British off guard, and despite air and surface attacks the ships got through.

The Royal Navy's Fleet Air Arm sent six Swordfish aircraft for a torpedo attack led by Lieutenant-Commander Eugene Esmonde, who had led the first attack on the *Bismarck*. They attacked without waiting for the arrival of their Spitfire escort. No Swordfish returned and none scored a hit on the German ships. Of the eighteen crewmen, thirteen were killed and five were rescued. Esmonde was awarded a posthumous Victoria Cross. However, both the *Scharnhorst* and the *Gneisenau* hit mines in the later stages of the journey. It took six months to repair the *Scharnhorst*, and the *Gneisenau* was subsequently hit by a British air raid while under repair at Kiel and was never re-commissioned: once again, air attack had been decisive.[37]

The *Scharnhorst* was subsequently deployed in Alten Fjord in northern Norway for use against the Allied supply convoys to Russia. When intelligence reports indicated that it and an escort of destroyers were readying to intercept an Arctic convoy, Admiral Sir Bruce Fraser deployed units of the Home Fleet to sink it. This was successfully accomplished on 26 December 1943. It was one of the few examples of a German capital ship being dispatched by a surface naval engagement.[38] Churchill wrote in *The Second World War*, '. . . [this] removed the worst menace to our Arctic convoys . . .'[39] But the worst menace to all Allied convoys was that of the U-boats.

U-BOATS

More responsibly, Churchill wrote: '. . . the only thing that ever really frightened me during the war was the U-boat peril'. He also wrote that 'this mortal danger to our life-lines gnawed my bowels'. He was correct: the threat posed by the *Unterseeboot*, or U-boat, of the Kriegsmarine during World War II was critical. However, Churchill underestimated the vulnerability of surface vessels to the submarine, just as he had to air attack.[40] Hitler knew that the umbilical cord enabling Britain to prosecute the war was its merchant sea lanes across the Atlantic. If sufficient merchant vessels could be sunk, Britain would be finished. Thus, winning what Churchill called the 'Battle of the Atlantic' was essential.

The significance of the campaign was well understood in Berlin. Germany had conducted the same strategy in World War I, and by 1917 had been very close to defeating Britain. Surprisingly, the Kriegsmarine was poorly equipped to undertake such a task in 1939, with only 56 operational submarines deployed. Hitler said he was a 'hero on land, but a coward at sea' and it required Admiral Karl Dönitz to persuade him of the virtues of submarine warfare.[41]

The German occupation of Norway and France provided forward bases, permitting U-boats to undertake longer-range patrols into the Atlantic than would have been possible from bases in Germany. They were supported by Focke-Wulf FW 200 Kondor four-engine long-range reconnaissance aircraft, which provided essential intelligence information for the U-boats as well as being able to undertake limited attacks on Allied merchantmen themselves.

The British response was to provide convoys with naval escorts. Royal Navy warships were equipped with ASDIC (named after the Anti-Submarine Division, and later known as sonar) for the detection of submerged U-boats. This system emitted an acoustic signal that would bounce off a metallic object, identifying its location and range. However, Churchill overestimated its effectiveness and deliberately exaggerated the U-boat losses.[42] The Royal Navy was very short of suitable escort vessels, and was helped by the provision of 50 American destroyers under President Roosevelt's lend-lease programme. Although Churchill increased the production of small destroyers and improved defences against magnetic mines, his obsession with German battleships was diverting resources from the one critical component of the sea war. It was against the U-boat threat that the resources needed to be concentrated.

The six-month period from June to Christmas 1940 was critical for Britain, as some three million tons of Allied merchant vessels were sunk by U-boats, mines and attacks by surface vessels and aircraft. German tactics were improved still further at Christmas, when Dönitz introduced 'wolfpacks' – massed attacks by U-boats on the surface at night. They were extremely effective and led to the Kriegsmarine submariners referring to this as the 'happy time'. Britain's ability to address the problem proved to be limited. Corvettes and trawlers were deployed to provide additional escorts, but once again Churchill was culpable in failing adequately to predict the escort shortage and deal with it.

It was the backroom boys who would help to rescue him. The British development of the 'cavity magnetron' was critical in shifting the balance of power to the Allies in the U-boat war. It permitted the development of lightweight short-wave radar systems, capable of being carried on aircraft and detecting surfaced U-boats. Submarine technology of the period provided only very limited underwater endurance, so U-boats frequently had to recharge their batteries and replenish their air supply, and as the surface performance of their diesel engines was so much better than the electric power used when submerged, U-boats were obliged to spend long periods on the surface. Once aircraft were equipped with portable radar systems they could detect U-boats on the surface and attack with machine guns, bombs and depth charges. More U-boats could now be sunk with relatively fewer resources. Thus the U-boats had to spend much more time underwater, with a considerable reduction in their offensive capability as a result.

Intelligence was also crucial, and Churchill was an enthusiastic supporter of its use. The breaking of the Enigma codes, at the Government Code and Cypher School at Bletchley Park, produced intelligence information to which Churchill referred as being *ultra* secret: thus it acquired the name 'Ultra'. The capture of a German Enigma coding machine from the U-110 on 9 May 1941 helped considerably in this regard.[43] It was said that the Battle of Waterloo was won on the playing fields of Eton; it is only a slight exaggeration to say that World War II, or at least the Battle of the Atlantic, was won at Bletchley Park.

AMERICA ULTIMATELY PROVES DECISIVE

Much of the work in the Battle of the Atlantic was left to the United States, and Churchill had done much to cultivate the relationship with the American President (see chapter 17). From April 1941 President Roosevelt decided that the US Navy should take responsibility for escort duties on the American side of the Atlantic, despite the fact that the USA was still officially neutral in the war. On 4 September an RAF Sunderland flying boat spotted a U-boat off Iceland, close to a US Navy destroyer, the USS *Greer*. The Sunderland signalled the *Greer* accordingly but its commanding officer was under orders not to attack unless threatened. The U-boat commander was under similar orders from Dönitz. The Sunderland, which was low on fuel, jettisoned its depth charges and left the scene. The U-boat commander thought the depth charges had originated from the *Greer* and fired a torpedo, which missed. The destroyer now replied with depth charges but failed to hit the U-boat. This episode proved to be crucial, for the United States was now in a shooting war with Germany and subsequently its navy would openly escort convoys. Fortunately for Churchill, the United States was precipitated into the Battle of the Atlantic even before it was officially in World War II, and the Americans saved Britain from being starved of vital resources.[44]

When the Americans first entered the war, they failed to 'black out' coastal towns or to introduce a comprehensive convoy system. Consequently, in the first six months of 1942, more than three million tons of shipping was sunk. This was the second 'happy time' for the U-boat crews.[45] Churchill was keen to criticize the United States for this in *The Second World War*:

> All this destruction, far exceeding anything known in this war, though not reaching the catastrophic figures of the worst period of 1917, was caused by no more than twelve to fifteen boats working in the area at any one time. The protection afforded by the United States Navy was for several months hopelessly inadequate. It is surprising indeed that during two years of the advance of total war towards the American continent more provision had not been made against this deadly onslaught.[46]

In early 1943 Dönitz had a fleet of 400 U-boats, and the Allies had a problem producing merchant vessels faster than they were being sunk. The United States therefore developed 'Liberty Ships', which were constructed on a mass-production basis. Another problem was the 'mid-Atlantic gap' between the radii of operation of land-based planes operating from Britain and North America. The introduction of American-built light escort aircraft carriers in September 1941 was crucial to address this, as was the introduction to RAF Coastal Command of the American Consolidated B-24D Liberator, a very long-range four-engine aircraft equipped with radar and a 'Leigh Light' – a high-power searchlight that could illuminate a surfaced U-boat at night. These aircraft proved to be very effective. By mid-April 1943 Dönitz still had as many as 193 U-boats deployed in the Atlantic, but many of the most experienced crews were dead, and the reliance on newly trained crews drastically reduced operational performance. Faced with these problems, Dönitz was obliged to withdraw most of his U-boats in May 1943. The Germans developed much more advanced long-range U-boats, Types XXI and XXIII, but by the time they became operational it was too late for them to have any impact on the outcome of the war.[47]

The Battle of the Atlantic cost the lives of between 75,000 and 85,000 Allied seamen. It also accounted for two-thirds of the 28,000 deaths of U-boat crewmen, out of the total of 41,000 who served during the war.

TIRPITZ

Despite the U-boat war constituting the real threat, Churchill would not let go of his obsession with battleships: he wanted to sink the *Bismarck*'s sister ship, the *Tirpitz*. In a letter to Major-General Ismay for the Chiefs of Staff Committee on 25 January 1942, he wrote: 'The destruction or even the crippling of this ship is the greatest event at sea at the present time.'[48]

However, the *Tirpitz* never fired a shot against an Allied ship in the entire war. The Germans stationed it in Alten Fjord in Norway, fenced in with anti-submarine netting precisely because of its vulnerability. The ship made only three offensive sorties during its long period based in Norway, two of which took place in 1942 and the third the following year. But *Tirpitz* caused paranoia in Churchill. When in 1942 the Admiralty received a report – which turned out to be false – that it had left Norway to attack a convoy taking supplies to Russia, it ordered the withdrawal of the convoy's cruiser escort and the dispersal of the convoy itself. U-boats and German aircraft had a field day, sinking 23 out of the 34 ships in the convoy.[49]

The *Tirpitz* was attacked in September 1943, in Operation Source. This involved the use of midget submarines – X-craft – which laid explosive charges beneath the ship's hull and disabled it. Repairs to *Tirpitz* took a few months. In April 1944 Operation Tungsten was mounted against it, involving much of the Home Fleet. A Fleet Air Arm attack was made by Fairy Barracuda torpedo planes from no less than six aircraft carriers. It caused many casualties among *Tirpitz*'s crew, but the only damage to the ship was to the superstructure, plus some flooding, and it took two months to repair. Three more attempts were planned for April and May but cancelled because of the weather. Operation Mascot, another air raid, was mounted in July 1944, again by Barracudas, this time launched from three aircraft carriers. But the Germans had introduced smokescreen apparatus and the raid was a failure. Four more attempts were made in late August by the Fleet Air Arm with five carriers: Operations Goodwood I, II, III and IV. The net result of these was one unexploded bomb, which German sailors dealt with by opening it up and shovelling out the explosives. However, a Royal Navy aircraft carrier was damaged by a U-boat, so seriously that it was beyond repair.[50]

The Navy having had a go – both with submarines and aircraft – it was now the turn of the RAF. Operation Paravane took place on 15 September, with 5,400kg (12,000lb) 'Tallboy' bombs, designed by Barnes Wallis, the inventor of the 'bouncing bomb'. They were dropped by Avro Lancasters of 617 'Dam Buster' Squadron and 9 Squadron (see chapter 16). *Tirpitz* sustained some damage, but once again the smokescreen offered protection. The Germans now moved *Tirpitz* to Tromsö, where Tallboys were again used on 28 October, but cloud cover was the problem this time. Finally, Operation Catechism was executed on 12 November 1944, and without a working smokescreen apparatus installed at Tromsö, the Tallboy attack was successful and *Tirpitz* capsized in shallow waters.[51]

From the very beginning of World War II, armoured warships were inherently vulnerable. The submarine and the aircraft carrier had already become the principal capital vessels for the world's major navies, but Churchill lacked the vision to appreciate the significance of this.

10
NORTH AFRICA: CHURCHILL'S DISPERSIONIST STRATEGY TAKES HOLD

The North African campaign was another example of the war being taken to the Germans in an area of no strategic importance, though the Germans did oblige by contesting it. It was part of Churchill's dispersionist strategy: as in the Norway campaign, forces were not concentrated directly against Nazi Germany but were dispersed around the periphery. Churchill reasoned that Britain, by itself, lacked the necessary resources to conduct a land campaign against the Germans in Western Europe, so North Africa was seen as a suitable surrogate. However, when the North African strategy was implemented, the danger of a German invasion of Britain was still real. General Sir John Dill, the CIGS, wrote on 6 May 1941: 'It is the United Kingdom . . . and not Egypt that is vital, and the defence of the United Kingdom must take first place. Egypt is not even second in order of priority . . .'[1] Churchill would sack Dill the following November.

The only importance the North African campaign had for the Germans was that it held down British forces so they were not available in more important theatres.[2] Churchill was playing directly into Hitler's hands. As he admitted in *The Second World War*, the German High Command was rather uninterested in the campaign: 'If the enemy had chosen they could have spared and ferried, at an accepted cost, the forces necessary to make our position untenable.'[3] Later, the Americans were also drawn into this campaign. After the Japanese attack on Pearl Harbor it is utterly incredible that they could have thought that their priority was to engage in combat in Morocco. Yet, under Churchill's influence, they did.

However, Churchill's initial reason for an offensive operation in North Africa was not to oppose Hitler but to thwart the ambitions of Mussolini. In *The Second World War*, he wrote:

> With the disappearance of France as a combatant and with Britain set on her struggle for life at home, Mussolini might feel that his dream of dominating the Mediterranean and

rebuilding the former Roman Empire would come true. Relieved from any need to guard against the French in Tunis, he could still reinforce the numerous army he had gathered for the invasion of Egypt.[4]

Even writing after the war, Churchill still had not grasped how inconsequential Mussolini had been. The principal objective of the war effort had to be the defeat of Hitler: once that was accomplished the threat from Mussolini would simply fall away. Mussolini's declaration of war and his invasion of North Africa had all to do with his trying to grab some spoils of war while the grabbing was good. Without Hitler and Nazi Germany, Mussolini could not have posed any significant geopolitical threat to the Allied powers. This was clearly evident by the time Churchill was writing his account.

In the early stages of the North African campaign, before the United States entered the war, the Western Desert Force – renamed XIII Corps – under Lieutenant-General Richard O'Connor was first pushed back by the Italians, then successfully mounted a counterattack, Operation Compass. It was initiated on 9 December 1940, and by 7 February 1941 over 130,000 Italian and Libyan prisoners had been taken, along with 180 medium tanks, 200 light tanks and 845 artillery pieces. But just when O'Connor was in a position to take Tripoli, the Libyan capital, and clear Italian forces out of North Africa altogether, Churchill obliged his commanding officer, General Archibald Wavell, to withdraw much of XIII Corps for operations in Greece. The advance in North Africa, which could have defeated the Axis powers, was halted.[5]

In fact, long before the prize of Tripoli was abandoned, Churchill was already minded to withdraw forces from the campaign in Cyrenaica and Tripolitania (Libya) and sacrifice even the conquest of Benghazi, the capital of Cyrenaica. In an 'appreciation' that he drew up for Major-General Sir Hastings Ismay and the Chiefs of Staff Committee on 6 January 1941, when not even the strategically important port of Tobruk had been taken, let alone Benghazi or Tripoli, he wrote:

> It may be possible for General Wavell, with no more than the forces he is now using in the Western Desert, and in spite of some reduction in his Air Force, to conquer the Cyrenaica province and establish himself at Benghazi; but it would not

be right for the sake of Benghazi to lose the chance of the Greeks taking Valona, and thus to dispirit and anger them, and perhaps make them in the mood for a separate peace with Italy. Therefore the prospect must be faced that after Tobruk the further westward advance of the Army of the Nile may be seriously cramped. It is quite clear to me that supporting Greece must have priority after the western flank of Egypt has been made secure.[6]

To justify his position, in *The Second World War*, Churchill quoted a letter to himself from General (later Field Marshal) Jan Smuts, the South African Prime Minister, on 8 January 1941: 'Magnificent victories in the Middle East open up a field of speculation regarding our future course. Flowing tide will soon carry Wavell to Tobruk. Should he go farther? Tripoli is much too far.'[7] Churchill cabled Wavell on the 10th: 'Nothing must hamper capture of Tobruk, but thereafter all operations in Libya are subordinated to aiding Greece, and all preparations must be made from the receipt of this telegram for the immediate succour of Greece . . .'[8] In consequence, the following forces were moved to the support of Greece after Tobruk had fallen: a squadron of infantry tanks, a regiment of cruiser tanks plus ten regiments of artillery and, from the RAF, five squadrons.[9]

Now there was vacillation, as Churchill wrote:

> . . . the Greek Government were unwilling that any of our troops should land in Salonika until they could do so in sufficient numbers to act offensively. On receipt of this telegram the Chiefs of Staff telegraphed on January 17 that there could be no question of forcing our aid upon the Greeks. In consequence we modified our view of the immediate future, decided to push on to Benghazi . . .[10]

Then Churchill wrote to the chiefs of staff on 31 January concerning North Africa, the worsening Greek situation and his old hobbyhorse, Turkey:

> The advance to Benghazi is most desirable . . . Nevertheless only forces which do not conflict with European needs can be employed . . . For instance, the air support promised to Turkey

cannot be delayed till then. It may however be possible to reconcile both objectives.'[11]

But it was not possible. Tobruk had indeed been taken on 21–2 January, and Benghazi on 6–7 February. British forces had pushed even further west, but this plan proved to be disastrous. Churchill wrote to Wavell on 12 February:

> In the event of its proving impossible to reach any good agreement with the Greeks and work out a practical military plan, then we must try to save as much from the wreck as possible. We must at all costs keep Crete and take any Greek islands which are of use as air bases. We could also reconsider the advance on Tripoli. But these will only be consolation prizes after the classic race has been lost. There will always remain the support of Turkey.[12]

But in *The Second World War* he wrote: 'The Desert Flank was the peg on which all else hung, and there was no idea in any quarter of losing or risking that for the sake of Greece or anything in the Balkans.'[13] However, on 10 March 1941 he had written to Roosevelt: 'Although it was no doubt tempting to try to push on from Benghazi to Tripoli . . . we have felt it our duty to stand by the Greeks . . . We are therefore sending the greater part of the Army of the Nile to Greece, and are reinforcing to the utmost possible in the air.'[14] These are two of the few occasions on which Churchill admits the original aim was Tripoli at all.

BRITISH FORCES ARE PUSHED BACK

A certain Generalleutnant Erwin Rommel, who would subsequently rise to the rank of Generalfeldmarschall, headed the riposte by the Afrika Korps on 31 March. His first reinforcements landed unopposed, because O'Connor's advance had been halted by the loss of his forces to Greece. Rommel then pushed back British forces some 800km (500 miles) to where they had started, capturing O'Connor in the process. All of the British advantage had been lost, precipitated by Churchill's decision to withdraw

British forces at the crucial moment.

Churchill's priority shifted to Crete when the British forces were defeated in mainland Greece (see chapter 11). However, by 18 April the chiefs of staff were trying to shore up the North African front as British troops were evacuated from Greece.[15] Not only was Tripoli not attained, but all the territory that had been gained in North Africa was now lost, and Greece, Crete and the Greek islands would be lost as well. Not only the 'classic race' but all the consolation prizes had been well and truly lost. Both the North African and Greek campaigns had proved to be tragedies, and trying to run both simultaneously had made matters worse.

Churchill wrote to Eden on 3 April 1941: 'Far more important than the loss of ground is the idea that we cannot face the Germans and that their appearance is enough to drive us back many scores of miles. This may react most evilly throughout Balkans and Turkey.'[16] But not being able to 'face the Germans' was precisely what was happening. On 14 April he wrote to the chiefs of staff: 'If the Germans can continue to nourish their invasion of Cyrenaica and Egypt through the port of Tripoli and along the coastal road they can certainly bring superior armoured forces to bear upon us, with consequences of the most serious character.'[17] He thus revealed the pivotal significance of Tripoli, and underscored the folly of trying to conduct a North African campaign, yet withdrawing forces for Greece and abandoning the original objective of Tripoli. Now it would be necessary to conduct a naval bombardment of Tripoli to attempt to deal with the problem that way.

The commander-in-chief of the Mediterranean fleet was Admiral Sir Andrew Cunningham. His responsibilities were often undermined by operational interference by Churchill, whom Cunningham described as 'a perfect nuisance', though he found the Prime Minister 'very amusing.'[18] The naval task he now faced proved to be a grave matter, as a communication to him from the Admiralty on 15 April 1941 made clear:

> It is evident that drastic measures are necessary to stabilise the position in the Middle East. After thorough investigation it is considered that air action alone against Tripoli will not sufficiently interrupt the flow of reinforcements which are entering Libya chiefly through that port.[19]

What the Admiralty suggested was that a naval bombardment should be undertaken by 'block ships' as they approached the harbour, sacrificing the battle-cruiser *Barham*, no less. Cunningham didn't like this at all and chose instead to risk the whole battle fleet in a naval bombardment: he got away with it for no other reason than that the Luftwaffe were busy elsewhere. And all because Tripoli had not been taken in the first place.

In *The Second World War* Churchill wrote: 'The beating of our Desert Flank while we were full-spread in the Greek adventure was however a disaster of the first magnitude. I was for some time completely mystified about its cause . . .'[20] He was unquestionably correct about the magnitude of defeat, but that he should have been mystified as to its cause is most surprising. He went on to say that he asked Wavell to explain the problem, and that Wavell told him 'this and that' had gone wrong. Yet the real problem was a fundamental failure of strategy: taking on two futile campaigns that could not be won simultaneously and withdrawing forces from North Africa just when the crucial prize of Tripoli was within Britain's grasp.

DISPERSIONISM EXTENDED

The events in North Africa were a sideshow to the war to liberate German-occupied Europe. However, while they were occurring, Churchill initiated a sideshow to the sideshow. The Italians had occupied Abyssinia in the late 1930s and Churchill wanted to get them out. He also sanctioned military action in the Sudan and Somaliland, where the Italians had forces and where, in the latter case, both Britain and France had been imperial powers. British Somaliland was regained, but French Somaliland presented a problem as British forces were now in conflict with Vichy France.[21]

This was a dispersionist policy of the highest order, where the very limited forces at Britain's disposal were dispersed across disparate elements of the Italian empire with, at best, little strategic gain if they were successful. And the dispersionist strategy would be widened to include dealing with a pro-German government in Iraq, where British forces were needed to secure the city of Basra, and fighting the Vichy French again, this time in Syria. But Churchill was not finished yet: Iran would be added to this panoply of military objectives, even though the forces were already very thinly stretched.[22]

Unbelievably, Churchill's mistake in withdrawing forces at the critical moment was repeated when, much later, British forces pushed the Germans back for a second time: Churchill transferred forces to the campaign in the Far East just as the Allies were on the cusp of eliminating Axis forces from Africa altogether. As a result Rommel was able to push the British back for a second time. British forces had now been back and forth across North Africa on two separate occasions.

THE TECHNICAL PROBLEMS

Part of the problem was the modest design quality of British tanks and the later American tanks that augmented them. By contrast, when a captured German tank was sent back to England, it was found that its armour was case-hardened and could withstand British anti-tank gun assault.[23] Another problem for the British was their lack of tank transporters, which meant they had to travel everywhere on their own tracks. While muddy terrain is ideal for tanks, as water is a lubricant, desert conditions increase wear on moving components, and as the British tanks spent so much time on their tracks, their reliability was poor. Also, whereas the Germans would recover their knocked-out tanks from the battlefield and repair them, the British tended to abandon theirs. Yet Churchill pressured his commanders to attack despite these crucial deficiencies.

Undoubtedly the tactics were a problem too. While the British would attack with tanks firing on the move, the Germans recognized that tanks function most efficiently in 'hull-down' positions, awaiting an enemy assault. If their tanks were caught out in the open, they were used to decoy the enemy tanks on to their defensive anti-tank batteries – in Germany's case the formidable Krupp 88mm. Recounting the defects of the North African campaign to Churchill, Wavell wrote on 25 April 1941:

> I did not become aware till just before the German attack of the bad mechanical state of the cruiser [tank] regiment, on which we chiefly relied. A proportion of these tanks broke down before reaching the front, and many others became casualties from mechanical defects during the early fighting. The same seems to have occurred with the other cruiser regiment of the 2nd Armoured Division, which went to Greece.

> Our light tank was powerless against German tanks, which
> were all armed with guns [cannons – compared with the
> machine guns fitted to the British light tanks].[24]

Churchill, replying to Wavell on the 28th, wrote: 'We seem to have had
rather bad luck. I expect we shall get this back later.'[25] Of course 'luck' had
nothing to do with it.

The wisdom of conducting the North African campaign was also
questioned by the logistics. The simple solution would have been to provide
supplies through the Straits of Gibraltar, which Britain controlled, and
via the Mediterranean. But the Mediterranean was a hotbed of Italian and
German naval and air activity, so most supplies for Allied forces in Libya
had to come around the Cape of Good Hope and through the Suez Canal.
This was a crippling distance to travel, and exposed shipping to U-boat
attack in the Atlantic as well as the threat of mines in the inshore areas.

Operation Battleaxe was executed on 15 June 1941 by XIII Corps,
under Lieutenant-General Sir Noel Monson de la Poer Beresford-Pierse.
Its objective was to defeat the Germans and Italians in eastern Cyrenaica
and to lift the siege of Tobruk. It failed as it was a hasty operation and
the British forces were ill prepared. More than half the British tanks
were destroyed or disabled on the first day alone. Rommel initiated his
counterstroke on the second day, and on the third British forces were
withdrawn to avoid encirclement.[26] This situation would characterize
much of the campaign, with the British repeatedly beaten by the Germans
(though not by the Italians).

CHURCHILL SACKS HIS GENERALS

Churchill's response to defeat was to sack his generals until he found
one who would win. He had believed that Wavell's disposition made
him better suited to be chairman of a golf club or a Conservative Party
association than a senior military officer.[27] Inevitably, with the failure of
'Battleaxe', Wavell was to be sacked, and in a communication on 21 June
1941 Churchill asked General Sir Claude Auchinleck ('the Auk') to replace
him: Wavell and Auchinleck were to swap jobs, with Wavell becoming
commander-in-chief in India.[28] Yet Churchill would subsequently sack

Auckinleck too.

Churchill required success quickly, despite the facts that North Africa was new to Auchinleck, it was about the size of India, the new forces just arrived from Britain were inexperienced and required training, the existing forces were tired and dispirited, and the equipment was inferior to that of the Germans.[29] This was characteristic of Churchill: pushing hard for action, but in so doing precipitating a rash and premature attack before British forces and their commanders were ready.

No sooner had Churchill appointed 'the Auk' than he had serious misgivings. First, Auchinleck made it clear that he was not confident of the defence of Tobruk after September, then a wrangle developed over the use of non-British troops. Churchill wrote in *The Second World War*, 'I was sensitive to the hostile propaganda which asserted that it was the British policy to fight with any other troops but our own and thus to avoid the shedding of United Kingdom blood.'[30] Thus he had the 50th British Division transferred to Egypt, but Auchinleck deployed them to Cyprus; Churchill was immediately upset that he had not thrown them into the fight in North Africa. The real problem was the usual one: 'the Auk' wanted to take time to prepare for attack, while Churchill wanted action quickly, particularly while Hitler was preoccupied in Russia.[31] But Hitler would be occupied with the Russians until the end of the war and time was necessary for effective preparation.

On 23 July Auchinleck wrote to Churchill: 'I entirely agree as to the desirability of using present German preoccupation in Russia to hit enemy in Libya, but . . . to launch an offensive with the inadequate means at present at our disposal is not, in my opinion, a justifiable operation of war . . .' Auchinleck asked for complete discretion in these matters, particularly for his planned main assault, Operation Crusader, planned for 1 November. But Churchill wanted to control him from London.[32] He wrote to him on 29 September: 'All now depends upon the battle . . . Every day's delay is dearly purchased in the wider sphere. The prize is Turkey, whose action may well be determined by victory in Cyrenaica.'[33] Turkey, yet again!

In a letter to Roosevelt on 20 October, Churchill enunciated his hopes for Operation Crusader: 'His [Auchinleck's] object will be to . . . capture Benghazi as quickly as possible,' and if successful, 'a further rapid advance upon Tripoli may be carried out.' The latter operation, to occupy Tripolitania more generally, was codenamed Operation Acrobat.[34]

The Eighth Army came into being on 26 September 1941. Its principal elements were XIII Corps, under Lieutenant-General Henry Godwin-Austen, and XXX Corps under Lieutenant-General Sir Willoughby Norrie; Auchinleck placed it under the command of (acting) Lieutenant-General Alan Cunningham. Churchill thought that new equipment could be used as soon as it was delivered to a theatre, and so hurried Cunningham to take the offensive. The Eighth Army had some 770 tanks, including the American Stuart light tank and the British Crusader cruiser tank, which inspired the name of the operation. The Afrika Korps under Rommel consisted of the 15th and 21st Panzer Divisions plus the ZBV (later named 90th Light) Division, with seven Italian Divisions. Rommel had 174 medium tanks plus 146 Italian tanks.[35]

OFFENSIVE ACTION AGAIN

Operation Crusader was launched by the Eighth Army on 18 November from Mersa Matruh, with a subsidiary attack launched from Tobruk. However, the Eighth suffered a defeat at Sidi Rezegh and Rommel counterattacked into Egypt behind the British main force. Cunningham wanted to withdraw, but Auchinleck refused. This proved to be tactically correct, as Rommel's bold stroke failed to come off because he outran his supply lines. The Auk's decision to hold fast was the turning point, and on 7 December the Afrika Korps was in full retreat.

Cunningham was replaced by Auchinleck's deputy chief of staff, Major-General Neil Ritchie, promoted to the rank of lieutenant-general. The Afrika Korps had to retreat past Benghazi and all the way back to El Agheila by 30 December, from where Rommel's attack had begun in March. However, on 21 January 1942 he would counterattack again and drive the Eighth Army back to Gazala, where both sides dug in. Rommel sensed that the British were overextended: suddenly Benghazi was threatened and shortly it was back in German hands.[36] So the Eighth Army had pushed Rommel back to his starting point, but Rommel's counterattack meant that everybody went back the other way again. In *The Second World War* Churchill wrote:

> This extraordinary reversal of fortune and the severe military disaster arose from the basic facts that the enemy had gained virtually free passage across the Mediterranean to reinforce

and nourish his armour, and had brought a large part of his Air Force back from Russia. But the tactical events on the spot have never been explained.[37]

Thus the failure to take the port of Tripoli so long before caused a fundamental failure in this episode, and the tactical events *were* known.

Over the next four months Churchill, as usual, demanded of Auchinleck that he press hard against the Germans. However, crucially, three divisions were withdrawn from Auchinleck's forces, together with much of the Desert Air Force, for use in Burma, and equipment that Auchinleck had been promised had still not been supplied. Once again Churchill was removing vital forces from his desert commander just at the moment when victory could have been accomplished. Defeat was not so much Auchinleck's responsibility as Churchill's.[38]

As usual, Churchill was keen to precipitate a renewed assault in North Africa before his commander was ready and despite denuding him of forces. He wrote in *The Second World War*:

> During February it became apparent to us that General Auchinleck proposed to make another four months' pause in order to mount a second set-piece battle with Rommel. Neither the Chiefs of Staff nor I and my colleagues were convinced that another of these costly interludes was necessary. We were all sure it was lamentable that British and Imperial armies, already numbering over six hundred and thirty thousand men on ration strength, with reinforcements constantly arriving, should stand idle for so long a period at enormous expense while the Russians were fighting desperately and valiantly along their whole vast front. Moreover, it seemed to us that Rommel's strength might well grow quicker than our own.[39]

Auchinleck took up a defensive line at Tobruk. But Rommel's counterstroke came and he was pushed back, leaving Tobruk isolated behind German lines – for the second time – and supplied only from the sea. Having run back and forth across North Africa several times, British control of Tobruk had been threatened more than once. Finally, on 21 June

1942, it fell to Rommel. Ritchie had left an open flank in his defence of Tobruk, which allowed Rommel to attack through it. Auchinleck had not taken direct command of the Eighth Army, as he had done previously when things were looking sticky, though he would do so belatedly four days after Tobruk fell.[40]

Churchill was in Washington with President Roosevelt at the time, and he recounted in *The Second World War*:

> Presently a telegram was put into the President's hands. He passed it to me without a word. It said, 'Tobruk has surrendered, with twenty-five thousand men taken prisoners.' This was so surprising that I could not believe it.

This was yet another body blow, as Churchill had set such great store by the defence of Tobruk. He went on:

> This was one of the heaviest blows I can recall during the war. Not only were its military effects grievous, but it had affected the reputation of the British armies. At Singapore eighty-five thousand men had surrendered to inferior numbers of Japanese. Now in Tobruk a garrison of twenty-five thousand (actually thirty-three thousand) seasoned soldiers had laid down their arms to perhaps one-half of their number. If this was typical of the morale of the Desert Army, no measure could be put upon the disasters which impended in North-East Africa. I did not attempt to hide from the President the shock I had received. It was a bitter moment. Defeat is one thing; disgrace is another.[41]

CHURCHILL FACES A HOUSE OF COMMONS CENSURE

Having faced a vote of confidence in January, Churchill was now obliged to face a censure motion in the House of Commons, shortly after he had returned from Washington on 25 June 1942. Tabled by Sir John Wardlaw-Milne, it was seconded by Admiral of the Fleet Sir Roger Keyes and supported by Leslie Hore-Belisha, the former Secretary of State for War.

On the government's side, Sir Stafford Cripps, the Leader of the House, took responsibility for organizing the riposte, but he made the mistake of selecting a new boy in the Commons, Oliver Lyttelton, to undertake the arduous task of replying for the government. Lyttelton was insufficiently familiar with either the normal practices of the House or the personalities of the influential members to reply effectively. Churchill faced opposition from both right and left in such figures as Admiral Keyes and Aneurin Bevan (who would create the National Health Service after the war). Bevan was right when he pointedly remarked that Churchill won every debate but lost every battle.[42] But Sir John Wardlaw-Milne then made the incredible suggestion that the Duke of Gloucester should be appointed Commander-in-Chief of the British Army. Few could take this seriously and it fatally undermined the case against Churchill. Only 25 votes went against him, with 475 in favour. Churchill insisted that if people were patient it would come right in the end.[43] Well, victory was achieved in the end, but by the USA and USSR, rather than by Churchill.

Just before this debate the government had lost a by-election in Malden, Essex, in spectacular fashion. There was a 22 per cent swing against the government, and the independent candidate Tom Driberg, a journalist on the *Daily Express*, run by Lord Beaverbrook, took the seat. He argued for government reorganization and more effective assistance to Russia.[44]

CHURCHILL SACKS AUCHINLECK

After the defeat at Tobruk, XXX Corps were withdrawn to a new defensive line at El Alamein. They were joined there by XIII Corps and the two divisions of X Corps, the latter having counterattacked from Mersa Matruh on 27 June, without success, before being withdrawn.[45]

Churchill sacked Auchinleck on 5 August. Having won territory in North Africa he had then lost it to Rommel, and Churchill sacked him largely for this reason, despite his success in the first Battle of El Alamein in July. In fact, at El Alamein he had chosen the natural tactical position to defend, with the Qattara Depression on his left – with its thin crusty surface, which was unable to sustain the weight of armoured vehicles – and the sea on his right. Rommel was at the end of his supply lines and could not outflank the British. Churchill did not understand a defensive battle, yet it was precisely

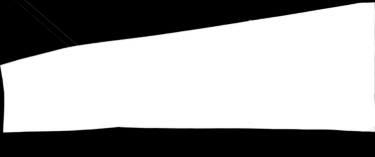

this that was to be the turning point of the desert war. The rot was stopped.

Hiving off the responsibilities of Persia and Iraq from the Middle East Command, Churchill offered this reduced office to Auchinleck, but he turned it down and returned to India. He was unemployed for some time before being re-appointed to his old post of Commander-in-Chief of the Indian Army under Wavell, who had been appointed Viceroy. Churchill appointed General Sir Henry Maitland 'Jumbo' Wilson to the Persia and Iraq Command, and replaced 'the Auk' with General Sir Harold Alexander as head of Middle East Command. Bernard Law Montgomery, 'Monty', then a lieutenant-general, was appointed head of the Eighth Army.[46]

MONTY IN CHARGE

Wisely, Monty resisted Churchill's pressuring for an early assault. Instead he amassed a vast force to attack Rommel in the second Battle of El Alamein, which began on 23 October. The fact that Rommel could not outflank at El Alamein of course meant that Monty could not outflank Rommel either. Operation Lightfoot was thus to be a frontal assault through Rommel's minefields by XXX Corps, under Lieutenant-General Sir Oliver Leese, and XIII Corps, under Lieutenant-General Sir Brian Horrocks, followed by the two armoured divisions of X Corps under Lieutenant-General Sir Herbert Lumsden to exploit a breakthrough. Progress was slow, with counterattacks made by the 15th Panzers at Kidney Ridge, but the Allied victory was helped by the fact that Rommel was unwell and back in Germany, and General Georg Stumme, in command in his absence, died of a heart attack during the battle. When Rommel returned to command the Afrika Korps on 25 October he was furious that they had not counterattacked immediately while Monty's force was negotiating the minefield. At Kidney Ridge fierce fighting took place through 27 and 28 October. Monty, with the offensive faltering, reorganized his forces into a renewed assault, Operation Supercharge, on 2 November. In 24–48 hours the battle was won and the Afrika Korps was in full retreat, pinching its Italian allies' transport to so do. Rommel would be pushed back across North Africa for the last time, and Tripoli finally taken on 23 January. It was a victory that could have been won so long before.[47]

What Monty did, apart from meticulous planning, was simply to hit

Rommel with a bigger club. He insisted from the start on the necessary equipment in the necessary quantities, and this was supplied. He had a quarter of a million men, twice as many as Rommel had at his disposal. If Churchill had seen to it that the North African campaign had received the necessary supplies in the first place, the victories would have come sooner, even without replacing commanders. Pressuring generals into a premature assault and sacking them after yet another failure did not address the underlying reason for those failures.

Monty was able to exercise considerable influence over Churchill, largely because Churchill could not afford to continue to sack generals indefinitely. If victory was to be achieved in North Africa, Monty's requirements for materiel had to be met and not suddenly withdrawn at the crucial moment, as had happened twice before. Monty was promoted to full general and knighted. Churchill had not at first wanted Monty at all, but Major-General William 'Strafer' Gott, but as Gott was killed shortly after Churchill made his decision Monty got the job.[48] Thus, Monty was appointed not because Churchill's prescience enabled him to see how capable a general he was, but because after appointing a series of generals whose results had not come up to his expectations, he arrived at Monty at the end of that line, largely by chance. As the historian Piers Brendon put it, 'Churchill was too egotistical to be a sound judge of men. He was always inclined to mistake picturesqueness for originality, rashness for bravery, glibness for ability, restlessness for energy.'[49]

CHURCHILL PERSUADES THE AMERICANS

When the Americans came into the war, Churchill argued vociferously for prioritizing the war against Germany first – particularly in North Africa – and Japan second. To some extent President Roosevelt and his chiefs of staff were already minded towards a 'Germany First' strategy. Its principal supporters were General George Marshall, the Army Chief of Staff, and Admiral Harold Stark, Chief of Naval Operations (1940–2) and later Naval Commander-in-Chief European Theatre (1942–5). This policy was secretly discussed with the British in January 1941 and was represented in the secret plans, Rainbow 5 and Plan Dog.

The issue of the North African campaign was more ticklish. Given

Roosevelt's naval background, and the fact that Stark was personally more approachable than Marshall, he tended to lean towards the navy's view. The US Navy had enunciated concerns about the possible establishment of German bases in north-west Africa, particularly after the loss of France and its colonial territories in that region. Colonel Frank Knox, the US Navy Secretary, had suggested, albeit as an extreme case, that the USA might occupy one of these bases, at Dakar. Also, there was a joint US Army–Navy memorandum suggesting that the Mediterranean, as well as the Atlantic, was an important part of the European theatre, and that North Africa might constitute a theatre of action. Roosevelt, when in conversation with Clement Attlee, the Deputy Prime Minister, said that he would like to have troops in Algiers.[50]

However, this was no more than a tentative interest. It was far from the commitment Churchill had wanted: namely, the concentration of forces in the Mediterranean, rather than a Second Front in France. More importantly, there were vociferous opponents of the strategy, principally General Marshall and the US Secretary of War, Henry Stimson. They saw the Mediterranean campaign as a peripheral strategy distracting from a necessary direct thrust across the English Channel to France, the Ruhr and the heart of Germany.[51]

It was at the Washington Conference codenamed Arcadia, held from late December 1941 to mid-January 1942, that the matter was seemingly settled. Marshall's attention was distracted from the central issue, as he had to focus on the creation of an integrated command structure for Anglo-American operations. Thus it is perhaps unsurprising that his views were not well represented, and this weakened Stimson's position. The conclusion of Anglo-American discussions resulted in an agreement that:

> . . . in 1942 the main object will be to strengthen the ring [round Germany] by sustaining the Russian front, by aiming and supporting Turkey, by increasing our strength in the Middle East, and by gaining possession of the whole North African coast . . . It does not seem likely that in 1942 any large-scale land offensive against Germany . . . will be possible. In 1943 the way may be clear for a return to the Continent, across the Mediterranean, from Turkey into the Balkans, or by landings in Western Europe.[52]

It is clear that Churchill had got what he wanted: a postponement of any cross-Channel operation, a concentration on the Middle East and particularly North Africa, and when Germany was eventually to be assaulted, maybe this would be undertaken via southern Europe or Turkey.

Although Marshall and Stimson did not get their way at the Arcadia Conference, both understood that the agreement was necessarily provisional and fluid in response to events, particularly in the Pacific and also concerning the help needed by the Russians. So they felt they might get a second bite at the cherry, which indeed they did. The effort to oppose the Japanese advance and supply the Soviets caused a hiatus in preparations for a Mediterranean adventure, and during it Marshall and Stimson put forward proposals for a cross-Channel landing in France during 1942 – Operation Sledgehammer – and a major offensive there in 1943, Operation Roundup. This naturally created a problem for Churchill and the British chiefs of staff, who had their hearts set on a joint North African operation and would be stalwart in their opposition to both Sledgehammer and Roundup. In consequence Churchill sent Vice-Admiral Louis (Dickie) Mountbatten to see Roosevelt in order to prepare a second Washington conference for the summer of 1942.[53]

Mountbatten was a good choice to send to Washington, for unlike other senior British servicemen whose caution, timidity and failure had created a certain prejudice against them in American minds, Mountbatten's lack of caution, indeed his recklessness, conveyed a very different impression to the Americans. Whether they were wise to regard him in this way was another matter. He had been the captain of the destroyer HMS *Kelly*, which had been sunk by the Germans. Mountbatten's biographer Philip Ziegler said that if you could leave skid-marks with a destroyer, Mountbatten would have left them all over the ocean. It was also said of him, 'There is no one I would rather have in a tight corner than Dickie Mountbatten – and no one who would get me into one sooner.'[54]

Mountbatten was head of Combined Operations, responsible for all landings and raids, and this gave him a degree of credibility. He was thus able to see Roosevelt alone, to the discontent of the American chiefs of staff. He pointed out to Roosevelt that at this stage of the war, the American contribution to Operation Sledgehammer would necessarily be small, and the Germans could easily defeat it. Thus, he told Roosevelt, the only practical alternatives were to prepare for Roundup in 1943, reinforce

British forces in the Middle East, attack North Africa, or attack Norway – which, not surprisingly, was Churchill's idea.

Roosevelt had already promised the Soviet Foreign Minister, Vacheslav Molotov, that there would be a Second Front in 1942 to offer relief to the Russians, so merely preparing for Roundup or reinforcing the Middle East was insufficient. This left North Africa or Norway. At this time the possibility of a German breakthrough in the Caucasus and into Egypt seemed real. Also, a Japanese advance into India, eventually leading to a joining up of German and Japanese forces, seemed possible. So North Africa had it. The second Washington Conference in June 1942 was thus ready to produce agreement between Roosevelt and the British on this. Marshall and Stimson, who had previously convinced Roosevelt of the virtues of Sledgehammer, were furious. But events would intervene.[55]

During the conference, Tobruk fell, and not only did this weaken the British position with the Americans but General Sir Alan Brooke, the CIGS, wavered over mounting any major new operation in 1942. One crumb of comfort for Churchill came from the meeting: Admiral Ernest King, the new Chief of US Naval Operations (replacing Admiral Stark) and General Hap Arnold, Commander-in-Chief US Army Air Forces, accepted that a North African operation was feasible from sea and air. Marshall, the army chief, was now isolated. So although the conference ended with an inconclusive result, it still left the door open for North Africa. However, King's position was not what it appeared. He was primarily interested in what was happening in the Pacific, and a North African operation would bleed fewer resources away from there than Sledgehammer or Roundup. It would also appear much more of a British operation, since the British were already fighting there, and it could be argued that the British should be left to get on with it.[56]

With the decision on North Africa still not finally settled, Roosevelt dispatched Marshall and King to London to resolve the matter. With Roosevelt's imperative that there must be some kind of front in 1942 to take the pressure off the Russians, and with Churchill and the British chiefs opposed to Sledgehammer, the choice was between North Africa and Norway. Both the Americans and the British chiefs found no merit in Churchill's pet project of Norway, and so North Africa it was. On 24 July 1942 the American chiefs formerly agreed to go ahead with the British idea. The fact that this decision was taken despite the opposition of Marshall and Stimson, let alone others in the US administration and military, was in the end down to Roosevelt. His predisposition, both for dealing with Germany first and for a Mediterranean operation, overrode the opposition. It was the only time he vetoed Marshall. It was not the wisest of judgments, for the North African campaign not only prevented the speculative adventure of Sledgehammer, it ruled out the much more feasible project of Roundup in 1943, as forces were now to be concentrated in the Mediterranean theatre, rather than built up for a cross-Channel invasion.[57]

THE AMERICANS JOIN THE NORTH AFRICAN CONFLICT

Operation Torch (originally called Gymnast) – the joint assault on North Africa – would have the Americans in the conflict, and with the Soviet Union already in the war, there really would be a 'grand alliance'. Operation Torch was the first jointly planned and executed Anglo-American military operation in the war. But George Marshall and Henry Stimson still believed that an invasion of France was the appropriate way ahead, so that the basic strategy of Torch continued to be questioned at the highest level in the United States. Stimson believed that the whole North Africa operation was designed to put off a Second Front, and pointed out, 'The success of "Torch" depended on a multitude of suppositions – that Spain would remain neutral; that the French would not resist strongly; that the Germans would not seize the African airfields.' The situation was compounded by the fact that French sources had told the Allies that the Germans were aware that an Allied attack on North Africa at Casablanca or Dakar was imminent and were warning the Vichy French to oppose it.[58]

Despite this information, landings were to be made in the French North African countries of Morocco and Algeria before daybreak on 8 November 1942. The victory at El Alamein in the same month constituted an important spur to the operation. The choice of landings, in north-west rather than north-east Africa – closer to German forces – reflected Marshall's concern that Spain might be drawn into the war, and Spain's commanding position over the Straits of Gibraltar risked cutting off American forces in the Mediterranean if they were landed too far east. Thus, ironically, it was Marshall's caution that prolonged the

North African campaign and prejudiced what would have been the decisive Operation Roundup.[59]

In Churchill's mind, the function of Torch was to constitute a stepping-stone to Sicily and thus to Italy. For him this was the 'soft underbelly of Europe', through which Germany could be more readily attacked and defeated than via a Second Front in France. So committed was Churchill to Torch that some of his comments bordered on the wild: 'Torch offers the greatest opportunity in the history of England . . . It is the one thing that is going to win the War.'[60] He was about the only person who thought so. However, consistency didn't impinge on his thinking; in one outburst he insisted, 'We should be able to rip at Hitler's mouth [in France] at the same time as we are ripping at the Axis belly [in the Mediterranean].'[61] In fact, it was precisely the 'mouth' that Churchill wanted to avoid, yet for now, not only should the 'belly' be attacked but the 'mouth' as well! If the problems of attacking the mouth were so great, how could both be attacked simultaneously, with all the problems, not least of logistics, this would incur?

The Americans' vacillation over the precise detail of the plan indicated a weakness in their decision-making procedure, which shows why Churchill was able to influence them so significantly. As Lieutenant-General Mark Clark, who would be deputy commander of Torch, said of his fellow Americans, 'I was getting awfully tired of the mind-changing that kept going on at home. It seemed to me that it showed timidity and uncertainty that might make our African venture more difficult because it would be on too small a scale to encourage quick French assistance.'[62]

THE PROBLEM OF THE FRENCH

Approximately 60,000 French troops were stationed in Morocco, with a modest French fleet at Casablanca. France's North African colonies were under the authority of Vichy, capital of the French collaborationist government, and Torch would require the engagement of the French forces on the Allied side. Initial communications were established by the US Consul in Algiers, Robert Daniel Murphy, followed up by a clandestine meeting in Cherchell, Algeria, when Lieutenant-General Clark was sent by submarine to meet the French on 21 October 1942. It was hoped that General Henri Giraud might attend the meeting, as he appeared to be the most probable candidate to lead the Free French forces and co-operate with the Allies.[63] Murphy indicated that Admiral Jean-François Darlan, a highly placed minister in Philippe Pétain's Vichy government, was considering switching sides and going to Africa with the French fleet. However, Giraud took the view that Darlan could not be trusted as he was a German collaborator and was switching sides opportunistically. Another eminent French figure, General Charles Emmanuel Mast, supported Giraud and not Darlan, arguing that the French forces would support Giraud and that Torch could thus be undertaken without the French firing a shot against the Allies if he were in command. When Clark arrived for the clandestine meeting at Cherchell, it was Mast, with five staff officers, who met him, representing Giraud, to discuss the outline of Torch. The Allies would thus use Giraud as a figurehead to lessen the likelihood of French resistance to Torch.[64]

General Dwight Eisenhower was appointed overall commander of Torch, with Clark as his deputy. The operation was to involve several landings. The Western Task Force of 35,000 troops was to land close to Casablanca on 8 November at Safi, Rabat and Mehdia, under the command of Major-General George S Patton. At Oran the Central Task Force was to land with 18,500 troops under Major-General Lloyd Fredendall. Finally, the Eastern Task Force of 20,000 troops under Major-General Charles Ryder was to land at Algiers. More than 400 ships, 1,000 planes and a total of 107,000 men were deployed in the operation.

Now that the Americans had entered the fray the logistical problems became much worse, as Clark described at length:

> There were unexplained shortages, particularly in spare parts for weapons and motor vehicles. There were whole shiploads of equipment that seemed to get sidetracked in the United States, and, of course, there were the inevitable losses of ships to enemy submarines. One cargo of vitally needed combat equipment for the 1st Division started out three times from New York, and each time was lost or otherwise diverted. There were never enough ships either to supply our needs in the United Kingdom on schedule or to assure that the great mass of supplies essential to the success of the invasion would be kept moving steadily to Africa after our landings.
>
> So confused was the logistical situation that by mid-

September it became obvious that it would be impossible to launch the invasion at the beginning of November.[65]

And yet on 8 November the invasion did in fact take place. Many of these problems would have occurred anyway, but far from the North African campaign making things easier, it compounded the problems.

As the Allied expectation was that French forces would co-operate, it was expected that none of the landings would be opposed; consequently no preliminary bombardment of shore positions was planned. However, French forces did oppose the invasion, in every case but one. French coastal batteries engaged Allied transport ships, and this required the return of fire by Allied warships. Once on land, French sniper fire was encountered and carrier-based strike planes engaged the French forces on the beaches. However, Patton was in Casablanca by the 10th. At Oran, the shallow waters caused damage to the landing craft; French naval forces attacked the landing fleet and had to be engaged by Allied forces. The Americans undertook their first large-scale airborne operation of the war at Oran with the 509th Parachute Regiment. French troops surrendered on 9 November and Algiers was in Allied hands by 6.00pm. Negotiations continued until the 11th before there was an end to French resistance and their co-operation was gained. The fact that the Allies received not support but opposition from the French exposed another basic flaw in Churchill's North African plan. Britain was now fighting its own Allies, never mind the enemy.

More than 150,000 German troops were shifted to Tunisia from Sicily, and they halted the Allied advance before it reached Tunis. Having recovered from his defeat by Monty at El Alamein, Rommel initiated an offensive operation against the Torch forces on 14 February 1943. His aim was to turn the south flank of the British First Army, under Lieutenant-General Sir Kenneth Anderson, and to capture the Allied base near Tebessa.

The Germans inflicted upon the Americans the biggest defeat they had yet suffered, resulting in their retreat via the Kasserine Pass, and advanced nearly 160km (100 miles) before the Allies were able to stop the rot on 22 February. The Germans then withdrew to their starting point, but in early March they initiated a more limited offensive against the British First Army and another against the Eighth. These were repulsed. The Allies then took the initiative with the US II Corps, newly under the command of

Patton, and elements of the Eighth Army. They advanced through Bizerte and Tunis, and concluded the battle on 12 May 1943.

THE CONSEQUENCES

The benefits of the North African and Mediterranean campaigns were modest by comparison with what the Soviets were accomplishing. In North Africa the western Allies held down about 25 German divisions, while the Soviets were holding down 214. The Tunisian campaign yielded some 275,000 German and Italian prisoners; the Soviets took over three million.[66]

It is ironic that Monty eventually took Tripoli: Churchill could have had Tripoli so much earlier under O'Connor, had he not stripped him of forces for yet another ill-fated adventure, the one in Greece. Churchill had made the classic mistake of expecting success too quickly and too easily, and had paid the price with a protracted campaign in a theatre of no strategic importance whatsoever. The result was unnecessary losses, and efforts diverted from the crucial theatres of the war: the Eastern Front, where the Soviets would decisively defeat Hitler, and the strategic bombing campaign plus the Second Front, which was the responsibility of the western Allies, above all Churchill.

As the Allies liberated the French imperial possessions in North Africa from Axis control, a decision was needed as to who would govern them. Roosevelt's candidate was Giraud, but the man who would become the hero of France, Charles de Gaulle, got the job. Roosevelt thought de Gaulle a prima donna and opposed him. Churchill had a difficult relationship with de Gaulle, but was more right about him than Roosevelt, recognizing his outstanding qualities as well as his irritating ones.

When the Tunisian campaign ended in May, Churchill wanted further action in the Mediterranean, while the Americans wanted to undertake a Second Front in France. As chapter 14 will recount, Churchill and the British chiefs would get their way.[67]

11
THE BALKANS:
CHURCHILL'S OBSESSION

The Balkan region was yet another objective of little or no strategic importance, and the consequences of fighting there were dire. Its mountainous terrain, and its history of internecine conflict and political instability, meant that it was another costly campaign. Yugoslavia, Greece and Crete were all lost to the Germans, and Turkey remained neutral until very near the end of the war – despite all Churchill's efforts to bring it in. The Balkan countries were important to Churchill for the same reason that Italy was: he believed that Germany could be defeated by an assault through 'the soft underbelly of Europe'. His obsession was fuelled further by his romantic rhetoric about Greece being the cradle of democracy. However, these campaigns only helped to delay the inevitable and necessary Second Front – the cross-Channel invasion of France.

GREECE

The modern state of Greece, with its rich heritage drawn from ancient Greece and the Byzantine Empire, had been founded as an independent state in the 1820s after nearly four centuries of Ottoman rule. From 1935 Greece was ruled by King George II, who was greatly concerned at the prospect of a Communist-inspired coup, and so appointed the Minister of War, General Ioannis Metaxas, as Prime Minister in 1936. Metaxas would take on dictatorial powers.

The Italians were the first to invade Greece. On 28 October 1940 they gave an ultimatum to the Greeks, but Metaxas famously rejected it with the single word *Oxi* ('No'). The Italian invasion was mounted with forces drawn from its occupation of Albania. Mussolini had been keen to demonstrate to Hitler that Italy was a worthy Axis partner and so had occupied Albania in 1939. Lieutenant-General Alexander Papagos was the Greek Chief of the General Staff, and despite the fact that the Italian and Greek forces were evenly matched in numbers, under his stewardship the Greek forces defeated the Italian advance. The Greeks not only expelled the Italians from their homeland but within two months had pursued them into Albania. The Italians counterattacked on 9 March 1941 but were defeated within a week.

On 10 January 1941 Churchill wrote to the head of Middle East Command, General Sir Archibald Wavell: 'Destruction of Greece will eclipse victories you have gained in Libya, and may affect decisively Turkish attitude, especially if we have shown ourselves callous of fate of allies.'[1] So Greece was to be defended for reasons that included its effect on Turkey and other small, no doubt noble, nations – none of which had any central strategic significance for the defeat of Germany.

TURKEY

The Republic of Turkey was created out of the dissolution of the Ottoman Empire in the aftermath of World War I by Mustafa Kemal Pasha, better known as Mustafa Kemal Atatürk ('Father of the Turks'), who became its first President. After his death in 1938, Mustafa Ismet Inönü replaced him as President.

Just as with Gallipoli in World War I, Churchill wanted an adventure in Turkey during World War II. In 1939 Hitler had sent Count Franz von Papen, a former German Chancellor, as his ambassador to Turkey to try to influence the Turks to join the Axis powers. President Roosevelt and Joseph Stalin, like Churchill, favoured Turkey entering the war on the Allied side, and given Churchill's belief in Turkey as strategically important to the Soviet Union, he was keen to push the issue with Stalin.[2] Churchill wrote to him on 21 September 1941: 'It seems to me that the most speedy and effective help would come if Turkey could be induced to resist a German demand for the passage of troops, or better still, if she would enter the war on our side. You will, I am sure, attach due weight to this.'[3] More than a year later Churchill was still at it; he wrote again to Stalin on 24 November 1942:

> It seems to me that we ought all of us to make a new intense
> effort to make Turkey enter the war on our side in the
> spring . . . If we could get Turkey into the war, we could not

only proceed with operations designed to open a shipping route to your left flank on the Black Sea, but we could also bomb heavily from Turkish bases the Rumanian oil fields which are of such vital importance to the Axis.[4]

The following day Churchill wrote to the chiefs of staff: 'A supreme and prolonged effort must be made to bring Turkey into the war in the spring.'[5] But this did not happen the following spring or even the following Christmas. Churchill and Roosevelt conferred with President Inönü during the second Cairo Conference, codenamed Sextant, in December 1943, but Inönü wouldn't commit.[6] It was not until 23 February 1945, when the war was virtually won, that he finally brought Turkey into the war on the Allied side, largely because of concerns about the post-war threat the Soviet Union posed to Turkey. Thus, after the war Turkey joined the United Nations and, most pointedly, the North Atlantic Treaty Organization (NATO), to gain American protection against the Soviets.

YUGOSLAVIA

Yugoslavia had been created out of the collapse of the Ottoman and Habsburg Empires after the end of World War I. It was a federation of Serbs, Croats and Slovenes under a constitutional monarchy, and was thus potentially unstable from the outset. It had begun to disintegrate after the assassination of King Alexander in 1934, after which it became a regency under Prince Paul, because the new monarch, King Peter II, was still a child.

Yugoslavia had developed relationships with France and Czechoslovakia, but it attempted to remain neutral in the coming hostilities. However, following the *Anschluss*, Hitler attempted to persuade Yugoslavia to ally itself with Germany. The Yugoslavs were all too aware of the fate of France and consequently, on 11 December 1940, they signed a 'Friendship Treaty' with Germany – something short of a pact. Hitler met the Yugoslav Prime Minister, Dr Dragiša Cvetkovic, on 14 February 1941, impressing him with Germany's military capability and its closeness to the Soviet Union (though Germany would soon invade the Soviet Union), but failing initially to persuade him to sign the Tripartite Pact between Germany, Italy and Japan. The following day, Churchill attempted to persuade Prince Paul to resist the overtures from Hitler, but this was to no avail.

On 1 March Bulgaria signed the Tripartite Pact and German forces were deployed along the border with Serbia. With this direct threat upon his border, Cvetkovic finally signed the Tripartite Pact in Vienna on 25 March 1941. A coup two days later resulted in the overthrow of the Council of Regency, deposing Prince Paul. There were some local demonstrations in support of this change. Now King Peter II, just 17 years of age, was served by a new government under the Chief of Staff of the Air Force, General Dušan Simovic.[7]

Churchill wrote to President Inönü of Turkey on 27 March 1941: 'The dramatic events which are occurring in Belgrade and throughout Yugoslavia may offer the best chance of preventing the German invasion of the Balkan peninsula.'[8] However, precisely the opposite was to occur. The coup precipitated the very thing Churchill did not want: Hitler issued 'Directive No 25', the plan for the invasion of Yugoslavia and Greece. This risked delaying Barbarossa – the invasion of the Soviet Union – the very action that would ultimately result in the defeat of Germany.

CHURCHILL'S BALKAN STRATEGY

In *The Second World War* Churchill wrote:

> Our limited hope was to stir and organise united action.
> If at the wave of our wand Yugoslavia, Greece and Turkey
> would all act together, it seemed to us that Hitler might
> either let the Balkans off for the time being or become so
> heavily engaged with our combined forces as to create a
> major front in that theatre.[9]

Yet France had been defeated despite the fact that its armed forces, augmented by the British Expeditionary Force, were large by comparison with those of the small Balkan countries. Thus it seems naive to have supposed that Hitler would balk at attacking these small nations, particularly given the logistical problems that Britain faced trying to help them – problems it had not faced when fighting in France in 1940.

Churchill wrote to his Foreign Secretary, Anthony Eden, on 20 February 1941, prior to a visit Eden and the CIGS were to make to Athens: 'Do not consider yourselves obligated to a Greek Enterprise if in your hearts you feel it will only be another Norwegian fiasco.'[10] But 'another Norwegian fiasco' it was going to be.

British forces were deployed to support Greece directly, in Operation Lustre, in March and April 1941. In a message to Eden on 28 March Churchill commented: 'Together, Yugoslavia, Greece, Turkey, and ourselves have seventy divisions mobilised in this theatre. Germans have not yet got more than thirty.'[11] And in a cable to the Australian (acting) Prime Minister, Sir Arthur Fadden, on 30 March, he wrote, '. . . we may cherish renewed hopes of forming a Balkan front with Turkey . . . This is of course by no means certain yet. But even now it puts "Lustre" in its true setting, not an isolated military act, but as a prime mover in a large design . . . Result unknowable . . .'[12] Despite this apparent Allied superiority in armed forces, and the 'large design', there was no successful policy to organize and co-ordinate the forces of these nations, and the Germans would enjoy a quick victory. This consequence was certainly 'knowable', at least to Hitler. Like Churchill, Eden claimed that the consequences of the policy 'could not be foreseen';[13] in other words he hoped it might have beneficial consequences but in reality the outcome of the policy had never been thought through.

In *The Second World War,* Churchill wrote that Generalfeldmarschall Wilhelm Keitel, in his evidence to the Nuremberg Trials after the war, 'confirms our view that the greatest danger to Germany was "an attack upon the Italian Army from the rear."'[14] He then wrote, 'There was however open to Yugoslavia the chance . . . of striking a deadly blow to the naked rear of the disorganised Italian armies in Albania.'[15] Even writing years after the events, Churchill still did not realize that the Italians were never important to the outcome of World War II. Also, the Balkan countries had limited capacity to perform this function, and partly because of the logistical problems, Britain could not and did not help them defeat Germany via this route either. In a letter to the Yugoslav Prime Minister, Dušan Simovic, just two days before the German invasion, Churchill wrote, 'The one supreme stroke for victory and safety is to win a decisive forestalling victory in Albania, and collect the masses of equipment that would fall into your hands.'[16] Had the Yugoslavs taken Churchill's advice, they would been undertaking this task in Albania, in the south-west, while the Germans invaded from Bulgaria, in the south-east.

In *The Second World War* Churchill admitted the logistical problems faced by Britain in offering support to Greece:

> On 4 March Admiral Cunningham left us in no doubt as to the considerable naval risks in the Mediterranean which were involved in the move of the Army and the Royal Air Force to Greece. This meant continuous convoys of men, stores and vehicles for the next two months. Destroyers in particular would have to be very heavily worked, and fighter and anti-aircraft defence would be very weak for some time to come. If the Germans started an air offensive from Bulgaria we must expect losses in the convoys both at sea and at their ports of disembarkation. Nor could we rule out surface action by the Italian Fleet. This could be met by our battleships based at Suda Bay in Crete, but only at the expense of weakening the destroyer escort for the convoys and leaving the supply line to Cyrenaica [Libya] practically unprotected. All this in its turn would increase the strain on Malta. The vulnerability of the Suez Canal to magnetic and acoustic mines gave cause for much anxiety just when these big movements of troops and convoys were starting. All offensive plans, including the combined operations against Rhodes, must, the Admiral said, be postponed. His resources would be taxed to the limit . . .[17]

Although despite all this Cunningham would assent to the plan, the logistical problems were a nightmare by comparison with those of the BEF in France the previous year, which had ended in the debacle of Dunkirk.

By early March 1941 the folly of the proposed campaign to support the Greeks was becoming evident to the chiefs of staff, as the situation in Greece deteriorated. Churchill himself admitted this in *The Second World War*. Of the chiefs he wrote:

> They first emphasised the main changes in the situation: the depression of the Greek Commander-in-Chief; the omission

of the Greeks to carry out their undertaking of twelve days earlier to withdraw their troops to the line we should have to hold if Yugoslavia did not come in; the fact that thirty-five Greek battalions were to have helped us hold this line, and that now there were to be only twenty-three at most, all newly formed, untried in battle, and lacking in artillery. In addition it had been expected that the Greeks would be able to withdraw some divisions from the Albanian front. 'General Papagos now says that this cannot be done, as they are exhausted and outnumbered.'

Turning to our own difficulties, the Chiefs of Staff pointed out that they had always expected that Rhodes would be captured before or simultaneously with, the move to Greece; instead, this could not now be done till the move was over. This would mean that instead of our being able to concentrate our air forces against the German advance we should now have to conduct 'considerable' air operations against Rhodes in order to protect our lines of communication to Greece. Finally, the Suez Canal was for the moment completely blocked by mines, and was not expected to be cleared until March 11. Half the ships carrying motor transport were north of the Canal and all the personnel ships south of it.[18]

Clearly this was a policy in serious trouble, and its consequences to the Allied war effort would not be long in coming. However, consistency of argument did not trouble Churchill. In a letter to Eden on 6 March 1941 he wrote: 'Loss of Greece and Balkans by no means a major catastrophe for us, provided Turkey remains honest neutral.'[19] Churchill's belief that Turkey was pivotal in the war, as he had believed in World War I, would continue to distract attention from the genuinely important matters. But his comment that Greece and the Balkans were not pivotal was both correct and yet contradicted by his policy of trying to defend them.

But much worse than this, with a German invasion of Greece anticipated by the Allies, Churchill diverted much of Wavell's XIII Corps from North Africa to Greece, and by so doing halted an Allied advance in North Africa that could have defeated the Axis powers there, as we saw in chapter 10.[20] The strategy was in vain, however, as by the end of April the Germans would have successfully occupied both the Greek mainland and most of the Greek islands, as well as Yugoslavia.

THE GERMANS INVADE

The German invasion of Greece and Yugoslavia simultaneously, Operation Marita, started on 6 April 1941. It was led by Generaloberst Paul von Kleist commanding 1st Panzer Group. The German forces had moved from Bulgaria to mount the initial attack against Greek positions at the 'Metaxas Line', which consisted of 19 fortified positions in Eastern Macedonia plus two in Western Thrace. The 2nd Panzer Division launched an assault from the Strumica Valley in Bulgaria into Yugoslavia, turning south to follow the Vardar/Axios River and thus bypassing the Yugoslav defensive positions and capturing the port of Thessalonika on 9 April. The Greek forts in Eastern Macedonia were thereby cut off, and the forces occupying them wanted to surrender as a result. On 10 April they received permission from the Greek High Command, and the surrender was duely concluded. On the same day German forces moved from Yugoslavia into Western Macedonia. The Germans faced two divisions and one armoured brigade of Commonwealth forces plus two Greek divisions, and on 11–12 April defeated them.

On 11 April, Italian and Hungarian Army divisions joined the Germans in the assault on Yugoslavia. Generaloberst von Kleist took the Yugoslav surrender the following day, and two days later King Peter II fled with British help. An armistice was signed in Belgrade on the 17th by the Foreign Minister, Dr Aleksander Cincar-Markovic, and representatives of the various regions of Yugoslavia. Fewer than 200 Germans died in the Yugoslavian campaign.

As German forces pursued the British southwards, 14 divisions of the Greek Army, which were engaged with the Italians in Albania, were now threatened from the rear. The Greeks felt increasingly compromised and by 23 April they were obliged to capitulate despite the Greek High Command's desire for Greek forces to cover the British retreat. King George II of Greece and his government embarked for Crete.

Meanwhile, the Commonwealth forces made a last ditch effort at Thermopylae, but were then forced to retreat to the ports of the Peloponnese.

German forces were in Athens on 27 April and occupied all mainland Greece and many of the Greek islands within a few days. The Allied retreat had been rushed, with German forces harrying them, and the Royal Navy was obliged to conduct the withdrawal in chaotic fashion – it was another 'Dunkirk'. Many of the Allied troops were deposited on the island of Crete, augmenting the 14,000-strong garrison there. All Churchill could say in *The Second World War* was, 'Through no fault of ours we had failed.'[21]

CRETE IS NEXT

On 25 April Hiter issued Directive No 28, to invade and occupy Crete. At Churchill's insistence, on 9 May, Wavell reinforced Crete with six infantry tanks and 15 light tanks (equipped with machine guns only).[22] This penny packet shipment of largely inferior tanks was entirely insufficient. The German invasion, Operation Mercury, occurred on 20 May 1941.

The general in charge of Allied forces on Crete was a New Zealander, Bernard Freyberg. Churchill had appointed him as he was a personal friend: they had known each other since World War I. Despite having won a Victoria Cross in World War I, Freyberg's tenure in this command was not to be a happy one. The Allies, including Freyberg himself, assumed that the Germans would undertake a seaborne assault; however, Crete was invaded by German paratroopers, the 7th Flieger Division, under Generaloberst Kurt Student. It was the largest-scale airborne attack undertaken by the Germans in World War II.

The fundamental failure to provide adequate air defence was something Churchill admitted in *The Second World War*: 'But of course it was only our weakness in the air that rendered the German attack possible. The R.A.F. strength early in May was twelve Blenheims, six Hurricanes, twelve Gladiators, and six Fulmars and Brewsters of the Fleet Air Arm, of which only one half were serviceable.'[23] It was rather appropriate that aircraft with the name 'Blenheim' were deployed in this theatre, named as they were after the great victory by Churchill's ancestor, the 1st Duke of Marlborough. However, this lightly armed, militarized version of a civilian transport aeroplane had already proved hopelessly vulnerable to Luftwaffe attack. The Gladiators were biplanes and entirely obsolete. The Fulmars were a navalized version of the RAF's Fairey Battles, which had been annihilated by the Luftwaffe in the Battle of France. The Brewsters were modest Australian aircraft. Only the Hurricanes were state-of-the-art, but there were only six of them – when they were serviceable.

German assaults were made against Crete's three principal airfields in the north, at Maleme, Rethimnon and Heraklion. Effective resistance was encountered from British, ANZAC and Greek forces, plus local civilians, and the German invasion came precious close to failure: by the end of the first day German forces had failed to accomplish any of their objectives and had endured approximately 4,000 casualties. Only the vigorous intervention of Student produced victory for the Germans. Over the following day, poor Allied communication and a failure to grasp the situation helped the Germans to occupy the airfield at Maleme. Student used this facility to bring in several thousand additional troops and so occupied the western part of Crete. The scale of German reinforcement caused disillusionment among the Allies, and once again the Royal Navy was obliged to conduct a withdrawal over the four nights of 28–31 May – yet another evacuation! Approximately 17,000 troops were successfully withdrawn. However, more than 5,000 British and Imperial forces remained on the island, variously to surrender or to survive as best they could. Some were protected by Greek villagers, who suffered at the hands of the Germans in consequence.[24]

The Royal Navy suffered very significant losses in Cretan waters at the hands of the Luftwaffe. It was during this operation that Lord Louis Mountbatten, then captain of the destroyer *Kelly*, had his ship sunk by dive-bomber attack (he survived unscathed). In *The Second World War* Churchill wrote:

> Thus in the fighting of May 22 and 23 the Navy had lost two cruisers and three destroyers sunk, one battleship, the *Warspite*, put out of action for a long time, and the *Valiant* and many other units considerably damaged. Nevertheless the sea-guard of Crete had been maintained. The Navy had not failed. Not a single German landed in Crete from the sea until the battle for the island was ended.[25]

But the Germans did not need to land forces from the sea to take the island – and take it they did. It was another humiliating defeat for the British, though they had been, at one point, quite close to victory. After this successful invasion by German paratroopers, Churchill would again come to the wrong conclusion: he now wanted the British to have paratroopers. But the Cretan experience, with the heavy casualties endured by the elite 7th Flieger Division, enabled Hitler to see how vulnerable paratrooper operations were, and he thus forbade such operations in the future. Student called Crete a 'disastrous victory' and 'the graveyard of the German paratroopers'. Hitler's judgment would be borne out by the catastrophic failure of Operation Market Garden at Arnhem in Holland in 1944, where British, American and Polish paratroopers suffered so much: Major-General Robert 'Roy' Urquhart, commander of the British Airborne Division, went into Arnhem with 10,000 paratroopers, and ended up with fewer than 2,000.

THE DODECANESE

It was in October 1942 that Churchill first envisaged an operation to occupy the Dodecanese Islands in the Aegean: principally Rhodes, Kos, Samos and Leros, which had been controlled by the Italians. He also wanted to reoccupy Crete. The purpose was to deny these islands to German use, employ them as forward bases from which to mount further operations in the Balkans and encourage Turkey to join the Allies in the war. This would create a route through the Dardanelles to supply Russia, rather than via the Arctic. So it was a prelude to Gallipolli all over again!

In January 1943 at the Casablanca Conference, codenamed Symbol, the Americans initially assented to Churchill's plan, and on 27 January he asked the military brass to develop detailed plans for Operation Accolade. An attack on Rhodes was planned with three infantry divisions plus an armoured brigade; however Crete, occupied by the Germans, was deemed too heavily fortified to assault, so plans for it did not proceed. Air cover was a problem: the Germans had plenty of it with the Luftwaffe's X Fliegerkorps, whereas Allied air bases were far away in Cyprus and the Middle East. Also the invasion of Sicily (Operation Husky) was already under way, to be followed by the invasion of Italy (see chapter 14), and this competed for resources.

As the Italian surrender loomed, and so seemingly a split with Germany, Accolade was scaled down. It was now to be based on the 8th Indian Division, and hoped-for air cover from American-supplied Lockeed

P-38 Lightning long-range twin-engine fighters. However, at the Quebec Conference, codenamed Quadrant, in August, the Americans put their foot down, seeing this as another harebrained scheme that distracted from more important operations and diverted men and materiel away from them. The Americans said the British would have to go it alone.

Hitler anticipated the Italian surrender and moved forces to occupy the islands, principally from Greece, notably the Sturmdivision Rhodos of 7,500 officers and men under Generalleutnant Ulrich Kleemann. On 9 September 1943 Lord Jellicoe, at the head of a British delegation, was parachuted into Rhodes, the principal island, in an attempt to persuade the Italian commander, Admiral Inigo Campioni, and the 40,000-strong garrison to join the Allies. However, the same day Kleemann attacked, forcing an Italian surrender two days later.

Despite this catastrophe Churchill pressed ahead with the occupation of Kos, Samos and Leros. With the 234th Infantry Brigade shipped in from Malta under Major-General FGR Brittorous, these and smaller islands in the group were occupied between 10–17 September. The German response was swift: by 19 September many of the smaller islands were in German hands, and four days later the German 22nd Infantry Division under Generalleutnant Friedrich-Wilhelm Müller, based in Crete, was given orders to wrest Kos and Leros from British control. The only airfield on Kos held by the British was already being bombed by the Luftwaffe on 18 September, and on 3 October the Germans mounted an opposed landing jointly by sea and air – Operation Polar Bear. German forces reached the capital the same day, and the British withdrew from the island. Meanwhile, aerial bombardment of Leros from 26 September was the prelude to a German assault by Müller on the island on 12 November, Operation Typhoon, which was followed by the British surrender four days later.

As ever, Churchill would get an idea into his head about the vital and overriding importance of some objective with little or no strategic significance and worry it like a dog with a bone until he drove those around him to distraction. He would not give up Rhodes even if the Germans did now occupy it, and did not seem concerned about the effect on the operations being conducted simultaneously in Italy. Sir Alan Brooke, the CIGS, recorded on 6 October 1943: 'PM by now determined to go for Rhodes without looking at the effects on Italy or at any rate refusing to look the implications square in the face.' And the following day he noted:

Another day of Rhodes madness . . . The same arguments brought up again and again! . . . He next broke the news to me that on Saturday (today being Thursday evening 11 pm) I was to start with him for a conference in Tunis!! and that we should come back on Tuesday!! This is all to decide whether we should try and take Rhodes which he has set his heart on! He is in a very dangerous condition, most unbalanced, and God knows how we shall finish this war if this goes on.

On the day after that Brooke picked up the theme again:

I am slowly becoming convinced that in his old age Winston is becoming less and less well balanced! I can control him no more. He has worked himself into a frenzy of excitement about the Rhodes attack, has magnified its importance so that he can no longer see anything else and has set his heart on capturing this one island even at the expense of endangering his relations with the President and with the Americans, and also the whole future of the Italian campaign. He refuses to listen to any arguments or to see any dangers! He wired to the President asking for Marshall to come out to the Mediterranean for a conference in Tunis to settle the matter, hoping in his heart to be able to swing the meeting by his personality. However, the President sent him back a very cold reply asking him not to influence operations in the Mediterranean. This did not satisfy him and he wired back again asking [the] President to reconsider the matter. The whole thing is sheer madness, and he is placing himself quite unnecessarily in a very false position! The Americans are already desperately suspicious of him, and he will make matters far worse.

Meanwhile it is nearly midnight Friday and we none of us yet know whether we are to start for Tunis tomorrow or not! It is quite maddening and all most futile, but the worst of the whole matter is that I am afraid matters will go on deteriorating rather than improving. If they do I shall not be able to stick it much longer![26]

Brooke later added in retrospect, 'It should be remembered that the Americans always suspected Winston of having concealed desires to spread into the Balkans. These fears were not entirely ungrounded! They were determined that whatever happened they would not be led into the Balkans. At times I think that they imagined I supported Winston's Balkan ambitions, which was far from being the case.'[27] He recorded in his diary for 18 November 1943:

> He [Churchill] is inclined to say to the Americans, all right if you won't play with us in the Mediterranean we won't play with you in the English Channel. And if they say all right well then we shall direct our main effort in the Pacific, to reply you are welcome to do so if you wish! I do not think that such tactics will pay . . . There are times when I feel that it is all a horrid nightmare which I must wake up out of soon. All this floundering about, this lack of clear vision, and lack of vision! PM examining war by theatres and without perspective, no clear appreciation of the influence of one theatre on another! Then he discusses Command and Commanders and has never yet gained a true grasp of Higher Command organization and what it means.[28]

Retrospectively he added:

> First of all the new feelings of spitefulness which had been apparent lately with Winston since the strength of the American forces were now building up fast and exceeding ours. He hated having to give up the position of the dominant partner which we held at the start. As a result he became inclined at times to put up strategic proposals which he knew were unsound purely to spite the Americans. He was in fact 'cutting off his nose to spite his face'. It was usually fairly easy to swing him back on the right line and to get rid of these whims. There lay, however, in the back of his mind the desire to form a purely British theatre when the laurels would be all ours . . . Austria or the Balkans seemed to attract him for such a front.

Winston's views on command always remained confused throughout the war. He could not or would not follow how a chain of command was applied. He was always wanting a Commander-in-Chief to suddenly vacate his post and concentrate on commanding one individual element of his command at the expense of all the rest.[29]

As ever, the Americans did not see the virtue of the Balkan operations. While Roosevelt was on his way to meet Churchill for the Sextant Conference in Cairo in November 1943, the President complained about 'chaotic conditions developing in the Balkans', where it appeared that resistance groups were more interested in fighting each other than the Germans.[30]

Churchill's operation for the Dodecanese had lasted from 8 September to 22 November 1943. The result was catastrophic, with huge naval as well as military losses. It was a complete defeat for the British and the last major German victory of World War II. Once again it was Churchill's preoccupation with the Balkans and with Turkey that constituted the problem. But the tide was turning: not only between the Allied and Axis powers, but between Churchill and Roosevelt. The American President listened to Churchill less and less.

THE COMMUNIST INFLUENCE

Churchill minuted to Eden on 4 May 1944, '. . . broadly speaking the issue is: are we going to acquiesce in the Communisation of the Balkans . . .?'[31] In terms of Yugoslavia, Churchill's policy had helped in accomplishing precisely that. From 1943 Churchill had supported the Communist Marshal Josip Broz Tito and his partisans, or National Liberation Movement, over non-Communist groups. They most certainly helped in fighting the Germans, as did non-Communists, but Churchill's support enabled them to take control of Yugoslavia after the war. Now, Churchill would help bring about Communism in Romania.

In *The Second World War* he wrote, 'On May 18 the Soviet Ambassador in London called at the Foreign Office to discuss a general suggestion which Mr. Eden had made that the U.S.S.R. should temporarily regard

Romanian affairs as mainly their concern under war conditions while leaving Greece to us.'[32] The Russians, of course, were delighted to hear this, but only if Washington agreed. When Churchill subsequently consulted Washington – having failed to do so at the outset – Cordell Hull, the Secretary of State, was concerned about anything that 'might appear to savour of the creation or acceptance of the idea of spheres of influence'. Churchill would attempt to deny any attempt to create such spheres in a letter to Lord Halifax – then Ambassador to Washington – on 8 June.[33] But this is precisely what it was, and the Soviets had no intention of restricting this influence only to 'war conditions'. Like a naughty schoolboy, Churchill tried to retrieve the situation in a communication to Stalin on 11 July:

> Some weeks ago it was suggested by Eden to your Ambassador that the Soviet Government should take the lead in Roumania, and the British should do the same in Greece. This was only a working arrangement to avoid as much as possible the awful business of triangular telegrams, which paralyses action. Molotov [the Soviet Foreign Minister] then suggested very properly that I should tell the United States, which I did, and always meant to . . .[34]

Churchill's attitude to the Communists in Greece would be decidedly at variance with his attitude towards them in Romania and Yugoslavia. By the end of August 1944 he had asked Brooke to devise a plan to take Greece in the event of a German withdrawal. Operation Manna would be commanded by Lieutenant-General Sir Ronald Scobie. As German troops were withdrawn from Greece, British forces moved in. However, the Communist organization, the Greek National Liberation Front (EAM) and its military wing, the People's Army of Liberation (ELAS), wanted to fill the political power vacuum. Churchill wrote to Scobie on 5 December:

> You are responsible for maintaining order in Athens and for neutralising or destroying all E.A.M.–E.L.A.S. bands approaching the city. You may make any regulations you like for the strict control of the streets or for the rounding up of

any number of truculent persons. Naturally E.L.A.S. will try to
put women and children in the van where shooting may occur.
You must be clever about this and avoid mistakes. But do not
hesitate to fire at any armed male in Athens who assails the
British authority or Greek authority with which we are
working . . . Do not hesitate to act as if you were in a
conquered city where a local rebellion is in progress . . .
We have to hold and dominate Athens. It would be a great
thing for you to succeed in this without bloodshed if
possible, but also with bloodshed if necessary.[35]

This communication, was routinely copied to the American Ambassador in
Rome, and thence it went to the State Department in Washington. It seems
that the American government leaked it to the press. What appeared to be a
reactionary quasi-colonialist policy caused a whole swathe of criticism both
in the United States and in Britain.[36]

Tito, not content with creating a Communist regime in Yugoslavia,
wanted to annex the city of Trieste and the entire region of Istria,
part of which had been Italian before the war. He and his forces hoped to
take Trieste before the British and Americans had secured it, and indeed he
would enter the city on 30 April 1945. Tito also hoped that the remaining
7,000 German troops would surrender to him and that he would thus
acquire their equipment. However, on 2 May, Allied forces, General Sir
Bernard Freyberg's New Zealanders entered the city and took the German
surrender themselves. Three days later, Field Marshal Sir Harold Alexander,
who was responsible for ground forces in Italy, sent a telegram to Churchill:

Tito . . . now finds himself in a much stronger military
position than he foresaw when I was in Belgrade. He hoped to
step into Trieste when finally I stepped out. Now he wants to
be installed there and only allow me user's right.

We must bear in mind that since our meeting he has been
to Moscow. I believe he will hold to our original agreement if
he can be assured that when I no longer require Trieste as a
base for my forces in Austria he will be allowed to incorporate
it in his New Yugoslavia.

In his reply the following day Churchill wrote, 'Tito, backed by Russia, will push hard . . .'[37] And he admitted in *The Second World War*: 'If Tito succeeded he would probably claim parts of South Austria, Hungary and Greece . . . to engage in uncontrolled-land grabbing or tactics which were all too reminiscent of Hitler and Japan.'[38]

So Tito, whom Churchill had supported, was now in league with the Soviets, trying very hard to augment Yugoslav territory, and was to be compared with the totalitarians who had run Germany and Japan. In fact, Tito he succeeded in annexing the entire region of Istria, including the Italian part. After the war most of the Italian population of Istria would leave to escape repression by Tito's Communist regime.

Churchill did not have quite as much prescience about the looming threat from the Soviet Union as the myth gives him credit for. In 1942 he wrote to President Roosevelt: 'The balance of power [at the end of the war] will favour the Anglo-Americans, and the Russians will require our help more than we theirs.'[39] But by the later stages of the war, when Soviet hegemony in Eastern Europe was becoming obvious to anyone who was focused on these events, he did become concerned and strove to persuade the Americans of the virtue of containing the Soviets by advancing through the Balkans. At first he believed that the Dodecanese were the key to this; later he thought that the Italian campaign could facilitate it via the Ljubljana Gap, or by landing troops on the Adriatic to enable the western Allies to invade what would shortly become the Soviet satellite states of Central and Eastern Europe.[40] The difficulties with this strategy were the considerable logistical problems already seen in the earlier Balkan adventures, and that it would have drained away essential forces required for the defeat of Germany via the Second Front. Churchill wanted to protect Greece, Crete, Yugoslavia and Austria from Soviet hegemony after the war. Despite the failure of the Dodecanese campaign, Greece, Crete and Austria did not become Soviet satellite states, although Yugoslavia was not fully integrated into the Soviet system and was reasonably open to the West.

CHURCHILL'S POST-HOC JUSTIFICATION

In *The Second World War* Churchill posited a revisionist exposition of the Balkan conflict in order to try to justify his actions. He wrote:

> If Hitler had been able, with hardly any fighting, to bring
> Greece to her knees and the whole of the Balkans into his
> system and then force Turkey to allow the passage of his
> armies to the south and east, might he not have made terms
> with the Soviets upon the conquest and partition of these vast
> regions and postponed his ultimate, inevitable quarrel with
> them to a later part of his programme? Or, is it more likely,
> would he not have been able to attack Russia in greater
> strength at an earlier date?[41]

Regarding the first point, Hitler *did* bring 'Greece to her knees' – 'with hardly any fighting'. As for Hitler conquering the 'whole of the Balkans', he took as much of it as he wanted and would have taken Turkey had he had the same fetish for it as Churchill had. Hitler could have carved up the Balkans with Russia as part of the Molotov–Ribbentrop Pact, just as he did with Eastern Europe. In which case Churchill's actions would have been irrelevant, for, as with Poland in 1939, the Germans and Russians could have carved up the Balkans without any hope of British intervention preventing it. Could Hitler have attacked Russia earlier than he did by taking the Balkans? Unlike Churchill, Hitler wanted to do the logical thing of attacking Russia directly, not via a circuitous route through the Balkans in the way Churchill had tried and failed to defeat Germany via Turkey in World War I. Hitler had amassed sufficient forces in place to assault Russia.

Churchill was motivated to support the Balkan campaign because of his romance with the role of Greece in developing democratic government in antiquity, and, more importantly because the Balkan strategy was consistent with his 'soft underbelly' theory. At the end of the war, the Balkan countries thanked Churchill for his attempts to liberate them. Yet they would have thanked him more had the war ended a year earlier because forces had been used in a Second Front in France in 1943, rather than squandered in Churchill's dispersionist campaign in the Mediterranean. The only way to defeat Germany was via the Soviet advance on the Eastern Front, combined with the Second Front undertaken by the western Allies. Had the latter occurred in 1943 in place of the dispersionist campaign, Axis forces occupying the Balkan countries would then have capitulated at the end of the war, as actually occurred with those occupying Norway and Denmark. The whole Allied Balkan campaign was thus wasteful.

12
DIEPPE:
CHURCHILL'S FOLLY

In sanctioning the Dieppe raid on 19 August 1942, Churchill broke his rule of attacking targets of no strategic importance. Dieppe was unquestionably strategically important, but the raid was deeply ill considered, with insufficient forces marshalled against a well-defended target and a shingle beach on which tank tracks lacked purchase and quickly malfunctioned. There was a withdrawal within five hours, and two-thirds of the men were left dead, wounded or in captivity.

It was (acting) Vice-Admiral Lord Louis Mountbatten, who on Churchill's instructions had replaced Admiral of the Fleet Sir Roger Keyes as Chief of Combined Operations, who had responsibility for planning the raid. Operation Rutter, later renamed Jubilee, was to be a hit-and-run raid on the port of Dieppe on the north-west coast of France. Churchill had sanctioned a small raid on the French coast before: shortly after Dunkirk, and the day after Hitler signed the armistice with the French in June 1940, 120 commandos had spent a short time ashore, with very limited results. When they returned to England they were mistakenly arrested as deserters and spent a night in jail.[1]

Operation Rutter was in response to the Soviet Union's demand that the western Allies should launch a Second Front to relieve its armies in the east, and a response to American demands for direct action against Germany in 1942. Congressional elections were scheduled for November, and the Roosevelt administration might have had difficulty carrying the 'Germany First' policy with the US electorate without some direct action. Yet this raid would not be a proper lodgement on the French coast, which could assist the Russians by siphoning off substantial German forces from the Eastern Front; its objectives were much more limited, largely confined to information gathering. The Luftwaffe aerodrome was to be searched for papers, as were the barracks, the coastguard facility, the Palais de Justice, the post office, the railway station, a dozen hotels and the prison. French prisoners were to be released from the latter at the same time. A list of telephone subscribers was to be obtained, as were samples of French bread![2]

The Dieppe raid was referred to by some officials as the greatest 'return ticket' operation of the period.[3] This was an unfortunate phrase, for so many were unable to avail themselves of the return portion of the ticket. It actually turned out to be a massive sacrifice of Allied servicemen in return for learning some lessons about undertaking an opposed landing, a few of which were really rather obvious. Churchill's attitude to the raid was at once contradictory and ill thought through. General Sir Alan Brooke noted in his diary for 23 May 1942, some three months before the raid:

> Went round to 10 Downing St at 12.30 after COS [chiefs of staff meeting] where Mountbatten and I had [a] long interview with [the] PM discussing invasion possibilities. He was carried away with optimism at times and establishing lodgements all round the coast from Calais to Bordeaux, with little regard to strengths and landing facilities.[4]

However, Churchill and the British chiefs of staff had vociferously opposed the more extensive plan for a lodgement, Operation Sledgehammer, which was favoured by the head of the US Army, General George Marshall (see chapter 15). At the Washington Conference codenamed Argonaut, Churchill sent a memo to Roosevelt on 20 June 1942 in which he argued against Sledgehammer; his comments were an unwitting portent of Rutter's failure:

> . . . the British Government would not favour an operation that was certain to lead to disaster for this would not help the Russians whatever their plight, would compromise and expose to Nazi vengeance the French population involved and would gravely delay the main operation in 1943 [the proposed Second Front, Operation Roundup].[5]

He could just as well have been writing this about Rutter, as the Dieppe raid was a weak interpretation of Sledgehammer. (He would later oppose the 1943 cross-Channel invasion, Operation Roundup, to which he also referred.) On 8 July, and also on the 14th, just a month before Rutter's execution, Churchill again told Roosevelt that Sledgehammer was impossible and the British could not support it.[6] Then, on 14 August, just five days before the Dieppe raid, he told Stalin:

> [Sledgehammer] would be a hazardous and futile operation. The Germans have enough troops in the West to block us in this narrow peninsula with fortified lines . . . In the opinion of all the British Naval, Military and Air authorities, the operation could only end in disaster . . .[7]

Once again, Churchill's exposition of the futility of such an assault applied almost exactly to the Dieppe raid. Since the Germans had sufficient troops in the west to block Sledgehammer, they could equally block the Dieppe raid. Just as Sledgehammer would have ended in disaster and wastefully and wantonly used up key men, so this would be the case at Dieppe. So why did Churchill think Rutter was likely to be successful, whereas the more robust Sledgehammer was not? As it proved, Rutter would be a catastrophe.

Churchill also told Stalin: 'All the talk about an Anglo-American invasion of France this year has misled the enemy, and has held large air forces and considerable military forces on the French Channel coast.'[8] So he knew that substantial German forces were now being held for deployment against the Allied raid on Dieppe. Yet he still authorized it.

The adventure would subsequently be spun into a necessary rehearsal for the Second Front in France, Operation Overlord, when it finally came nearly two years later. Mountbatten would spend the rest of his life arguing that this had been its function. He had travelled to Washington not long before the operation in order to tell the President that Sledgehammer was not possible, as neither the troops nor the landing craft were available. Yet they *would* be available for the admittedly smaller Operation Rutter. However, Sledgehammer and Rutter were not too different: both were less than the proposed full-scale invasion for 1943 – Roundup – or the actual landings in 1944.[9] Rutter's problem was that it was neither large enough to inflict a decisive strategic defeat on the Germans, nor small enough to be a commando raid with the advantage of surprise to give it a chance of success.

OPERATION RUTTER

Rutter would be a simple frontal assault and would lack any substantial air bombardment, as French civilian casualties were feared. Montgomery, then a lieutenant-general in charge of South-Eastern Command, initially had responsibility for the operation, but it was clear he had no enthusiasm for it. The Canadian 2nd Division, some 5,000 strong, under the command of Major-General John Hamilton Roberts, would constitute the main force, while British parachute units, 1,000 strong, assaulted German artillery batteries on the Canadians' flanks. A Royal Marine Commando contingent, plus a nominal 50 US Rangers, would also be deployed in the operation. Air Vice-Marshal Trafford Leigh-Mallory, then Air Officer Commanding No 11 Group Fighter Command, was appointed air force commander and Captain John Hughes-Hallett was appointed as naval force commander. Despite his relatively junior rank, Hughes-Hallett replaced the original choice, Rear-Admiral Tom Baillie-Grohman, because of his planning role in Combined Operations.[10] The assault phase would be mounted from five ports, from Southampton to Newhaven, with 237 surface vessels including landing craft; 66 fighter squadrons plus eight other squadrons would be in support for small-scale aerial bombardment.

The fact that the principal contingent of armed forces in the raid would be Canadian created a political problem. Once the United States had entered the war, Churchill formed the Combined Chiefs of Staff with the Americans without even informing, let alone consulting Mackenzie King, the Canadian Prime Minister, and his Cabinet. This committee would determine the use of all Allied forces, including those of Canada, yet King would not discover this until he read the newspapers. He was having difficulty introducing conscription in Canada, as it split the country along English- and French-speaking lines. Churchill's attitude did nothing to help this, or Canadian participation in the war generally; nor did the recriminations after the Dieppe raid, when so many Canadians were taken prisoner, wounded or dead.[11]

King had sent a volunteer Canadian force to Britain, which had remained idle for some time. Although Canadian forces had seen fighting in Hong Kong when it capitulated to the Japanese, there was increasing clamour from the Canadian press, who wanted to see Canada's forces productively employed in the war effort. King could see the electoral advantage of a Canadian military success, and one or two of his generals wanted the chance to command in action. Thus King and some of his military brass had pushed hard for Canadian involvement, and the Dieppe raid was the dubious result.

Planning and intelligence for the raid were poor. Only pre-war holiday snaps were used to assess the suitability of the beaches for the assault, and reconnaissance had not picked up on German gun emplacements cut into the cliffs. German intelligence, on the other hand, was good: their Y-service (radio monitoring) picked up increased Allied radio traffic, reconnaissance spotted the naval preparations and double agents also gave the game away.

Failings in the initial rehearsal for the raid were a portent of things to come, but the second rehearsal was sufficiently satisfactory for Monty to give the go-ahead. The decision was taken on 1 July to enact the raid on the 4th if the weather was good, or as soon after that date as the weather would permit. However, poor weather caused a decision to be taken to delay the operation on the 3rd – the day after Churchill had defeated a vote of no confidence in the House of Commons by 475 to 25.

With the Germans expecting a raid, the Luftwaffe had been ordered to undertake reconnaissance missions to detect preparation for it. British intelligence knew about this and informed Churchill. The 8th was the last possible date that the tides would permit the raid. Plans were revised on the 6th and a commitment was made to remount the operation later if the weather made a further cancellation necessary. Then one of the Luftwaffe pilots assigned to the reconnaissance operation, leading a flight of four Focke-Wulf 190 fighter-bombers and flying under the radar, discovered the Allied assault force in harbour in the Solent. They attacked, causing some damage to the force, and in consequence on the 7th the Dieppe raid was cancelled. Monty was concerned that if the operation was to be remounted at a later date details of the raid would leak out (given that the Germans had now discovered it anyway) and argued that it should be cancelled altogether. As a result his direct superior, Lieutenant-General Sir Bernard Paget, decided to bypass Monty in the command chain for the operation, so his involvement with the Dieppe raid was over. A little later he was dispatched to North Africa – no doubt much to his relief.[12]

The new command structure would be very Canadian: Paget gave Monty's role to Lieutenant-General Andrew McNaughton, who in turn selected another Canadian, Lieutenant-General Henry Crerar, commanding the First Canadian Corps, to take on overall responsibility.

OPERATION JUBILEE

The cancellation of Rutter on 7 July marked a critical point in Churchill's relations with both the Americans and the Russians, for earlier that same day he and the British chiefs had finally said 'No' to Sledgehammer. So now Churchill was offering precisely nothing in terms of a direct cross-Channel assault in 1942. Six days later he resurrected Rutter, now renamed Jubilee.[13]

During the postponement, the plan for small-scale aerial bombardment was reduced still further. A naval bombardment was then planned, but the fear was that battleships would be too vulnerable operating close inshore, so it was decided to employ eight destroyers for the task, as these were more dispensable, despite the fact that their small-calibre guns meant the bombardment would now be inadequate. The threat of another cancellation caused by the weather resulted in the abandonment of the use of British parachute units and they were replaced by No 3 and No 4 Army Commando units. After the initial assault, it was decided that Royal Marine Commandos were to land by motorboat to destroy dock installations, raid the port office and remove secret documents from the safe. Conveniently, one Marine had been a burglar before joining the armed forces.

The Allied force faced the German 10th Panzers. Not only was this unit at full strength, it had been deployed just 65km (40 miles) from Dieppe. Intelligence reports had conveyed this fact to the British even before Rutter had been cancelled. Subsequent reports indicated that two SS divisions were located 80km (50 miles) from Dieppe. Hitler had redeployed these units from the Russian front precisely because of his concern about an Allied landing in the Dieppe–Le Havre area. He then capped it all by appointing his most able defensive commander, Generalfeldmarschall Gerd von Runstedt, as Commander-in-Chief West. With around half a million German troops in France and all leave cancelled in August, the opposition to a limited raid such as Jubilee was formidable. On 20 July intelligence reports of the strengthening of German defences of northern French ports was disseminated to the chiefs. Although British Intelligence was supplying a great deal of precise detail to Churchill and his chiefs personally, little of this information was passed on to Jubilee's planners. This was for security reasons, but it placed great responsibility upon Churchill and the chiefs to see the dangers for Jubilee when the planners could not.[14]

When the raid finally went ahead at 4.50am on 19 August, the element of surprise was immediately lost as Allied naval elements were obliged to fire on German ships they encountered just over an hour before the landings. Only four destroyers, each armed with four 105mm (4in) guns, provided the naval bombardment. The bomber assault had been cancelled when it was decided that the necessary accuracy could not be guaranteed, though Allied fighters did provide a preliminary attack with cannon and machine gun fire.[15]

Despite this, No 4 Commando accomplished its objective in full. However, No 3 Commando managed to deploy only 18 of its men in the correct target area and had to withdraw. The Canadians fared disastrously: of the 543 men of the Royal Regiment, only 60 returned in the withdrawal. Of the South Saskatchewan Regiment, many did not land in the target area, and only a few accomplished the prescribed objectives. The Queen's Own Cameron Highlanders of Canada managed to advance further than any other unit, but were quickly defeated. Subsequently the Essex Scottish Regiment and Royal Hamilton Light Infantry were deployed in their assault phase, together with the 14th Canadian Army Tank Regiment deploying 27 Churchill tanks. The tracks of most of the tanks were compromised by the shingle beach, leaving them hopelessly vulnerable to anti-tank fire; the few that retained mobility were faced with impassable concrete obstructions. The infantry on the beaches were mown down. Major-General Roberts had his view of the fiasco obscured by his own covering smokescreen, and unaware of what was happening he deployed his two reserve units into the withering fire. The scene was now set for withdrawal, which occurred between 11.00am and 2.00pm.

A total of 3,367 Canadians and 275 British commandos were killed, wounded or taken prisoner. The Royal Navy suffered 550 dead and wounded and lost one destroyer plus 33 landing craft. The RAF suffered 106 aircraft shot down. German casualties were 591, and they lost 48 aircraft. Churchill would remark that it had been a 'not unfruitful reconnaissance in force'.[16]

THE RECRIMINATIONS BEGIN

Mysteriously, no written record exists of the approval of the mission; Churchill wrote in *The Second World War* that this was to ensure secrecy, but all such operations required secrecy, yet all did not lack records.[17]

A meeting of the Supreme War Council in Paris in June 1940: (left to right) Churchill; General Sir John Dill, Chief of the Imperial General Staff; the Labour Party leader, Clement Attlee; and the French Prime Minister, Paul Reynaud.

Churchill, near Tripoli in North Africa during the height of World War II at the headquarters of General Sir Bernard Law Montgomery – 'Monty' (centre), and with the Chief of the Imperial General Staff, General Sir Alan Brooke (right).

Churchill in Italy in September 1944 with the Yugoslav communist leader 'Tito' (left). Despite warning of the scourge of communism, Churchill helped Tito to power.

Lord Louis Mountbatten. Churchill appointed him to high office during World War II – with mixed results.

Churchill (right) in Normandy, fourteen days after the D-Day landings on 6 June 1944. Churchill had prevaricated over mounting a Second Front in France at all.

The US Army Chief of Staff, General George Marshall (left) and US Secretary of War, Henry Stimson (right) flank Churchill at a demonstration of US forces at Fort Jackson, Louisiana in June 1942. Neither American believed in Churchill's 'dispersionist' strategy, but firmly believed in mounting a Second Front in France.

US generals, Mark Clark (left) and Dwight Eisenhower in 1942. Eisenhower led
the American assault in North Africa with Clark as his deputy. Later, Clark would
lead allied forces in the Italian campaign, and Eisenhower would be Supreme Allied
Commander for the D-Day landings in France in 1944. Both Americans were sceptical
of Churchill's strategy.

Sir Arthur 'Bomber'
Harris led the British
strategic bombing
offensive against Hitler.
Churchill wanted to
make it appear that the
unseemly consequences
of area bombing were the
responsibility of Harris
and not himself.

Churchill and the President of the United States, Franklin Roosevelt (left) with the President's son Elliott (centre) aboard a US warship at Placentia Bay in Newfoundland, Canada in August 1941. Churchill's only policy for victory in World War II was to try and bring the virtually unlimited productive capacity of the United States into the war. The President's personal envoy to Churchill, Harry Hopkins said that Churchill seemed to believe 'he was being carried up into the heavens to meet God.'

In Morocco for the Casablanca conference in January 1943, Churchill and President Roosevelt are with the Free French leaders: General Henri Giraud (left) and Charles de Gaulle (third from left). The President favoured Giraud, Churchill supported de Gaulle. Churchill was right and the President wrong on this issue.

The 'Big Three': Churchill with Roosevelt and the Soviet Premier, Joseph Stalin (right) at their first conference, in Tehran, Persia (Iran) in late 1943. Churchill thought he could do business with Stalin, but later warned of the threat of Soviet communism.

A conference at Allied Forces headquarters in North Africa in June 1943: (left to right) the Foreign Secretary, Anthony Eden; the Chief of the Imperial General Staff, General Sir Alan Brooke; Air Chief Marshall Sir Arthur Tedder, who would become Deputy Supreme Allied Commander for the 'D-Day' landings the following year; Admiral Sir Andrew Cunningham; General Sir Harold Alexander; US Army Chief of Staff, General George Marshall; General Dwight Eisenhower and 'Monty'.

The 'Big Three' conference at Yalta in the Crimea in February 1945. The President's deteriorating health is evident, he died shortly after the conference. Churchill had already been sidelined, so in reality it was the 'Big Two' and the 'Little One'.

Churchill giving an election speech during the general election campaign in 1945; an election he didn't want and one he would lose catastrophically.

No. 10 Downing Street was Churchill's official home for nine years in all. Here he is seen retiring – against his will – in 1955 at the age of 80.

Churchill was replaced as Prime Minister by Anthony Eden (right), who he had already undermined by setting in train the 'Suez Crisis' which would engulf Eden a year later. No Prime Minister had made it so difficult for their successor to take office.

Churchill and his principal chiefs now sought a scapegoat. Mountbatten had been appointed by Churchill to the Chiefs of Staff Committee to join Sir Charles Portal (RAF), Sir Dudley Pound (RN) and Sir Alan Brooke (army). The other chiefs disliked him, seeing him as unqualified for his job. Brooke said, 'Mountbatten considered that he was there to express his views on all subjects, most of which he knew nothing about.'[18] The lack of any records meant that Churchill and the chiefs could blame Mountbatten. However, Mountbatten insisted that Churchill and the other chiefs had sanctioned the raid and thus they were ultimately responsible.[19]

Churchill wrote to the War Cabinet on 21 August, just after the raid: 'My general impression of "Jubilee" is that the results fully justified the heavy cost.'[20] On 8 September he made a statement to the House of Commons that he 'gave his sanction,' and 'personally regarded [the raid] . . . as an indispensible preliminary to full-scale operations'. But shortly thereafter he distanced himself from the raid. It was three months after this speech that he launched his first attempt to deny that he had been involved in the debacle. He asked Lieutenant-General Sir Hastings Ismay, chief of staff to the Minister of Defence (Churchill himself) in December 1942 about the plans for the raid:

> Who approved them? At first sight it would appear to a layman very much out of accord with the accepted principles of war to attack the strongly fortified town front without first securing the cliffs on either side. I was not consulted about the resumption as I was away . . . I think I had already started for Cairo and Moscow.[21]

In truth, Churchill had cabled Ismay while on that trip to ask for the date of the raid and to give instructions about it. He had also told Stalin of the raid while in Moscow, stating, 'There will be a more serious raid in August. It will be a reconnaissance in force. Some 8,000 men with 50 tanks will be landed.'[22]

In 1950, when Ismay was helping Churchill with the fourth volume of *The Second World War*, the general said of Dieppe: 'My recollection is that you had approved the raid in principle before you left for Cairo, but that the decision to launch the operation was taken after you had left. Mountbatten certainly pressed hard for it, but he did not have the deciding voice.' Ismay then wrote a passage that he suggested Churchill include in his book; it read, 'Before I [Churchill] left England, I had approved an operation against Dieppe and I anxiously awaited news. Accordingly, I telegraphed to General Ismay, "Please report if and when Jubilee takes place."' But Churchill was not happy and instead drafted a passage that said, 'On the initiative of Admiral Mountbatten, the project was revived.' Sir William Deakin, who assisted Churchill with his literary works, said that he was inclined to cover up his mistakes: he did this over Trondheim and Singapore as well as over Dieppe.[23]

However, Mountbatten himself said of Churchill's involvement, 'You were (as ever) the moving spirit. You and the Chiefs of Staff went into the revived plans carefully . . . there were no written records because you and the Chiefs of Staff agreed to this on account of the extraordinary secrecy.'[24] Churchill was thus forced to back down and so the final published version became: 'After the Canadian authorities and the Chiefs of Staff had given their approval I personally went through the plans with the C.I.G.S., Admiral Mountbatten . . .' But Churchill's account still emphasized that the Canadian authorities (which in fact had been most vociferous in their criticism of the raid) should be identified as having given their approval first, the CIGS second, and he only third, as though his involvement had been minor.[25] His official biographer, Martin Gilbert, pointed out, 'Churchill or the Chiefs of Staff could have cancelled the raid anytime in August, and right up to the day it was mounted. The fact that they didn't means they accepted it.'[26]

THE EFFECTS OF THE RAID

Many able servicemen and planners argued that the detailed lessons from Dieppe were a great help, but for the most part this was for one of two reasons: either to placate the Canadians by conveying that their sacrifice had not been in vain, or because they were planners who had been responsible for the raid and thus had a vested interest in justifying what they had done. Mountbatten himself was the principal figure in the latter category, and many Canadians, including Crerar, were in the former. In his speech on 7 June 1944 Crerar said:

> I think it is most important that, at this time, all of you should realize what a vital part the gallant and hazardous operation of the raid in force on Dieppe has played in the conception, planning and execution of the vast 'Overlord' [Second Front] Operation.
>
> . . . Although at the time the heavy cost to Canada, and the non-success of the Dieppe operation, seemed hard to bear, I believe that when this war is examined in proper perspective, it will be seen that the sobering influence of that operation . . . was a Canadian contribution of the greatest significance to final victory.[27]

Also in the placating category was Eisenhower, who signalled Mountbatten from the Normandy beaches at the time of the Second Front: 'Except for Dieppe and the work of your organisation we would have been lacking much of the special equipment and much of the knowledge needed for the invasion.' On 10 June 1944 a letter was sent to Mountbatten concerning the Second Front that read, '. . . the success of the venture has its origin in developments effected by you and your staff of Combined Operations.'[28] This was signed by placaters: the American chiefs – General Marshall, Admiral King and General Hap Arnold of the US Air Force – and those who had been directly responsible for the raid, Brooke and Churchill himself.

It is clear that, in light of the Dieppe raid, plans were changed for the North African and Italian opposed landings as well as for the Second Front in France. As we have seen, when Churchill gave his House of Commons speech about Dieppe on 8 September 1942 he said that his sanctioning of the raid was to obtain vital information for major operations in the future.[29] But since, as chapter 15 will explore, he had been opposed to the Second Front, he would hardly have conducted the Dieppe raid in order to improve the chances of its success.

Although Jubilee did draw German divisions from the Eastern Front, its effect there was much too small to be of any real significance. When Churchill travelled to Moscow in August 1942 for five days of talks, to persuade Stalin a Second Front was not possible, he managed to get Stalin to say, 'Dieppe will be explained by Torch [the joint Anglo-American operation in North Africa].'[30] So Dieppe was just a distraction from Churchill's Mediterranean strategy.

The effect of the raid on Hitler was to cause him to reinforce the French coast, drawing forces away from other theatres, so to some extent it acted as a decoy for the North African operations. However, although the combined Anglo-American assault had yet to take place, British forces had been fighting in North Africa for some time; thus, the fact that fighting was to continue in this theatre could hardly have surprised Hitler, so it seems that Dieppe could have had little effect as a decoy. But the reinforcement of coastal defences in France did mean that when the Second Front eventually came, Allied forces faced far more robust German defences. Dieppe was thus detrimental to Allied strategic interests.

It can be argued that the Dieppe raid reinforced Hitler's belief that when the Second Front was eventually mounted it would be focused at a port, and the need for short communications meant it would have to be in the Pas-de-Calais region. Yet Dieppe is in Normandy, an alarming indicator to Hitler of what would be the actual location of the Second Front when it came two years later. Despite this, it seems Hitler never assumed that Normandy would be the eventual target. But even though Allied planners had yet to evolve the plan for the Second Front, the Dieppe raid did nothing to dissuade Hitler from the idea that this might be its ultimate location.

Publicly at least, Canadian reaction was muted at the time, with restraint among Canadian politicians and the military brass; even the minutes of the Canadian War Cabinet for the last few months of 1942 contain few references to the raid. However, Churchill's behaviour weakened Britain's ties with Canada. It would help to loosen the grip of Empire, which had been central to Churchill's interests for most of his political career. It would do little to help the Allied war effort – far from it. Dieppe was no more than a pinprick raid, another part of Churchill's dispersionist strategy.

13
THE FAR EAST: CATASTROPHIC DEFEAT

Britain first began to regard the Japanese as a threat from 1922, with the ending of the Anglo-Japanese Alliance, though Churchill was very slow to realize it. The Japanese military government embarked on a policy of colonial expansion in the 1930s, so the increasing threat was not too difficult to see. Yet on 28 April 1941, just a few months before the Japanese attack on the American Pacific Fleet at Pearl Harbor, Churchill wrote to the War Cabinet:

> Japan is unlikely to enter the war unless the Germans make a successful invasion of Great Britain, and even a major disaster like the loss of the Middle East would not necessarily make her come in, because the liberation of the British Mediterranean Fleet which might be expected, and also any troops evacuated from the Middle East to Singapore would not weaken the British war-making strength in Malaya. It is very unlikely, moreover, that Japan will enter the war either if the United States has come in, or if Japan thinks that they would come in consequent upon a Japanese declaration of war . . .[1]

Churchill himself observed, 'Political ability is the ability to foretell what is going to happen tomorrow, next week, next month and next year. And to have the ability afterward to explain why it didn't happen.'[2]

Japan's occupation in World War II of Britain's colonial possessions in the Far East – Hong Kong, Singapore, Malaya and Burma – constituted a significant part of its overall objective of gaining exclusive access to raw materials and developing into a regional hegemonic power. Yet Churchill obstinately insisted on outlandish plans for their recapture, distracting the attention of the service chiefs from planning an effective strategy and threatening the crucial Anglo-American relationship.

In the summer of 1941 Churchill appointed General Sir Archibald Wavell to the post of Commander-in-Chief India; he also had responsibility for defence in the Far East. Churchill had previously sacked Wavell as commander of the North African forces because of his decisive defeat at the hands of Rommel, so the omens were not propitious for the Far East.

THE INVASION OF MALAYA

On 8 December 1941, one day after the attack on Pearl Harbor, the Japanese 25th Army launched an assault from Indochina, landing at Kota Bharu in northern Malaya. Two days later, in the Gulf of Siam, the Japanese Air Force sank the battleship *Prince of Wales* and the battle-cruiser *Repulse* (see chapter 9). This left not only the east coast of Malaya exposed, but the seas of the entire region.

The Japanese invasion of Malaya was opposed by the Indian Army's III Corps and by a number of British Army battalions. Although the Japanese were outnumbered by the Allied forces in both Malaya and Singapore, they enjoyed superior close air support, and good armour for their ground forces, while Allied forces were hampered by having no tanks. The Japanese Air Force had fewer aircraft than the Allies but possessed technically superior fighters, particularly the Mitsubishi Zero, and thus gained the crucial advantage of air superiority. However, the Japanese benefited most of all from their superior tactics, borne of greater experience. Japanese forces rapidly surrounded the Indian units defending the coast and advanced down the Malay Peninsula. Despite their greater numbers, the Allies were overwhelmed and the Japanese forces advanced towards Singapore. As Churchill recounted in *The Second World War*:

> It is at least arguable whether it would not have been better to concentrate all our strength on defending Singapore Island, [rather than] merely containing the Japanese advance down the Malayan peninsula with light mobile forces. The decision of the commanders on the spot, which I approved, was to fight the battle for Singapore in Johore [the southern region of Malaya close to Singapore].[3]

This was Churchill being wise after the event. The occupation of Malaya provided the Japanese with rubber, routes westward via Burma into India and south to the great island 'fortress' of Singapore at the southern tip of Malaya, plus control of the Strait of Malacca and the Java Sea. Across this sea to the south-east of Malaya lay the Dutch East Indies, poorly defended and with substantial natural resources.

HONG KONG IS LOST

When the Japanese attacked China, they occupied Guangzhou on 21 October 1938, and thus effectively cut off Hong Kong. Churchill had written in a letter to Stanley Baldwin as far back as 15 December 1924, '. . . suppose we had a dispute with Japan about something in China and we declared war upon her . . . Hong Kong would of course be taken by Japan in the early days.'[4] Although it was not Britain's dispute with Japan over 'something in China' that had now resulted in war, Hong Kong would indeed be gone as quickly as Churchill had predicted. The British defence studies already undertaken concurred with Churchill that it would not be practicable to defend Hong Kong if the Japanese chose to attack. The defence cuts Churchill had made in the 1920s, as Chancellor of the Exchequer, helped to make this more certain. Nevertheless, the defence of Hong Kong was deemed of sufficient priority in the mid-1930s, during Churchill's 'wilderness years', for the government to initiate work on developing its defences. However, by 1940, as Churchill came to power, the Hong Kong garrison was reduced to nothing more than a symbolic defence force.

It was the commander-in-chief of the British Far East Command, Air Chief Marshal Sir Robert Brooke-Popham, who argued that a defence of Hong Kong would delay a Japanese attack elsewhere and so gain crucial time. Thus, in the autumn of 1941 Britain accepted a Canadian Government offer to provide two infantry battalions and a brigade headquarters, totalling nearly 2,000 personnel, to reinforce the Hong Kong garrison. The contingent was known as 'C Force' and arrived on 16 November 1941. It did not have all its equipment, as some had been diverted, and in November Brooke-Popham was to have been replaced by Lieutenant-General Sir Henry Royds Pownall, but he did not arrive in Singapore until 27 December.[5]

It was a little after 8am, Hong Kong time, on 8 December 1941, less than eight hours after the attack on Pearl Harbor, that the Japanese attacked Hong Kong. The British commander, Major-General Christopher Maltby, had six battalions of British, Canadian and Indians under his command, plus Hong Kong Volunteer Defence forces. The Japanese had three divisions under Lieutenant-General Sakai Takashi, outnumbering by two to one the Allied forces, who were quickly overwhelmed.[6] There was an RAF station at Hong Kong's Kia Tak Airport, but it had only three obsolete Vickers Vildebeest torpedo-reconnaissance aircraft plus two slow Supermarine Walrus amphibious planes. Twelve Japanese bombers destroyed four of these five planes, plus all but two aircraft used by the Hong Kong Volunteer Defence Corp Air Unit. From then on the RAF and Air Unit personnel fought as ground troops. Royal Navy vessels were then ordered to leave Hong Kong for Singapore.

In two days the Allied lines were breached by the Japanese and the Allied evacuation from Kowloon was initiated the day after that, on 11 December. By the 13th, the last Allied troops had withdrawn to Hong Kong Island, and the Japanese demanded a surrender. This was rejected, as it would be for a second time four days later. On 18 December the Japanese assaulted the island, and within two days the Allied forces controlled no more than the Stanley Peninsula and western portions of the island. The Japanese took control of the water supply, and naturally denied water to the Allies. On the afternoon of Christmas Day it became clear that the game was up, and the Governor of Hong Kong, Sir Mark Aitchison Young, offered the Allied surrender to the Japanese. Thus, after 18 days of fighting, Hong Kong became the first British Crown Colony in history to be surrendered to an enemy.

THE FALL OF SINGAPORE

'Fortress Singapore', as Churchill called it, would be the biggest single loss in British military history. This occurred a few days after Churchill won a vote of confidence in the House of Commons by 464 votes to 1. Already, on the day of the Pearl Harbor attack, the Japanese had bombed Singapore Harbour: the harbour lights had guided the Japanese bombers to their target and remained switched on during the entire raid because no one knew how to switch them off!

Singapore was the base for the American–British–Dutch–Australasian Command (ABDACOM), which replaced the British Far East Command, and was the very first joint command of Allied forces in World War II. Wavell was appointed to command this new organization, and Pownall, who had only just replaced Brooke-Popham as Commander-in-Chief Far East, now found himself as Wavell's chief of staff. This Allied reorganization came at a critical time, and weakened the command structure. The Allied commander of defence forces for Singapore was Lieutenant-General Arthur Percival; his commander-in-chief was Pownall, who now had a diminished position, while Wavell could spend only part of his time providing assistance to Percival in Singapore.[7]

As late as 12 December 1941 Churchill was reorganizing the political heirarchy in Singapore. Alfred Duff Cooper, the Chancellor of the Duchy of Lancaster, was to be in charge. Churchill set down his functions as 'Resident Minister of Cabinet Rank at Singapore for Far Eastern Affairs'. He was to 'serve under and report directly to the War Cabinet' and would preside over a war council in Singapore.[8] But this evolution of the political structure did nothing to address the deficiencies in Singapore's defence.

Percival had a total of 85,000 soldiers under his command. Of these, some 70,000 were frontline troops, comprising 38 infantry battalions plus three machine-gun battalions. Many units lacked training and experience, there was no Allied bomber force of significance and only very limited artillery. A substantial contingent of British reinforcements had arrived in Singapore the day before the Japanese invasion, ready to go straight into Japanese captivity having fired hardly a shot. Churchill telegrammed General Wavell on 15 January 1942:

> Please let me know your ideas of what would happen in event of your being forced to withdraw into the island [Singapore].
>
> How many troops would be needed to defend this area? What means are there of stopping landings [such] as were made in Hong Kong? What are defences and obstructions on landward side? Are you sure you can dominate with fortress cannon any attempt to plant siege

batteries? Is everything being prepared . . . ? It has always seemed to me that the vital need is to prolong the defence of the island to last possible minute, but of course I hope it will not come to this . . .

Everyone here is very pleased with the telegrams you have sent, which give us all the feeling how buoyantly and spaciously you are grappling with your tremendous task.[9]

So preparations were being made, yet along with such confidence there was that ominous statement about prolonging the defence to the last possible minute. Singapore had no fixed defence to the landward side, but on the seaward side there was one battery of three and another of two 380mm (15in) guns. These could fire either armour-piercing or high-explosive shells, but were equipped mainly with the former as they were intended for defence against a naval assault. These batteries were capable of being turned to face inland, and were indeed used against the Japanese invading force. However, their location on the seaward side and the fact that most of their ammunition was armour-piercing meant they were inadequate for this purpose.

It seems that, just as with the French Maginot Line, where the Germans were expected to impale themselves on fixed fortifications, a force attacking Singapore was expected to impale itself on the seaward-facing guns. Little regard was given by anybody, including Churchill, to the notion that an assaulting force would simply land elsewhere on the peninsula and attack from the poorly defended rear. This was despite the fact that in World War I, in exactly this manner, Lawrence of Arabia and an irregular force of Arabs had taken the North African port of Aqaba, which also had only fixed artillery emplacements on the seaward side and no adequate defence from the landward side.

On 31 January 1942 the last Allied forces finally withdrew from Malaya, blowing up the causeway linking it with Singapore in the process. The Japanese commander, General Tomoyuki Yamashita, had more than 30,000 troops in three divisions, and he enjoyed good intelligence of Allied troop dispositions. At 8.30pm on 8 February the Japanese initiated their assault with 4,000 troops against Singapore, and Australian machine-gunners offered resistance. The Japanese were able to take advantage of gaps in the Allied lines in the north-west. By midnight one of the

Australian brigades was obliged to retreat. The Japanese reinforced their forces in the north-west of Singapore at 1.00am and the last Australian reserves were committed. Percival believed that the Japanese would undertake landings in the north-east, so failed to reinforce the north-west. Then on 9 February Japanese landings were undertaken in the south-west. Two days later, with Japanese supplies running perilously low, Yamashita attempted to bluff Percival, telling him to 'give up this meaningless and desperate resistance'.

As the battle raged, Sir Alan Brooke noted in his diary on 12 February:

> News of Singapore far worse, and that of Burma rapidly deteriorating. We are bound to lose the former before long and I am getting very nervous about the latter! We are paying very heavily now for failing to face the insurance premiums essential for security of an Empire! This has usually been the main cause for the loss of Empires in the past.[10]

On the same day, Churchill cabled Roosevelt: 'A fierce battle is raging at Singapore and orders have been given to fight it out.'[11] However, just two days later he cabled Wavell, then Supreme Commander South-West Pacific: 'You are of course sole judge of the moment when no further result can be gained at Singapore and should instruct Percival accordingly. C.I.G.S. concurs.'[12]

By 13 February the Japanese had captured the bulk of the Allies' ammunition and fuel, and controlled the water supplies, which they had taken with ease. With Allied strength weakening, Percival's officers advised surrender in order to minimize civilian casualties. Percival sought higher authority to surrender but this was denied.

The Japanese overwhelmed the Allied forces on the morning of 15 February, and with the Allies running out of food, with ammunition low and anti-aircraft ammunition gone, the game was finally up. Percival consulted his unit commanders then met Yamashita at the Ford car factory, and just after 5.15pm formally surrendered to him. So much for Churchill's statement to Roosevelt that British forces were ordered to 'fight it out'.

Approximately 80,000 Allied troops went into captivity, joining 50,000 who had been captured in Malaya. The Indian Army alone lost 67,450 men at Singapore. The Japanese had sustained about 10,000 casualties in effecting this stunning victory. Many of the Allied prisoners of war were held in Changi Prison in Singapore, and thousands more were transported in 'hell ships' to camps elsewhere in Asia, including Japan. They became slave labourers on projects such as the Siam–Burma Railway, best known for the infamous 'Bridge on the River Kwai'. Many would die in consequence, some 12,000 on the Siam–Burma railway alone.

Churchill's bodyguard wrote of him: 'He shared the impression generally held in this country that Singapore was impregnable. He had, I remembered, expressed this view without qualification at a Press Conference when I was present in Ottawa some six weeks previously.' Churchill was deeply shocked and surprised; he had no idea that Singapore would offer hardly any resistance and was not in fact a fortress at all. His bodyguard added, 'When friends asked the Prime Minister what had happened at Singapore, he would shake his head dismally and say, "I really don't know".'[13] When Churchill reported these dire events to the House of Commons, he said it was 'the greatest disaster to British arms that history records'. On this occasion Churchill's rhetoric gave true dimension to the magnitude of the catastrophe.

Churchill could not be blamed for the inadequate development of Singapore's defences as the threat from Japan grew during the 1930s, but when he did have the chance, and the Japanese threat was clear and imminent, he still brushed the problem aside. The reorganization of the command structure at the crucial time had been disruptive, Percival was clearly not up to the job, and indeed all the principal command appointments and lesser ranks had been filled by the second eleven. This was all the responsibility of Churchill and his chiefs of staff. While in Japanese captivity, Percival was asked why he had not fortified 'fortress Singapore', and replied that he thought it would be damaging for civilian morale![14]

In *The Second World War* Churchill wrote, '. . . it had never entered my head that no circle of detached forts of a permanent character protected the rear of the famous fortress. I cannot understand how it was I did not know this.' He continued, 'I do not write this in any way to excuse myself. I ought to have known. My advisers ought to have known and I ought to have been told, and I ought to have asked.'[15] The eminent historian AJP Taylor said of this passage, 'I am sorry to say that the records show his advisors told him, and Churchill pushed their warnings aside.'[16] Churchill could only conclude, '. . . the possibility of Singapore having no landward defences no more entered into my mind than that of a battleship being launched without a bottom.'[17]

This would not simply be the largest single loss in British military history, but the most shameful of defeats. Singapore and Hong Kong constituted the bulwark of British and Commonwealth opposition to the Japanese advance in the Far East, yet both had fallen quickly and easily. These failures would add considerably to the cost in American, British and Commonwealth lives in the subsequent defeat of the Japanese and recapture of the lost colonial possessions. Churchill had failed to grasp any of the realities of this situation prior to the catastrophe. Afterwards he refused to hold an inquiry by Royal Commission into the matter while the war was on. Clearly he had no intention of revealing his own culpability.[18]

BURMA, THE DUTCH EAST INDIES AND CEYLON

Early in 1942 the Japanese mounted air raids on Rangoon, the capital of Burma, and then initiated a land invasion of Burma from Siam (Thailand). The British, Indian and Burmese forces were decisively defeated and undertook the longest withdrawal in British military history. Rangoon fell on 9 March; by early April the Japanese had inflicted a decisive defeat on the Chinese, and in May the British and Indian forces were rolled back into India itself. Burma provided the Japanese with oil, rice and rubber. It also acted as a forward base from which to assault India and China.

The Japanese attacked the Dutch East Indies on 11 January 1942. They landed on Celebes and Tarakan Island off Borneo, and headed rapidly west through the Moluccas, Timor and Bali to Java and Sumatra, stopping on each island for as long as it took to establish a garrison and construct an airfield. They were in Java by 28 February. On 9 March the Dutch forces surrendered, and the Dutch East Indies passed under Japanese control.

On 5 April the Japanese mounted an attack on Colombo in Ceylon (Sri Lanka) with more than 300 carrier-based aircraft, doing great damage though missing the Royal Navy's ships, which had recently been deployed elsewhere. Subsequently however, Japanese dive-bombers were to sink the aircraft carrier HMS *Hermes* and two cruisers, HMS *Cornwall* and HMS *Dorsetshire*.

South-East Asia Command (SEAC) was set up as a combined Allied organization under Vice-Admiral Lord Louis Mountbatten to undertake the function of expelling the Japanese from these territories. It would cause much friction with the Americans, who dubbed SEAC 'Save England's Asian Colonies'. Once again, Churchill insisted on trying to interfere with military strategy, as General Brooke was acutely aware. A recurrent, indeed obsessive, theme for Churchill in the Pacific war was the prospect of an Allied landing on the northern tip of Sumatra, Operation Culverin. Referring to the Anglo-American Operation Torch in North Africa, he wrote in *The Second World War*, '. . . "Culverin" would be the "Torch" of the Indian Ocean.'[19] On 30 November 1942 Brooke noted in his diary, 'Cabinet from 5.30pm to 8pm and now off for another meeting with him [Churchill] from 10.30 to God knows when, to discuss more ambitious and impossible plans for the re-conquest of Burma!' On 10 May 1943 Brooke recorded:

> We . . . went . . . to the PM at 11.30 and discussed the Far East strategy till 1.30pm. A thoroughly unsatisfactory meeting at which he again showed that he cannot grasp the relation of various theatres of war to each other. He always gets carried away by the one he is examining and in prosecuting it is prepared to sacrifice most of the others. I have never in the 1½ years that I have worked with him succeeded in making him review the war as a whole and to relate the importance of the various fronts to each other . . . It was not long before we were drawn off again to his pet of the moment in the shape of an attack on Northern Sumatra or Penang!![20]

Three months later, the notion that Sumatra was the key to operations in South-east Asia continued to obsess Churchill, and despite Brooke's best endeavours he would not let go. On 19 August 1943 Brooke wrote:

> We went to . . . see the PM to discuss South East Asia operations. I had another row with him. He is insisting on capturing the top of Sumatra Island irrespective of what our general plan for the war against Japan may be! He refused to accept that any general plan was necessary, recommended a purely opportunistic policy and behaved like a spoilt child that

wants a toy in a shop irrespective of the fact that its parents
tell it that it is no good! Got nowhere with him, and settled
nothing! This makes my arguments with the Americans
practically impossible!

   . . . Winston was by now revolving round the northern end of
Sumatra as he had done over Trondheim in the past! He had
discovered with a pair of dividers that we could bomb Singapore
from this point and he had set his heart on going there. It was
not a suitable base for further operations against Malaya, but I
could not get any definite reply from him as to what he hoped
to accomplish from there. When I drew his attention to the fact
that when he put his left foot down he should know where the
right foot was going to, he shook his fist in my face, saying, 'I do
not want any of your long term projects, they cripple initiative!'
I agreed that they did hamper initiative, but told him that I
could not look upon knowing where our next step was going as
constituting a long term project! I told him he must know
where he was going, to which he replied that he did not want to
know! All this made arguing impossible, and made it difficult
to stop him chasing this hare at this critical moment. We were
having difficulties enough with the Americans to arrive at an
agreement on our Burma operation without bringing in extra
complications such as Sumatra.[21]

This obsession of Churchill's would become increasingly serious and was
to jeopardize the development of overall plans for the defeat of Japan. The
following day Brooke wrote:

We struggled with the war with Japan till after 1pm in our
morning COS meeting without arriving at any very definite
conclusions. The problem is a very difficult one and made all
the more difficult by the PM's childish attitude of selecting
one operation and wishing to close his eyes to all the rest![22]

On the day after that, when they met again, Brooke wrote of Churchill,
'. . . He was more reasonable, and did accept the fact that an overall plan
for the defeat of Japan was required, but still shouted for the Sumatra

operation like a spoilt child!'[23] Patience was not a virtue Brooke possessed in abundance, and he gave full vent to his feelings in his diary. By this time he was getting to the end of his tether. His entry for 23 August reads:

> ... a peevish temperamental prima donna of a Prime Minister, suspicious to the very limits of imagination, always fearing a military combination of effort against political dominance, the whole matter becomes quite unbearable! He has been more unreasonable and trying than ever this time. He has ... in a few idle moments become married to the idea that success against Japan can only be secured through the capture of the north tip of Sumatra! He has become like a peevish child asking for a forbidden toy. We have had no real opportunity of even studying the operation for its merits and possibilities and yet he wants us to press the Americans for its execution![24]

Throughout the war, Brooke was obliged to spend a disproportionate amount of his time constraining Churchill, which naturally restricted his ability to focus on the crucial planning for the war. On 28 September 1943 he recorded:

> COS at which we discussed PM's wild minute about proposed operations in the Indian Ocean. Now in addition to the impossible Sumatra operation he hopes to do Akyab, Ramree and the Rangoon operation all in 1944!! If Germany is defeated by the end of this year, there may be some hope of doing something out there, but Germany is not yet defeated and his wild schemes can have only one result, to detract forces from the main front. Cabinet at 5.30 which lasted till 7.45. We then had a COS meeting from 9 to 10.30 to prepare for the PM's meeting which lasted from 10.30 to 1am. We did practically nothing, or at any rate nothing that could not have been finished in an hour. He was in a foul mood and convinced that we are finding every excuse we can to avoid doing the Sumatra operation.[25]

On 1 October Brooke recorded:

> A rushed morning with COS till 12 noon, then meeting with
> PM, COS, Dickie Mountbatten and Pownall [Mountbatten's
> chief of staff]. This resulted in an hour's pitched battle
> between me and the PM on the question of withdrawing
> troops from the Mediterranean for the Indian Ocean
> offensive. I was refusing to impair our amphibious potential
> in the Mediterranean in order to equip Mountbatten for
> adventures in Sumatra. He [Churchill] on the other hand
> was prepared to scrap our basic policy and put Japan before
> Germany. However I defeated most of his evil intentions in
> the end![26]

It was at the beginning of the dry season early in 1944 that the Fourteenth
Army, under General Sir William Slim, conducted a major offensive into
the Arakan Peninsula of Burma. The Fourteenth would be the largest
Commonwealth army in World War II, with almost a million men by late
1944, many from India but also from several other British colonies. Slim
would comment that all his battles seemed to be conducted uphill and at
the intersection of two or more maps. It was Slim who doggedly conducted
a highly successful campaign against the Japanese while Churchill fretted
about Sumatra.

While the Allies were conducting this offensive, the Japanese launched
a diversionary attack into the Arakan, codenamed *Ha-Go*, while their main
attack (*U-Go*) of some 80,000 men was conducted westward into Assam
in north-eastern India. This was to produce memorable battles at Imphal
and Kohima. By February 1944 the Battle of Kohima had turned into a
siege, which would last 64 days. On 30 March Imphal was also besieged
until on 22 June the Allies finally prevailed, and the *U-Go* offensive was
stopped. There were nearly 18,000 Allied casualties, while the Japanese
sustained 53,000.

However, Churchill was still at it. Brooke recorded on 24 February 1944,
'. . . tomorrow promises badly as we then discuss the Pacific strategy with
the PM and he will wish to fasten onto the tip of Sumatra like a limpet.'[27]
On 7 March he wrote:

> Most of our COS meeting was devoted to preparing notes for
> tomorrow evening's meeting with the PM concerning the

South East Asia strategy. He has produced the worst paper I have seen him write yet. Trying to make a case for an attack on the top of the island of Sumatra! He compared this plan to our outline plan for the defeat of Japan operating with Americans and Australians from Australia through New Guinea towards [the] Philippines, Formosa etc. He has now taken Eden [the Foreign Secretary], Attlee [the Deputy Prime Minister] and Oliver Lyttelton [Minister of Production] in tow, none of whom understand anything about it at all, but who are useful as they are prepared to agree with him! We shall, I feel, have a royal row about this matter.[28]

The following day Brooke recorded:

An unpleasantly heavy day! First a COS meeting where we discussed papers prepared to counter the PM's wild statements about the Pacific strategy . . . and finally at 10pm off for our meeting with the PM on the Pacific strategy.

The meeting consisted of the PM, who had brought with him to support him Attlee, Eden, Oliver Lyttelton and [Lord Frederick] Leathers [Minister of War Transport]! Our party consisted of Chiefs of Staff. Portal as usual [was] not too anxious to argue against [the] PM, and dear old Cunningham [was] so wild with rage that he hardly dared let himself speak!! I therefore had to do most of the arguing and for 2½ hours, from 10pm to 12.30am I went at it hard arguing with the PM and 4 Cabinet Ministers. The arguments of the latter were so puerile that it made me ashamed to think they were Cabinet Ministers! It was only too evident that they did not know their subject, had not read the various papers connected with it, and had purely been brought along to support Winston! And damned badly they did it too! I had little difficulty in dealing with any of the arguments they put forward. Finally . . . we had got him [Churchill] to realize that his plans for the defeat of Japan must go beyond the mere capture of the tip of Sumatra.[29]

But Brooke found that Churchill was still not finished. On 17 March he recorded:

> He [Churchill] then informed us that he had discovered a new Island just west of Sumatra, I think it is called something like Simmular [Simeulue]. He has worked out that the capture of this island, when once developed, would answer as well as the top of Sumatra and would require far less strength!! However, by the time he had asked Portal his view he had discovered that from the point of view of the air he had little hope of building up his aerodromes and strength before being bumped off [by the Japanese]. From Cunningham he found out that from a naval point of view, with the Jap fleet at Singapore he was courting disaster!!! Both Portal and Cunningham were *entirely* correct, and I began to wonder whether I was Alice in Wonderland, or whether I was really fit for a lunatic asylum! I am honestly getting very doubtful about his balance of mind and it just gives me the cold shivers. I don't know where we are or where we are going as regards our strategy, and I just cannot get him to face the true facts! It is a ghastly situation.[30]

The strain of handling Churchill increasingly told on Brooke, and on 20 March 1944 he recorded:

> One of the worst of Cabinet meetings with Winston in one of his worst moods! Nothing that the Army does can be right and he did nothing but belittle its efforts in the eyes of the whole Cabinet. I cannot stick any more meetings like it! He has now produced an impossible document on the Pacific strategy in which he is overriding our opinions and our advice![31]

The following day he wrote:

> We discussed at the COS how best to deal with Winston's last impossible document. It is full of false statements, false deductions and defective strategy. We cannot accept it as it stands, and it would be better if we all three [Brooke,

Cunningham and Portal] resigned rather than accept his
solution . . . I don't know how tiresome he will insist in being.
He may perhaps see some reason, otherwise we may well be
faced with a very serious situation.[32]

And on 24 March:

American wire stating that we should push on in Burma and
give up all thoughts of Sumatra. PM's reaction was to wire
direct to Mountbatten saying if you will conform to American
requirements in Burma I shall back you in Sumatra and see
that you are allowed to carry out the operation!!! We stopped
the wire, but heaven knows where we are going. I feel like a
man chained to the chariot of a lunatic!! It is getting beyond
my powers to control him.[33]

Finally, on 24 May Brooke could record, 'I think we have at last got him
swung to an Australian based strategy as opposed to his old love of the
"Sumatra tip"!'[34] However, the problem of managing Churchill was not
to diminish. On 6 July Brooke noted in his diary:

. . . at 10pm we had a frightful meeting with Winston which
lasted till 2am!! It was quite the worst we have had with him.
He was very tired as a result of his speech in the House . . . he
had tried to recuperate with drink. As a result he was in a
maudlin, bad tempered, drunken mood, ready to take offence
at anything, suspicious of everybody, and in a highly vindictive
mood against the Americans. In fact so vindictive that his
whole outlook on strategy was warped. I began by having a bad
row with him. He began to abuse Monty because operations
were not going faster, and apparently Eisenhower had said he
was over cautious. I flared up and asked him if he could not
trust his generals for 5 minutes instead of continuously
abusing them and belittling them. He said that he never did
such a thing. I then reminded him that during two whole
Monday Cabinets in front of a large gathering of Ministers, he
had torn Alexander to shreds for his lack of imagination and

leadership in continually attacking at Cassino [in Italy]. He was furious with me, but I hope it may do some good in the future.

He then put forward a series of puerile proposals, such as raising a Home Guard in Egypt to provide a force to deal with the disturbances in the Middle East. It was not till after midnight that we got onto the subject we had come to discuss, the war in the Far East! Here we came up against all the old arguments that we have had put up by him over and over again. Attlee, Eden and Lyttelton were there, fortunately they were at last siding with us [the chiefs of staff] against him. This infuriated him more than ever and he became ruder and ruder. Fortunately he finished by falling out with Attlee and having a real good row with him concerning the future of India! We withdrew under cover of this smokescreen just on 2am, having accomplished nothing beyond losing our tempers and valuable sleep!![35]

If Brooke ever had hopes that Churchill would drop his Sumatra strategy, they were forlorn. On 8 August he wrote:

We have been discussing the Pacific strategy, recommending the capture of Burma by a landing at Rangoon combined with a Pacific strategy of naval, air and Dominion forces operating from Australia. Winston still hovers back to his tip of Sumatra and refuses to look at anything else.

1am – Just back from our evening conference with the PM. It was if anything worse than any of the conferences of the day. I believe he has lost the power of giving a decision. He finds every possible excuse to avoid giving one. His arguments are becoming puerile, for instance he upheld this evening that an attack on the tip of Sumatra would force a withdrawal of Japanese forces in northern Burma and would liquidate our commitment in this area. We have conferred for 7 hours!!! with him today to settle absolutely nothing. Nor has he produced a single argument during the whole of that period that was worth listening to. I am at my wits' end and can't go on much longer![36]

Churchill himself once observed, 'A fanatic is one who can't change his mind and won't change the subject.'[37]

General Slim mentioned Churchill little in his post-war account, *Defeat into Victory*, save to say that he never met the Prime Minister before or during the long Burma campaign.[38] However, Slim made one decorous comment on Churchill's pet obsession: 'Mr. Churchill . . . strongly urged an amphibious operation against Sumatra . . . It was, however, decided that, with the resources available, it could not be undertaken . . . There was then no alternative but to abandon the Sumatra operation.'[39]

On 5 September 1944, while on board the *Queen Mary* on the way to the Quebec Conference, Brooke recorded:

> I am not looking forward to this journey. Winston is still always set on capturing the tip of Sumatra, he has agreed to our airborne campaign on lower Burma, but limits his sanction to the capture of Rangoon alone, without the clearing of the rest of Burma. This makes the expedition practically useless and converts it into one which cannot appeal to the Americans since it fails to affect upper Burma where their air route is situated. I should have a difficult enough task to get the Americans to agree to the Burma plans. But with the PM in the background it becomes relatively impossible.[40]

Brooke later added, 'I was in for a series of the most difficult conferences with Winston on this journey. Conferences where he repudiated everything he had agreed to up to date.' During the Quebec Conference itself things deteriorated further, as Churchill suspected that Brooke and the other British chiefs were siding with the American chiefs and the President. Brooke continued, '[Churchill] kept on sending for me to find out what we were settling, and trying to alter every decision. It was a ghastly time from which I carried away the bitterest of memories.'[41]

On 8 September, Brooke recorded that Churchill insisted he had not been informed that shifting additional troops to Burma would be possible only after the defeat of Germany: an accusation that Brooke insisted was false. Churchill also said he had originally been told by the chiefs that only one division would be required for operations in Burma, but that they were now insisting that five divisions were necessary. Brooke insisted that this was also a false accusation. Churchill accused the chiefs of wanting to go to the Quebec Conference only to obtain 20 landing craft from the Americans with which to undertake an amphibious assault against Istria (on the coast of Slovenia) in order to capture Trieste. Brooke noted, 'It was hard to keep one's temper with him but I could not help feeling frightfully sorry for him. He gave me the feeling of a man who is finished, can no longer keep a grip of things, and is beginning to realise it.'[42] The following day Churchill made the Istria accusation again and then repudiated an agreement for a possible British task force under US General Douglas MacArthur, an agreement to which he had assented weeks before and which had already been submitted to the Americans with Churchill's approval.

In December 1944 the Fourteenth Army under General Slim made its decisive attack in the Arakan Peninsula, capturing Kalewa and the port of Akyab by January 1945. The Irrawaddy River was crossed north of Mandalay, Kangaw and Rangoon were captured by 3 May, and Burma was once more in the hands of the Allies.

THE CONSEQUENCES

The Burma campaign was the largest land campaign fought against the Japanese in World War II, but much of this might have been avoided had Churchill not interfered. At the Sextant Conference in November 1943, President Roosevelt had promised the Chinese leader, Chiang Kai-shek, that there would be a major amphibious assault in the Andaman Islands in the Indian Ocean, Operation Buccaneer, which in turn would facilitate a landing at Rangoon. He did this without consulting Churchill, who, when he learnt of the proposal, opposed Buccaneer as it would bleed resources from the Mediterranean theatre and most particularly from his Dodecanese campaign (see chapter 11). Yet Churchill would be obliged to abandon that campaign. Had Buccaneer been implemented it is possible that it would have been a more effective strategy for the defeat of Japan than the protracted and costly campaign in Burma.[43]

The fall of Hong Kong, Singapore, Malaya and Burma led their populations to lose faith in Britain's ability to defend them. The perceived frailty encouraged the rise of indigenous separatist movements. Churchill's actions led ineluctably to the decline of the British Empire after the war.

14
ITALY: THE 'SOFT UNDERBELLY' OF EUROPE

After Torch, the North African operation, came Husky, the landings in Sicily on 9–10 July 1943, and this was followed by the invasion of mainland Italy. It was 'a glorious opportunity', as Churchill put it, to capitalize on the Allied successes in North Africa.[1] He had originally wanted to do it earlier and had codenamed the plan Whipcord, but it was never properly developed.[2] He had written to the chiefs of staff on 25 November 1942: 'The paramount task before us is first, to conquer the African shores of the Mediterranean . . . [then] using the bases on the African shore to strike at the under-belly of the Axis in effective strength and in the shortest time . . .'[3]

In order to represent German-occupied Europe diagrammatically, Churchill sketched a crocodile fashioned from the map of Europe. Its mouth was facing Britain, its belly was southern Europe and its tail pointed at the Soviet Union. He showed this to Stalin and said that the Mediterranean was the 'soft underbelly of the crocodile'. He told US Lieutenant-General Mark Clark, who would command forces in Italy, that the objective was to 'slit this soft underbelly of the Mediterranean',[4] and argued that Italy was thus an ideal route by which to attack Germany.

However, Churchill's 'soft underbelly' picture of Europe was a false one. In reality the mouth of the crocodile faced the USSR, as this was where most of the German divisions were – some 214, compared with the 59 that were later deployed against the western Allies at the Second Front in France. It was on the Eastern Front that World War II in Europe would ultimately be decided, yet Churchill would mention the Soviet war effort hardly at all in his post-war books.[5]

The soft underbelly theory was also fundamentally flawed by a failure to consider the geography of the region. The Italian Alps were ideal for defence; indeed they were effectively impassable, with their high peaks and deep passes, offering plenty of opportunities for forces to secrete themselves and attack the Allies as they advanced. Armoured fighting vehicles are particularly vulnerable when attempting to negotiate narrow mountain passes; they require open country to move swiftly and effectively. As the use of ground attack aircraft is difficult in mountain passes, Allied air superiority was of limited benefit, while strategic bombing was of little use against anything other than large targets such as the historic abbey of Monte Cassino, which the Germans had occupied. German tanks, operating 'hull down' from concealed positions along with artillery and machine gun posts, could wreak havoc among the Allied advance. There were better ways of causing the attrition of German forces. Yet the Italian campaign would bog down along the spine of Italy long before it even got to the Alps.

Churchill's Italian strategy also presented a logistical nightmare. A long chain of communications was required, either via the eastern Atlantic, Gibraltar and the Mediterranean or, because of the threat from Wehrmacht forces, via the very much longer route around the Cape of Good Hope and through the Suez Canal. A Second Front in France, on the other hand, needed only a short chain of communication.

The US Army Chief of Staff, General George Marshall, was not at all convinced by Churchill's strategy; he wanted the Second Front in France, Operation Roundup, to occur in 1943 instead of Husky. On 14 December 1942 Field Marshal Sir John Dill reported this to Churchill: 'He [Marshall] is . . . getting more and more convinced that we should be in a position to undertake a modified "Round-up" before the summer [of 1943] if, as soon as North Africa is cleared of Axis forces, we start pouring American forces into England . . . Such an operation would, he feels, be much more effective than . . . "Husky" . . .'[6]

Churchill was reluctant to overrule his chiefs of staff, but he did sack them if they didn't agree with him. He had already sacked Sir John Dill as CIGS and sent him off to the United States. General Sir Alan Brooke replaced him and proved similarly obstructive, but his saving grace in Churchill's eyes was that he fully supported his dispersionist Mediterranean strategy.[7] Churchill, aided and abetted by such military brass, persuaded the Americans reluctantly to agree to this strategy.

The Second Front was still being resisted by Churchill, but Husky was intended to relieve pressure on the Russian front. This was decided at the Casablanca Conference, codenamed Symbol, between Churchill and Roosevelt in January 1943. The Americans agreed to support the British

Mediterranean campaign because British prevarication had meant that Roundup could now not take place in 1943. They insisted that it should take place the following year, but this meant that, without an Italian campaign, the western Allies would not be engaging the Germans at all until the summer of 1944, and with so many forces already deployed in the Mediterranean theatre, Churchill argued that it would be foolish not to continue to use them there. Also, Mussolini fell from power on 25 July, when he was outvoted in his own Fascist Grand Council and dismissed by King Emmanuel III. Thus it seemed that Italy was about to ask for terms or indeed to change sides.[8]

Therefore Churchill had got his way. Harold Macmillan summed things up with the remark, 'We are the Greeks in the New Roman Empire', meaning that while the Americans had the military and industrial facility, the British had the brains. The Americans were not all that comfortable with the result, and one of their planning staff, Albert Wedemeyer, commented, 'We came, we saw, we were conquered.'[9] The situation was made worse by Churchill's irascible nature, as Brooke recorded in his diary on 24 May 1943:

> At 4.45 pm went to the White House, first to be photographed, and then to attend conference with [the] President and PM. There the PM entirely repudiated the paper we had passed, agreed to, and been congratulated on at our last meeting!! He wished to alter all the Mediterranean decisions! He had no idea of the difficulties we had been through and just crashed in 'where angels fear to tread'. As a result he created [a] situation of suspicion in the American Chiefs that we had been behind their backs, and has made matters far more difficult for us in the future!! There are times when he drives me to desperation![10]

Brooke explained that the British chiefs had been obliged to concede certain points when originally drafting the paper, in order to gain American support on other issues. With Churchill's repudiation, it looked now as though they were using Churchill to try to get the Americans to reverse their decisions on points the British had already conceded. The American chiefs knew that Roosevelt would never have acted in this way unless they themselves had briefed him to do so, and thus they falsely assumed that Churchill would not act without the express approval of the British chiefs. Brooke therefore called Churchill's intervention 'tragic'.

OPERATION HUSKY

Sicily was defended by two German divisions (some 35,000 men) and ten Italian divisions (some 315,000 men), including five infantry divisions and five for the fixed coastal defences. All were under the command of General Alfredo Guzzoni. The fixed fortifications were not particularly robust, and there were few tanks, but the terrain was formidable – an ominous portent of things to come in mainland Italy.

General Dwight Eisenhower was appointed Allied Commander, General Sir Harold Alexander was Eisenhower's deputy and commanded the land forces, 15th Army Group. Admiral Sir Andrew Cunningham was responsible for seaborne forces, and Air Marshal Sir Arthur Tedder was in charge of the air forces: a British command structure with the Americans in overall charge of an Anglo-American force. Cunningham and Tedder had separate HQs, which led to poor communication, and Eisenhower and Mountbatten (at Combined Operations) were both in Malta.[11]

The British Eighth Army landed on the south-east coast of the island, with the US Seventh Army under the command of George Patton, now a lieutenant-general, landing just to the west for the capture of the airfield at Gela.[12] The objective was Messina, a short distance across the sea from the Italian mainland. Naturally the landings were opposed, but poor weather and an Allied deception plan had put the defensive forces off guard, so early resistance was muted. However, the airborne landings were scattered. At first the British advance was rapid; Syracuse was taken on 10 July and Augusta three days later. However progress then became costly as they faced the Hermann Göring Division, and fierce resistance at Catania – halfway to Messina – held them up for some time. The American forces advanced to Gela where they met a counterattack, but by 22 July Patton had entered Palermo. At the end of the month the advance would momentarily grind to a halt at Mount Etna before eventually entering Messina. The hold-ups in Sicily, however, would be nothing compared with the problems in mainland Italy.

THE 'TOUGH OLD GUT'

After the *hors d'oeuvre* of Sicily came the main course of Italy itself – Operation Avalanche – initiated on 9 September 1943. Its objective was the capture of Naples via an assault at Salerno Bay.

Although Mussolini had been overthrown on 25 July, it required protracted negotiations before the new Italian government, under the elderly Marshall Pietro Badoglio, arranged an armistice on 3 September.[13] Churchill had predicted this possibility back on 25 November 1942: 'If there is a revolution in Italy and an Armistice Government came into power, it is at least arguable that the German interests would be as well served by standing on the Brenner [Pass] as by undertaking the detailed defence of Italy against the wishes of its people, and possibly of a provisional Government.'[14] On 26 July 1943 he wrote to the War Cabinet concerning his thoughts on the fall of Mussolini:

> The fate of the German troops in Italy, particularly of those south of Rome, will probably lead to fighting between the Germans and the Italian army and population. We should demand their surrender . . . It may be, however, that the German divisions will cut their way northwards in spite of anything that the Italian armed forces are capable of doing. We should provoke this conflict as much as possible, and should not hesitate to send troops and Air support to assist the Italians in procuring the surrender of the Germans south of Rome.[15]

The Salerno attack was, then, intended to take the Germans by surprise while their Italian allies chased them out of Italy. However, it would do nothing of the sort. Luftwaffe Generalfeldmarschall Albrecht von Kesselring, in charge of German forces in the region, had already anticipated the possibility of attacks at Salerno and Gaeta between 6–9 September, as the moon entered its second quarter. Furthermore, as it was the only suitable landing area defended by Italians, the Germans realized that the collapse of Italy would make it an ideal Allied target. Thus, far from the Italian collapse being an advantage to the Allied cause, it gave the whole game away. The Germans were fully aware of the Allied task force leaving Sicily, and Axis forces were put on alert for an imminent landing at 15.40 on 8 September.

Although Italy was no longer 'officially' an adversarial belligerent, Hitler re-installed Mussolini as the head of the 'Republican Fascist Government', a puppet regime controlled from Berlin. This called the effectiveness of the Badoglio government into question. President Roosevelt did not believe support should be given, either to King Victor Emmanuel III, who had appointed Mussolini as Fascist Prime Minister in 1922, or to the Badoglio government, which he had now appointed. Churchill didn't agree, but attempted to compromise with Roosevelt by saying that support should be maintained for the regime at least until Rome had been taken by Allied forces.[16]

Churchill wrote to Stalin on 21 September: 'I propose . . . to advise the King to appeal on the wireless to the Italian people to rally round the Badoglio Government and to announce his intention to build up a broad-based anti-fascist coalition government'.[17] But when German forces approached Rome, Badoglio and his associates jumped into their cars and fled! The fact that Italy was now officially out of the war had at once become almost irrelevant, for while Badoglio's government had hoped for the support of the Italian people, the conflict in Italy would continue unabated no matter what they or Churchill wanted.

In *The Second World War* Churchill wrote of Avalanche: 'The Combined Chiefs of Staff advised the President and me to accept this plan, and to authorise the seizure of Sardinia and Corsica in second priority. We did this with alacrity; indeed it was exactly what I had hoped and striven for.'[18] The dispersionist tendencies are clearly evident here: the islands were of little strategic importance, yet he desired their occupation with 'alacrity'.

Eisenhower had appointed Lieutenant-General Mark Clark to take charge of Avalanche with command of the American Fifth Army – really a joint Anglo-American force. It had been formed in January 1943 and was divided into two corps, the British X Corps and the US VI Corps, a total of more than 30,000 men, to be delivered in 700 ships. On 3 September, six days prior to Avalanche, Monty and the Eighth Army initiated a diversionary assault, Operation Baytown, close to the Calabrian town of Reggio. Ranged against the Allied forces were the German Tenth Army, under Generaloberst Heinrich von Vietinghoff, and the 222 Italian Coastal Defence Division at Salerno bay. The Tenth Army was newly formed but

Vietinghoff himself had extensive combat experience. In all, the Germans had 45,000 men ready to oppose the Salerno landings. Opposing Monty's Eighth Army at Calabria they had 30,000 men. A further 17,000 were available on the Adriatic. As Hitler had anticipated the Italian collapse, he ordered Panzers to replace the Italian coastal defence forces.

Whereas Husky had been largely a surprise because of the Allied deception plans and the weather, Avalanche was nothing of the kind. Clark referred to it as a 'near disaster'.[19] The underbelly of Europe was supposed to offer less resistance than the French coast, but the onslaught by the Luftwaffe during the first three days took a massive toll on the Allied fleet. There had been little opposition to Baytown, as Kesselring realized that this was a diversionary feint, so the Germans chose simply to delay Monty's advance with tactics such as the demolition of bridges. Monty had originally opposed the whole idea of Baytown for precisely this reason, predicting correctly that the Germans would see it for what it was and refuse to engage the Eighth Army in serious battle. What it did accomplish was to place the Eighth Army some 480km (300 miles) south of Salerno, a distance they then had to march while being harried by the Germans all the way.

From the outset of both operations, the logistical problems created by the terrain were crippling. The US Fifth and the British Eighth Armies were too large to fight together in the narrow 'toe' of Italy, but the geography would permit only a single supply operation. Also, the assault assumed a swift advance by Monty, who was not known for moving quickly at the best of times; the terrain, supply restrictions and German harassment made this far from the best of times. By the evening of 12 September the Panzers had established a salient between the American and British forces, attacking both. German positions used the high ground to advantage and the Allied beachheads were exposed. Kesselring's counterattack had been launched the previous day and would continue until the 18th. The Allies were hard pressed to avoid being pushed back into the sea. Soon, anybody who could carry a gun was pressed into service on the Allied side.

When progress was eventually made, the obvious fact that the mountainous terrain offered opportunities for defence while exposing attacking forces as they moved along roads and passes became very apparent. The American GIs referred to Chiunzi Pass as 'Hellfire' or '88 Pass' because of the opposition from the Krupp 88mm artillery. The battle here lasted 18 days. Eventually, Kesselring gradually withdrew towards Rome, but by 18 September the casualties at Salerno told their own story: the Allied figure was 8,731, of which 4,736 were wounded, 2,430 missing and 1,565 confirmed dead; German casualties were 1,649, of which 835 were wounded, 589 missing and 225 dead.

Exemplifying the whole campaign was the decision to bomb the German stronghold of Monte Cassino, made because the Allies had mounted a land assault three times and had been defeated three times, losing 4,000 New Zealanders in the process. This demonstrated how difficult it was to attack yet how ideally suited conditions were for defence. Even after the bombing the Germans simply moved into the rubble and fought on tenaciously. As Clark subsequently said, far from being the soft underbelly of Europe, Italy was 'a tough old gut'.[20] At the turn of the year 1943–4, Clark recounted:

> Churchill had always had his eyes on the soft underbelly of the Axis, and that included the Balkans. He was not pleased when he saw that plans for the cross-Channel invasion of France were already sucking men, ships, and material away from the Mediterranean, and that the situation would be intensified later on. At the Christmas conference he overrode all objections, including Eisenhower's, who warned Churchill that the Germans would probably not withdraw, but would fight it out, as they did.[21]

The Gustav Line was a formidable German defensive line occupying the high ground at the Italian peninsula's narrowest point. The Apennine Mountains were particularly rugged, so the terrain was ideally suited to defensive warfare and almost prohibited an armoured assault. Kesselring planned to hold the Gustav Line for at least the next six months. This prevented the Allied Fifth Army from moving forward into the Liri Valley and on to Rome. As Eisenhower and Clark predicted, the Germans were intent on fighting out the Italian campaign.

With poor weather in the winter of 1943–4, Eisenhower and the Combined Chiefs of Staff appreciated that the advance was now effectively halted. So difficult was the campaign becoming that a seaborne operation had to be devised to circumvent German land forces in southern Italy. Thus the idea to bypass the Gustav Line with an amphibious landing near Rome began to take shape from late October 1943. This would enable a direct assault on the Italian capital, or so it was hoped. Churchill was prepared to halve the modest rations of the British people in order to release shipping to, as he put it, 'strike at the knee', rather than crawl up the Italian leg 'like a harvest bug'.[22]

ANZIO

On 8 November, General Sir Harold Alexander, who commanded the 15th Army Group, consisting of the Fifth Army under Clark and the Eighth under Monty, ordered Clark, on behalf of the Combined Chiefs of Staff, to develop a plan to land one division at Anzio on 20 December. However, due to American disquiet, the operation was momentarily shelved on 18 December. Then in January Eisenhower relinquished responsibility for Allied forces in the Mediterranean to take up his duties for Overlord – the Second Front in France – and the command structure for the Mediterranean now became British. General Sir Henry Maitland 'Jumbo' Wilson took over Eisenhower's responsibilities, and US Army Chief of Staff George Marshall, the principal American military opponent of the British strategy, was thus effectively out of the loop. Sir Alan Brooke and the British chiefs now had responsibility for planning in the theatre, so the Anzio plan was back on – and now in enlarged form. In early January 1944 Churchill persuaded the Americans to slow down the transfer of amphibious craft to southern England for the Second Front to enable the Anzio assault to take place. It was codenamed Operation Shingle.

Churchill had wider ambitions for Shingle, though with the deteriorating relationship with Roosevelt he could hardly confide in the American President. Once Rome had been taken, Churchill hoped a further advance could be undertaken to the Pisa–Rimini line, then on into the Po Valley, then via the Ljubljana Gap to Vienna, Prague and Budapest. The Americans were constantly suspicious of Churchill's desire for adventure in the east, and as it would do little to defeat Germany but rather take men and materiel away from the Second Front, it remained no more than a dream.[23]

Churchill supported Anzio, despite the fact that, as Clark recounted, the senior intelligence officer:

. . . was sceptical of the advisability of the operation, because he knew the political importance of Rome to Hitler; he knew that there were German divisions in France and Yugoslavia not too busily engaged during this winter period; and he also knew that the enemy could move those divisions to Italy if they were needed. All of these factors added up to a dangerous undertaking. In spite of all this Churchill was ready to accept the obvious hazards of the landing because the prize to be gained by seizing Rome justified a calculated risk.[24]

Indeed, intelligence reports suggested that the 29th Panzer Grenadier Division had been moved close to Rome and threatened the Anzio beachhead directly. Clark wrote: 'President Roosevelt was anxious not to undertake any operation that would delay or damage the invasion of France, but Churchill felt that it was desirable to take Rome at almost any cost.'[25] As well as this, Churchill was now, as ever, pressurizing Clark and the others for an early date for Anzio on a familiar pretext. As Clark recounted, 'The Germans were putting up such a successful defence of Rome. This, he [Churchill] believed, was having an unfavourable effect on both Turkey and Spain; it was, therefore essential that the Italian capital should be captured, and soon.'[26] Turkey again!

Anzio had been picked as it offered reasonably good terrain and was within the radius of Allied air cover. The beachhead selected was 25km (15 miles) wide, only the Alban Hills were between Anzio and Rome, and around these there were two major trunk roads. The operation was now slated for late January, and was to be one of three undertaken. Clark picked US Major-General John Lucas to lead the Anzio operation. He gave him only vague orders, reflecting the fact that both men were increasingly sceptical about the British plan, particularly with the limited availability of forces, and the expectation – which turned out to be false – that the landing would be opposed by significant German units. So Clark wanted to leave Lucas the scope for advancing only as far as he felt prudent in the circumstances.

The operation was to be undertaken by the Fifth Army's VI Corps. The British contributed the First Infantry Division and the 46th Royal Tank Regiment plus two commando battalions. From the air, the XII Tactical Air Command, the British Desert Air Force, the Coastal Air Force and the

Tactical Bomber Force were all employed. The naval component consisted of, on the American side, two task forces: 81 and X-Ray, commanded by US Rear-Admiral Frank Lowry; the former encompassed 250 vessels to make the assault and the latter 74 vessels to support the beachhead. On the British side, Rear-Admiral Thomas Troubridge commanded Task Force Peter, comprising 52 ships intended to deliver and support the British land forces.

Ten days before Anzio, elements of the Fifth Army consisting of the US II Corps, British X Corps, and French Expeditionary Corps, were to attack the Gustav Line directly, crossing both the Garigliano and Rapido Rivers and defeating von Vietinghoff's Tenth Army at Cassino. They were then to advance through the Liri Valley to join the Anzio assault forces. While this was happening, the Eighth Army would attack the Adriatic flank, pinning down German forces there. In fact, the French Expeditionary Corps attacked Cassino, while the British X Corps attacked at the Garigliano River, but both attacks failed to breach the Gustav Line. On 20 January, the US II Corps attempted to cross the Rapido River, but failed after two days of intense combat.

Operation Shingle was instigated in the early hours of 22 January 1944 by VI Corps with landings near Anzio and Nettuno. German resistance was light, as German forces had been sent south to reinforce the Gustav Line, and complete surprise was thus accomplished. The British and American forces achieved their first day's objectives by midday, and had advanced 5–6km (3–4 miles) inland by nightfall. Of course it could not have been foreseen that the Germans would fail to oppose the landings: the prospect of such opposition had been real, yet the entire Italian campaign had been initiated precisely to avoid the prospect of an opposed landing – this was why Churchill was opposed to the Second Front.

In a telegram sent on 8 February 1944 to Sir John Dill, Churchill's representative in Washington, to be conveyed to General Marshall, Churchill included an exchange between himself and General Wilson. Churchill had asked, 'Why was no attempt made to occupy high ground and at least the towns of Velletri, Campeleone and Cisterna twelve or twenty-four hours after the unopposed landing?' Wilson had responded:

> This was not due to lack of urging from above as Alexander and Clark visited beachhead in first 48 hours to speed up advance. Attributed to: (1) failure of Corps Commander to

appreciate value of surprise he had achieved and to take advantage of it. (2) A Salerno complex in that task was to beat off inevitable counter-attacks as a prelude to success. (3) Disinclination to risk advance without considerable backing. In this case arrival of combat team of 1 U.S. Armoured Division.[27]

Churchill's riposte was, 'Senior commanders should not "urge" but "order".' He then commented on the lessons that could be learnt for the Second Front in France, which was, by this time, certain to go ahead. As we have seen, Clark was not at all convinced that such an advance would not have been defeated. Far better to dig in, establish a beachhead and bring up reinforcements to undertake an effective attack against Kesselring's most capable opposition.

In Berlin the OKW had been expecting such a landing for some time, but was surprised by the location and speed of it. However, Kesselring quickly ordered units of the 4th Parachute and Hermann Göring Divisions to interdict the Allied forces. The 3rd Panzer Grenadier and 71st Infantry Divisions were soon engaging Allied forces at Anzio, and these were rapidly reinforced as Hitler moved forces from other parts of Italy, from Yugoslavia, France, and from Germany itself. Kesselring, Generalmajor Siegfried Westphal, his chief of staff, and Generaloberst Eberhard von Mackensen, whose 14th Army would have responsibility for repelling the Allies, soon had matters in hand. Some 70,000 German servicemen would halt the Allied advance.

The Anzio campaign lasted for four months, and VI Corps endured some 4,400 killed, 18,000 wounded, and 6,800 prisoners or missing in action, plus 37,000 non-combat casualties. The German 14th Army suffered about 5,500 killed, 17,500 wounded, and 4,500 prisoners or missing in action.

There was stalemate until the spring, with an old-fashioned World War I-type trench system. Kesselring used this hiatus to create a new defensive line, the Caesar C Line, to contain the Allied beachhead. On the Allied side, US Major-General Lucian Truscott replaced Lucas on 22 February to command VI Corps and prepared for Operation Diadem, the next offensive against the Gustav Line. Diadem would fail to destroy German resistance and the Allies would have to fight until May 1945, during which time the US Fifth and British Eighth Armies endured some 44,000 casualties. But the prize of Rome still beckoned and Clark insisted that VI Corps should go for it:

> We not only wanted the honour of capturing Rome, but felt that we deserved it . . . Not only did we intend to become the first army to seize Rome from the south, but we intended to see that people at home knew that it was the Fifth Army that did the job, and knew the price that had been paid for it.[28]

Go for Rome they did, and Clark would enter it as liberator. Yet when the battle was raging at a bridgehead south of Rome, Churchill could not prevent himself from interfering with the detailed command structure at a critical time. Alan Brooke wrote in his diary on 16 February 1944:

> I had hardly arrived in the office when I was sent for by [the] PM who wanted to send Alexander to command the troops in the bridgehead and Wilson to command the main front! I am afraid I rather lost my temper with him over this and asked him if he could not for once trust his commanders to organise the command for themselves without interfering and upsetting all the chain and sequence of command. He gave up his idea for the present, but may well return to the attack!![29]

By October 1944 the reality was coming home to Churchill. On the 10th he telegrammed Eisenhower, whose Second Front forces were entering Germany:

> On the way to Naples with Generals Wilson and Alexander. I was much distressed by their tale. The fighting has been very hard. Our losses since the battle opened have been about 30,000 . . . Our men are tired and there are no fresh divisions to put in. It seems so much has been taken away from our Italian front against Germany as just to deny a complete victory in this theatre . . . Thus Kesselring may bring us to a standstill in the Apennines until they are wrapped in snow. He could then withdraw five or six divisions to resist

Eisenhower on the Rhine. The German fighting here has been of utmost tenacity, and troops he could withdraw would be of high class.[30]

Churchill continued by pleading for more forces. But he had given the game away by admitting that Eisenhower's Second Front forces were already on the Rhine, whereas Churchill's campaign in Italy was going precisely nowhere.

THE ENDGAME

The fundamental problem with the entire Italian campaign was that the country's geography necessitated amphibious landings: this was the only way to circumvent the restrictions presented by the narrow, circuitous routes up the east and west coasts, which were the only ones available to an assaulting force. But the whole campaign quickly fell into stalemate anyway, causing the kind of attrition seen in World War I.

What Anzio did was ensure that the flow of forces directed to Italy slowed down the process of organizing a Second Front in France. By 1945 it had certainly become important to keep Italy out of Soviet hands, but as Italy would have collapsed after the defeat of Germany the Allies could have walked into it in 1945 with no opposition. Italy would have collapsed anyway, in much the same way as the German occupation of Norway and Denmark was ended non-violently after the collapse of Germany.

It is sometimes said that the real Allied victory in the Italian campaign was to inflict half a million German casualties. But Churchill's purpose for the Italian campaign was not the attrition of German forces, but the defeat of Germany by attacking through the soft underbelly of Europe, and it was precisely on this issue that he was wrong. The spine of Italy was almost impossible to fight through, and the Italian Alps were impassable. Eventually forces had to be withdrawn for the western Allies to undertake the real battle against Germany, via Normandy. Allied forces had reached Trieste by April 1945, but by this time Germany had already been effectively defeated by the Soviet Union and the Second Front in France, while the Alps remained unpenetrated. Italy proved not to be a route to Germany at all. The American generals were quite right to concentrate on the Second

Front to defeat Germany. Defeat Germany and Italy would collapse, defeat Italy and Germany still had to be defeated.

In reality, without the defeat of Germany, fighting continued in Italy to the bitter end. The *Linea Gotica*, or Gothic Line, renamed the Green Line in June 1944, was Kesselring's final line of defence along the Apennines. Although Allied forces penetrated it on the Adriatic side and in the central area by autumn 1944, Kesselring's forces managed to retire in a successful defensive movement so that the Allies were unable to make a decisive breakthrough until the spring of 1945. It was not until 29 April that von Vietinghoff, then commanding Army Group C, signed the surrender, and the war in Italy was over on 2 May. The war in Italy had lasted almost as long as the war against Germany.

Churchill's response was to blame the American insistence on Operation Anvil, later renamed Dragoon – the invasion of the South of France – which was undertaken to support the cross-Channel invasion and had drawn forces away from the Italian campaign. In his own post-war historical account he wrote:

> Many of the forces needed for the operation – that is to say, for the full-scale invasion as opposed to a feint or threat – would have to come from our armies in Italy. But these had first to accomplish the arduous and important task of seizing Rome and the airfields. Until this was done little could be spared or taken from Alexander's forces. Rome must fall before 'Anvil' could start.
>
> All turned on the capture of Rome. If we could seize it quickly all would be well. Troops could then be withdrawn from the Italian front and 'Anvil' launched in good time. If not, a feint landing would suffice.[31]

The Americans wanted more than just a 'feint', as will be seen in the next chapter, but this shows how vital the Italian campaign was in Churchill's mind. Yet his 'soft underbelly' theory was now dead: the Allies could not defeat Germany by this route. Rome was a sideshow; the war was being won by the western Allies in France and by the USSR in the East. The Italians were already out of the war anyway, so Rome was not a priority at all. Churchill attempted to justify his position by continuing:

The important descent at Anzio to accelerate the capture of Rome had drawn eight or ten German divisions away from the vital theatre, or more than was expected to be attracted to the Riviera by 'Anvil'. This in effect superseded it by achieving its object. Nevertheless the Riviera project went forward as if nothing had happened.[32]

According to this, the Italian campaign was not to defeat Germany via the soft underbelly of Europe, but Churchill had accepted the American position that the need was to draw German forces away from the 'vital' theatre in northern France. However, given the Allies' substantial logistical problems in supplying the Italian campaign, and because the topography favoured the defensive German tactics, this was not the most efficient way to degrade German forces. More resources should have been committed to the strategic and tactical bombing campaign (see chapter 16), given that the Allies had total air superiority by this period in the war. Churchill did not appreciate that landings in France were simply a better way to defeat Germany than fighting up the spine of Italy.[33] His strategy, and the prevarication over a Second Front in France, prolonged the war and helped the Soviets gain substantial territory in Eastern Europe, which they would rule until the end of the 1980s.

15
THE SECOND FRONT: CHURCHILL PROCRASTINATES

Churchill argued in *The Second World War* that he had always been in favour of a Second Front in France. However, using his image of German-occupied Europe as a crocodile (or later an alligator) with its teeth in France, he wrote, 'When Stalin asked me about crossing the Channel I told him, "Why stick your head in the alligator's mouth at Brest when you can go to the Mediterranean and rip his soft underbelly." So why was he in favour of a Second Front in France if he thought it meant attacking the teeth rather than the soft underbelly?[1]

Churchill's suggestion that he had always endorsed a Second Front in France is quite inconsistent with his dispersionist strategy. He had a proclivity to attack in areas of no strategic importance, yet France was of central strategic importance. In reality the whole purpose of the Italian campaign was to avoid a Second Front in France altogether. Indeed for Churchill, the Italian campaign *was* the Second Front. But it was clearly impossible to defeat Germany through Italy, and a Second Front in France had to occur at some time. Churchill's procrastination and President Roosevelt's failure to veto him simply postponed the inevitable.

It has been argued that the Germans endured a considerable attrition of their resources in Italy, depleting their ability to prosecute the war as a whole. Indeed they did, but so did the Allies. The procrastination did have one beneficial effect on British casualty numbers: it meant that the Soviet Union had to do most of the fighting, suffer most of the casualties and take most responsibility for victory in the European war. It also meant that at the end of the war the Soviets had advanced further west than they otherwise would have, and thus more Central European citizens found themselves in Communist one-party states controlled from Moscow than need have done.

General Sir Alan Brooke, was, like Churchill, opposed to a Second Front in France, recognizing that Britain had insufficient forces to conduct a direct assault on continental Europe any time soon. Like Churchill,

Brooke was in error not to see that the almost infinite industrial capacity of the USA made a Second Front feasible in 1943, if not 1942, or that it was necessary to obviate the enormous number of additional deaths in the European war that would result from its postponement to 1944. However, he played an invaluable role in constraining Churchill, who would insist on flights of fancy with operations Brooke knew were not feasible. Brooke noted in his diary on 27 May 1942, 'At 5.30 went to 10 Downing St to discuss establishing of Western Front. PM in very good form and quite ready to appreciate that it is impossible to establish a front with landing craft only capable of lifting 4,000 men [in] first flight. He was very amenable to reason, but inclined to transfer the scene of action to Northern Norway!'[2]

SLEDGEHAMMER AND ROUNDUP

General George Marshall had all along been convinced that the only way to defeat Germany was by a Second Front in France. Thus, it was on Marshall's advice that in 1942 Roosevelt forced Churchill to accept America's intention that a Second Front be mounted.[3] Two alternative plans were proposed: one was for a lodgement on the French coast, scheduled for the autumn of 1942 and codenamed Sledgehammer; the second was for a full-scale invasion in 1943 codenamed Roundup. Finally the plan would become Overlord (though 'Millennium'[4] had been the original codename reserved for it), which would be executed on 6 June 1944.[5]

On 28 May 1942 Churchill sent Roosevelt a summary of his talks with the Soviet Foreign Minister, Vyacheslav Molotov. It is clear from this that Churchill was already opposed to Sledgehammer. After receipt of the summary, Roosevelt himself held talks with Molotov. He then approved a communiqué which said, among other things, 'In the course of the conversations full understanding was reached with regard to the urgent tasks of creating a second front in Europe in 1942.' It is not at all clear whether Roosevelt seriously meant this or just endorsed the communiqué to placate the Soviets, but it was consistent with the American position that an early Second Front was deemed essential.[6]

Roosevelt sent Churchill a message on 1 April 1942 stating that Marshall and Harry Hopkins (Roosevelt's unofficial, but crucial, emissary to Churchill and Stalin) would travel to London to inform him of American intentions for a cross-Channel invasion. In addition to Marshall and Hopkins, Henry Stimson, the US Secretary of War, was an architect of the plan, codenamed Modicum, which referred to both Sledgehammer and Roundup. Although Churchill wrote back in effusive terms it is clear that his primary aim was to steer Roosevelt away from both Sledgehammer and Roundup.[7] He gave an entirely false impression to Marshall and Hopkins, who then conveyed it back to the President. Major-General Sir Hastings Ismay, Churchill's representative to the chiefs of staff, attended the meeting, and recalled:

> Our American Friends went happily homewards under the mistaken impression that we had committed ourselves to both ROUNDUP and SLEDGEHAMMER . . . When we had to tell them, after the most thorough study of SLEDGEHAMMER, that we were absolutely opposed to it, they felt that we had broken faith with them . . . I think we should have come clean, much cleaner than we did, and said, 'We are frankly horrified because of what we have been through in our lifetime . . . We are not going into this until it is a cast-iron certainty.'[8]

However, Churchill wrote to the President on 17 April, after Hopkins and Marshall had left for the USA:

> We wholeheartedly agree with your conception of concentration against the main enemy, and we cordially accept your plan with one broad qualification . . . It is essential that we should prevent a junction of the Japanese and the Germans. Consequently, a proportion of our combined resources
> must . . . be set aside to halt the Japanese advance . . .
>   The campaign of 1943 [Roundup] is straight forward, and we are starting joint plans and preparations at once. We may, however, feel compelled to act this year. Your plan [Sledgehammer] visualised this . . .

Churchill went on to mention Marshall's concern that there might be insufficient American air cover for Sledgehammer, but provided this could be rectified, he wrote, 'We are proceeding with plans and preparations on that basis.'[9] He had assented to either plan, yet in fact he supported neither.

One of the purposes of a Second Front was to relieve the pressure on the Russians, but in this regard Churchill revealed his cold feet. He wrote to Roosevelt on 1 June 1942: 'Like you I am anxious about Russia and also China in the next few months. It is often easier to see dangers gathering than to have the power to ward them off, and very often they don't happen.'[10] Unfortunately, in this war the dangers often *did* happen.

Now Churchill reversed his position on Sledgehammer. At the Washington Conference codenamed Argonaut, he sent a memo to Roosevelt on 20 June 1942:

> Arrangements are being made for a landing of six or eight Divisions on the coast of Northern France early in September. However, the British Government would not favour an operation that was certain to lead to disaster for this would not help the Russians whatever their plight, would compromise and expose to Nazi vengeance the French population involved and would gravely delay the main operation in 1943 [Roundup]. We hold strongly to the view that there should be no substantial landing in France this year unless we are going to stay.
>
> . . . No responsible British military authority has so far been able to make a plan for September 1942 which had any chance of success unless the Germans become utterly demoralised, of which there is no likelihood.[11]

Brooke was also opposed to Sledgehammer, as he recorded on 1 July 1942:

> One might think we were going across the Channel to play baccarat at Le Touquet, or to bathe at Paris Plage! Nobody stops to think what you can possibly do with some 6 divisions against a possible 20 to 30! PM is well aware of all the implications. And yet for all that we are likely to be forced to undergo all the handicaps of taking up the necessary shipping and sacrificing the required training in order to prepare for an operation which we are convinced is impracticable.[12]

Churchill wrote to Roosevelt on 8 July 1942 extolling the virtues of his North African operation Torch (originally Gymnast), rather than Sledgehammer:

> No responsible General, Admiral or Air Marshal is prepared to recommend SLEDGEHAMMER as a practical operation in 1942 . . . According to Mountbatten [Chief of Combined Operations], if we interrupt the training of the troops we should . . . delay ROUNDUP . . . for at least two or three months even if the enterprise were unsuccessful and the troops had to be withdrawn after a short stay.
>
> In the event of a lodgement being effected and maintained it would have to be nourished and the bomber effort on Germany would have to be greatly curtailed . . . I am sure that GYMNAST [Torch] is by far the best chance for effective relief to the Russian front in 1942.[13]

This proved to be an extremely dangerous statement. The Americans were not surprised and Marshall said to Admiral Ernest King: 'If the British position must be accepted, the US should turn to the Pacific for decisive action against Japan.'[14] In fact this was precisely what happened: from September 1942 Marshall began to reduce his support for the entire notion of 'Germany First' – that Germany should be dealt with before Japan – and enabled King to start shifting resources to the Pacific theatre, the very thing Churchill did not want.

Operation Bolero, the build-up of American forces in Britain in preparation for a cross-Channel invasion, was now compromised. The estimate in the autumn of 1942 was that by the following spring only about half a dozen American divisions would be combat-ready in Britain, whereas it had been envisaged that at least 27 would be needed for Roundup. Indeed Bolero was to be reduced by around a million US servicemen. Churchill was understandably alarmed, but Roosevelt was clear that demands in the Pacific made this necessary. The net result was that the United States, the stronger partner, fielded fewer combatants in the European theatre during 1943 than Britain. American ground forces would not exceed the British until the following year. Forces were now being bled away from the European theatre, and there would be no cross-Channel invasion for the foreseeable future. The prospect for the citizens of occupied Europe was bleak.[15]

But Churchill wouldn't let up. On 14 July 1942 he wrote to Roosevelt: 'I have found no one who regards Sledgehammer as possible. I should like to see you do Gymnast as soon as possible, and that we in concert with the Russians should try for JUPITER. Meanwhile all preparations for ROUNDUP in 1943 should proceed at full blast . . .'[16] However, Churchill would renege on Roundup; Operation Jupiter was the invasion of Norway!

Marshall, Hopkins and King were dispatched by Roosevelt to London, arriving on 18 July 1942. Despite Churchill's request that they go directly to the Prime Minister's country retreat of Chequers, the Americans headed for Claridge's in London, where they set up their headquarters and worked on their strategy. When they met Churchill and the British chiefs, they argued that a Second Front in France was essential to keep the eight million Russian combatants in the war. However, the British wouldn't have it. By 22 July it was clear that neither side would budge. Marshall cabled Roosevelt accordingly and then asked Eisenhower, who would ultimately command the Second Front, to mediate. He said, 'I hardly know where to start . . . [this] could well go down as the blackest day in history.' In the end Roosevelt sided with Churchill in order to maintain unity, and the North African invasion went ahead instead.[17]

Consistency never troubled Churchill, however, and he wrote to Roosevelt on 27 July 1942, 'We must establish a second front this year and attack at the earliest moment.'[18] Having said 'No' to Sledgehammer, and been most insistent, he was now saying 'Yes'. In the end the Americans would kill Sledgehammer. US Lieutenant-General Mark Clark wrote:

> [Churchill] stressed to us that he was in favour of postponing the cross-channel operation and undertaking an invasion of North-west Africa at the earliest possible date. A European operation, even of a limited nature, would be too hazardous, he said, until a later time. Both Ike [Eisenhower] and I felt that direct action was the best idea, and that it was necessary to carry the war to the Continent as directly and as quickly as possible. We were therefore non-committal about Churchill's suggestions, because we felt that his Africa plan would detract from whatever hope there was of striking directly at Europe with a limited invasion programme in 1942, or of mounting a large-scale invasion operation in 1943.[19]

Thus Eisenhower, Clark, and indeed Marshall, and much of the senior American brass along with Hopkins and Stimson, were in favour of the Second Front in France as the primary mechanism to defeat Nazi Germany, although, Clark wrote:

> . . . it was finally agreed that, while plans for 'Round-up' would be continued, the main immediate effort would be directed towards the Mediterranean theatre. We were therefore instructed to be prepared as fully as possible for an emergency attack against the French coast late in 1942 if the Russian situation became so critical that such action was essential, and we were told to proceed with broader plans for a 1943 invasion of Europe. But it was soon obvious that our real effort at this time was going to be against North Africa.[20]

There was grave disquiet at the highest level in the USA, as Clark wrote:

> I found the Secretary of War, Henry L. Stimson, worried, however, about the success of the African invasion. He was also apprehensive that it would have the effect of greatly delaying any invasion of Europe, which, he believed, must be executed. He suggested doubts of the soundness of Churchill's judgment regarding the 'soft belly' of the Axis.[21]

Churchill had accomplished his task, for Torch and the subsequent Italian campaign would put off Roundup.

When Churchill first met Stalin for a conference in Moscow from 12–17 August 1942, Stalin immediately insisted on a Second Front in France by the end of the year. The Soviets had endured more than four million casualties in 1941. In talks with Molotov, Churchill vacillated, saying that it would require a lot of preparation. Well it would, but the Soviets' exasperation is understandable: in the end it would take almost two more years' preparation, while they were undertaking the bulk of the fighting. Churchill sent a memo to Stalin on 14 August saying that a Sledgehammer-type operation was not realistic and insisting that the North African operation, Torch, was the only practicable solution for the relief of pressure on the Soviet armies. He wrote:

Compared with 'Torch', the attack with 6 or 8 Anglo-American Divisions on the Cherbourg Peninsular and the Channel Islands would be a hazardous and futile operation. The Germans have enough troops in the West to block us in this narrow peninsula with fortified lines . . . In the opinion of all the British Naval, Military and Air authorities, the operation could only end in disaster . . . It would also be far more a running sore for us than for the enemy, and would use up wastefully and wantonly the key men and the landing craft required for real action in 1943.[22]

However, he did give a personal promise to Stalin on the final evening of their conference that there would be a Second Front – of some sort.[23]

Churchill misinterpreted a communication from the Americans, wrongly thinking they had changed their stance on the cross-Channel invasion. Thus, in a telegram to the President on 24 November 1942, as though butter wouldn't melt in his mouth, he wrote:

We had no knowledge that you had decided to abandon for ever 'Roundup', and all our preparations were proceeding on a broad front under 'Bolero' . . . It seems to me that it would be a most grievous decision to abandon 'Roundup'. 'Torch' is no substitute for 'Roundup' and only engages 13 divisions as against the 48 contemplated for 'Roundup'. All my talks with Stalin, in Averell's [Averell Harriman, the President's envoy] presence, were on the basis of a postponed 'Roundup'. But never was it suggested that we should attempt no second front in Europe in 1943 or even 1944 . . . Surely, Mr. President, this matter requires most profound consideration. I was deeply impressed with all General Marshall's arguments that only by 'Roundup' could the main forces be thrown into France and the Low Countries, and only in this area could the main strength of the British Metropolitan and United States Overseas Air Forces be brought into action. One of the arguments used against 'Sledgehammer' was that it would eat up in 1942 the seed-corn needed for the much larger 'Roundup' in 1943 . . . Only by the building up of a 'Roundup' force here as rapidly as other urgent demands on shipping allow can we have the means of coming to grips with the main strength of the enemy and liberating the European nations. It may be that, try as we will, our strength will not reach the necessary levels in 1943. But if so it becomes all the more important to make sure we do not miss 1944 . . . Even in 1943 a chance may come. Should Stalin's offensive reach Rostov-on-Don, which is his aim, a first class disaster may overtake the German southern armies. Our Mediterranean operations following on 'Torch' may drive Italy out of the war. Widespread demoralization may set in among the Germans, and we must be ready to profit by any opportunity which offers.[24]

The President replied, 'We, of course, have no intention of abandoning "Roundup"'.[25] Churchill's reference to Stalin is important: he was always stung by Stalin's jibes that he was afraid to endorse a cross-Channel invasion. So his concern was partly Stalin's reaction to a cancellation of Roundup. Churchill's comment that, 'never was it suggested that we should attempt no Second Front in 1943' is at variance with his own position and that of the British chiefs as enunciated in this chapter. His reference to Stalin's recent offensive and how that might be exploited is blatant opportunism – not a coherent plan to defeat the Axis powers. But his enthusiastic endorsement of the basic idea of the cross-Channel invasion was inconsistent with his whole 'soft underbelly' theory.

Churchill's procrastination increasingly concerned Stalin, who telegrammed him on 28 November 1942 saying that he hoped he had not changed his mind regarding 'your promise given in Moscow to establish a second Front in western Europe in the spring of 1943'.[26] Brooke noted in his diary for 30 November 1942:

COS [Chiefs of Staff meeting] at which we examined [the] most recent ideas of PM for re-entry into the Continent in 1943, and where he is again trying to commit us to a definite plan of action. After lunch interview with S of S [Secretary of State for War] on [the] new proposed manpower cuts of [the] PM. He never faces realities, at one moment we are reducing our forces, and the next we are invading the Continent with vast armies for which there is no hope of finding the shipping. He is quite incorrigible and I am quite exhausted![27]

However, Churchill's conception of Roundup was fundamentally different from Marshall's. Churchill saw Roundup, not as a Second Front, but simply as another operation to be conducted as part of his dispersionist strategy. It was never to be the principle, decisive assault by the western Allies, but one of many pinpricks around the periphery of Hitler's fiefdom. The historian Warren Kimball observed:

> [Churchill] tried to make up in rhetoric what his forces could not do in the field. Bringing 'the war home to Mussolini and his Fascist gang with an intensity not yet possible', hardly substituted for an assault against the main enemy – Germany. 'Continuous preparations' to 'keep the Germans pinned in the Pas-de-Calais' and Allied bombers 'blasting Germany with ever increasing violence' were a far cry from a confrontation with the enemy's armies. Such measures would 'tighten the halter upon the guilty doomed', but the Soviets would continue to suspect that the Anglo-Americans were deliberately delaying the Second Front. Those suspicions could eventually lead to Soviet–German peace talks, which left Churchill on the horns of a dilemma, a dilemma made worse by the initial Soviet success at Stalingrad; for if they no longer needed Anglo-American assistance to expel the Germans from the Soviet Union, such negotiations would become even more feasible.[28]

Kimball is not quite right: Soviet–German peace talks were never likely unless there was stalemate. If the Soviets had been defeated at Stalingrad the Germans might have been in an unassailable position, and the Second Front would have come too late. But with the Soviet victory at Stalingrad the Germans were likely to be beaten by the Soviets alone. Thus if the Second Front had never come, or had simply been a dispersionist measure rather than a concentrated and decisive *Schwerpunkt*, Stalin's forces might have brought Western as well as Eastern Europe under Communist hegemony.

On 3 December, Churchill wrote to the War Cabinet and the chiefs of staff:

In April last General Marshall unfolded to us the plan subsequently called 'Roundup', of which 'Bolero' is the administrative counterpart. A massive argument was that 'Roundup' is the only way in which large American and British forces can be brought into direct contact with the enemy, and the British Metropolitan and United States Overseas Air Forces exercise their maximum power. American military opinion was solidly ranged behind this enterprise, and since then preparations under 'Bolero' have gone forward steadily, subject only to 'Torch'. As an addition to 'Roundup', 'Sledgehammer' was proposed in July. It was agreed by the combined staffs that 'Torch' should be executed instead of 'Sledgehammer'. Meanwhile 'Bolero' was to continue with preparations for a retarded or opportunist 'Roundup' . . . However, the opinion was held by the American Staffs that the abandonment of 'Sledgehammer' and the adoption of 'Torch' in fact rendered 'Roundup' impossible in 1943, even though retarded. One reason for this was the probability of Russia being so seriously weakened that Hitler could bring back very large armies from the east, thus making the forces available for 'Roundup' in 1943 altogether insufficient. They also founded their opinion on the fact that the assembly of forces for 'Roundup' would be so delayed by the diversion of shipping to 'Torch', that we should not be strong enough during the 1943 season to effect an entry into the Continent, even against comparatively weak forces. The American Military Staff thus foresaw their troops being held idle in the United Kingdom, a situation which the President and General Marshall were anxious to avoid . . . 'Torch' is in full progress with its serious demands on shipping . . . the Russians having been led to believe that we were going to open 'a Second Front in 1943', 'Roundup' was explained to them by me in the presence of the United States representative, Mr. Harriman. These conversations at Moscow were duly reported to the President. I fell that Premier Stalin would have grave reasons to complain if our land offensive against Germany and Italy in 1943 were reduced to the scale of about 13 divisions instead of nearly 50, which have been mentioned to him. Moreover, apart from any Russian obligations, I feel that our offensive war plans for 1943 are on altogether too small a scale compared with the resources and power of Britain and the United States.[29]

So now Roundup was impossible because of the dispersionist Mediterranean campaign, and it was an American decision, not Churchill's. But the dispersionist campaign was always his, and by his own admission it was sucking away vital shipping as well as forces from Roundup; thus Torch was preventing Roundup. Yet Churchill admitted that larger-scale operations were necessary. On the same day Brooke recorded in his diary:

> COS meeting at which we were faced with a new paper written by the PM. Again swinging back towards a western front during 1943!! After having repeatedly said that North Africa must act as a 'springboard' not as a 'sofa' to future action! After urging attacks on Sardinia and Sicily he is now swinging away from these for a possible invasion of France in 1943!

He subsequently added:

> At that afternoon meeting after saying that the Army would have to fight the German Army in 1943, he said, 'You must not think that you can get off with your "sardines" (referring to Sardinia and Sicily) in 1943, no – we must establish a western front, and what is more we promised Stalin we should do so when in Moscow!' To which I replied, 'No, we did not promise!' He then stopped and stared at me for a few seconds, during which I think he remembered that if any promise was made it was during that last evening when he went to say goodbye to Stalin, and when I was not there! He said no more . . .[30]

Momentarily, Churchill became so optimistic that he thought that conquest of Tunis and Tripoli in North Africa would be quickly followed by either Sicily or Sardinia in the Mediterranean. Turkey was to be brought into the war and Roundup could be conducted in August 1943. It was the usual Churchill fantasy – in his mind suddenly all these tasks could be accomplished readily.[31] He had undergone a *volte face* from his previous position and soon he would undergo a *volte face* back again. In 1926, while Chancellor of the Exchequer, he had said in an exchange in the House of Commons, 'To improve is to change; to be perfect is to change often.'[32]

It is clear that Brooke believed in the easier option of Mediterranean operations, as he noted on 8 December 1942: 'Finished off COS fairly early. We were busy deciding [the] line of action to adopt in order to influence the PM to abandon ideas of [the] invasion of France in 1943 for more attractive prospects in the Mediterranean.' And on 16 December 1942 he recorded, 'As the paper we put in went straight against Winston, who was pressing for a western front in France, whilst we pressed for amphibious operations in the Mediterranean, I feared the worst!! However [the] meeting went well from the start and I succeeded in swinging him round.'[33]

The North African campaign was dragging on and the Bolero projections indicated that only 21 US Divisions would be in Britain by the summer of 1943, whereas at least 27 were needed for Roundup. So at the Casablanca Conference codenamed Symbol in January 1943, Churchill and the British chiefs of staff concurred that Roundup was not possible. On the American side, Marshall still argued for it, but as he had been overruled over Sledgehammer and consequently had allowed the Pacific war to take the very resources needed for Roundup, there would now be no cross-Channel operation for 1943. Admiral King was content with this because he did not believe in the 'Germany First' policy anyway. No Roundup meant less competition for forces for the Pacific theatre.[34]

THE ATLANTIC WALL

Hitler had proclaimed in 1942 that Europe would be turned into a Nazi fortress, but in fact little of substance was done at that time to achieve this. It was not until November 1943 that he took seriously the possibility of an Allied landing on the French coast, and measures to fortify that coastline – the Atlantic Wall – were started in earnest. Hitler's Directive No 51 resulted in the appointment of Generalfeldmarschall Erwin Rommel to undertake direct responsibility for the defence of the Atlantic Wall, with Generalfeldmarschall Gerd von Rundstedt in overall command.

This meant that the Atlantic Wall was particularly open to a concerted Allied Second Front until late 1943. Without the Allied distraction of the Mediterranean campaign, Roundup could have been undertaken. With German resources occupied principally on the Eastern Front and against the air war of Bomber Command and the US Army Air Forces, France was never more open. Far from deferring the Second Front to reduce the casualties endured, the actions of Churchill and the British chiefs had simply made large casualties more likely. Of course preparations for an earlier invasion attempt would have stimulated Hitler to fortify the Atlantic Wall more quickly, but it would have allowed less time and so made it more difficult. The procrastination of Churchill and his chiefs of staff delayed the Second Front until the summer of 1944 – just long enough for the Germans to reinforce the Atlantic Wall.

The problem for the Germans was that the Atlantic Wall stretched from Norway to southern France, and with most of their troops deployed on the Eastern Front, it was impossible to defend the entire wall adequately. The basic difficulty was that they did not know where the Allies would make their landing, though naturally the Pas-de-Calais was the most natural spot, as it was the shortest distance from England. But they could not be sure an attack would not come elsewhere. The Allies therefore enjoyed a significant advantage, as they could strike where they wished. This naturally made things extremely difficult for Rommel, who had to spread his resources very thinly along the French coast. His task was made worse as he and his direct superior, von Rundstedt, each believed in very different tactics. Rommel believed that the Allied invasion would have to be stopped at the water's edge if it was to be stopped at all. Von Rundstedt believed that forces should be held further back until the exact location of the invasion was identified. Once it had begun, German forces could be concentrated in a *Schwerpunkt* to try to defeat it.

In a sense they were both right, and here lies the German dilemma. Rommel was right because tactically the most efficient place to defeat an opposed landing is by pushing the invading forces back into the water, where they are at their most vulnerable as the infantry are exposed and the heavy equipment is not yet ashore. Von Rundstedt was right because, without knowing for sure where the invasion would come, Germany had insufficient forces to deploy in every possible location. This problem was made worse as Hitler insisted that there could be no major troop movements without his express approval. Von Rundstedt wryly commented that the only troop movements he had within his own discretion were the sentries at his own gate. All this made the Atlantic Wall inherently vulnerable.

Rommel found the existing defences woefully inadequate and began a substantial fortification programme. He oversaw the laying of over three million mines, the construction of fixed devices below water level – known as 'Rommel's asparagus' – to tear the hulls of landing craft, and the flooding of low-lying inland areas to deny their use as paratrooper landing zones. Pillboxes were constructed with interconnected trenches to create an effective defensive line, with guns offering overlapping fields of fire across the beaches. The divisions of German soldiers were augmented with Soviet conscripts from prisoner-of-war camps and pro-Nazis from countries under German occupation. By May 1944, the German defence of France had thus been strengthened to 59 divisions – over 200,000 men.

OVERLORD IS PLANNED

Plans for a Second Front had been hashed around since 1941, but were not given serious impetus until the meeting between Churchill and Roosevelt at the Casablanca Conference in January 1943. At this, Churchill and Brooke opposed the Americans and argued for yet more delay for fear of another Dunkirk. Nevertheless, it was decided to create an Allied staff planning group under a 'Chief-of-Staff to the Supreme Allied Commander' (COSSAC). In mid-March, Lieutenant-General Frederick Morgan was appointed to this post and a planning group was formed.

At the Washington Conference, codenamed Trident, in May 1943, Roosevelt and his chiefs insisted on a target date for the Second Front: it was to be 1 May 1944. The operation was to be larger than Sledgehammer but not as large as Roundup, and it would be codenamed Roundhammer. Because of Churchill's continual procrastination over the Second Front, there was a joke doing the rounds in Washington: Stalin telephones Churchill and says, 'It's Joe here.' Churchill says, 'Joe who?' 'Joe Stalin' is the reply. Churchill says, 'Hello Joe, where are you?' Stalin replies, 'Oh I'm in Calais.'[35]

By this time the 'Germany First' policy had been abandoned by the Americans, and resources were flowing equally to the Pacific and European theatres. Churchill remonstrated with Roosevelt, but the President would have none of it. This time Roosevelt told Churchill that if he did not commit himself to the Second Front and instead wanted to continue to concentrate forces in the Mediterranean, this would prejudice Bolero, the build-up of forces in Britain. In other words, the US would concentrate on the Pacific war and leave Germany to Churchill. The implied threat was clear and Churchill was obliged to back down. This moment was decisive: for the first time Churchill could not influence the Americans in their decision and it marked the end of Churchill's, or indeed Britain's, ability to determine major global events.[36]

After the Washington Conference Roosevelt and Churchill met again at Quebec in August 1943 for the Quadrant Conference, where they discussed the first COSSAC outline plan, submitted by Morgan to the War Cabinet on 15 July. In November they met yet again, in Cairo for the Sextant Conference, this time to confirm the principal aspects of the plan and organize the command structure.

In August 1943 Churchill withdrew his proposal, which he had made three times before, that Brooke should be supreme commander of the operation, instead suggesting that it should go to an American. The proposal of a British general had been lunacy: Britain would be contributing only one quarter of the men and materiel to the operation. But not only should Churchill never have suggested it in the first place, he also handled his change of position badly, alienating Brooke in the process. Brooke had naively hoped that he was to be appointed, and when Churchill simply changed his mind and failed to let him down carefully it was devastating for Brooke, for whom the post would have been the summit of his career.

In his heart of hearts the 'soft underbelly' theory remained Churchill's preference and in a letter to General Sir Harold Alexander on 25 September 1943 he wrote, 'You will see that I have announced in Parliament that the Italian campaign is the "Third Front". The Second Front is here in Great Britain, in potential but not yet engaged. This form of statement should be adhered to, as it is less disagreeable to the Russians and avoids arguing with them as to whether the Italian campaign is the Second Front or not.'[37] He could have added that it was less disagreeable to the Americans as well.

At the Foreign Ministers' Conference in Moscow during October 1943 the commitment to the operation taking place the following spring was underscored by the Foreign Secretary, Anthony Eden. However, Churchill was worried about the siphoning off of resources from his Mediterranean campaign and asked Eden to see Stalin about a postponement. It did not take long for Stalin to take the American side, particularly at the 'Big Three' Conference in Tehran, codenamed Eureka, later in the year. Churchill's request had done nothing for Anglo-Soviet relations, but it had sent Anglo-American relations through the floor. Although the Americans admitted that Mediterranean operations were holding down about 40 German divisions, and therefore could not simply be abandoned, the apparent lack of commitment to the operation on Churchill's part was a fundamental miscalculation. This episode confirmed the end of the influence Churchill had over Roosevelt.[38]

Largely as the result of this episode the Americans insisted on an invasion of the South of France, Operation Anvil, to divert German resources from the Second Front and act as a pincer movement. Naturally, Churchill opposed this, as it would take even more resources from his Mediterranean campaign. But the Americans would not be moved, and Churchill was forced to acquiesce.[39]

The Supreme Headquarters Allied Expeditionary Force (SHAEF) was created in London in December 1943. Eisenhower took command in the following January, as Supreme Commander Allied Expeditionary Force. He was the obvious choice: an American, but a general who was more of a diplomat than a field commander and could thus keep the whole multinational force together. Air Chief-Marshal Sir Arthur Tedder was appointed Deputy Supreme Allied Commander. This was another sensible choice for what was essentially a fictional role: a British officer reflecting Britain's large, but secondary, contribution to the Front. Tedder was emollient and would thus not cause friction with the Americans. General Walter Bedell Smith would be Eisenhower's chief of staff. American ground forces would be under the command of Lieutenant-General Omar Bradley, and the British would be under 'Monty', who would have complete control of land forces during the initial assault. Rear-Admiral Alan Kirk would command the American naval forces, and Admiral Sir Philip Vian would command the British, with Admiral Sir Bertram Ramsay (of Dunkirk fame) in overall naval command. The American air force operation would be under Lieutenant-General Lewis Brereton, with the British under Air-Marshal Sir Arthur Coningham and with Air Chief-Marshal Sir Trafford Leigh-Mallory in overall command.

While Eisenhower had been obliged to conduct campaigns in North Africa and Italy, no clear plans for a Second Front had been developed. Churchill's procrastination over the Second Front had thus ensured that vital planning was delayed. Vast numbers of landing craft were needed, and most of the existing ones were in Italy. Even now Churchill persuaded the Americans to delay shifting amphibious craft from the Mediterranean theatre so as not to prejudice the landings at Anzio (see chapter 14), and he would force a postponement of the operation from May to June. Detailed planning did not start until January 1944; an entire year had been lost since Casablanca, during which only a general outline had been produced. In that outline Morgan had wanted to avoid well-defended harbours and other strong points and to land on the beaches east of the Cotentin Peninsula – in Normandy.

Churchill could not prevent himself from interfering with the plan, to the chagrin of Brooke, who wrote in his diary on 8 February 1944:

> A day spent almost continuously with the PM! . . . A great deal
> of this was concerned with a proposed wild venture of his to
> land 2 Armoured Divisions in Bordeaux 20 days after the cross
> Channel operations. I think we have ridden him off this for
> the present. Next a wild scheme for raising additional
> transport planes for the airborne airlift.[40]

The following day he wrote, '. . . At 5.15 pm I was handed a 5 page telegram which [the] PM had drafted for [the] President covering the whole strategy of the war, and most of it wrong!'[41]

Also in February, Roosevelt made it clear that Churchill was wrong to suggest that there would be insufficient resources to conduct both Anvil – the invasion of the South of France – and the Second Front, and overruled Churchill's wish for another meeting of the chiefs of staff to argue the matter. Churchill wanted at least to continue the Italian operations rather than undertake Anvil, and he threatened to resign if he didn't get his way, but the Americans would not have it.[42]

Meanwhile the experts were developing the initial detailed plan for Operation Overlord. Originally three divisions were to land on the first day, but Monty argued that five were necessary for the initial landings, and this was accepted. Thus two divisions each from the USA and Britain, plus one Canadian one, would be landed at beaches codenamed Utah and

Omaha (American), Gold and Juno (British) and Sword (Canadian). In the original plan two airborne brigades were to be deployed in the initial stages, but Monty argued for three divisions; thus, what would be the greatest airborne landing ever undertaken was planned. Artificial harbours were to be constructed to facilitate the landing of further divisions and their heavy equipment, and two 'Mulberry harbours' were built and towed across the Channel, one for the American forces, one for the British.

In a letter to Marshall on 11 March 1944 concerning Overlord, Churchill wrote, 'I am hardening very much on this operation as the time approaches, *in the sense of wishing to strike if humanly possible even if the limiting conditions . . . are not exactly fulfilled . . .'* [43] (Churchill added the emphasis himself when he reproduced the letter in *The Second World War*.) It is extraordinary, first, that he would choose to use the term 'if humanly possible' at a time when Overlord was going ahead anyway, and second, that he should emphasize this very passage when he was trying to defend the case that he had supported the operation all along. On 15 May, at a meeting at Monty's headquarters in London in the presence of King George VI, Eisenhower and the chiefs of staff, Churchill would again use the phrase, 'I am hardening on this operation.' [44] This was astonishing, as Overlord's execution was just three weeks away. Eisenhower, in his post-war account *Crusade in Europe*, interpreted it as evidence that Churchill had previously been opposed to the Second Front. [45] In *The Second World War* Churchill claimed that Eisenhower had been wrong to suggest this, and in an attempt to justify his position after the event he even repeated the suspect phrase, 'if humanly possible', plus the subsequent phrase, 'even if the limiting conditions . . . are not exactly fulfilled.' [46] However, limiting conditions are hardly ever exactly fulfilled in any such operation, and neither of these phrases would be uttered by a man who was entirely convinced of the correctness of a course of action. They would, however, be used by one who knew the operation was going ahead anyway and was now grudgingly resigned to it.

OVERLORD IS EXECUTED

The Allies reinforced a belief that Hitler and his military staff already held – that the main Allied landings would occur at the Pas-de-Calais. This was to ensure that the German Fifteenth Army was retained in this location.

To accomplish this, the Allies had created the fictitious 'First US Army Group' (FUSAG), under Lieutenant-General George Patton, as part of the deception plan, codenamed Fortitude South. There was decoy equipment for German reconnaissance flights to observe and false radio traffic for their Y-service (radio monitoring service). Another fictitious outfit had been created called Fortitude North, which was intended to deceive the Germans into thinking an Allied landing would be undertaken in Norway and so hold down German forces deployed there.

Overlord would land 156,000 Allied troops, 600,000 tons of stores and 200,000 vehicles in 5,000 ships and landing craft. Special-purpose tanks created paths through the minefields, and large naval vessels called Rhinos landed vehicles, heavy weapons and other supplies once the beaches had been secured. Sixteen divisions were landed in the first two weeks, with a final total of 23 landed in Normandy altogether. Fuel was supplied via the 'Pipe Line Under The Ocean' (PLUTO) direct from England. The Allied heavy bomber force was used against tactical targets in France between 1 April and 5 June, to make it difficult for German reinforcements to reach Normandy. Some 195,000 tons of ordnance were delivered by 11,000 aircraft, of which 2,000 were lost.

The sea crossing was codenamed Neptune, and was set for 5 June 1944: D-Day. However, some of the worst ever summer weather resulted in its postponement. The Chief Meteorologist, Group Captain James Stagg, said there would be a window in the poor weather on the 6th. Otherwise they would have to wait two weeks until the moon was full again and the tide low, to ensure the landing craft were not impaled on the underwater obstacles close in to shore. With so many units embarked ready to go, Eisenhower agreed with his senior commanders and on 6 June they went. The first landings took place at 12.05am, with gliders delivering British forces at Pegasus Bridge across the Seine and into Normandy. The seaborne landings took place from 5.00am, with the main American force arriving at 6.30am and the British an hour later. Churchill wanted to go across with the first wave: this was a problem for Eisenhower, who was obliged to stop him yet strictly did not outrank him and so could not order him not to go. The problem was solved by King George VI, who insisted that if Churchill was to go, he would go as well. Churchill backed down as a result.

When early indications of an Allied invasion became apparent to the Germans, Oberst Walther Pluskat of the 352nd Infantry Division went to observe events in a bunker on Omaha Beach. He reported to his commanding officer that there were 5,000 Allied ships heading his way. His CO replied: 'Don't worry, Pluskat, the Allies haven't got that many ships.'

At Omaha, German opposition was serious, as the 352nd Division was highly experienced from the Russian campaign, and Allied intelligence had not been aware of its presence. At one point it looked as though US forces might have to be withdrawn. The Canadians also took substantial casualties initially but progressed off the beach quickly nevertheless. Elsewhere it was different: the British faced only minor opposition at Juno and Gold, and at Utah the Americans landed and moved inland quickly with no more than 200 casualties. The beachheads were secured, and the 'Longest Day' was a success for the Allies.

Once the invasion had secured a good foothold and it was clear it was not going to be thrown back into the sea, the fate of Germany was certain. Only the United States and perhaps the Soviet Union were capable of fighting on two fronts and winning. Now, what Germany had always feared had occurred: two determined opponents would crush it for certain. Perhaps the Soviet Union could have done so by itself, but Overlord removed any doubt.

OPERATION ANVIL

Despite the American insistence on Anvil (renamed Dragoon), the operation in the South of France, Churchill, who had opposed it from the start, was still intent on prevarication. It now became increasingly important as fresh American forces were brought to Europe directly from the United States, and Marshall pointed out that logistically it made more sense to capture ports in the ill-defended South of France and land them there directly.[47] Churchill wrote to Roosevelt on 4 August:

> The course of events in Normandy and Brittany . . . give good prospects that the whole Brittany peninsula will be in our hands within a reasonable time. I beg you will consider the possibility of switching 'Dragoon' into the main and vital theatre.[48]

So now, rather than concentrating on the Italian theatre, Churchill was insisting that France was where the *Schwerpunkt* should occur, and it should not be dispersed with an assault on southern France. He was coming round to the view that Marshall and the others had held years earlier. Churchill wrote, 'I visited Eisenhower at his headquarters near Portsmouth and unfolded to him my last hope of stopping the "Dragoon" operation.'[49] Once again, consistency didn't trouble him: he now wanted to replace Anvil with a raid on the west-coast town of Bordeaux, with troops taken from Italy through the straits of Gibraltar. But Eisenhower and the President were unmoved.

However, Churchill was still at it. In a communication to Field Marshal Jan Smuts, Prime Minister of South Africa, on 26 August, he wrote:

> So far 'Anvil' has had the opposite effects for which its designers intended it. Firstly, it has attracted no troops away from General Eisenhower at all. On the contrary, two and a half to three divisions of German rearguard troops will certainly reach the main battle-front before the Allied landed troops. Secondly, a stage of stagnation has been enforced here [Italy] by the breaking in full career of these two great armies, the Fifth and the Eighth, and by the milking out of the key personnel in them. The consequence of this has been the withdrawal from the Italian front of three German divisions, including one strong Panzer having an active strength of 12,500. These have proceeded direct to the Chalons area. Thus about five divisions have been deployed against Eisenhower, which would not have happened had we continued our advance here in the direction of the Po and ultimately on the great city [Vienna]. I still hope that we may achieve this. Even if the war comes to an end suddenly I can see no reason why our armour should not slip through and reach it, as we can.[50]

However, the landings in the South of France were a logical way to get ashore those fresh forces arriving directly from the USA. If attrition of German forces was how Churchill now saw the Italian campaign, there were more efficient ways of accomplishing this than by scrapping Anvil and keeping massive forces in Italy.

CHURCHILL'S FINAL LEGACY

The dispersionist strategy in the Mediterranean prevented Bolero from effecting the necessary troop and materiel build-up needed to conduct the Second Front in 1943, in Operation Roundup. Both Churchill and Brooke were culpable in this regard, as both subscribed to the dispersionist strategy. However, Brooke was a practical and experienced soldier and understood the distinction between practical military operations and the impatient eccentricity that characterized so many of Churchill's ideas. Brooke consistently performed the invaluable function of constraining Churchill by opposing his wild strategies. However, Brooke's vision was limited and he failed to understand the true extent of America's ability to conduct industrialized warfare. The USA provided the overwhelming majority of the troops and materiel for Overlord, and it *could* have done so for Roundup.

In the final year of the war, approximately ten million people died.[51] If Roundup had been undertaken and the war in Europe finished by the summer of 1944, many of those lives could have been saved. The western Allies could also have fought further east before meeting the Soviet forces and so reduced the extent of post-war Communist hegemony. Ironically, Churchill decided he wanted the Allies to drive further east *after* the Second Front finally took place (see chapter 17). But it was primarily his procrastination and Roosevelt's failure to overrule him that ensured that neither of these things was to happen.

In *The Second World War*, Churchill wrote,

> The reader . . . must not be misled by a chance phrase here and there into thinking (a) that I wanted to abandon 'Overlord', (b) that I wanted to deprive 'Overlord' of vital forces, or (c) that I contemplated a campaign by armies operating in the Balkan peninsula. These are legends. Never had such a wish entered my mind.[52]

16
THE BOMBER OFFENSIVE: THE LOST OPPORTUNITY

At the beginning of the war, the Secretary of State for Air, Sir Howard Kingsley Wood, said that the Royal Air Force could not bomb German factories, because they were private property. How things would change.[1]

Sir Charles Portal was Air Officer Commanding-in-Chief (AOC-in-C) of Bomber Command from April until October 1940, when he replaced the retiring Sir Cyril Newall as Chief of the Air Staff. He was replaced as AOC-in-C of Bomber Command by Air Chief Marshal Sir Richard Peirse. In April 1942 Portal was promoted to air chief marshal, and in January 1944 to marshal of the Royal Air Force. The relationship between Churchill and Portal would be pivotal in the bombing campaign, as Major-General Sir John Kennedy, Director of Military Operations, stated: 'The bombing policy of the Air Staff was settled almost entirely by the Prime Minister himself in consultation with Portal, and was not controlled by the Chiefs of Staff.'[2]

As AOC-in-C of Bomber Command, Portal initially attempted to conduct precision bombing raids, a policy favoured by both Newall and Peirse. However, early in the war, navigation and bomb-aiming equipment proved to be insufficiently sophisticated for such raids. Thus, as Chief of the Air Staff, Portal would advocate the area bombing of German cities, a policy to which Churchill assented.[3] It is clear that Churchill was already minded towards an area bombing policy when he wrote on 8 July 1940:

> When I look round to see how we can win the war I see that there is only one sure path. We have no continental army which can defeat the German military power. The blockade is broken and Hitler has Asia and probably Africa to draw from. Should he be repulsed here or not try invasion, he will recoil eastward, and we have nothing to stop him. But there is one thing that will bring him back and bring him down, and that is an absolutely devastating, exterminating attack by very heavy bombers from this country upon the Nazi homeland.[4]

Of course Britain lacked the capacity to do this in 1940, because heavy bombers were not yet available, but the idea was clear. On 3 September 1940 Churchill wrote: 'The bombers alone provide the means of victory.' On 2 November, in a letter to the Air Ministry, he said: 'We have seen what inconvenience the attack on the British civilian population has caused us, and there is no reason why the enemy should be freed from all such embarrassments.'[5] And in December 1940, his view was accurately summed up by the Ministry of Information: 'All the evidence goes to prove that the Germans, for all their present confidence and cockiness will not stand a quarter of the bombing that the British have shown they will take.'[6] This view had been endorsed by Churchill's scientific advisor, Professor Frederick Lindemann.[7]

DE-HOUSING

And so the policy of eroding civilian morale through 'de-housing' was initiated. By the end of the war, 3.37 million homes would have been destroyed and 593,000 German civilians killed by bombing.[8] However, by September 1941 Churchill had changed his mind about the bombing as the result of a scientific report on its results, which had been prompted by Lindemann (now Viscount Cherwell). The report, which was drawn up by David Bensusan-Butt of the War Cabinet Secretariat, was presented on 18 August 1941:

> An examination of night photographs taken during night bombing in June and July points to the following conclusions:
> 1. Of those aircraft recorded as attacking their target, only one in three got within 5 miles.
> 2. Over the French ports, the proportion was two in three; over Germany as a whole, the proportion was one in four; over the Ruhr it was only one in ten.
> 3. In the full moon, the proportion was two in five; in the new moon it was only one in fifteen . . .
> 4. All these figures relate only to aircraft recorded as *attacking* the target; the proportion of the *total sorties* which reached within 5 miles is less by one-third . . .
>   The conclusion seems to follow that only about one-third

of aircraft claiming to reach the target area actually reach it.[9]

Churchill wrote to Portal in September:

> It is very disputable whether bombing by itself will be a
> decisive factor in the present war. On the contrary, all that
> we learnt since the war began shows that its effects, both
> physical and moral, are greatly exaggerated . . . The most that
> we can say is that it will be a heavy and I trust a seriously
> increasing annoyance.[10]

His view had changed from area bombing winning the war, to it doing
no more than 'annoying' the Germans. On 2 October 1941 Portal
wrote in response:

> . . . if the most we can hope to achieve with our bomber force
> is a heavy and increasing annoyance, then, as I see it, the
> strategic concept to which we have been working must
> dissolve, and we must find a new plan . . . The worst plan of all
> would be to continue our present preparations after we have
> ceased to believe in the efficacy of the bomber as a war-
> winning weapon.

The Secretary of State for Air, Sir Archibald Sinclair (who had replaced
Kingsley Wood) thought Portal's comments 'masterly' and 'audacious'.[11]
Portal also pointed out to Churchill that just a few weeks earlier he had
assented to a chiefs of staff document that stated, 'It is in bombing on a
scale undreamt of in the last war that we find the new weapon on which we
must principally depend for the destruction of economic life and morale.'
Churchill replied to this at length – something he invariably did when he
was caught out – but he only reinforced his new proposition that bombing
alone was unlikely to win the war.[12]

However, Churchill did nothing to change the policy he now believed
defective – far from it. Yet his comments missed the point: it was 'precision'
bombing that was not working; 'area' bombing was another matter, and
this was happening by 1941 anyway. On Portal's recommendation, to
which Churchill agreed, Air Marshal (Acting) Arthur 'Bomber' Harris

replaced Peirse as AOC-in-C Bomber Command on 22 February 1942. He concurred with the policy of area bombing and implemented it – vehemently.

By 1942, with the Americans in the war and the Soviets fully engaged with the Germans on the Eastern Front, the air offensive took on another role in Churchill's mind: it was a way of delaying the landings in northern France and so letting the Soviets take the bulk of the casualties. Bomber Command would lose nearly 56,000 men in World War II, but the Soviet Union's total losses would be 20–25 million.[13] However, as losses mounted and German economic collapse failed to materialize, the whole de-housing policy of Bomber Command was coming under scrutiny again; it would be Lord Cherwell whose arguments would sustain it. He undertook an analysis of the bombing of British cities and on this basis calculated the effects of the bomber offensive on Germany, given the predicted production output of British bombers, their bomb-carrying capacity and expected survival rate. Based on his findings he wrote to Churchill on 30 March 1942:

> Investigation seems to show that having one's home demolished is most damaging to morale. People seem to mind it more than having their friends or even relatives killed. At Hull signs of strain were evident, though only one-tenth of the houses were demolished. On the . . . figures we should be able to do ten times as much harm to each of the fifty-eight principal German towns. There seems little doubt that this would break the spirit of the German people.[14]

Sir Henry Tizard, former scientific advisor to the Ministry of Aircraft Production, expressed doubt about this argument in a note to Cherwell on 15 April, and the Navy's chief scientist Professor Patrick Blackett argued that Cherwell's figure for the extent of the damage was 600 per cent too high! Tizard provided a detailed account of his reasoning on 20 April, explaining that while Cherwell had assumed bomber production of 10,000 heavy bombers by June 1943, official figures said 8,000 (Cherwell later said he had picked a round number because it wouldn't tax Churchill's brain), and that on the basis of past experience only 7,000 were likely to be delivered. Given that no more than 25 per cent of bombs dropped would actually fall on the intended target area, this would result in 50,000 tons delivered. Tizard therefore said, '(a) That a policy of bombing German towns wholesale in order to destroy dwellings cannot have a decisive effect by the middle of 1943, even if all heavy bombers . . . produced are used for this purpose. (b) That such a policy can only have a decisive effect if carried out on a much bigger scale than envisaged.'[15]

Towards the end of 1942 Churchill had shifted his position yet again. Now he thought bombing would be crucial to eroding morale, even though it could not win the war alone. He wrote, 'The severe, ruthless bombing of Germany on an ever increasing scale will not only cripple her war effort . . . but will also create conditions intolerable to the mass of German population . . . We must regard the bomber offensive against Germany at least as a feature in breaking her war-will . . .'[16]

In a dictatorship such as Nazi Germany the authorities continuously exercised martial law, and this reduced the adverse effect on the war effort of a decline in morale. German workers went back to their factories after the mass bombing raids despite the enormous destruction and the loss of their homes and loved ones.[17] It was the material damage the bombing did to the German war effort that was important. Germany was finally defeated in combat, not because the people lost the will to fight. The material degradation of German factories and manpower through area bombing played a vital role in this defeat.

THE THOUSAND-BOMBER RAID

In May 1942 Bomber Command was equipped with 16 squadrons of Vickers Wellingtons, two squadrons of the unreliable Avro Manchesters and two of the antiquated Handley Page Hampdens – all twin-engine aircraft. Of the four-engine heavy bombers, there were five squadrons of the inefficient Short Stirlings, six squadrons of Handley Page Halifaxes, and just six squadrons of the most efficient bombers, the Avro Lancasters. This gave a total frontline strength of only 350 serviceable aircraft.

When Harris came up with the notion of a thousand-bomber raid this seemed far-fetched, as previously the maximum ever sent on a single raid had been 228. But Air Vice-Marshal Robert Saundby, Harris's deputy, pointed out that a thousand-bomber force was possible if aircraft and crews were provided by the Operational Training units, the heavy conversion units, plus other parts of Training Command, as well as Coastal Command, which had its own fleet of rather inefficient Armstrong Whitworth Whitleys, Lockheed Hudsons and Handley Page Hampdens – all twin-engine.

Churchill agreed to Harris's suggestion, and Harris said, '[Churchill] was prepared for a loss of a hundred bombers on this operation.'[18] Harris was all too well aware of the risks: his entire training programme could be wrecked in one operation, as could his plan for expansion, and routine training would be badly disrupted. There was also the spectre of losing an alarming proportion of his bomber force in one night, for there was no guarantee that Churchill's arbitrary loss figure would not be exceeded, perhaps substantially. However, if it inflicted a decisive blow and the loss figures were acceptable, it would provide the political impetus for expansion and place renewed emphasis on the bomber force.

The raid was given the codename Millennium (the name originally reserved for the Second Front),[19] and on the night of 30 May 1942 Cologne was targeted: one of the criteria employed to select the target was the use of the electronic navigational aid 'Gee', which had a restricted range. The raid would be mounted by 1,046 aircraft and would drop 1,455 tons of high explosives and incendiaries.

The loss rate turned out to be well within Churchill's figure, with 40 aircraft lost. However 116 were damaged, 33 of them seriously, and a dozen had to be written off. The first reconnaissance sorties, at 5.00am the morning after the raid, found the target still obscured by smoke to a height of 4,600m (15,000ft). What the reconnaissance made clear was that some 250ha (600 acres) of Cologne had been laid waste, with the destruction of more than 250 factories central to the German war machine. Even the German assessment was spectacular: 1,500 industrial and commercial facilities destroyed, some 36 major plants, plus 300 damaged. As regards de-housing, 13,000 homes had been destroyed and 6,000 badly damaged, with some 45,000 people made homeless, though remarkably the death toll was only 469 plus 5,027 injured. Reichsmarschall Hermann Göring could not believe the figures coming in from Cologne; indeed he insisted that they must be wrong. Hitler, on the other hand, was inclined to believe them and the reports in British newspapers. Churchill was naturally delighted, as well he might have been.[20]

On 1 June 1942, Essen was raided with 956 aircraft, though with unanticipated cloud cover the city got off lightly. On 11 June Harris was created a Knight Commander of the Bath and celebrated on 25 June by sending 1,006 bombers to Bremen, but again cloud cover reduced the raid's effectiveness.[21]

This should have put renewed energy into the bomber offensive, and Harris certainly argued vociferously for it in a detailed paper for Churchill on 28 June. However, in October the Army's victory at El Alamein in North Africa diverted Churchill's energies back to the land campaign. Consequently Bomber Command's raids were scaled down to 200–300 aircraft, not much different in number to what they had been before the thousand-bomber raids. An opportunity to cripple the German war machine decisively was thus missed.[22]

Viscount Trenchard, the founder of the Royal Air Force in 1918, quite naturally endorsed the vital importance of air power in winning the war. In a paper sent to Churchill on 29 August 1942 he wrote:

> *Time is short and we are at a parting of the ways.* The risk is that we shall try to go down two roads, and that our air-power will be inextricable entangled in large schemes and protracted operations of two-dimensional warfare . . .
>
> For the country to get mixed up this year or next in land warfare on the continent of Europe is to play Germany's game – it is to revert to 1914–18. It is to bring in against us the one enormously powerful military asset remaining to the enemy – namely, the German Army. Our strength and advantage over Germany is in the air – the British and the American Air Force . . .
>
> The strategy of warfare to-day is undergoing a greater change than that caused by the invention of gunpowder or the coming of the modern battleship. The power of the air grows every day. It has progressed enormously since 1939. The bombs and the bomber to-day are vastly different from those in use when war broke out . . .
>
> Britain and America are growing stronger in the air every day. There is no realisable limit to the power we can achieve in this arm *if we concentrate our efforts on a policy which realises what we can do – and do quickly* . . .
>
> As the enemy conquered Poland and France by their 'tank blitz', so we can smash the German machine by the

'bomber blitz' . . .[23]

In a communication sent by both Churchill and Roosevelt to Stalin on 27 January 1943, they wrote: 'As you are aware, we are already containing more than half the German Air Force in Western Europe and the Mediterranean.'[24] Indeed, so significant was the bomber offensive to the Allied war effort that it has been estimated that more than one-third of British national resources were devoted to it.[25] However, on one occasion when Churchill received the usual reports from Harris of the previous night's attacks, he remarked, 'I'm sick of these raids on Cologne.' Harris replied, 'So are the people of Cologne.'[26]

Churchill employed Britain's commitment to the bomber offensive as a ploy to deflect the Soviet desire for the western Allies to mount a Second Front in France. He wrote to Stalin on 6 April 1943, 'I am deeply conscious of the giant burden borne by the Russian armies and their unequalled contribution to the common cause, I must emphasise that our bombing of Germany will increase in scale month by month . . .'[27] But with resources squandered in the Mediterranean, this ambition could not be fulfilled.

THE CASABLANCA DIRECTIVE

On 21 January 1943 at the Casablanca Conference, codenamed Symbol, Churchill and Roosevelt determined the strategy for Bomber Command for the remainder of the war. The Casablanca Directive was conveyed to Bomber Command in a letter from the Air Ministry on 4 February:

> Your primary object will be the progressive destruction and dislocation of the German military, industrial and economic system, and the undermining of the morale of the German people to a point where their capacity for armed resistance is fatally weakened.
>
> Within the general concept, your primary objectives, subject to the exigencies of the weather and of tactical feasibility, will for the present be in the following order of priority:
> (a) German submarine construction yards
> (b) The German aircraft industry
> (c) Transportation

(d) Oil Plants

(e) Other targets in enemy war industry

. . . Moreover, other objectives of great importance . . .
must be attacked. Examples of these are:

(i) Submarine operating bases on the Biscay coast . . .

(ii) Berlin . . . when conditions are suitable for the
attainment of specially valuable results . . .

Harris duly attacked the French towns where the submarine bases were
located. The bombproof pens that protected the U-boats meant that time
after time the bombers plastered them with no appreciable effect. Admiral
Karl Dönitz told the German Admiralty, 'No dog or cat is left in these
towns, nothing remains but the U-boat pens.' On 6 April Harris was finally
ordered to abandon this hopeless struggle, which had done nothing but
delay the vital battle against the Ruhr.[28]

Between March and August 1943 the Battle of the Ruhr raged, in which
Bomber Command concentrated on the principal area of German industrial
production. Although the days of the thousand-bomber raids had gone,
and most attacks were made with less than half that number, the effect
was nevertheless devastating, as Joseph Goebbels, the German propaganda
minister, noted in his diary for 10 April after a visit to the Ruhr city of Essen:

> We went to the hotel on foot because driving is quite
> impossible in many parts of Essen. This walk enabled us to
> make a first-hand estimate of the damage inflicted by the last
> three air raids. It is colossal and, indeed ghastly . . . The city's
> building experts estimate that it will take twelve years to repair
> the damage . . . Milch [Göring's deputy and Chief of the
> German Air Staff] believes that the English could lay a large
> part of the Reich in ruins, if they go about it the right way.[29]

THE DAM BUSTERS

The most famous of Bomber Command's raids on the Ruhr, or indeed
in the whole of World War II, was the 'Dam Buster' raid, Operation
Chastise, on the night of 16–17 May 1943. This was the attack on the

Mohne, Eder and Sorpe dams in the Ruhr Valley. The brilliant inventor, Barnes Wallis, had produced a paper in March 1941 called, innocuously, 'A note on a method of attacking the Axis powers'.[30] This was classic English understatement, as it actually set out in great detail a method of shortening the war. The idea was to destroy the Ruhr Valley's hydroelectric production, which powered the Krupp works, which in turn provided the bulk of the material Germany required to prosecute the war. If the Germans were denied the means to fight a modern industrial mechanized war, their defeat was certain. The idea was sound. Churchill's scientific adviser Lord Cherwell said in September 1942 that he 'doubted if the dams were of any consequence',[31] but Sir Henry Tizard became a supporter.

To accomplish the task Wallis had developed a 'bouncing bomb', which was in fact a cylindrical mine. Electric motors were fitted in the bomb bays of each aircraft to rotate the mines as they were dropped. This created 'backspin', which caused the bombs to bounce in a controlled way when they hit the water and then cling to the dam wall as they went down. A hydrostatic pistol in each mine then exploded the charge at a depth of 9m (30ft). The incompressibility of the water concentrated the explosive force against the dam wall and so breached it.

The raid was seen as a curiosity by Churchill, and when Air Vice-Marshal Saundby presented the idea, Harris dismissed it as 'tripe'. However, with Churchill's approval, Portal ordered the raid to take place, and once the decision had been made Harris committed all the necessary resources to try to make it a success.[32] A new elite squadron, 617, was created, equipped with the most efficient of the four-engine heavies, the Avro Lancaster, and using many of the best crews in Bomber Command. It was to be led by the 24-year-old 'veteran', Wing Commander Guy Gibson, who would be awarded the Victoria Cross.

The Mohne and Eder dams were successfully breached, and the Sorpe was damaged. After the raid, with the Ruhr Valley partly flooded, German military production was momentarily attenuated. Goebbels noted in his diary: 'The attacks of British bombers on the dams in our valleys were very successful. The Führer is exceedingly impatient and angry about the lack of preparedness on the part of the Luftwaffe. Damage to production was more than normal.'[33]

It was now essential to conduct a concentrated series of attacks on the Ruhr immediately, preferably in thousand-bomber raids with conventional ordnance to frustrate German attempts to rebuild the dams. Such raids would have had a much more profound effect than bombing Berlin. Harris, as we have already seen, wanted to employ such raids routinely, albeit principally against large cities. But Churchill, although he had ordered the Dam Buster raid, failed signally to see that if sufficient resources were employed to follow it up, the war could be shortened. Yet as early as 1935 he had recognized the vulnerability of Germany to the bombing of the Ruhr. In *The Second World War* he referred to notes he had written on 23 July 1935: 'A large part of German munitions production is concentrated in the Ruhr, which is easily accessible to enemy bombing.'[34] His failure to see this in May 1943 threw away a golden opportunity, just when the Germans were still at the height of their powers.

Albert Speer, Hitler's armaments minister, was a brilliant man, but even he could not have coped with a supremely concentrated onslaught on Germany's munitions production. Yet, although the Battle of the Ruhr continued until August, attention was then switched to Hamburg. The Germans were allowed to recover, which, under Speer's direction, they did surprisingly quickly. In consequence, instead of a decisive blow against the heart of the enemy, as Wallis had originally envisaged, the Dam Buster raid has been interpreted by some historians as achieving no more than boosting British morale.

However, the real problem was that the Sorpe, the largest dam, had not been breached because the bouncing bomb was not suited to the task of breaching an earth dam. It had only suffered damage to its very top. Even so, if the damage had extended just 0.5m (18in) more, the water would have started to escape and led to the catastrophic loss of the dam. This was crucial, as Speer recognized: the Sorpe was the principal dam in the system and if it had gone the cooling system for the Ruhr steel mills would have gone with it. Speer said later, 'If the water supply had broken down the steel industry would have been suffering for months and months.'[35] The raid had come that close to a remarkable victory.

The Eder dam, Speer pointed out, was comparatively unimportant. Breaching it caused a 9 per cent reduction in the output of the Dortmund coking plants, but little else.[36] The great irony was that the significance of the Sorpe and the irrelevance of the Eder dams was known to the Ministry of Economic Warfare in London. Yet instead of concentrating on breaching the Sorpe, 617 Squadron was ordered to attack the Mohne first, the Eder second and the Sorpe last, with those few remaining bouncing bombs the Lancasters had not already used, and which were not designed to destroy an earth dam like the Sorpe anyway.[37]

Wallis would develop two more important weapons during the war, the 5,400kg (12,000lb) Tallboy and 10,000kg (22,000lb) Grand Slam earthquake bombs. Cherwell thought these weapons were unsound, but he was wrong. They were designed to penetrate deep into the earth and use the soil's limited compressibility to focus the blast and so create a mini-earthquake. However, they became operational late in the war so their effect was limited. Had their development been hurried, particularly the first one, Tallboy, it is interesting to speculate whether it could have been used to breach the Sorpe dam and thus shorten the war appreciably. Instead, Churchill's pet project was to use Wallis's genius to destroy the German battleship, *Tirpitz*, which, as we have seen, did not shorten the war by one second.[38]

The Dam Buster raid was astonishing technologically, in terms of its execution and for the bravery of the men who carried it out (53 out of the 133 airmen were killed), but it had only a momentary effect, as the Germans were allowed to clear up and repair the mess. The British predicted that the Eder could not be repaired before winter, but Speer had its reconstruction completed by September, and that of the Mohne at about the same time. However, the raid did result in taking 50,000 men away from the construction of the Atlantic Wall, and also diverted many anti-aircraft guns to the region.[39]

POINTBLANK

On 10 June 1943 the Pointblank Directive came into effect for both Bomber Command and the US Eighth Army Air Force. Based on the Casablanca proposals and those of USAAF Lieutenant-General Ira Eaker, it established the joint bombing offensive that would lead up to the Second Front. When, at the Washington summit in May, it had been finally agreed, Churchill had done nothing but wave it through, despite the fact that it required a precision bombing campaign, long abandoned by Bomber Command. Harris effectively ignored the 'precision' element anyway.[40]

On the night of 24–25 July 1943, Bomber Command executed Operation Gomorrah – the raid on Hamburg. This did not really satisfy the Pointblank

Directive, but it was a large industrial city within relatively easy reach, and its docks and lakes would show up well on the RAF's terrain-mapping airborne radar, codenamed H2S. The force consisted largely of four-engine heavies: 347 Avro Lancasters, 247 Handley Page Halifaxes and 125 Short Stirlings; plus 73 twin-engine Vickers Wellingtons – some 792 aircraft in all. They carried 1,454 tons of high explosive bombs plus 1,006 tons of incendiaries. The raid created a firestorm over some 10.5sq km (4 sq miles); a total of 210km (130 miles) of streets were ablaze, along which were 1,600 apartment blocks. American Boeing B17 Flying Fortresses attacked the following day.[41]

It is often stated that aerial campaigns cannot win wars. Bomber Harris alluded to this during the war and added, 'but we shall see'. Speer wrote of the Hamburg raid:

> Hamburg had put the fear of God into me. At the meeting of Central Planning on 29 July [1943], I pointed out: 'If the air raids continue on the present scale, within three months we shall be relieved of a number of questions we are at present discussing. We shall be simply coasting downhill, smoothly and relatively swiftly . . .' Three days later I informed Hitler that armaments production was collapsing and threw in the final warning that a series of attacks of this sort, extended to six more major cities, would bring Germany's armaments production to a total halt.[42]

Generalfeldmarschall Erhard Milch said:

> It's much blacker that Speer paints it. If we get just five or six more attacks like these on Hamburg, the German people will just lay down their tools, however great their will power. I keep saying, the steps that are being taken now are being taken too late. There can be no more talk of night fighters in the East, or of putting an umbrella over our troops in Sicily or anything like that. The soldier on the battlefield will just have to dig a hole, crawl into it and wait until the attack is over. What the home front is suffering now cannot be suffered much longer.[43]

Yet Speer wrote that Hitler responded, '"You'll straighten all that out again," . . . In fact Hitler was right.'[44]

The Battle of Berlin was a less successful strategy. Beginning on 18 November 1943 and lasting until 24 March 1944, it encompassed 9,111 sorties. Berlin was a long haul and it possessed the best anti-aircraft defences in Europe. The attrition of British bombers was thus considerable: 492 bombers were shot down, and an additional 95 were written off on their return, with a further 859 damaged. Berlin, as the enemy's capital, was an obsession with Harris, and those around him failed to argue the point that it was not the best target. As Speer pointed out after the war, Berlin was not that important for war production. Churchill also failed to understand this.[45]

Despite the inadequacy of the Battle of Berlin, the bombing of the German capital continued on a less substantial scale, and the campaign was so serious that by April 1945 Hitler had to retreat to his bunker. The air war had crippled Berlin and other German cities – particularly Hamburg – before the ground forces ever engaged these targets.

The air campaign was also essential against Hitler's V-weapons. The V-1 flying bomb could be interdicted by the most advanced fighters in the RAF, especially the Hawker Tempest and the Gloster Meteor, the only Allied jet plane to see service in World War II. However, the V-2 ballistic missiles, of which Cherwell, as usual, had been sceptical, could be destroyed only at their launch sites, and at the development facilities at Peenemünde on the German Baltic coast. The strategic bomber force was crucial for this.

DRESDEN

It was said that when Dresden was selected as a target it was because Churchill and the chiefs wanted a city that would burn. With an old city of timber buildings it was possible to raise a 'firestorm' by dropping incendiaries containing magnesium, phosphorus or napalm. These would generate enormous temperatures in the target area, and as the hot gases rose, they would suck in cold air and so fuel the fire. Dresden, the capital of Saxony, was a historic city with many old timber-framed buildings and narrow streets: it was known as 'Florence on the Elbe'.

Churchill was motivated to bomb Dresden because he had been asked to by the Soviets, and was stung by Stalin's jibes that he had been afraid to mount a Second Front, so that most of the fighting had been left to the Soviets. The Dresden raid was a foolish attempt to display British virility. Dresden had little strategic importance and not a great deal of its industry had been employed for military production. Nevertheless, it was a communications link and had been on Harris's list, along with Chemnitz and Leipzig, for precisely this reason. However, Dresden was at the far end of the range of Harris's four-engine heavy bombers, with all the additional attendant risks for his crews.[46]

On 25 January 1945 Churchill asked the Secretary of State for Air, Archie Sinclair, about a possible bomber offensive against the German retreat from Breslau. Sinclair responded guardedly the following day, to which Churchill gave a short-tempered riposte: 'I did not ask you about plans for harrying the German retreat from Breslau. On the contrary I asked whether Berlin, and no doubt other large cities in East Germany, should not now be considered especially attractive targets. Pray report to me tomorrow what is going to be done.'[47] This executive urgency prompted the raid; the misgivings of the service chiefs and others were overridden at the express insistence of Churchill himself, even though American co-operation had yet to be sought.

Dresden had not been attacked prior to this raid and had virtually no anti-aircraft defence. Refugees fleeing the Soviet advance had swelled the population of the city from its usual 650,000 to about a million. The raid, Operation Thunderclap, occurred on 13–14 February, and consisted of 773 Lancasters and 527 American four-engine heavies. The Americans had agreed to open the assault, but due to poor weather the American raid was postponed for 24 hours and Harris's force went in first. The second wave could see the target from some distance as it was still on fire and smoke was rising to high altitude. No one knows the death toll; early estimates were as high as 200,000 but more recently it has been put between 35,000 and 40,000.

The raid killed a lot of refugees as well as many of the indigenous population, but that was about all. It was retrospectively justified on the grounds that there were German military production facilities in the city, including the largest ball-bearing factory. But German military production was virtually everywhere. In March, after the raid, Churchill minuted:

> It seems to me that the moment has come when the question of
> bombing of German cities simply for the sake of increasing the

terror, though under other pretexts, should be reviewed. Otherwise we shall come into control of an utterly ruined land . . . the destruction of Dresden remains a serious query against the conduct of Allied bombing . . . I feel the need for more precise concentration upon military objectives rather than on mere acts of terror and wanton destruction, however impressive.[48]

The implication was that it was beginning to look as though Britain was committing war crimes, and Churchill intimated that Harris was responsible. Portal was incandescent, and supported by Sinclair, forced Churchill to withdraw it. Dresden was a target imposed upon Harris ultimately by Churchill; it was a disgrace that he had attempted to blame Harris. Churchill had been an architect of the area bombing campaign from the outset, and it was he almost alone, save Portal, who determined the overall conduct of the bomber offensive.[49]

The reasons for suggesting that the raid was a war crime were Dresden's lack of clear strategic importance, the fact that Germany was well on its way to being beaten, the presence of so many refugees, and the fact that the RAF bombers had successfully whipped up a firestorm. If Churchill thought this amounted to a war crime, and if he had been concerned about British forces committing such a crime, he should never have ordered Harris to undertake the raid. The fact that the war would have been won just as quickly without such an attack made the raid shameful.

As has already been noted, precision attacks were not possible early in the war, but by the time of Dresden they were, though Harris resisted them, wanting to stick to the area bombing philosophy. Nevertheless, precision squadrons had already been introduced: the Pathfinder squadrons in 1942, and 617 – the Dam Buster squadron – the following year both demonstrated that high-precision bombing was possible. However, it took Dresden to make Churchill seriously question area bombing.

THE ASSESSMENT

Churchill made his Victory in Europe 'VE' Day speech to the nation on the afternoon of 13 May 1945. In it he made no mention of Bomber Command's contribution to victory in World War II, save a very brief mention of the damage done to Berlin.[50] He wished to distance himself, not simply from the Dresden raid, but from the entire Bomber Command area bombing campaign. This was a disgrace for three reasons. First, he had been one of its architects and as Prime Minister had authorized it. Second, it played a fundamental role in the outcome of World War II. And third, his omission was a betrayal of the airmen who risked and lost their lives fighting for their country while doing his bidding. In all, the British bomber force lost 55,573 air crew, of which virtually all were officers and NCOs. This was greater than the loss of officers by the British Army in the whole of World War I. The losses were nearly one-seventh of all British combatant deaths in World War II.[51]

Although Harris was promoted to marshal of the Royal Air Force on 1 January 1946, unlike the other principal war leaders he was not awarded a peerage in the 1946 New Year's honours list. In fact he had held only 'acting' ranks of air marshal and air chief marshal during the war: his last substantive rank had been air vice-marshal at the war's outset. In *The Second World War*, Churchill wrote a reasonable amount about Bomber Command in the early volumes, much less so in the later ones. In the last volume, Harris is mentioned only once and then critically.[52] This treatment of Harris was reprehensible. Churchill wanted to make it seem that the consequences of Bomber Command's policies were the responsibility of Harris and not himself. Yet again, things Churchill didn't like were someone else's fault, not his own.

The British and American forces conducted largely independent bombing campaigns, and although each believed in the validity of their respective strategies at the time, doubts grew when the post-war assessment was undertaken. After the war, the official British historians claimed that the plastering of Hamburg cost the Germans only 1.8 months' worth of lost production. The raids on the Ruhr region cost a little less, and all the raids on the Krupp factories at Essen only three months. The problem, as Speer pointed out after the war, was that Bomber Command did not return to the cities they had laid waste, quickly and in sufficient numbers to prevent their recovery, and they failed to do the same to other cities, except for Berlin where the risks were too high and the benefits too little. When the US Eighth Army Air Force attacked the ball-bearing plants at Schweinfurt, production fell by 38 per cent after the first raid and 67 per cent after the second, but the cost in American aircraft was high and the Germans quickly started to disperse production. The Americans also failed to follow up the raids quickly and on a large scale. Speer was amazed that it was not until the spring of 1944 that the Americans targeted Germany's synthetic oil plants, and that Bomber Command did not target them at all.[53] The German fighter ace and night-fighter commander, General Adolph Galland, said of the targeting of oil plants, that it was 'the most successful operation of the entire Allied strategical air warfare'; he couldn't understand 'why the Allies started this undertaking so late . . . Right from the start, fuel had been the most awkward bottleneck for the German conduct of war.'[54] This is how Harris justified not participating in the campaign:

> The largest oil plants were restored to full production in a
> few weeks and were often able to produce a fair proportion of
> their former output in little more than a week after a highly
> successful attack. The dispersal of small oil plants above and,
> to some extent, below ground, taxed our intelligence services
> to the utmost and it was not surprising to me that during
> the offensive we got news of additional oil sources almost
> every day.[55]

But after the war Harris was not so sure. Speer had told Hitler in July 1944, 'that by September all tactical movements would necessarily come to a standstill for lack of fuel'. But much later he said:

> In my memoranda to Hitler I was stating what the experts, the
> historians, are now saying, that with these attacks on oil our
> forces in September 1944 won't be able to move at all, but this
> was not the real effect. We had quite a high stock of supplies of
> gasoline and to my astonishment this stock was sufficient even
> to supply the tanks in the winter and spring of 1944 to '45.[56]

However, the important point is that the large-scale raids were not immediately followed up with others to prevent the recovery of these plants and the reorganization of production. Resources squandered on the Mediterranean campaign could have been employed more effectively in performing this task.

For Speer, it was the bombing of transport and communications that had the most significant effect. After the war he said:

> The attack on the traffic was certainly the most effective one.
> First of all, I could no more produce anything regularly. Then
> the whole German economy came to a standstill because we
> hadn't any more coal. Then, with the ruined traffic system our
> military moves were very difficult.[57]

It was precisely because of this bombing campaign that Speer sent a memo
to Hitler in November 1944 stating, 'We are finished.'[58]

The United States Strategic Bombing Survey of their offensive over
Germany, conducted at the end of the war, doubted the effectiveness of its
achievements. The survey argued, 'every 15,000 tons of bombs dropped . . .
resulted in a loss of one per cent of the annual production of Germany as
a whole'. However, recovery would be remarkably swift and it was often
mostly non-essential production that was affected.[59] Yet Speer responded
to the official American history:

> It seems to me that the book misses the decisive point. Like all
> other accounts of the bombing that I have so far seen, it places
> its emphasis on the destruction that air raids inflicted on
> German industrial potential and thus upon armaments.
> In reality the losses were not quite so serious . . . The real
> importance of the air war consisted in the fact that it opened a
> second front long before the invasion of Europe. That front
> was the skies over Germany . . . The unpredictability of the
> attacks made the front gigantic . . . Defence against air attacks
> required the production of thousands of anti-aircraft guns, the
> stockpiling of tremendous quantities of ammunition all over
> the country, and holding in readiness hundreds of thousands
> of soldiers . . . As far as I can judge from the accounts I have
> read, no one has yet seen that this was the greatest lost battle
> on the German side.[60]

During Speer's interrogation by the Allies immediately after the war (before
he wrote this passage), he held the belief that bombing had really made a
significant contribution to the defeat of Germany only in the late stages of
the war. And in his memoirs, *Inside the Third Reich*, written later, he returned

to this more pessimistic view of the Allied bombing campaign. Yet when he discussed the matter in a television broadcast in 1973, after he had published his memoirs, he said of the Schweinfurt raids, 'If there had been a couple more similar raids conducted immediately afterwards . . . this would have been extremely serious for Germany.' And most significantly, of the Bomber Command assault on Hamburg, 'Six more raids like this and it would have finished the war.'[61] What is clear is that more effort could have been decisive, and if Churchill had been truly prescient he would have understood this. Even so, Speer would comment that from early 1943 the bombing campaign constituted a Second Front in its own right. But so much more could have been accomplished.

At the end of the war Professor (later Lord) Solly Zuckerman reported on the effects of the bombing campaign. His report demonstrated that Lord Cherwell's notion of eroding morale was wrong, but Cherwell's prediction concerning the number of homes that would be destroyed was only 1.4 times the actual figure. This was far less inaccurate than that of Sir Henry Tizard, one of his critics. Tizard was correct however, that de-housing would not have a decisive effect on the German war effort by the summer of 1943, as had been hoped. Professor Blackett, another of Cherwell's critics, was also right when he said that de-housing could not win the war, but his prediction of the deaths caused by bombing was only about 2 per cent of the actual figure.[62]

The most important outcome of Zuckerman's report was to corroborate Speer's view of the importance of targeting the communications infrastructure. Of Hamburg he wrote:

> The crucial blow inflicted to Hamburg's economy was . . . the transportation difficulties that resulted from . . . raids against railroad and canal installations. These raids – and the whole series of air attacks on the Ruhr region – prevented Hamburg's factories from receiving (1) raw materials and finished parts they needed from the Ruhr industries, (2) vital supplies of coal, and (3) electrical power which is normally produced in Hamburg from Ruhr coal.[63]

To have had a decisive effect on the outcome of the war, the bombing would have needed to be concentrated on these targets, but it would also have needed to be undertaken on a more substantial scale. Back in 1941 the air staff had proposed a plan to win the war against Germany with the bomber offensive alone, requiring 4,000 bombers. In a minute to Portal on 16 June 1941, Archie Sinclair, the Air Minister, reported that other ministers were 'reluctant to commit themselves to so big a concentration of effort upon one means of winning the war'.[64] Yet this was the only way Britain could have won the war. Although he never overtly signed up to the 4,000-bomber programme, Churchill did exhort ever-increasing production towards this hoped-for target. On 7 September, shortly after he had received the Butt report concerning the inaccuracy of RAF bombing, he wrote:

> In order to achieve a first-line strength of 4,000 heavy and medium bombers, the RAF require 22,000 to be made between July 1941 and July 1943, of which 5,500 may be expected to reach us from American production. The latest forecasts show that of the remaining 16,500, only 11,000 will be got from our own factories. If we are going to win the war, we cannot accept this position.[65]

So bombers were going to win the war, despite the Butt report's concerns and Churchill's pessimistic response to it. However, it was precisely his Mediterranean strategy, which committed such a high proportion of Britain's resources first to the North African and subsequently to the Italian campaigns, that denuded Britain's ability to take the war effort decisively to the heart of the German war machine. If Hitler's cities and war production could have been attacked decisively with such a force, it would have had a much more significant effect on shortening the war than Churchill's dispersionist strategy.

The bombing campaign, taken in the round, was central to the war effort, as Speer pointed out after the war. He made it clear that the air war amounted to a Second Front from 1943, as it took thousands of guns, a hundred thousand men and millions of shells from the Eastern Front.[66]

The European war was, of course, won by land armies in the end, but the one in Japan ended with two Boeing B29 Super Fortresses – each with an atomic bomb – targeting Hiroshima and Nagasaki. In fact, however, the victory was already largely won through the use of massed formations of B29s dropping conventional ordnance. Thus for Japan the air war was decisive. Had the European war gone on longer it is likely that the same result would have occurred, with or without the need for an atomic bomb to end it. In his memoirs Harris wrote,

> If we had had the force we used in 1944 a year earlier, and if we had then been allowed to use it together with the whole American bomber force and without interruption, Germany would have been defeated outright by bombing as Japan was . . . The allied war leaders did not have enough faith in strategic bombing . . . We were always being diverted from the main offensive by the demands of other services . . . Without these diversions . . . there would have been no need for the invasion.[67]

But crucially Harris should have added that immediate, repetitive, large-scale attacks were needed on strategic targets, including the transport and oil-producing infrastructure. In 1940 some 13,000 tons of bombs were dropped on Germany; in 1941 it was 32,000 tons and in 1942, 46,000 tons. It was only in 1943 that the campaign was massively increased to 157,000 tons, but these mostly fell on civilian targets. In 1944 the figure was a truly massive 526,000 tons, and only then did the campaign significantly target the transport and oil facilities.[68] This corroborates both Harris and Speer: both of them understood that the bomber assault should have been larger and taken place earlier to have been truly effective. This was something Churchill did not see.

Churchill believed that Britain lacked the necessary resources to attack Germany directly until the Second Front in 1944, when the USA was well and truly in the war and the Germans had been partly beaten by the Soviet Union. Thus taking the war to the Germans in some other theatre was necessary prior to this. But this caused a disproportionate use of resources in dispersionist campaigns that denuded Bomber and Coastal Command of vital resources. If, instead of so much effort being concentrated on campaigns in Norway, the Balkans, North Africa and Italy, Britain had concentrated more effort directly on the German war machine with the bombing campaign, the war could have been won more quickly. Most of the senior politicians and military brass failed to see this – Churchill among them.

17
THE 'BIG TWO' AND
'BIG THREE' CONFERENCES

Most of the conferences between the leaders of Great Britain, the USA and the Soviet Union were in fact 'Big Two' conferences, either between Churchill and Roosevelt, or occasionally between Churchill and Stalin. There were only three 'Big Three' conferences, and they did not start until the meeting at Tehran in Persia (Iran) during the latter part of 1943; the second was at Yalta in the Crimea at the beginning of 1945 and the last at Potsdam outside Berlin that summer. Roosevelt attended only the first two of these: his death in spring 1945 meant that the new President, Harry Truman, represented the United States at the last one. During that last Big Three conference at Potsdam, the British general election results were announced and the new Prime Minister, Clement Attlee, replaced Churchill as the British representative partway through the conference.

RIVIERA

Churchill met Roosevelt for a conference codenamed Riviera, from 9–12 August 1941, at Placentia Bay in Newfoundland, Canada. However, he neither informed nor consulted the Canadian Prime Minister, William Lyon Mackenzie King, let alone inviting him to the conference, despite the fact that King had been his greatest ally after the fall of France. Churchill travelled across the Atlantic aboard the battleship HMS *Prince of Wales*, which would be sunk in the next few months when he sent it to face the Japanese. During the crossing, radio silence prevented him from transmitting orders to his forces, so he read CS Forester's *Captain Hornblower RN*.[1]

In truth Churchill and Roosevelt had met once before, in 1918 at Gray's Inn in London, when Roosevelt was Assistant Secretary of the Navy. But Churchill claimed he had no memory of this, something that rather irked the President. Also present on that earlier occasion had been

Joseph Kennedy, the father of a later president, who said that Roosevelt had commented that Churchill was rude and a 'stinker . . . lording it all over us.'[2]

When they met in Canada, Roosevelt said, 'At last – we have gotten together,' and Churchill replied, 'We have.'[3] According to the President's aid and personal envoy to Churchill, Harry Hopkins, Churchill seemed to believe 'he was being carried up into the heavens to meet God'.[4] Roosevelt would say some time later that Churchill had a hundred ideas a day, only four of which were any good. When informed of this remark Churchill said that Roosevelt never had any ideas at all.[5] The United States, of course, was not yet at war. Churchill was keen that Roosevelt should get his country into it, but the President would not commit himself. Isolationist sentiment at home prevented him, and he had been obliged to fight the 1940 presidential election on an anti-war ticket.

Already Churchill and the British chiefs of staff were promoting their dispersionist strategy: that forces should be committed in the Mediterranean and the Middle East rather than mounting an assault against German forces in France. The head of the US Army, General George Marshall, opposed this policy from the outset. He wanted a Second Front in France and to supply the Russians in their battle on the Eastern Front.[6]

At the conference the two leaders created a vision of the post-war world, and to this effect they negotiated and became signatories to the Atlantic Charter, which was issued as a joint declaration on 14 August:

> The President of the United States of America and the
> Prime Minister, Mr. Churchill, representing His Majesty's
> Government in the United Kingdom, being met together,
> deem it right to make known certain common principles in
> the national policies of their respective countries on which
> they base their hopes for a better future for the world.
>
> First, their countries seek no aggrandizement, territorial
> or other;
>
> Second, they desire to see no territorial changes that do not
> accord with the freely expressed wishes of the peoples
> concerned;

Third, they respect the right of all peoples to choose the form of government under which they will live; and they wish to see sovereign rights and self government restored to those who have been forcibly deprived of them;

Fourth, they will endeavor, with due respect for their existing obligations, to further the enjoyment by all States, great or small, victor or vanquished, of access, on equal terms, to the trade and to the raw materials of the world which are needed for their economic prosperity;

Fifth, they desire to bring about the fullest collaboration between all nations in the economic field with the object of securing, for all, improved labor standards, economic advancement and social security;

Sixth, after the final destruction of the Nazi tyranny, they hope to see established a peace which will afford to all nations the means of dwelling in safety within their own boundaries, and which will afford assurance that all the men in all lands may live out their lives in freedom from fear and want;

Seventh, such a peace should enable all men to traverse the high seas and oceans without hindrance;

Eighth, they believe that all of the nations of the world, for realistic as well as spiritual reasons must come to the abandonment of the use of force. Since no future peace can be maintained if land, sea or air armaments continue to be employed by nations which threaten, or may threaten, aggression outside of their frontiers, they believe, pending the establishment of a wider and permanent system of general security, that the disarmament of such nations is essential. They will likewise aid and encourage all other practicable measures which will lighten for peace-loving peoples the crushing burden of armaments.

Regarding point 1, the Americans wanted a commitment from Churchill that he had not undertaken any secret agreements concerning post-war territorial acquisitions. Such secret agreements had been entered into at the end of World War I, and the Americans had only discovered this at the Versailles peace conference. Churchill failed to give such a commitment.[7]

Regarding point 4, Britain had a system of 'Imperial Preference' protecting its trading relationship with its empire. This had originally been proposed by Joseph Chamberlain at the beginning of the century, but it had not then gained a Parliamentary majority and become law – ironically, at that time Churchill had believed in free trade. It eventually became policy in 1932 with the General Tariff, when one of Joseph Chamberlain's sons, Neville, was Chancellor of the Exchequer (see chapter 2). Churchill now defended this policy. The US Secretary of State, Cordell Hull, saw free trade as a condition of peace. Churchill insisted that he also believed in free trade but that there was opposition at home, and he would anyway have to consult the Dominions before he could take a policy stance. Yet this was a red herring: British trade policy really didn't have the benefit of the Dominions as its objective, and Churchill was deploying troops from those very Dominions to further his wartime policies without much reference to their own interests. When Roosevelt pressed Churchill on the matter, he insisted that the current pattern of trade should continue because it had made Britain great.[8]

Roosevelt then raised an even more contentious issue with regard to point 3: colonialism. He insisted that all peoples of the world should be freed from the yoke of colonialism after the war. This was too much for Churchill, who asked, 'What about the Philippines?' This was, of course, one of the USA's very few possessions. Churchill insisted that the British Empire was 'the foundation of our greatness'. But Roosevelt was adamant: an end to despotism was needed.[9]

ARCADIA

The two leaders next met at Christmas 1941 in Washington for the Arcadia Conference, which lasted from 22 December until 14 January. At first, Roosevelt did not wish to conduct it so soon after the Japanese attack on Pearl Harbor, but this was precisely why Churchill wanted to meet.

He sailed to the United States aboard the battleship *Duke of York*, sister ship of the *Prince of Wales*, and the only mishap on the trip was that they ran out of white wine. It was on this trip that Churchill would further develop his dispersionist strategy for the war.[10]

Churchill knew that the relationship with Roosevelt was vital to winning the war; the policy of engaging the United States, with its unlimited industrial capacity, in the conflict was the only way he could see that Nazi Germany could be defeated. During the conference he addressed a joint session of the US Congress, making much of his American mother. He then addressed the Canadian Parliament, where he alluded to the warning given by France's General Weygand that in three weeks England would have its neck wrung like a chicken, to which he added, 'Some chicken,' then after a pause, 'Some neck.'[11] Returning to Washington he was signatory to the creation of the United Nations Organization and the Grand Alliance treaty encompassing 26 nations, all opposed to the Axis powers. Immediately after Pearl Harbor, Hitler invoked the tripartite Axis pact and declared war on the USA, as Japan was now at war with it. It was a great irony that after all Churchill's cajoling to get the Americans into the war, it was the Japanese and Hitler who had made it happen.

During the conference there was an episode when Roosevelt went into Churchill's rooms at the White House; he was told that Churchill was in the bathroom and that he should go right in, which he did. Churchill was in the bathtub and Roosevelt apologised and started to leave, but Churchill stood up and said, 'The Prime Minister of Great Britain has nothing to conceal from the President of the United States.' Churchill later denied this story, but it constitutes a good metaphor for the political reality of Churchill's situation.[12]

When the summit officially opened, the Americans underscored the 'Europe First' policy, the chiefs of staff saying, 'Once Germany is defeated, the collapse of Italy and the defeat of Japan must follow.'[13] However, Churchill's policy –which would at least initially prevail – was not that the collapse of Italy should follow the defeat of Germany, but just the other way around. The reason for the Americans' compromise is perhaps best summed up by a remark Roosevelt made to Marshall: 'I am responsible for keeping the Grand Alliance together. You cannot, in the interests of a more vigorous prosecution of the war, break up the alliance.'[14] However, Roosevelt momentarily swung back when after the conference he consulted with the Russians and supported the plans of the American chiefs for an invasion of France, though this would change yet again. After the conference, with continuing bad news about the British position in the war, Churchill was 'hitting out blindly, like a child in a temper,' according to his doctor, Charles Wilson.[15]

SHUTTLING BETWEEN THE RUSSIANS AND THE AMERICANS

In May 1942, Churchill discussed the matter of the Second Front with the Russians when he entertained the Soviet Foreign Minister, Vyachaslav Molotov, and his delegation at Chequers. Buoyed up by apparent American support, the Russians argued for it vociferously. Churchill said that plans were going ahead for just such an assault later in that year, but played down its expected effect. This was of course because he opposed it anyway.[16]

Churchill and Roosevelt then met on 18 June at the President's home, Hyde Park, New York. Here Churchill argued the case against Operation Sledgehammer, General Marshall's proposed opposed landing in France scheduled for that autumn. He was strongly supported by General Sir Alan Brooke, the CIGS. They argued that the operation could not be conducted due to the lack of landing craft and that the Germans would have to endure a serious defeat at the hands of the Russians for it to be possible at all.[17]

The two leaders met again in Washington immediately afterwards for another formal conference from 20–25 June. Here Churchill argued that Allied forces should not wait idly in the Mediterranean while preparations were made for Sledgehammer or the bigger landing, Operation Roundup, proposed for 1943. Instead the Allies should mount a major campaign in North Africa, putting Sledgehammer pretty much out of the question. And thus Churchill got his way. Yet the Americans argued that such a strategy would not result in Germany shifting any forces away from the Russian front. As Sir John Dill, head of the British Joint Services Mission to Washington, put it, the American chiefs of staff thought they were being led 'down the Mediterranean garden path to a cul-de-sac'.[18] It was then announced that Tobruk had fallen to the Germans, and Churchill left the conference early.

Churchill travelled to Moscow with Averell Harriman, representing Roosevelt, for a meeting with Stalin from 12–17 August 1942. Faced with the problematic task of telling the Soviet leader that there would be no Second Front in 1942, he said it was 'like carrying a large lump of ice to the North Pole'.[19] Stalin said that the Germans were not supermen and that Britain need not be afraid of them. Churchill insisted that the bombing campaign would sap German morale – something it really never did – and that it wasn't necessary for the Second Front to be in France. He then told Stalin of the Anglo-American plans for North Africa and the Mediterranean, using his analogy of Europe as a crocodile. But the crocodile's snout was pointing at the Soviet Union, as Stalin was all too well aware: 10,000 Russians were dying on the Eastern Front each day, and Stalin insisted that the Allies ought to be able to land six or eight divisions around Cherbourg to relieve the pressure.[20]

Churchill was in a bad mood and in private moments vented his despair at the British Ambassador to Moscow, Archibald Clark Kerr, who said of him, 'I felt like giving him a good root up the arse. My respect for him and faith in him have suffered sadly.'[21] The senior Foreign Office diplomat Alexander Cadogan said of Churchill when he attended a party given by Stalin, 'He was like a bull in the ring maddened by the pricks of the picadors.'[22]

SYMBOL

Churchill met Roosevelt again at the Casablanca Conference, codenamed Symbol, which ran from 14–24 January 1943. Stalin was much preoccupied with the Battle of Stalingrad and did not attend. The military gains that his forces would make meant his position would be strengthened by meeting the other two later.[23] At the conference the familiar story unfolded, with Churchill, supported by Brooke, arguing for an invasion of Sicily followed by Italy, while Marshall argued for the cross-Channel Operation Roundup. The head of the US Navy, Admiral Ernest King, said that Churchill and the British had 'definite ideas as to what the next operation should be, but [did] not seem to have an overall plan for the conduct of the war'. King was inclined to think that the British were just waiting for the Russians to defeat Hitler, in which case he believed it would be prudent for the United States to provide additional military aid to Russia rather than participating in British-inspired operations in the Mediterranean. Once again, to keep the alliance together, Roosevelt came down in Churchill's favour.[24]

It was, however, decided that the accumulation of armed forces in Britain should continue, and that a Second Front could be initiated 'in the event that the German strength in France decreases, either through withdrawal of her troops or because of an internal collapse'. Neither of these events was particularly likely, of course. There was planning involving operations in Burma and an attempt to encourage Turkey into the war. Churchill had got his way.

Roosevelt opposed Churchill's support for the Free French leader, General Charles de Gaulle. Roosevelt thought him an upstart, and instead backed Henri Giraud as the man to represent the French. The two Frenchman, who both attended the conference, could not have been more opposed: Giraud had connections with the German-sponsored Vichy government controlling the southern part of France, while de Gaulle was adamantly opposed to the Vichy regime. Yet at Casablanca Roosevelt forced de Gaulle to shake the hand of his adversary, in what was a very public humiliation, and tried to make them work together. Roosevelt was wrong about de Gaulle, and despite the fiery relationship between de Gaulle and Churchill, the latter rightly backed the great Frenchman. This would have important implications for France after the war, though not to the benefit of Britain.[25]

As the President reflected on the two Frenchman he said that it was like arranging co-operation between Grant and Lee, the Union and Confederate commanders in the American Civil War. He added, off the cuff, that Grant was referred to as 'Old Unconditional Surrender'. Crucially, he then said that unconditional surrender was what was required of the Axis powers. Churchill complained that he should have been consulted before the President announced such a policy decision. Although Roosevelt's son Elliott said that the matter had been mentioned at lunch, this marked a shift: the President was beginning to take a more independent line. He reflected privately to Elliott of the British:

> They must never get the idea that we're in it just to help them hang on to the archaic, medieval Empire ideas . . . I hope they realise they're not the senior partner; that we're not going to sit by, after we've won, and watch their system stultify the growth of every country of Asia and half the countries in Europe to boot . . . Great Britain signed the Atlantic Charter.

I hope they realise that the United States government means to make them live up to it.[26]

After the Casablanca Conference Churchill came down with a bout of pneumonia.[27] However, within a couple of weeks he was dining again on plovers' eggs, chicken broth and chicken pie, followed by chocolate soufflé, washed down by champagne, with port to finish and liberal quantities of brandy. He was back on form.[28]

TRIDENT

Churchill met Roosevelt again in Washington for a conference codenamed Trident, from 12–27 May 1943. His position was now a very familiar one. He argued that, once Sicily had been occupied, Allied forces should not remain idle and Italy should be the next objective. He made the extraordinary claim that it had been Bulgaria's decision to withdraw from the Central Powers in World War I that had led to the collapse of Germany in 1918, and that knocking out Italy now might cause Germany to collapse again. Needless to say this did not impress the Americans.[29]

Brooke, a strong supporter of the Mediterranean strategy, noted in his diary for 24 May:

> [Churchill] thinks one thing at one moment and another at another moment. At times the war may be won by bombing and all must be sacrificed to it. At others it becomes essential for us to bleed ourselves dry on the Continent because Russia is doing the same. At others our main effort must be in the Mediterranean, directed against Italy or [the] Balkans alternatively, with sporadic desires to invade Norway and 'roll up the map in the opposite direction to Hitler'! But more often . . . he wants to carry out ALL operations simultaneously irrespective of shortages of shipping![30]

It was at this conference that the Americans insisted that a date be set for the Second Front in France: it was to be 1 May 1944. Churchill was thus finally cornered into agreeing to the final assault on mainland Europe by the western Allies which, together with the Soviet advance from the east, would lead to the final defeat of Nazi Germany.

During Trident, Roosevelt conveyed a secret message to Stalin asking him to meet on a bilateral basis. Churchill was to be sidelined. The President had decided that the principal events that would shape the wartime and post-war periods could be addressed more effectively between the Big Two, with the 'Little One' added in later. Roosevelt was confident Churchill would be obliged to accept whatever decisions he made. Stalin almost agreed, but he was irritated by the fact that the date set for the Second Front at Trident meant yet another postponement of the operation, and he said 'No' to the meeting. However, this made it clear that, even before the Big Three met for the first time ever at Tehran at the end of 1943, Churchill had already been relegated to a secondary status.[31]

QUADRANT

Churchill and Roosevelt met again for the first of two conferences in Quebec, codenamed Quadrant, from 17–24 August 1943. It was also attended by the Canadian Prime Minister Mackenzie King, and the Chinese Foreign Minister, TV Soong. This conference saw the creation of a unified Allied China–Burma–India theatre, under Mountbatten. Roosevelt offered a limited recognition of the French Committee of National Liberation under the leadership of Charles de Gaulle and Henri Giraud, and there was also agreement to build the atomic bomb as quickly as possible.[32]

The contentious issue, however, was once again the Second Front. The US Secretary of War, Henry Stimson, reported to the President that Churchill and the British were only paying lip-service to it. In consequence, the Americans openly threatened to shift the force build-up from Britain to the Japanese theatre – something they had threatened before. Churchill had promised Brooke that he would command the Second Front, but the Americans would not agree to this, especially as Churchill and the British were hardly committed to it. In the end, the target date of 1 May 1944 that had been agreed at Trident was assented to and the codename 'Overlord' was specified. The Americans proposed a subsidiary landing in the South of France, which would become Operation Anvil and which Churchill didn't like at all, as it would detract from his Mediterranean strategy.[33]

Churchill was becoming increasingly peevish as he was progressively sidelined by the Americans. It did not help that it was also decided that his desire for operations in the Balkans should be confined to the supplying of resistance forces. Brooke noted in his diary for 30 August 1943:

> The Quebec conference has left me absolutely cooked. Winston made matters almost impossible, temperamental like a film star, and peevish like a spoilt child. He has an unfortunate trick of picking up some isolated operation and without ever really having looked into it, setting his heart on it. When he once gets in one of those moods he feels everybody is trying to thwart him and to produce difficulties. He becomes then more and more set on the operation brushing everything aside, and when planners prove the operation to be impossible he then appoints new planners in the hope that they will prove that the operation is possible. It is an untold relief to be away from him for a bit.
>
> I wonder whether any historian of the future will ever be able to paint Winston in his true colours. It is a wonderful character – the most marvellous qualities and superhuman genius mixed with an astonishing lack of vision at times, and an impetuosity which if not guided must inevitably bring him into trouble again and again. Perhaps the most remarkable failing of his is that he can never see a whole strategical problem at once. His gaze always settles on some definite part of the canvas and the rest of the picture is lost. It is difficult to make him realise the influence of one theatre on another. The general handling of the German reserves in Europe can never be fully grasped by him. This failing is accentuated by the fact that often he does not want to see the whole picture, especially if this wider vision should in any way interfere with the operation he may have temporarily set his heart on. He is quite the most difficult man to work with that I have ever struck . . .[34]

Brooke then continued this sentence in a different ink, intimating that he may have added a kinder reflection the following day: '. . . but I should not have missed the chance of working with him for anything on earth.'

SEXTANT

The next meeting between Churchill and Roosevelt was for the first of two conferences in Cairo, codenamed Sextant, from 21–26 November 1943. Two days later they went on to Teheran to meet Stalin collectively for the first time. Also present at Sextant was the Chinese leader, Chiang Kai-shek.

On his way to the conference, Churchill prepared the position he would argue in front of the Americans. It would be all too familiar. He wanted a renewed offensive in Italy and would complain that the existing problems were all to do with shifting forces away from that theatre in preparation for Overlord. He then wanted an assault on islands in the Aegean. His objectives were:

> (a) Stop all further movement of British troops and British
> and United States landing craft from the Mediterranean.
> (b) Use all possible energy to take Rome.
> (c) Bring Turkey into the war . . . Meanwhile prepare an
> expedition to take Rhodes before the end of January.
> (d) Seize a port or ports and establish a bridgehead on the
> Dalmatian coast, and carry a regular flow of airborne supplies
> to the Partisans. Use the British 1st Airborne Division and all
> the Commandos available in the Mediterranean . . . to aid and
> animate the resistance in Yugoslavia and Albania and also
> capture islands like Corfu and Kefalonia.
> (e) Continue and build up Overlord without prejudice
> to above.

The fact that the reference to Overlord comes last and only 'without prejudice' to the points listed above it indicates Churchill's prioritizing of his ambitious Mediterranean campaign over the Second Front. He stayed in Malta before continuing to Cairo. In front of Brooke, he threatened to withdraw from Overlord if the Americans refused to increase their deployment of forces in the Mediterranean, and said that if this led to the abandonment of the 'Europe First' policy, then so be it.[35]

The marginalization of Churchill now became very apparent. He was extremely keen to meet Roosevelt *à deux* in order to establish a united position before meeting Stalin at Tehran. However, the President said he did not wish to do this, as it would seem as though they were ganging up against Stalin. Yet this is precisely what Roosevelt would subsequently do with Stalin against Churchill at Tehran.[36]

Roosevelt had originally asked Stalin to attend the Cairo Conference, but he had refrained from telling Stalin that Chiang Kai-shek was to be present because the Soviet leader did not wish to provoke the Japanese by meeting the Chinese leader. Also, Stalin believed it necessary for only the Big Three to meet if important progress was to be made. However, Churchill leaked to Stalin the decision to invite Chiang, so Stalin refused to attend.[37]

Roosevelt met the Chinese leader on the first day of the conference, without Churchill being present and without him being told. Roosevelt would meet Chiang Kai-shek five times more during the conference, prioritizing discussion of the war in the Far East and so marginalizing European strategy. He promised the Chinese leader a British offensive in Burma and a major amphibious operation in the Indian Ocean, Operation Buccaneer. Churchill, like Mountbatten, was in principle in favour of Buccaneer but was alarmed at the priority being given to it over operations in the Mediterranean.[38]

Churchill and his chiefs tried to reopen the debate over the timing of the Second Front and the prioritizing of the Mediterranean campaign. This created much acrimony with the Americans. In particular, the arguments between Churchill and Marshall became very heated and soon pretty much the whole of the American and British delegations were at each other's throats. Churchill's doctor, Charles Wilson (now Lord Moran), commented in a diary entry, 'What I find so shocking is that to the Americans the P.M. is the villain of the piece; they are far more sceptical of him than they are of Stalin.'[39] Roosevelt and his chiefs had already effectively abandoned the 'Europe First' dictum – the very last thing Churchill had wanted – and it was Churchill's attitude towards Roosevelt and the American chiefs over the Second Front that had been principally responsible for this.[40]

The Americans had long held suspicions about Churchill's interests as an old-fashioned imperialist, as well as being opposed to his harebrained schemes in the Mediterranean and the Balkans. These suspicions had been fed by Stimson, Hull, Marshall and King. Even more importantly, they were being fed by Admiral William Leahy, the Presidential chief of staff and chairman of the US Joint Chiefs of Staff. These were a formidable, indeed the most formidable, array of senior US servicemen and politicians. Only Roosevelt's aid, Harry Hopkins, took a different view, and illness would attenuate his limited influence.[41] Increasingly the post-war world order would be determined principally by just two great powers, not three.

EUREKA

Churchill, Roosevelt and Stalin met for the first Big Three conference, codenamed Eureka, between 28 November and 1 December 1943, in Tehran. The Cairo Conference had ended without agreement; it was left to Tehran and Stalin to settle the matter, which Stalin did in the Americans' favour, as Roosevelt had clearly expected. The Second Front in France, not the Mediterranean, was to be prioritized, and the Americans would also concentrate resources in the Pacific theatre. At Tehran Roosevelt said to his son Elliott, 'Winston knows that he is beaten.'[42]

Roosevelt was anxious to establish a personal rapport with the Soviet leader, and to accomplish this he joked with Stalin directly at Churchill's expense. As Churchill scowled and his face reddened, Stalin smiled then laughed. Roosevelt had tapped into Stalin at a personal level and would conduct bilateral negotiations with him. He had chosen to stay in the Soviet Embassy with Stalin. This gave the Soviets the opportunity to eavesdrop on the President, but enabled him to meet Stalin at short notice to discuss essential matters without Churchill. Churchill learned only later of the content of these meetings. When he discovered that the other two were meeting without him, he asked Roosevelt to lunch, but the President declined, saying that he didn't want to meet Churchill alone without Stalin.[43]

When the three did meet they discussed the splitting up of Germany to prevent its re-emergence as a hegemonic power after the war. Stalin and Roosevelt favoured the dismemberment of Germany into five discrete parts. They also talked of Poland. Before Tehran, Churchill had agreed with Stalin that after the war the border between Russia and Poland should be along the 'Curzon Line', established back in 1920 and named after the former British Foreign Secretary. This meant that Stalin would keep all the Polish territory he had annexed under the Molotov–Ribbentrop Pact in August 1939. Churchill reaffirmed this at Tehran, but it would cause much dissention with the Americans.[44]

Also at Tehran, Churchill advocated an operation in the eastern Mediterranean to bring Turkey into the war. The other 'Two' of the Big Three were, of course, having none of it. As usual, Churchill wanted to fight in areas of little or no strategic importance. The Soviets knew all along that it was the land battle in central Europe that would be decisive, just as had been the case in World War I. All the expenditure of effort on the 'soft underbelly' and with Turkey was simply postponing the inevitable, a postponement that had already resulted in a considerable additional cost in lives. At dinner Churchill complained to Stalin that Britain was going pink, and Stalin retorted that this was the sign of good health.[45]

After the Tehran Conference Churchill came down with a second bout of pneumonia (as he had after the Casablanca Conference and as he would for a third time in August 1944). This time it was so serious that it looked as though he might die. But he recovered, not helped by his insistence on drinking whisky and smoking cigars,[46] and he and Roosevelt immediately travelled to Cairo for the second conference to be held there, from 4–6 December. Given the demands for war materiel, Roosevelt quickly forgot about Operation Buccaneer, which had been discussed at the first Cairo Conference. There would be sufficient resources for no more than one Mediterranean operation – Shingle, on the Italian coast at Anzio – to keep the campaign alive and German divisions pinned down.

For some time it had been expected that Roosevelt would appoint Marshall as supreme commander for Overlord, but he decided that he needed to keep Marshall with him in Washington and so chose General Dwight Eisenhower. Roosevelt asked Churchill and he approved. Certainly the diplomatic Eisenhower would be easier to get on with than the robust Marshall.[47]

The Turkish President, Mustafa Ismet Inönü, had been invited to the conference to get Turkey into the war. After three sessions and a total of 15 hours of discussion he declined, but he did kiss Churchill on the cheek at the conclusion. Eden commented that a kiss wasn't much of an outcome for the application of so much effort. Churchill subsequently commented that he was irresistible and Eden was jealous.[48]

OCTAGON

A second Quebec conference, codenamed Octagon, was held from 12–16 September 1944 and was attended by Roosevelt and Churchill. The overall strategy for the war and future plans for Germany were considered. While on the way to the conference aboard the *Queen Mary*, Brooke recorded in his diary on 8 September, 'According to [Churchill] we were coming to Quebec solely to obtain twenty landing ships out of the Americans to carry out an operation against Istria [coast of Slovenia] to seize Trieste; and there we were suggesting that with the rate at which events were moving Istria might be of no value.'[49] Churchill then accused his chiefs of conspiring against him with the Americans and secretly proposing a landing on the Adriatic. Brooke said this was absurd. When the conference was under way, on 13 September, Brooke recorded:

> At 11.30 we had a Plenary meeting, which consisted of a long statement by the PM giving his views as to how the war should be run. According to him we had two main objectives, first an advance on Vienna, secondly the capture of Singapore!

Brooke added retrospectively:

> It is worth noting that the two objectives he had named in the Plenary Meeting were neither of them in our plans. We had no plans for Vienna, nor did I ever look at this operation as becoming possible. Nor had we any plans for the capture of Singapore.[50]

On the second day of the conference Churchill suggested to Roosevelt that they should discuss the post-war American financing of the British economy, known as Lend-Lease Two. Roosevelt sent for Henry Morgenthau, the US Treasury Secretary, to be flown in to attend the session. The British economist John Maynard Keynes told Morgenthau that, although all the British spending on the war had been necessary, it was 'a story of financial imprudence which has no parallel in history'. Roosevelt was non-committal about providing finance for Lend-Lease Two, and in a characteristic outburst Churchill asked him, 'What do you want me to do? Get up on my hind legs and beg like Fala [Roosevelt's dog]?' Roosevelt agreed, though not in writing, that Britain should be provided with finance to cover 'reasonable needs'.[51]

At dinner on the 13th, Morgenthau outlined his plans for Germany after the war: that it should be de-industrialized and turned into an agricultural economy. Churchill at first violently opposed this, but Lord Cherwell, Churchill's scientific advisor and passionately anti-German, argued that Morgenthau's plan would open up former German export markets to British businesses. Eventually the Morgenthau Plan came to nothing.[52]

Churchill said to Roosevelt that the British and the Americans should use their Second Front to push much further east to ensure that more Central European territory came under Anglo-American control. He wanted the western Allies to capture the political prize, Berlin. This was surprising coming from Churchill, who had frustrated the Second Front from the outset, for it was only this that was now enabling this issue to be raised at all. If the Second Front had been initiated earlier, the western Allies might have been in a position to take Berlin, but left to Churchill and the British chiefs, they would still be trying to fight their way through the Italian Alps.

Churchill would return to this matter much later, in a letter to Roosevelt on 1 April 1945, very shortly before the President's death:

> I say quite frankly that Berlin remains of high strategic importance. Nothing will exert a psychological effect of despair upon all German forces of resistance equal to that of the fall of Berlin. It will be the supreme signal of defeat to the German people. On the other hand, if left to itself to maintain a siege by the Russians among its ruins, and as long as the German flag flies there, it will animate the resistance of all Germans under arms.

In the same letter he wrote:

> The Russian armies will no doubt overrun all Austria and enter Vienna. If they take Berlin will not their impression that they have been the overwhelming contributor to our common victory be unduly imprinted in their minds, and may this not lead them into a mood which will raise grave and formidable

difficulties in the future? I therefore consider that from
a political standpoint we should march as far east into
Germany as possible, and that should Berlin be in our grasp
we should certainly take it. This also appears sound on
military grounds.[53]

The Soviets simply were 'the overwhelming contributor to our common
victory', largely as a consequence of Churchill prevaricating over the
Second Front and forcing its postponement, which had forced the Soviets
to do the bulk of the fighting. In fact, Roosevelt had already considered
the issue of Berlin: while on his way to the Sextant Conference, he had
argued that there would be a race between the Russians and the Americans
for the German capital and that 'the United States should have Berlin'.
He continued that the United States would need to keep about a million
servicemen in occupation, 'for at least one year. Maybe two.'[54]

Ironically, the British intelligence services under Churchill had been
penetrated at a very high level by the 'Cambridge spy ring' of Kim Philby,
Guy Burgess, Donald Maclean and Anthony Blunt. They were responsible
for communicating to Stalin – via Lavrentiy Beria, the head of the NKVD
(the Soviet secret police) – the content of highly classified discussions
between Churchill and Roosevelt, and later Truman. This included
the western Allies' position on Berlin, giving Stalin an invaluable
advantage in negotiations.

Churchill wanted Berlin taken by the western Allies for prestige, but
Eisenhower was not willing to sacrifice Allied servicemen for this. There
was also the fear that Germany would mount a guerrilla war, and Churchill
argued that the psychological effect of the western Allies taking Berlin
would prevent this. But Eisenhower would not be moved by this argument
either.[55] There was a more important reason for leaving Berlin to the Soviets,
however. At the Yalta Conference the Big Three would decide to divide
Germany into zones at the end of the war, and Berlin would clearly be in the
middle of the Soviet zone. It would therefore be ridiculous for forces of the
western Allies to fight all the way to Berlin, incurring great casualties, only
to have to withdraw afterwards and hand the territory gained to the Soviets.
Eisenhower decided on a broad front, and in particular a targeting of the
Ruhr, where the German war machine could be dismantled and thus the war
finally concluded with the fewest Allied casualties.

TOLSTOY

Churchill next met with Stalin, but without Roosevelt, in Moscow
at a conference codenamed Tolstoy on 9 October 1944. Having been
marginalized by the Big Two, he now sought to establish Britain's place in
the post-war world in this bilateral conference with Stalin.[56] He knew he
was in for a difficult time, and once commented, 'Trying to maintain good
relations with a Communist is like wooing a crocodile. You do not know
whether to tickle it under the chin or beat it over the head. When it opens
its mouth, you cannot tell whether it is trying to smile or preparing to eat
you up.'[57] Beating the Soviets over the head was never going to work, and if
the croc was smiling it was because it was hungry. Mischievously Churchill
once said he could drink more than Molotov and Stalin put together.[58]

The purpose of this meeting was Churchill's proposal to carve up south-
eastern Europe into British and Soviet spheres of influence. He suggested
that the Soviet Union might have 90 per cent influence in Rumania, while
Britain had 90 per cent influence in Greece, with Yugoslavia split 50–50.
However, the Soviet Union's armed forces occupied much of Eastern
Europe at the time, and there were no British forces in Greece. History does
not record accurately what happened next: one version has it that Churchill
started to write down his plans in front of Stalin, another that Churchill
took out a piece of paper from his pocket with the information already
written on it and said, 'I have this naughty document here with some ideas
of certain people in London.' Either way, the paper stated that the division
of influence in Bulgaria should be 75 per cent for the Soviet Union, and
that Hungary should be split 50–50. Churchill passed the paper to Stalin,
who noted the information then took a pencil and ticked the corner of
the paper before passing it back to Churchill. For a moment it sat there in
front of them, and Churchill said, 'Might it not be thought rather cynical
if it seemed we had disposed of these issues so fateful to millions of people,
in such an off-hand manner?' Then he added, 'Let us burn the paper.' But
Stalin told him to keep it.[59]

Churchill, who had angrily condemned Stalin when he carved up
Eastern Europe with Hitler in 1939 under the Molotov–Ribbentrop Pact,
was now proposing to do precisely the same between Britain and the Soviet
Union. It is a deep irony that Churchill, of all people, believed that a piece
of paper assented to by a dictator constituted a binding agreement between

nations. It was only a very few years earlier that Neville Chamberlain had returned to London from Munich with just such a piece of paper. In that case it was a signed agreement between Chamberlain and Hitler that the latter had no more territorial demands in Central Europe, now it was an agreement between Churchill and Stalin that the latter had no more territorial demands in Central Europe. Churchill himself said, 'An appeaser is one who feeds a crocodile – hoping that it will eat him last.'[60]

This was not a 'naughty' document, but one that was both appalling and very silly. It had been a futile discussion with Stalin, as Britain would have no influence in these Eastern European countries, not even 10 per cent. Stalin, unlike Churchill, knew that the paper meant nothing. After the end of the war, his military presence in Eastern European countries would enable him to exercise control over them irrespective of what western leaders such as Churchill wanted, or thought Stalin had agreed to. Stalin knew that he could promise what he liked to get agreement with Churchill and Roosevelt, simply in order to placate them. It was only after the obvious fact had become apparent – that Stalin would do as he wished – that Churchill suddenly wanted to warn the world about the scourge of Communism.

Nevertheless, the charade of the naughty document was to be played out, but now it was delegated to the two foreign ministers, Eden and Molotov, who had to haggle over the percentages for all the relevant countries. Molotov wanted to increase Soviet influence in Yugoslavia and Hungary to 75 per cent. Understandably, from the British perspective Eden didn't like this, so Molotov suggested that Yugoslavia be 50–50, Bulgaria 90 per cent in Soviet favour and that Hungary be dealt with later. Eden made counterproposals and so the lunacy went on, with Eden tiring of it eventually, as well he might.[61]

After the conference with Stalin, Churchill got cold feet over the whole idea. His real fear was American reaction. The President's representative, Averell Harriman, learnt of the proposal, and it became clear that if Churchill persisted with this quasi-imperial carve-up of Europe it would prove potentially fatal to an already fractured relationship with the United States. Churchill would be risking his most important policy – Anglo-American co-operation – for something that was never going to happen anyway. It was a terrifying risk for Churchill to run.[62] As Lord Beaverbrook once commented, 'Churchill has the habit of breaking the rungs of any ladder he puts his foot on.'[63]

From the time of the German invasion of the Soviet Union in 1941, Stalin demanded that Churchill legitimize the Soviet annexations of Estonia, Latvia, Lithuania, eastern Poland, the Romanian province of Bessarabia sanctioned under the 1939 Molotov–Ribbentrop pact, and those border territories occupied in the Soviet–Finnish war of 1939–40. Initially, Churchill suggested that these issues should be settled in a post-war peace conference. However, by 1944, although he initially wanted free elections in Poland, he would end up accepting all Stalin's demands. Indeed, he would then function as the Soviet dictator's diplomatic representative to coerce the Polish government-in-exile in London to acquiesce to these demands. In a personal and secret message conveyed to Stalin on 25 April 1943, Churchill had written, 'I am examining the possibility of silencing those Polish newspapers in this country which attacked the Soviet Government and at the same time attacked Sikorski [who had been head of the Polish government-in-exile until his death in an air crash in 1943] for trying to work with the Soviet Government.'[64]

ARGONAUT

With the war in Europe approaching its climax, the Big Three met again, this time at Yalta in the Crimea. The conference, codenamed Argonaut, ran from 4–11 February 1945. It was called to discuss how to conclude the war and to determine post-war arrangements. It was only the second, and indeed the last Big Three conference that Roosevelt attended. He was clearly unwell and would die on 12 April.

Before the conference, Churchill made clear in a letter to his wife that he wanted to maintain India as the jewel in the crown of the British Empire; he wrote that he was not prepared to see our flag 'let down while I am at the wheel'.[65]

The British chiefs met on 30 January, before political discussions began. The minutes of Argonaut's first COS meeting read:

> SIR ALAN BROOKE gave an outline of the considerations
> which had impelled the British Chiefs of Staff to propose the
> reinforcement of General Eisenhower's forces in Western
> Europe by divisions drawn from the Mediterranean . . .

With the advance of the Russian armies in the East, operations across the Adriatic through Yugoslavia were unlikely to pay a substantial dividend . . . If we maintained our full present strength in the Mediterranean with a view to preparing an offensive in Italy in April or May, we were unlikely to earn the best dividend from the use of the forces at our disposal.[66]

So the Mediterranean strategy was finally dead. At last it was recognized that the defeat of Germany was to be accomplished via France and across the western borders of Germany as the Soviets advanced from the east. The 'soft underbelly of Europe' was finally revealed not to be so soft at all.

As the conference began, Eden noted in his diary, 'I am much worried that the whole business will be chaotic & nothing worthwhile settled, Stalin being the only one of the three who has a clear view on what he wants & is a tough negotiator. PM's all emotion in these matters.'[67] Indeed, Stalin wanted to create and secure an Eastern European buffer zone to protect the Soviet Union, to establish his country as a 'super power', and to remove the threat of Germany to the Soviet Union permanently. Churchill would be naive by comparison. In a Cabinet meeting in February he said that he had 'every confidence' in Stalin. Brendan Bracken once commented that Churchill had 'always been easily taken in'.[68] As the historian Piers Brendon wrote, 'Stalin could read Churchill . . . like an open book. The Prime Minister was as transparent as the dictator was enigmatic.'[69] This did not bode well for the negotiations.

On the conference agenda was the issue of the Soviet-occupied countries in Central and Eastern Europe. Churchill and Roosevelt wanted free elections in these countries. Stalin would promise free elections in Poland, and indeed said he would hold them even sooner than Churchill and Roosevelt had wanted. Of course, this was never to happen. Already, in 1943, Stalin had set up the Lublin Committee of Poles to ensure that the governance of Poland remained within Soviet control. Naturally the western Allies were reluctant to recognize this. With Stalin's January offensive making headway and being only 65km (40 miles) from Berlin, he was in a strong negotiating position. When the Americans later praised Churchill for his apparent prescience concerning the Soviets' expansionist intent, Eden wrote in his diary, 'This is almost all untrue and quite nauseating.'[70]

Churchill and Roosevelt agreed that democracy should be introduced after the war, yet Churchill privately stated that this would not apply to the British Empire. Roosevelt was gravely suspicious that Churchill would use the conclusion of the war for a land grab to augment the British Empire, just as had occurred after World War I.

The future of Germany after the war was also on the agenda. Stalin wanted a decision between his and Roosevelt's idea to split Germany into five parts, or Churchill's idea for Prussian and Austrian–Bavarian federations, with the Ruhr and Westphalia under international control. Churchill thought this could not be decided in such a short conference. It would in the end be decided by the advance of American and British forces from the west and the Soviets from the east, with Germany being split into two accordingly. As for occupation zones immediately after the war, originally there were to be Soviet, American and British zones, but Roosevelt and Churchill agreed to give France a zone created from the American and British areas. However, the French were not to be invited to participate in the Control Commission, which would govern Germany. Roosevelt also agreed to keep US forces in Germany for up to two years after the war.[71]

The fact that the Curzon Line had been assented to as the appropriate border between Russia and Poland at Yalta caused rumblings in the Conservative Party at home. Eden privately commented that he was mortified at the way Churchill had treated Poland. At the War Cabinet in February Churchill commented that Stalin 'meant well to the world and to Poland' and also 'that the Russians would honour the declaration [on Liberated Europe] that had been made.'[72]

The House of Commons debated the Yalta agreement for two days from 27 February, and it was very reminiscent of both the Norway and indeed the Munich debates years earlier. An amendment was put down by 21 Conservatives, displaying grave concern that there should be transference 'to another power' of 'the territory of an Ally'. It was defeated, with only 25 MPs supporting it and 398 against, but the result did not display the true depth of feeling, with many Conservatives abstaining and many voting in favour with great reluctance.

The future Prime Minister Alec Douglas-Home was one of those who opposed Churchill on this. Many years later, on the centenary of Churchill's birth on 30 November 1974, Douglas-Home would address the issue in a public broadcast. He recalled the events in the House of Commons all those years before, 'In a tense debate . . . I criticised our government's capitulation. In it Churchill had used a phrase which I could not let go by. He had seemed to accept a Russian occupation following victory as "an act of justice" – to use his words. I could recognise it as a fact of power but repudiated any suggestion of an act of justice.'[73]

On 27 March 1945 Churchill wrote to the War Cabinet:

> As you know, if we fail altogether to get a satisfactory solution on Poland and we are in fact defrauded by Russia, both Eden and I are pledged to report the fact openly to the House of Commons. There I advised critics of the Yalta settlement to trust Stalin. If I have to make a statement of facts to the House, the world will draw the deduction that such advice was wrong.[74]

Such a statement of admission to the House of Commons would hardly have destabilized Stalin in the Kremlin or altered the course of world events. All it did was to identify the fact that Churchill was indeed wrong. Yet he was not entirely naive. At Yalta he had toasted Stalin, 'whose conduct of foreign policy manifests a desire for peace', apparently then adding so that the interpreter could not hear, 'a piece of Poland, a piece of Czechoslovakia, a piece of Romania . . .'[75]

Also on the agenda at Yalta was the division of Berlin into four sectors controlled by the Soviet Union, Great Britain, the United States and France. The other principal issue was the creation of the United Nations organization. This would replace the defunct pre-war League of Nations for international peacekeeping. The United States Congress had never ratified American membership of the League, though President Woodrow Wilson had wanted it. As the USA retreated into 'splendid isolation' after World War I, the growth of political extremism in Europe and Japan drew it into the much bigger conflagration of World War II. Thus, by the time of Yalta, the USA had undergone a *volte face*: from now on it would be fully engaged in global affairs to prevent it having to fight World War III. Thus Roosevelt insisted that the first meeting of the new United Nations organization should take place in the USA, in San Francisco.

Roosevelt would die a few days before the Soviet Battle for Berlin. Churchill did not attend his funeral, giving the reason that many of his ministers were already abroad at the time and it was his duty to stay at home. When Churchill himself died 20 years later, the then President, Lyndon Johnson, did not attend his funeral.[76]

TERMINAL

The Big Three met again in Potsdam, on the outskirts of Berlin, between 17 July and 2 August 1945, for a conference codenamed Terminal. The result of the British general election was still not known, so Churchill took the Labour Party leader Clement Attlee with him. The two British leaders, with Churchill still officially Prime Minister, were to meet with Stalin and the new American President, Harry Truman.

Churchill was very worried about the parlous state of Britain's finances: he told Truman that Britain would be the biggest debtor nation on earth by the end of the war. Keynes commented that the financial aid Britain had received meant that it had spent £2 billion more each year than its domestic economy could produce, and if US aid was terminated Britain would be bankrupt.[77]

The threat from Stalin, in truth, was seen more clearly by Eden than by Churchill. At dinner on the first night of the conference Eden told Churchill 'not to give up our few cards without return'. In a memo, Eden wrote of Soviet policies as 'aggrandisement', saying they were 'clearer as they become more brazen every day.' Yet Churchill would repeat, 'I like that man [Stalin].' Churchill's doctor, Lord Moran, noted that he said, 'Stalin gave me his word that there would be free elections in countries set free by his armies. You are sceptical, Charles? I don't see why. We must listen to these Russians, they mobilised twelve million men, and nearly half of them were killed or are missing.' Yet Churchill would vacillate; the following day he said that the Soviets 'talk about the same things as we do, freedom and justice and that sort of thing, but prominent people are removed and not seen again'. Subsequently he said to Moran, 'I shall ask Stalin, does he want the whole world?'[78] If Stalin had said 'No', would Churchill have believed him?

Alexander Cadogan noted that Churchill failed adequately to read important government papers, and that he 'butts in on every occasion and talks the most irrelevant rubbish'. Cadogan also noted that Truman was 'most quick and business like.'[79] Churchill however, blamed Washington and the transition of power from Roosevelt to Truman for the gravity of the global problems after the war. He wrote in *The Second World War*:

> As a war waged by a coalition draws to its end political aspects have a mounting importance. In Washington especially longer and wider views should have prevailed. It is true that American thought is at least disinterested in matters which seem to relate to territorial acquisitions, but when wolves are about the shepherd must guard his flock, even if he does not himself care for mutton. At this time the points at issue did not seem to the United States Chiefs of Staff to be of capital importance ... They played a dominating part in the destiny of Europe, and may well have denied us all the lasting peace for which we had fought so long and hard. We can now see the deadly hiatus which existed between the fading of President Roosevelt's strength and the growth of President Truman's grip of the vast world problem. In this melancholy void one President could not act and the other could not know. Neither the military chiefs nor the State Department received the guidance they required. The former confined themselves to their professional sphere; the latter did not comprehend the issues involved. The indispensable political direction was lacking at the moment when it was most needed. The United States stood on the scene of victory, master of world fortunes, but without a true and coherent design.[80]

He set out his concerns in the following eight points:

> *First*, that Soviet Russia had become a mortal danger to the free world.
>   *Secondly*, that a new front must be immediately created against her onward sweep.
>   *Thirdly*, that this front in Europe should be as far east as possible.
>   *Fourthly*, that Berlin was the prime and true objective of the Anglo-American armies.

Fifthly, that the liberation of Czechoslovakia and the entry into Prague of American troops was of high consequence.

Sixthly, that Vienna, and indeed Austria, must be regulated by the Western Powers, at least upon an equality with the Russian Soviets.

Seventhly, that Marshal Tito's aggressive pretensions against Italy must be curbed.

Finally, and above all, that a settlement must be reached on all major issues between the West and East in Europe *before the armies of democracy melted,* or the Western Allies yielded any part of the German territories they had conquered, or, as it could soon be written, liberated from totalitarian tyranny.[81]

Given Churchill's view of the bankruptcy of US policy in this regard, it is rather surprising that contrary to his concerns in his eight points the Americans did recognize the Soviet threat and a 'new front' against Soviet advancement was created through the North Atlantic Treaty Organization (NATO) in 1949. The front could not be further east than it was without the risk of conflict with the Soviet Union. If the western Allies had attempted to take Berlin and Prague, they would have risked the possibility of World War III starting immediately at the end of World War II. Vienna and Austria were 'regulated' in the end only by the western powers. The aggression of Yugoslavia's Marshal Tito against Italy was helped by Churchill's support for him, as we saw in chapter 11. A 'settlement' was indeed accomplished, with US hegemony enacting the 'Truman Doctrine' of Soviet containment.

Seven days before the Potsdam Conference concluded, the British general election results came through: Churchill had lost, and Attlee replaced him at the conference. Churchill had gone.

18
GENERAL ELECTION DEFEAT AND INTO OPPOSITION

There had not been a general election in Britain since 1935. Churchill had been particularly keen that democracy should be the basis of the political systems in Eastern Europe, but during the war he was opposed to breaking up the British coalition government, which he referred to as 'the Grand Coalition'. He wanted to postpone the election until at least the defeat of Japan, and preferably to keep the coalition going, with him as its head. He himself was Prime Minister by dint of a House of Commons vote in 1940 and thus did not have a mandate from the electorate. Apart from by-elections, which the government often lost, democracy had been suspended in Britain for the duration of the war. It was the Labour Party and its leader, Clement Attlee, the Deputy Prime Minister, who decided they did not wish to continue in the wartime coalition government. Churchill's wife Clementine wanted him to retire now, at the apogee of his career, but he would have none of it.

Churchill had a precedent for not wanting to end a coalition government in such circumstances: at the end of World War I, Lloyd George had continued the wartime coalition initiated by Asquith in 1915. Churchill, as part of Lloyd George's government, had been one of those who wanted it to continue. He had a strong authoritarian streak and saw himself as a catalyst to ensure that both the sectionalist interests of trades unions and business and the national interest were served.[1] The Lloyd George coalition government ended only when the Conservatives decided to pull out of it in 1922. The committee that made this fateful decision became known as the 1922 Committee, and has played an important role in the Conservative Party ever since. Lloyd George was partly motivated to continue the coalition because, having replaced Asquith as Prime Minister, he had split the Liberal Party, and he knew that once the coalition fell he would have no chance of gaining power again. The Conservatives wished to end the coalition because they believed they could win power on their own – which is precisely what they did.

Towards the end of World War II, Churchill told Anthony Eden that he would not make what he saw as the same mistake of staying on after the war – yet stay on was what he really wanted to do. On 28 January 1945 he even told King George VI that, though there would be a general election, 'it is very likely that there will be a substantial Conservative majority in the new Parliament.'[2]

There had been a Conservative-dominated coalition or National government since 1931. In 1945 the circumstances were not the same as those for Lloyd George in 1918: there was no danger of the Conservatives not being able to form a government in the future, and indeed not only Churchill, but most people – including Attlee – believed that the Conservatives would win. Given the overt and shameful dictatorships of Hitler and Stalin, it seems a remarkably poor decision on Churchill's part not to have offered himself for re-election voluntarily rather than having to be pushed into it by the Labour Party. The United States did not suspend presidential elections during the war, let alone afterwards. It might be thought that Churchill's strong affinity with the USA (he was, after all, half American) would have taught him a vital lesson in democratic principles.

When it had become clear to Churchill that the coalition was to end, there was the question of timing. The conduct of the war remained the most significant determinant, and in May there was a threat to Trieste in Italy, when Marshal Tito's regime in Yugoslavia attempted to take control (see chapter 11). There was also a real fear of a land grab by the Soviets, and Churchill took the view that he could hardly expect Labour support in opposing such a thing and then promptly dissolve the coalition, so he wrote to Attlee and Sir Archibald Sinclair, the Liberal Party leader, on 18 May, asking them whether they favoured dissolving the coalition immediately or continuing it until after the defeat of Japan. Many Conservatives favoured a quick election, but Attlee and Ernest Bevin (who would become Foreign Secretary in the Labour government) wanted a delay. However, the Labour Party conference in Blackpool decided on the 19th for a quick dissolution of the coalition. Consequently, on 22 May Churchill requested the dissolution in a letter to the King and attended the Palace the following day, after which it was announced that a general election would take place on 5 July. Churchill led a brief caretaker Conservative government from 23 May while the general election was fought. The Labour Party would come to power on 26 July.[3]

Churchill was not well disposed to dealing with national politics and forming a caretaker Conservative ministry. He included a Liberal element, including Gwilym Lloyd George (son of the former Prime Minister) and Leslie Hore-Belisha, who had achieved some fame before the war as Transport Secretary, introducing 'Belisha' beacons on pedestrian crossings, as well as being a former Secretary of State for War. But the problematic appointments were the Conservatives. Churchill and Brendan Bracken quickly fell out over the former's ministerial choices, and Bracken, whom Churchill asked to take the presidency of the Board of Trade, refused to do so until Churchill defined his position on the American-sponsored 'Bretton Woods' requirement for sterling to be made convertible into other currencies. Eventually, Bracken did not take the position at all but ended up at the Admiralty. Lord Beaverbrook, who had been a close confidant of Churchill during the war, and had held positions in the wartime government, was offered a position but refused outright. Lord Woolton (Frederick Marquis), a non-party member of the government, who had been Minister of Food during the war, was made Lord President of the Council. But the portent for this government was ominous: Woolton said to Beaverbrook that most people were asking, 'Is he really interested in reconstruction and social reform?'[4]

During the war the Liberal politician Sir William Beveridge had been asked to undertake a study into social reform. Churchill had known Beveridge since his days as President of the Board of Trade in Asquith's government, when he had asked Beveridge to advise him on social reform. The Beveridge Report was published in 1942 and would lead to the post-war welfare state. But Churchill called Beveridge 'an awful windbag and a dreamer' and vacillated over the report, at once balking at it and then offering the prospect of trying to implement it.[5] Some Conservative politicians, such as Richard Austen ('Rab') Butler, Anthony Eden and Leo Amery, were in favour, but others, such as Sir Kingsley Wood (a Chamberlainite) and Lord Cherwell, were opposed. Wood was concerned that the scheme required 'an impractical financial commitment' and about the tax burden necessary to finance it. Indeed the post-war Labour government would impose income tax at 19s 6d in the pound on income over £2,000 per year – a marginal rate of 97.5 per cent – and would also introduce death duties. Cherwell warned that implementing such a scheme might cause the Americans to refuse aid after the war. In fact, when the post-war Labour government did implement it, Britain still received nearly a quarter of the total $13 billion 'Marshall Plan' aid, plus a $3.75 billion loan from the USA.[6]

However, the merchants of doom convinced Churchill, and although in the coalition government Labour had forced him to compromise by accepting the report in principle, he did not introduce legislation to bring it into effect. When the two parties went their separate ways in the summer of 1945, Churchill as Conservative leader and caretaker Prime Minister did not in the end sign up to the plan, whereas it formed the centrepiece of Labour's programme. The Conservative Party was split on the issue: the large Chamberlainite constituency remained opposed but the debate on the matter in February resulted in 45 Conservatives, including the Tory reform group and its leader Quintin Hogg, voting for the introduction of a Ministry of Social Security.[7]

Churchill found it difficult to get back into party politics and, amazingly, lacked effective communication with the public. He said to Lord Moran, 'I have no message for them.' Bracken had great influence in his bid to make the personality of Churchill himself the main focus of the Conservatives' general election campaign. The manifesto was imperiously entitled 'Mr. Churchill's Address to the Electors', and its contents emphasized foreign policy and British prestige internationally. It did include some reference to social reform, even the creation of a National Health Service and the maintenance of full employment, but this was buried in the document. The Labour Party did not make this mistake; their manifesto, 'Let us face the future', emphasized social and economic policy – precisely what the electorate was most interested in.[8]

The electioneering styles of the two main party leaders also contrasted strongly. Churchill and his entourage would turn up at a few grand meetings, whereas Attlee would be driven by his wife in the family car and eat sandwiches for his lunch. It was clear who was most interested in the mundane issues of the ordinary people.[9] Churchill said of Attlee that he was a 'sheep in sheep's clothing', 'He is a modest man who has a good deal to be modest about,' and, 'If any grub is fed on Royal Jelly it turns into a Queen Bee.' He is also purported to have said, 'An empty taxi arrived at 10 Downing Street, and when the door was opened Attlee got out,' though he would subsequently deny this last statement. Attlee said of Churchill, 'Fifty per cent of Winston is genius, fifty per cent bloody fool. He *will* behave like a child.'[10]

In a conversation with Roosevelt back in September 1942, Lord Beaverbrook had said that just as World War I saw the end of the Liberals, so this war would cost the Conservatives dear. Although the Conservative Party was not split in 1945 in the way that the Liberals had been during and after World War I, Churchill's obstinacy in refusing to allow the Conservatives to do anything to promote the Beveridge Report would realize precisely the outcome Beaverbrook had predicted.[11]

Churchill made another fatal error of judgment: in his first election broadcast on 4 June, he publicly announced that 'no Socialist Government conducting the entire life and industry of the country' could function without 'some form of Gestapo'.[12] This was, of course, absurd. Whatever people thought of Attlee, the Labour Party in 1945 and its policies, only a lunatic would believe that a Labour government would create such an organization. The welfare state policies the Labour Party was offering would be voted for voluntarily and welcomed by much of the electorate – violent coercion would never be required.

On 5 July, the day of the election, Eden wrote in his diary, 'Am beginning seriously to doubt whether I can take on F[oreign] O[ffice] work again. It is not work itself which I could not handle, but racket with Winston at all hours! He has to be headed off so many follies.'[13]

DEFEAT

In the two-week interval between the ballot and the announcement of the result, to allow the service vote to come in from overseas, the Potsdam Conference was held between the 'Big Three' (see chapter 17). Churchill, quite appropriately, took Attlee with him just in case of a Labour victory.[14] Apart from the conference, Churchill spent the time relaxing in the South of France. Two days after the election, on 7 July, he flew to Bordeaux with his wife and daughter Mary for a week's holiday.[15]

The summer of 1945 was the first time that the electorate had ever had the opportunity to vote for a Churchill-led government. The older voters did tend to vote for him, but there was a massive shift of the middle classes and first-time voters (who were many, after ten years without a general election) to Labour.[16] The 'median voter theorem' helps to explain Churchill's predicament. It assumes that the majority of voters have moderate political views and so will tend to support political parties towards the middle of the political spectrum. If there isn't a political party representing precisely the views of any voter, the electorate will vote for a party with policies that approximate most closely to its views. Thus, in order to attract sufficient votes to form a government, the major political parties tend to form moderate, centrist policies and cluster around the centre of the political spectrum, or the 'median voter'.[17] By 1945, with the Depression and the associated mass unemployment and social deprivation of the 1930s still fresh in the minds of many, the median voter had moved leftwards on the political spectrum. Churchill, given his belief in economic orthodoxy and his leadership in the war, was perceived as being on the right of the spectrum. This contrasted with Clement Attlee and the Labour Party, who embraced the Beveridge Report and wanted a universal welfare state, the maintenance of full employment and nationalization of major industries – policies in accordance with the beliefs of the median voter. In fact, the elements of the two parties' manifestos concerning economic and social policies were not dissimilar, but the electorate perceived them as very different, largely because of Churchill's chosen electoral strategy of promoting himself.[18]

The result was catastrophe for Churchill and the Conservative Party: they suffered their biggest electoral defeat since 1906. The party was reduced to just 213 MPs, even with its allied parties, whereas Labour had 393. After the result was announced Churchill wanted to challenge Attlee to defeat the Conservatives in a parliamentary vote. Wisely, Eden dissuaded him. Of those Conservative politicians who had served in Churchill's War Cabinet, only two survived the general election defeat: Eden and Oliver Lyttleton. Of the caretaker government, 29 ministers lost their seats. Bracken, Leo Amery and Churchill's own son Randolph were all out, as was Harold Macmillan, the future Prime Minister.[19]

Churchill told one of his staff that he would give him a brandy for each Conservative gain: the total amounted to three brandies. Labour had, for the first time in its history, a majority in the House of Commons, and what a massive majority it was.[20] Churchill said of the Labour Party, 'They are not fit to manage a whelk stall.'[21] In his own constituency of Woodford, Labour and the Liberals had chosen not to contest the seat out of respect for the old man, but an independent candidate, Alex Hancock, did stand, and 10,488 votes went against Churchill – a quarter of the total. Churchill resigned as Prime Minister on 26 July.

King George VI offered him the Order of the Garter, but as Churchill put it himself, he had just received the 'order of the boot', and did not see it as fitting to accept. Later on, however, he was knighted.[22] Clementine said to him that the general election defeat was probably a blessing in disguise; he responded, 'If it is a blessing, it is certainly very well disguised.' When he was asked to undertake a national tour so that the public could honour him, he said, 'I refuse to be exhibited like a prize bull whose chief attraction is his past prowess.'[23]

Despite the fact that the Conservative campaign emphasized the virtues of Churchill's wartime stewardship, the electorate was having none of it. The principal error was on policy: it was clear that the Labour Party's policies were very popular, but Churchill failed to appreciate the importance of the Beveridge Report. It would take six years of opposition before the Conservatives under Churchill were gradually won round to a set of policies that then formed the basis of a consensus between the major political parties, which lasted until the 1970s.

OPPOSITION LEADER

It might have been realistic to expect that, at the age of 70 and after a landslide general election defeat, Churchill would have wanted to retire. Clementine urged her husband to so do. Alternatively, Churchill could be imagined sitting down as leader of the opposition to map out, and then implement, a vigorous strategy to oppose the government. Neither of these transpired; rather, effective leadership of the party in opposition was left to Eden, while Churchill indulged his passion for painting to the full – often abroad – and began his own six-volume account, *The Second World War*, completing it during his subsequent peacetime ministry.

This left him out of touch with British politics, and most certainly derelict in his duty as leader of the opposition. He was behaving like a man in retirement, which in fact he was. Opposition didn't interest him and he was just waiting for another chance at government. It is hard to think of any other leader of a major political party whose colleagues would have tolerated this behaviour; it was only because of his unassailable position in the party by 1945 as a victorious war leader that he could get away with it. On 19 November 1945, the Labour government stated in the House of Commons that they intended to nationalize the electricity, gas and transport industries. This would be the major issue of contention between the two parties for much of the six years of the Labour government, yet at the time the statement was made only two Conservatives, Oliver Lyttleton and Oliver Stanley, were on the opposition front bench. There was an angry mood in the 1922 Committee concerning Churchill's absence at this pivotal time. But to no avail.[24]

The Labour government's nationalization of the iron and steel industry would prove very contentious, and it would be one of the very few nationalizations the Conservatives would reverse. When the government then announced its intention to nationalize the coal industry, it was Eden who led the Conservatives in the debate on 29 and 30 January 1946. It was Eden who led them again when in February, March and April the repeal of the 1927 Conservative Trades Disputes Act was debated. In neither case was his opposition particularly vociferous. There were many all-night sittings of the House of Commons; during that of 1–2 April a hundred Conservative members were present. Churchill was not among them.[25]

The Conservatives published their Industrial Charter on 11 May 1947, committing them to a mixed economy, the maintenance of full employment and the notion of central planning. This, to many Conservatives, was simply adopting the Labour agenda. At the Conservative Party conference in the autumn it would be patient work by Eden, Butler and Macmillan that ensured there was no rebellion.[26]

But Churchill was not idle. He entertained his shadow Cabinet to lunches at the Savoy on a fortnightly basis. One of its members, Sir David Maxwell Fyfe, commented that on one occasion Churchill ate a dozen oysters, a couple of helpings of roast beef and vegetables followed by a large plate of apple pie and ice cream, and washed it all down with a mixture of tomato juice and the obligatory wine and brandy.[27]

THE UNITED EUROPE MOVEMENT

In 1944 Churchill had told Charles de Gaulle, 'Each time we have to choose between Europe and the open sea, we shall always choose the open sea.'[28] But after the war he recognized that pan-Europeanism would constitute

an effective mechanism to create peace and stability in Europe, and he
became chairman of the Council of the United Europe Movement.
On 19 September 1946 he gave a speech on European unification in
Zurich, and talked of 'a kind of United States of Europe'. On 7 May 1948
at the movement's Hague Conference he talked of 'a merger of national
sovereignty'.[29] Between these two events, he gave a speech at the Albert Hall
on 14 May 1947 in which he quoted Clement Attlee's phrase, 'Europe must
federate or perish', and said, 'United Europe will form one major regional
entity.' He argued that the task was to 'smooth away' national frontiers and
that 'our aim is to bring about the unity of all nations of all Europe'.[30]
Of Britain's role he said:

> We have at once to set on foot an organisation in Great
> Britain to promote the cause of United Europe, and to give
> this idea the prominence and vitality necessary for it to lay
> hold of the minds of our fellow-countrymen to such an extent
> that it will affect their actions and influence the course of
> national policy . . . there is Europe, with which Great Britain
> is profoundly blended.'[31]

However, although Churchill was committed to Europe uniting, he
was not committed to Britain participating in such a union. The
primacy of the British Empire remained in his thinking. He saw Britain
as conducting a bilateral relationship with Europe as a whole, rather
than with individual European countries: he continued, 'His Majesty's
government, together with other governments, should approach the
various pressing continental problems from a European rather than a
restricted national angle.'[32]

Yet this apparently positive attitude towards European unification had
an ulterior motive. It was a divisive issue in the Labour Party, and Churchill
sought to exploit it. Edmund Dell, who would be President of the Board of
Trade in 1976–8, later commented:

> The truth is that, despite the brave European vapourings of
> Churchill and his colleagues . . . the Conservative Party's
> attitude in opposition was one of unprincipled opportunism.
> It began a tradition in which, with considerable damage to

British interests, opposition parties exploit the European question against the government of the day by making speeches and proposals to which they have no intention of living, once back in office.[33]

THE 'IRON CURTAIN' AND THE AMERICANS

In 1946 Churchill travelled to the USA as the honoured guest of President Truman and enjoyed a ticker-tape welcome. Posterity would now vouchsafe him the gift of foreseeing the post-war threat of Soviet Communism. On 5 March he made his famous speech, sanctioned by Truman, at Fulton, Missouri, when he said, 'From Stettin in the Baltic to Trieste in the Adriatic an iron curtain has descended across the continent [of Europe]'. In fact, Lieutenant-General Sir James Gammell, head of the British Military Mission in Moscow, had spoken to the Foreign Office the year before of an 'iron curtain now drawn across Eastern Europe'.[34]

It was decidedly late in the day to point out this obvious fact. Churchill had not warned of this threat in the 1930s or indeed in the early 1940s. His conversion was fairly late, and came only after Stalin had reneged on his promises and was imposing dictatorships in those Central and Eastern European countries under Soviet control. During a press conference in Cairo in 1943 Churchill had said, 'I always avoid prophesying beforehand, because it is much better policy to prophesy after the event has already taken place.'[35]

Stalin's murderous reputation was well understood from the inter-war years. However, in his European unification speech given at the Albert Hall in 1947, Churchill said that the United States, the USSR, Europe and Britain plus its Empire constituted the, 'four main pillars of the world Temple of Peace'.[36] So he was at once warning of the threat of the Soviet Union, yet assuming that the very same Soviet Union was to play a vital role in peace and security. To this end he was anxious that there should be a summit meeting between the Soviets, the Americans, the French and the British. In April 1945, while still Prime Minister, he had sent a telegram to Stalin enunciating his concern over the need for effective communication between east and west. In a speech during the election campaign for the 1950 general election Churchill said, 'Still I cannot help coming back to this idea of another talk with Soviet Russia upon the highest level. The idea appeals to me of a supreme effort to bridge the gulf between the two worlds, so that each can live their life, if not in friendship, at least without the hatreds of the Cold War.'[37] A year later in a speech during the 1951 election campaign he would say:

> If I remain in public life at this juncture it is because, rightly or wrongly, but sincerely, I believe that I may be able to make an important contribution to the prevention of a third world war and to bring nearer that lasting peace settlement which the masses of the people of every race and in every land fervently desire. I pray indeed that I may have this opportunity. It is the last prize I seek to win.[38]

LABOUR WINS AGAIN

When in February 1949 the Conservative candidate in the South Hammersmith by-election was defeated, there was a very great deal of hostility towards Churchill's stewardship of the party. At the 1949 party conference a letter was circulated stating that the party would be best placed to win the next general election under Eden. Opinion polls corroborated this view.[39] Churchill suffered a stroke in 1949, but even though he had his 75th birthday that year, he would remain as leader of the opposition and would face the general election the following year.[40]

With its landslide majority in 1945, the Attlee government was able to run its full five-year term, and called the next general election in 1950. It was Eden who led the Conservative campaign. The manifesto, 'The Right Road for Britain', emphasized less central government control, and it was Eden who broadcast on the BBC to promote it.[41]

The electorate had grown tired of austerity, though this would not appreciably diminish under the last Churchill government, as rationing would continue until 1954. Attlee's government was thus returned in 1950 with a majority in the House of Commons of only five MPs: Labour had 315 and the Conservatives 298. The Conservatives successfully exploited this small majority, and a year later Attlee called another general election, effectively telling the electorate that the Labour Party had had enough.

A FINAL CHANCE AT GOVERNMENT

The general election of 1951 was fought by the Conservatives principally on the issue of the rise in the cost of living under Labour. The Conservatives attempted to argue that this increase had been caused by the forced devaluation of sterling in the Bretton Woods exchange rate mechanism in September 1949. This devaluation had been by a massive 30 per cent, from $4.03, at which Britain had entered the mechanism in 1947, to $2.80 just two years later. Labour, on the other hand, insisted that the rise in the cost of living was to do with expenditure on the Korean War. Full employment was a less important issue in the campaign, not least because employment had remained full for the previous six years, as it had during the war. Surprisingly, nationalization was not a main issue, despite the Conservative opposition to it.[42]

The Conservative manifesto contained some generalizations that were very characteristic of Churchill: 'The prime need is for stable Government with several years before it, during which time national interests must be faithfully held far above party feuds or tactics.' It continued with the banality that so many political parties have offered the electorate over the years: 'A Conservative Government will cut out all unnecessary Government expenditure, simplify the administrative machine, and prune waste and extravagance in every department.'[43] Yet, Churchill, the believer in free trade, would put into the manifesto a commitment to continue Imperial Preference (see chapter 17), even though the Americans had already forced compromises on this. There was also reference to the creation of a united Europe. The rearmament programme, which the Attlee government had initiated, was to be continued, and house building was to be the principal social policy, in expenditure second only to defence. Regarding industrial policy, only iron and steel plus long-haul road freight haulage would be denationalized; the rest of the Attlee government's state ownership of industry would remain.[44]

After six years in opposition, not much of it effective, Churchill found himself back in power. But the problems had not ended; on the contrary, there would be many more to come.

19
THE LAST TIRED GOVERNMENT

Churchill won the general election on 25 October 1951: it was the only time he won as party leader, and he was almost 77 years of age. The victory had more to do with the electorate's realization that the Attlee government had run out of ideas and the will to govern, than a great desire to see another Churchill-led government. Indeed, it would vouchsafe his government a House of Commons majority of only 17: the Conservatives had 321 seats and Labour 295. The aggregate (or popular) vote for the Conservatives was in fact less than Labour's. In the local elections that followed in spring 1952, the Conservatives and those independent candidates with Conservative support gained 54 seats but lost 559, and results swung against the government in six of the nine by-elections held in 1952. The final Churchill government would last until the spring of 1955, just over three years and five months.[1]

There is a story that as Churchill was coming out of a House of Commons lavatory, a Member of Parliament noticed that none of his fly buttons were done up. The MP cleared his throat and discreetly uttered the euphemism, 'The guardroom door is open', to which Churchill replied, 'And is the sentry standing to attention, or lolling on a pair of sandbags?' When, on another occasion, someone pointed out to him the same omission, he replied, 'Dead birds don't fall out of their nests.'[2] But Churchill could still raise his game when it was required. The broadcaster and later BBC executive, Huw Wheldon, was entrusted with managing a live television broadcast from Downing Street for Churchill's 80th birthday on 30 November 1954. Wheldon later commented that he appeared '8,000 years old', that he seemed like a 'pterodactyl' and had 'skin like yellow leather'. He sat in the wrong chair and seemed to comprehend little of what was going on around him as various family members came in and out. Wheldon was appalled at how the British public were about to see him. But when it was time for the broadcast and Wheldon gave Churchill his cue, the old man suddenly galvanized himself to do the piece to camera. All his faculties at once seemed restored; he was focused and concentrating.

Wheldon said, 'It was like running into searchlights full on.' After the broadcast, Churchill said, 'I'm going to have a bath,' and, as Wheldon put it, he 'pushed off'.[3]

When Churchill's last ministry began in 1951, there was immediately tension within the government, as Eden was falsely led to believe that he would replace Churchill as Prime Minister in a year or so. Ironically it would be Eden's handling of the emerging Suez Crisis that Churchill would use to justify reneging on this understanding and hanging on to power.[4] Yet Churchill would be a particularly feeble peacetime Prime Minister, emerging from opposition during which he had left the party leadership predominantly to Eden.

Churchill immediately inducted his cronies into his Cabinet, regardless of their aptitude and experience, either for the jobs to which they were appointed or in politics and government. His wartime scientific adviser, Lord Cherwell, was brought in as Paymaster-General, and his chief of staff, Hastings Ismay, as Secretary of State for Commonwealth Relations. Harold Alexander was brought in after four months of government to replace Churchill himself in the post of Minister of Defence, which Churchill had occupied since the election, as he had during the war. A proper new Ministry of Defence had been created in 1947, but Churchill rarely went there and was not interested in making the important resource allocation decisions for the services. He hoped that Alexander would not object to his interference in strategic defence matters, while Alexander got on with the rest of the job. However, Churchill's first choice for the defence portfolio had been Charles Portal, head of the RAF during the war, who had turned it down. His political crony Brendan Bracken, also turned down a Cabinet post.[5]

Churchill appointed three co-ordinating ministers, or 'overlords', ostensibly to try to keep the Cabinet small and reduce the reliance upon committees, particularly when these were comprised of civil servants. However, the real reason was to enable him to make policy with a few trusted colleagues without their having the responsibility of running departments. The overlords were so named partly because of their role supervising several departments and partly because they were all to be drawn from the House of Lords. Churchill had originally planned to appoint four, but only three accepted: Lord Cherwell, officially as Paymaster-General, had the overlord responsibilities for co-ordinating scientific research and development, atomic research and production, and the Prime Minister's Statistical Branch. Lord Frederick Leathers was overlord for transport, fuel and power. Lord Woolton, officially Lord President of the Council, had overlord responsibilities for the separate Ministries of Agriculture and Fisheries and the Ministry of Food. Sir John Anderson was to have the fourth post and be given a Viscountcy, but he did not believe in the system and turned down the offer.

However, Churchill failed satisfactorily to define the constitutional position of these overlords; nobody seemed to know quite to which body they were responsible, nor were their functions precisely defined. Of the three, Woolton did best, because he did little. Leathers had not seen much of Churchill since they were in government together during the war and felt very much an outsider in the Cabinet. He was a man with qualities and experience ideally suited to dealing with detailed issues rather than the overarching co-ordination needed for the diverse ministries under his responsibility. Cherwell largely continued with what had been his wartime responsibilities, but Churchill's lack of interest in domestic affairs and the fact that he never took Cherwell's advice on foreign affairs reduced the breadth of his contributions and he hankered to return to his academic roots at Oxford. The overlord system lasted less than two years, after which the system of governance returned to normal.[6]

DOMESTIC POLICIES

Churchill achieved little of substance in his four-year stint as Prime Minister from 1951 to 1955. He was only really interested in foreign and defence policy and contributed little to detailed policy in domestic matters. The colossal political mistake he had made in 1945, in failing to endorse the Beveridge Report as central to Conservative Party policy, was now reversed, and the welfare state reforms of Attlee's government were accepted. Churchill's government thus largely adopted the social democratic socio-economic model the Attlee ministry had established, and this was somewhat against Churchill's own better judgment.
The government now also accepted the use, introduced by the Attlee government, of Keynes's theories as the basis of macro-economic policy. These were very different from the classical economic principles upon which Churchill had managed the economy as Chancellor in the 1920s. Churchill's Chancellor of the Exchequer, Rab Butler, adopted Labour

policies so closely that he and the previous Chancellor, Labour's Hugh Gaitskell, would have their names combined – in the term 'Butskellism' – to define the entire economic era.[7] This meant that in the entirety of his peacetime ministry, Churchill contributed virtually nothing in terms of domestic policy.

Rationing of basic consumption goods had remained in place until 1954, some nine years after the end of the war – continuing longer after the war than it had during it. Indeed, rationing was imposed for three years of Churchill's peacetime ministry and for eight out of the nine years he was Prime Minister. It had been introduced at the beginning of the war because of the German U-boat and surface fleet threat to Britain's supplies. It continued after the war because of Attlee's policy of 'export-led recovery': constraining domestic demand released productive output for export to generate a trade surplus and thus inflows of foreign revenue. This was needed both to finance post-war reconstruction and to repay the massive debts Britain had incurred, particularly with the USA.[8]

Nationalization of industry was the only significant policy issue over which there was much contention between the Churchill and Attlee ministries. Churchill had opposed Attlee's nationalization of the utilities, railways, coal, iron and steel and long-haul road freight transport. Although he continued to oppose it in principle, his government would denationalize only the iron and steel industry and long-haul road freight transport.[9]

There was, however, a dreadful legacy the Churchill ministry inherited from the Labour government. The balance of payments was in an appalling state; even the massive 30 per cent devaluation of the pound in 1949 by the Attlee government had not rectified this. Yet Churchill's government chose to increase expenditure on social policy.[10]

DEFENCE POLICY

When he became Prime Minister in 1951 Churchill inherited the Korean War from the Labour government; perhaps surprisingly, he was not overly interested in it, despite its continuance until 1953. During its final phase he did, however, manage to upset President Eisenhower and his Secretary of State, John Foster Dulles, by arguing that Syngman Rhee, the President of South Korea, should be prevented from using the issue of the repatriation of prisoners of war to slow negotiations for concluding the war.[11]

In the early days of Attlee's government the USA had terminated the bipartisan agreement with Britain over the 'Manhattan' programme to develop the atomic bomb. It introduced the McMahon Act, which prohibited the sharing of America's atomic secrets with any foreign power. If Britain was to have the bomb it would have to develop it itself, and the decision to go ahead was instigated by Attlee on the advice of his Foreign Secretary, Ernest Bevin, who felt that being a nuclear power would substantially increase Britain's influence over US policy. In the end, technical help from the USA to develop the bomb was both needed and eventually supplied. By the time Churchill returned as Prime Minister the programme, codenamed Hurricane, was so advanced that the first British atomic bomb was to be tested in 1952. Churchill was shocked to discover how advanced the British programme was. The issue interested him greatly, not because of its offensive potential against the Soviet Union, but, like Bevin, for the political leverage it would have with the Americans, and counterintuitively for the opportunity it gave for defence cuts.

Churchill's contribution to the programme was to maintain the scientific research that, continuing under his successors – Eden and Macmillan – would eventually yield a British thermonuclear or hydrogen bomb. On 8 November 1957, two and a half years after he had left office, Britain's first hydrogen bomb, codenamed Grapple, was successfully tested. However, even this was to further Britain's decline. The following year it caused the Americans, finally, to do what Churchill had hoped for: to restore a bilateral relationship on the development of such weapons. However, paradoxically, the Nuclear Co-operation Agreement led to the end of the independent British nuclear programme, as it was agreed that Britain would from then on use only what were effectively American designs. Thus Britain would progressively become a supplicant to the USA in nuclear defence, as in foreign and defence policy more generally.[12]

Due to the dire economic situation inherited from the Labour government, Churchill's Chancellor, Rab Butler, looked for immediate economies, and was keen to reduce the defence budget. To this effect, at Churchill's instigation the chiefs of staff developed the Global Strategy paper in 1952. This advocated the expansion of nuclear defence at the direct expense of conventional forces, because the great destructive power of nuclear weapons came at lower cost than the equivalent conventional forces. So the development of atomic weapons was to be viewed increasingly by the Churchill government not as a matter of national potency but as a way of economizing on defence expenditure. However, Churchill's involvement in policy development was limited. Colleagues complained that there were insufficient meetings of the Defence Committee, of which he was chairman, and that he was not as efficient and decisive as Attlee had been.[13]

These policies failed to reduce the strain on the economy, and so in the spring of 1952 the 'Robot' plan was proposed, which Churchill initially supported. 'Robot' was an acronym derived from the names of the plan's advocates: Sir Leslie Rowan, Second Secretary at the Treasury, Sir George Bolton, executive director of the Bank of England; and Richard (Otto) Clarke, Under-Secretary at the Treasury. The proposal was either to devalue the currency yet again in the US-sponsored Bretton Woods 'fixed' exchange rate system, and/or to make sterling convertible to non-sterling area holders in a flexible exchange rate arrangement and simply to let the exchange rate float down. Eventually Cherwell and Eden came down against the plan, and Churchill concurred. As finances were improving by 1952–3 the whole idea was abandoned.[14]

DECOLONIZATION

The Americans had forced Churchill to accept a decolonization policy, and Oliver Lyttleton as Colonial Secretary would continue the Attlee government's gradual if grudging decolonization programme.[15] In a letter to Eisenhower Churchill wrote: 'In this I must admit I am a laggard. I am a bit sceptical about universal suffrage for the Hottentots [a derogatory name for a South African tribe] even if refined by proportional representation. The British and American Democracies were slowly and painfully forged and even they are not perfect yet.'[16] This stance would fail to address the problem of white minority rule in South Africa, which would declare itself a republic in 1961 and sever its ties with the British Commonwealth. Southern Rhodesia – now Zimbabwe – would remain a problem for decades, initially, like South Africa, with white minority rule. In 1965 the government of Southern Rhodesia would make a 'Unilateral Declaration of Independence' (UDI) from Britain in order to retain white supremacy.

In Central Africa Churchill took little interest, but Northern Rhodesia, which was to became Zambia, progressed towards independence, eventually gaining it in 1964. In East Africa, Kenya endured a serious guerrilla war with the Mau Mau movement, which was brought to a conclusion by 1955 with some reorganization of the military command structure sanctioned by Churchill. However, the imprisoning of Jomo Kenyatta, Kenya's future leader, didn't help the decolonization process. Kenya finally gained independence in 1963. Tanganyika – modern-day Tanzania – and Uganda were also both some way from becoming independent, achieving this in 1961 and 1962 respectively. In West Africa, decolonization of the Gold Coast, which would become Ghana, continued, but would not be complete until 1957. Nigeria and Sierra Leone would finally become independent in 1960 and 1961 respectively – the latter with some reluctance on the part of the Colonial Office.

In South-east Asia there was a significant guerrilla war in Malaya and plans proceeded for its independence in 1957. Singapore became self-governing in 1959, and declared its independence in 1963 before briefly becoming part of Malaysia. Hong Kong would remain a British colony until 1997. None of these countries would gain independence before Churchill's retirement from government in 1955.[17]

EUROPEAN UNITY

Churchill's policy on Europe was to have negative effects on Britain. He was in favour of European unification but opposed to Britain's participation in it. In a Cabinet paper on 29 November 1951, he wrote:

> I never thought that Britain or the British Commonwealth should, either individually or collectively, become an integral part of a European Federation and have never given the slightest support to the idea . . . Our first object is the unity and consolidation of the British Commonwealth and what is left of the former British Empire. Our second, the 'fraternal association' of the English-speaking world; and third, United Europe, to which we are a separate, closely – and specially – related ally and friend.[18]

He represented his policy in terms of 'three spheres of influence': Britain and its Empire, the USA, and Europe, intersecting like a Venn diagram. With Soviet hegemony in the East, 'Europe' effectively meant continental Western Europe. What Churchill meant was that Britain and the USA were the controlling powers both strategically and economically, Europe was also of vital importance, and all three had important strategic and economic relations. However, they were all essentially separate.[19] An economically strong Europe, politically unified so as to remove the basis of conflict between the European nations, was in Britain's interests. Unlike those European nations, Britain had never coveted an empire in Europe, but it did fear the emergence of a dominant European power threatening its imperial interests around the world. This was why Britain had fought Napoleon in the 19th century and the Germans in both World Wars. European unification could help Britain by removing just such a potential threat. Britain had never kept a standing army in Europe but was now obliged to do so under its NATO commitments. Although the proximate cause of this commitment was containment of the Soviet Union, a unified, safe and secure Europe would diminish the need for such forces and could create a bulwark for Britain against the Soviets.

This policy would be fatally undermined. The most important condition for any dominant power is the size of its economy; it is this that enables it to project its strategic power. Churchill had been born into a Britain that was the richest country in the world, but he had helped to denude it of its wealth. Britain was bankrupt in 1945: the war had finished the job Churchill's economic mismanagement had helped to accomplish in the 1920s, and his last government failed to reverse the country's relative economic decline. This occurred as the Empire was being dismantled, because Britain was no longer capable of keeping it. The net result was that by the end of the 1950s Britain was beginning to examine the possibility of membership of the European Economic Community (EEC) – what is today the European Union.[20]

Economic growth is stimulated by trade between advanced industrial economies, because only they have the high real *per capita* incomes that cause high aggregate demand for imports. Much of Britain's trade was with its empire, much of which was comprised of developing economies with low real *per capita* income, which could not afford to demand much of Britain's industrial output. The EEC was a 'customs union', with tariff walls to protect it from external trade. Being inside it could stimulate the British economy and potentially reverse the relative economic decline.

When Harold Macmillan as Prime Minister applied to join the EEC in 1961, Britain was rebuffed by the French, as it would be when Harold Wilson tried again in the mid-1960s. The French President Charles de Gaulle believed, correctly, that Britain was not committed to the notion of European unification and would act as a conduit for American influence in European affairs.[21] The irony was that Britain had been asked several times to participate in European unification. First, Attlee, when Prime Minister, had declined to participate in negotiations to create the European Coal and Steel Community (ECSC), the precursor of the EEC; when Churchill succeeded him, he also refused to participate. The French proposed the European Defence Community, to create a European army. Churchill was in favour, but opposed to any British integration in the military command structure. The French eventually killed the plan.[22] Eden, when Prime Minister, said 'No' to participation in negotiations to develop the EEC itself, which culminated in the Treaty of Rome in 1957. It was then that the continental Europeans fashioned the EEC to address their own needs, not Britain's. Continental Europe had a large and politically significant agricultural sector, and the Common Agricultural Policy – a system of subsidies to support agriculture – was devised as a central element of the EEC. Britain, with its smaller, more efficient agricultural sector, would gain little from such a policy but would have to make a significant financial contribution to it.[23]

Churchill had helped to ensure that Britain was not part of the European unification process; his influence over Eden was corrosive. If he had encouraged Britain's participation in this process, Eden's government could have helped to fashion the EEC in Britain's interests. Churchill's policy would end in the worst of all possible worlds: Britain would eventually participate in European unification, in 1973, but on Europe's terms.

Of course, it could be said that Churchill did Britain a service by trying to keep it out of Europe, that with the Western European social model causing slow growth, and European political unification eroding Britain's national sovereignty, it was better to go it alone. The problem was that Churchill had no alternative model, no idea of how to reverse relative economic decline. His policies, which had helped imperial decline, helped to precipitate Britain into the EEC with its system of tariff barriers and quota restrictions, which were anathema to Churchill as an old liberal free trader. This was not the behaviour of a great visionary.

THE SUEZ CRISIS

There was one area of policy instigated by Churchill that would have disastrous effects after he left office: the Suez Crisis. In this he was clearly influenced by the Attlee government's loss of Palestine, India and the oil facilities in Iran. He undermined Eden's attempts at accommodation with the Egyptian government and was quick to identify such attempts with appeasement and the pre-war policy towards Germany. This bellicose policy of trying to hang on to a passing imperial world led to a crucial juncture in British history.[24]

The Suez Canal had been built by the French and opened in 1869. It was owned half by the Egyptian government and half by private French investors. Benjamin Disraeli had realized its immense strategic significance to Britain in its communications with its imperial possessions in the Indian sub-continent, the Far East, Australia and New Zealand, and in 1875 Britain had acquired the Egyptian-owned part of the company; military action conducted by Britain in Egypt in 1882 gave it *de facto* control over the canal. No longer did ships have to travel around the Cape of Good Hope; they could take the much shorter route through the Straits of Gibraltar – which Britain controlled – via the Mediterranean, the Suez Canal, the Red Sea and the Indian Ocean.

Though ostensibly a sovereign state, Egypt was bound to Britain by a bilateral defence treaty dating from 1936. Britain's dominance meant that Egypt was a supplicant, and the defence treaty enabled Britain to maintain a massive defence force in the Canal Zone. In fact, although the treaty facilitated this British presence, it permitted a maximum of only 10,000 personnel during peacetime, but eight times this number were actually deployed during Churchill's last ministry, so his position was precarious in international law. Egypt wanted all of these forces out.[25]

On 26 January 1952 the Egyptian capital was set alight by anti-British riots. This became known as 'Black Saturday' or the 'Burning of Cairo'. Eden had wanted to settle British differences with a moderate Egyptian government under King Farouk, and agree to withdraw British troops, but Churchill did not believe any negotiations should be undertaken with Egypt in this state. Of 'Black Saturday' he said:

> The horrible behaviour of the mob puts them lower than the
> most degraded savages now known. Unless the Egyptian

government can purge themselves by the condign punishment of the offenders and by the most abject and complete regrets and reparations I doubt whether any relationship is possible with them. They cannot be classed as a civilised power until they have purged themselves.[26]

In fact the British had killed some 50 Egyptians at Ismailia, but Churchill chose to ignore this. His comments set the bar far too high: it meant that a rift with Egypt was now entrenched and would set Britain on course, against Eden's better judgment, towards the final crisis.

With British forces increasingly subject to hostile Arab fedayeen (literally 'self-sacrifice') terrorist attacks, Churchill went to Washington to meet President Truman and, significantly, to discuss the growing crisis. Churchill referred to what was brewing as the 'Battle of the Canal Zone', and he wished to engage American forces in its defence. He saw the canal as of vital strategic and commercial importance to both America and Britain. The Truman administration saw it in no such terms, but recognized that it was of strategic importance to the British Empire. The State Department discussed the matter with the Cabinet Secretary and conveyed to him the importance of persuading Churchill not to bring the matter up in formal negotiations. The Americans had no intention of accepting his proposal and did not wish this to cause embarrassment on either side. Although Churchill assented to this wish, he was nevertheless motivated to bring it up in his address to Congress. His stance undercut the attempts the Foreign Office had been making since late 1951 to replace Egyptian technicians on the canal with Americans, French, Dutch and Norwegians. More fundamentally, it did nothing to help Anglo-American relations, either with the Democratic administration of Truman or with the subsequent Republican one under Eisenhower.[27]

Eden, however, was still keen to negotiate, on 10 March 1952 he wrote to Churchill:

The plain fact is that we are no longer in a position to impose our will upon Egypt, regardless of cost in men, money and international goodwill both throughout the Middle East and the rest of the world. If I cannot impose my will, I must negotiate. This is the best Government we have yet had to do so.[28]

A new Egyptian Foreign Minister, Abdel Fattah Amr, had been appointed, and as he had been a former ambassador to Britain, the appointment was viewed as a sign of the Egyptian government's willingness to negotiate. But Churchill was so hostile to him when he arrived in London in May that any chance of agreement was curtailed.

On 22 July 1952 a *coup d'etat* was enacted by the Egyptian military, which would eventually bring Colonel Gamal Abdel Nasser to power in 1954 as President in a republican Egypt. Churchill's government decided not to intervene and thus tacitly to permit the coup, effectively endorsing the overthrow of King Farouk by his own military. If Churchill expected this decision to improve Anglo-Egyptian relations he would be tragically disappointed.[29]

Between 22 January and 19 February 1954 Eden was obliged to go to Berlin to discuss Germany's future, and Churchill took this opportunity at the Cabinet meeting on 28 January to undertake a 'full review' of policy towards Egypt. He had made it clear to Eden that it might be necessary to take decisions without him in his absence from London. In fact, Selwyn Lloyd, then Minister of State at the Foreign Office, put forward a relatively conciliatory proposal, but Churchill's decision to exploit Eden's absence and go behind his back was most telling.[30]

As a corollary to his hostility towards Egypt, Churchill desired to maintain Israel as a potential military ally. This would be pivotal in the crisis when it came. Early in his last ministry, as the Suez Crisis began to brew, Churchill said, 'Tell them [the Egyptians] that if we have any more of their cheek we will set the Jews on them and drive them back into the gutter, from which they should never have emerged.'[31] He actively opposed the Foreign Office's policy of being sensitive to Arab opinion in order to placate Egypt over the canal, and he advocated support for Israel. In the spring of 1953 he said, 'The idea of selling Israel down the drain in order to persuade Egypt to kick us out of the Canal Zone more gently is not one which attracts me.'[32]

The issue now became immensely more significant than that of the mere presence of British forces in the Canal Zone. On 26 July 1956 President Nasser nationalized the canal, so that the toll revenues could be used to finance the building of the Aswan hydroelectric dam, and thus help to modernize the Egyptian economy. Nasser had asked Britain and the USA for finance to undertake this task, but after initial consideration of his request, both had withdrawn. Britain's imperial lines of communication were directly threatened by the loss of control over this crucial conduit. Eden, who for so long had been berated by Churchill for being insufficiently robust in his dealings with Egypt, particularly now that it was run by a military dictator, had the perfect pretext for intervention. It was thus Churchill's corroding influence over Eden that finally persuaded him to conduct a clandestine campaign for the return of the canal.

The heart of the Suez Crisis in 1956 was a secret deception plan hatched by the British and French governments – the former co-owners of the Suez Canal Company – to reverse the Egyptian nationalization of the canal: they would encourage an Israeli invasion of Egypt and use it as a pretext for an Anglo-French expedition, ostensibly to separate the belligerents, reoccupying the Canal Zone in the process. Israeli involvement was thus central to the plan.

The French were keen to participate, not only as former part-owners of the canal, but because Egypt was assisting rebels in French-controlled Algeria. Israel was keen to participate because of Palestinian fedayeen terrorist attacks and because Egypt was blockading the Straits of Tiran. Israel would invade Egypt across the Sinai Peninsula, and Britain and France would then give Nasser and Israel an ultimatum to stop fighting or military force would be used to 'protect' the canal.

The attack began on 29 October 1956. However, the United States had its eyes on the Soviet military invasion of Hungary to quell an uprising, and could hardly oppose this while sanctioning an Anglo-French invasion of Egypt. Much more importantly, the USA feared the possibility of a major conflagration in the Middle East because the Soviet Premier, Nikita Khrushchev, was openly threatening intervention, in support of Nasser, using 'all types of weapons of destruction' to attack London and Paris. Eisenhower threatened that the USA would sell its reserves of sterling, precipitating Britain's financial collapse. When the Arabs initiated an oil embargo against Britain and France, the USA refused help unless Britain and France withdrew. All these events precipitated a run on the pound on the foreign exchanges. Eden was thus obliged to call a ceasefire on 6 November, and would resign as Prime Minister due to 'ill health' in January 1957.

Churchill's former private secretary, Jock Colville, asked him not long before his death if *he* would have undertaken the Suez adventure. Churchill responded, 'I would never have dared, and if I had dared, I would never have stopped.' For someone who 'would never have dared', his statements, policies and his going behind Eden's back to prevent the appeasement of a dictator all seem very incongruous. If Churchill had dared and had not stopped, the Americans would most certainly have stopped him, if through no other mechanism than accelerating the run on the pound that was occurring anyway. Nearly £32 million was actually lost in this way, and had the adventure been pressed, Eisenhower would have seen to it that Britain's finances were bled away until it was forced to withdraw.[33]

Churchill's egging on of Eden helped to precipitate the debacle, which more than any other single event would convey to the British and to the world that Britain was no longer a hegemonic power. Britain's frailty would accelerate the decline of its empire, as its imperial possessions increasingly saw that, if pressed, it could be defeated. Churchill understood this when he said in 1953, 'What happens here [in Egypt] will set the pace for us all over Africa and the Middle East.'[34] The crisis would cause a momentous change in British policy. Harold Macmillan replaced Eden as Prime Minister in January 1957; he had been Chancellor of the Exchequer during the Suez Crisis and had originally backed the invasion, then reversed his position as he saw the adverse effect on the economy. As Prime Minister, he would make his 'wind of change' speech in Cape Town in February 1960, indicating that Britain was now formally to dismantle the British Empire.

Thus even when Churchill was gone – he was not quite gone. Out of office, he would loom up as a back-seat driver. It would be a most significant postscript to his last stint as Prime Minister. Churchill's own efforts, from his very first days in office – ironically as Parliamentary Under-Secretary for the Colonies in Campbell-Bannerman's ministry – to Suez, a span of just over half a century, would play a central role in Britain's decline – the very thing he had wanted least of all.

FOREIGN POLICY – THE LAST GASP OF THE 'BIG THREE'

Churchill believed that as Prime Minister he could restore the Anglo-American relationship of the early World War II years, but despite the fact that Britain now possessed atomic weapons, this relationship would never be restored. President Truman shut Churchill, and Britain, out of the main policy decisions. When Eisenhower replaced Truman, Churchill hoped that the man who had been Supreme Allied Commander under the political supervision of Roosevelt and himself during the war would restore that close relationship now he was President. Nothing of the kind was to occur. Roosevelt had already shut Churchill out by the time of the last 'Big Three' meeting he attended during the war, but had permitted Churchill too much influence prior to this. When Churchill emphatically promoted to Truman the notion of renewed Anglo-American co-operation in global affairs, the President said: 'Thank you Mr Prime Minister. We might pass that to be worked out by our advisers.'[35]

With regard to the Soviet Union, once the 'Iron Curtain' had descended across Europe, Stalin and his successors were going to hang on to their conquests with military occupation, quite immune from Churchill's blandishments. Thus the USA and the USSR were not going to have their differences brokered by a Churchill-led Britain; Churchill's hopes constituted naivety of an extraordinary order. Yet as soon as he became Prime Minister he sought a meeting of the 'Big Four': Britain, the USA, the USSR and France. Truman said that the issues should be discussed in the United Nations, which had been created for precisely this purpose; he continued that a 'Big Four' meeting would create false hopes and public clamour for foolish concessions.[36]

From 1950 until he became President, Eisenhower was Supreme Commander of NATO in Europe. In December 1951 he met Churchill for the first time since he had become Prime Minister; after that meeting he wrote: 'He simply will not think in terms of today, but rather only those of the war years . . . My regretful opinion is that the Prime Minister no longer absorbs new ideas . . .'[37] Eisenhower became US President in January 1953, and Churchill insisted that he was best placed to act alongside him.

Stalin died on 5 March 1953, and it now seemed to Churchill that the principal impediment to progress with the Soviet Union had gone. Churchill thus saw this as a golden opportunity to use his good offices to broker a settlement between the super-powers in a major peace conference. He pressed hard for a summit meeting of the major powers during that summer. Secret talks were held in the Soviet Embassy in London between Churchill's emissaries, John Colville and Christopher Soames, and the new Soviet Ambassador Jacob Malik. Washington, however, was becoming increasingly concerned about Churchill's actions. Churchill wrote to Eisenhower on 6 May 1953 concerning the new Soviet leaders: 'According to my experience of these people in the War we should gain more by good will on the spot . . . None of the four men who I am told are working together very much as equals, Malenkov, Molotov, Beria and Bulganin, has any contacts outside Russia, except Molotov. I am very anxious to know these men and talk to them as I think I can frankly and on the dead level.'[38]

Georgy Malenkov, Nikolai Bulganin, and the veteran Foreign Minister, Vyacheslav Molotov, all vied for power after Stalin's death. They would all oppose the emerging leader, Nikita Krushchev, and would be lucky that Krushchev spared their lives. Lavrentiy Beria was not so fortunate: as head of the NKVD – the secret police – he had been in large measure responsible for the purges of Soviet society in the 1930s and he was executed in 1953.

On 11 May 1953 Churchill made a speech to the House of Commons in which he said: 'I believe that a conference on the highest level should take place between the leading powers without long delay . . . The conference should be confined to the smallest number of powers and persons possible.'[39] Eisenhower requested a meeting with Churchill in Bermuda to discuss the summit plan, but Churchill had a very serious stroke on 23 June. He took a Cabinet meeting the following day. To some of those present, such as Harry Crookshank, the Lord Privy Seal, it was clear that he had had a stroke, but other ministers did not know and were not told until later. The public were told little. An item in *The Times* on 26 June said that Churchill had gone to Chartwell the previous day to prepare for the Bermuda meeting. On the 27th No 10 announced that the meeting was cancelled, and that Churchill was in need of complete rest. The signatories included his doctor, Lord Moran, and the announcement was published in *The Times* on the 29th. The public were not told of the stroke until two years later. In fact it had been so serious that his doctors were concerned that he would die. [40]

Churchill and Eden were at odds over the Soviets, with Eden believing that things had not appreciably changed from the Stalin era. Eden said: 'The Russians are making very great efforts by all sorts of means to drive wedges between us and the Americans.'[41] He agreed with Eisenhower that there was little purpose in a summit with the Russians. As he was about to go to Boston (to have corrective surgery after a botched operation), he said to his colleagues at the Foreign Office, 'Try not to allow too much appeasement of the Russian Bear in my absence.'[42] The Commonwealth Secretary and acting Foreign Secretary, Lord Salisbury, along with other

Foreign Office officials, supported Eden's position. Salisbury went to Washington in July 1953 and while he was there Eisenhower expressed the belief that the heads of government should not get engaged in detailed negotiations and bargaining with the Soviets. He wrote to Churchill: 'I do not like formally talking with those who only wish to entrap and embarrass us. I would prefer, at any rate in the first instance, to leave the initial approach to the Foreign Ministers on limited and specific lines . . .'[43]

Churchill, undeterred, was looking at September for a conference between the heads: he really wanted it between just the Soviet Union, the USA and Britain. Eisenhower suggested that it was essential to include the French. By widening any possible conference Eisenhower thus hoped to reduce its effectiveness and by so doing erode Churchill's enthusiasm for it. Eden now saw that only the Americans could stop Churchill and made the Americans aware of this. To this end the meeting in Bermuda was rescheduled for 4 December 1953, to be attended by the French as well as the British and the Americans. The Soviets upset the applecart when, on 27 November, they agreed to a conference, albeit on Eisenhower's suggested lines – including the French, but only at Foreign Minister level.[44]

At the Bermuda meeting Eisenhower made it clear that he was very cool about the matter, and the French were equally cool. There were more talks, this time in Washington from 25–29 June 1954, but Eisenhower refused a conference with the Soviets, though he said Churchill could meet with them bilaterally if he wished, while the US Secretary of State, John Foster Dulles, was opposed to the whole idea. Nevertheless, as Churchill returned home aboard HMS *Queen Elizabeth*, he dispatched a telegram to Molotov asking for a meeting. Eden was incandescent, saying the Cabinet should have been informed first. When Churchill attended a Cabinet meeting on his return the Cabinet revolted: Crookshank and Salisbury, particularly, argued that the Americans should have been consulted first. Churchill insisted that they already knew and had agreed, but the Cabinet was at war with him. Macmillan later noted that this event caused the Cabinet seriously to question Churchill's ability, and that if any such conference were to take place with Churchill representing Britain it might lead to a 'tragic ending'.

Churchill's precarious position was retrieved, ironically, by the Soviets. They sent a communication on 24 July to the USA, France, China and Britain calling for a European-wide security treaty, with all those European countries that wished to, conferring. The Western Europeans would reply collectively on 10 September, saying that no conference could be held unless the Soviets first agreed to free democratic elections in East Germany, as stated in the Austrian Treaty to which the USSR was not a signatory. This would kill the conference.[45]

But Churchill still would not give up. On 7 July 1954 he had written to Eisenhower, 'I thought it right to send an exploratory message to Molotov to feel the ground about the possibility of a Two Power Meeting.' In the message to Molotov he had said: 'Let me know if you would like the idea of a friendly meeting . . . to find a reasonable way of living side by side in growing confidence, easement and prosperity . . . our meeting . . . might be the prelude to a wider reunion where much might be settled.'[46] Eisenhower recognized Churchill's motivation when he wrote to him on 22 July:

> I am certain that you must have a very deep and understandable desire to do something special and additional in your remaining period of active service that will be forever recognised as a mile-stone in the world's tortuous progress towards a just and lasting peace. Nothing else could provide such a fitting climax to your long and brilliant service to your sovereign, your country and the world . . . As you know, while I have not been able to bring myself to believe wholeheartedly in the venture, I most earnestly pray that you may develop something good out of what seems to me the bleakest of prospects . . . I must also say that because of my utter lack of confidence in the reliability and integrity of the men in the Kremlin and my feeling that you may be disappointed in your present hopes, my mind has been turning toward an exploration of other possibilities by which you would still give to the world something inspiring before you lay down your official responsibilities . . . I suggest to you a thoughtful speech on the subject of the rights to self-government . . . (of the world's smaller nations).[47]

Given Churchill's old imperialist views, being fobbed off with such a task was hardly likely to distract him from his grand design. On 8 August 1954 he wrote to Eisenhower:

The mortal peril which overhangs the human race is never absent from my thoughts. I am not looking about for the means of making a dramatic exit or of finding a suitable curtain . . . I am however convinced that the present method of establishing the relations between the two sides of the world by means of endless discussions between Foreign Offices, will not produce any decisive result. The more the topics of discussion are widened, the more Powers concerned, the greater the number of officials and authorities of all kinds involved, the less may well be the chance of gaining effective results in time . . .

I have, as you know, since Stalin's death hoped that there could be a talk between you and me on the one hand, and the new Leaders of Russia, or as they might be, the Leaders of a new Russia, on the other.[48]

This was always going to be a fantasy, and the disagreements with the Americans didn't end there. On 29 March 1955 Eisenhower wrote to Churchill: 'We do not agree on the probable extent of the importance of further Communist expansion in Asia . . . Your . . . government seems to regard Communist aggression in Asia as of little significance to the free world future.'[49] This issue was increasingly exercising the Americans, and the Vietnam War was already brewing, but Churchill continued to think he could do business with the Communists. Far from brokering some kind of global settlement, however, his role would be entirely marginalized. Of the 'special relationship' Eisenhower wrote in his diary:

No such special relationship can be maintained or even suggested publicly. In public relationship all nations are sovereign and equal. This means that on the personal and informal basis we must find a way of agreeing with our British friends on broad objectives and purposes. Thereafter, each must pursue its own detailed methods of achieving these purposes.[50]

So in foreign policy Churchill would contribute little. He had established what he called Britain's 'special relationship' with the United States during the war, which would form the cornerstone of the foreign policy of all British governments from then on. But the inequality of wealth and strategic power between the two countries would ensure that Britain was the supplicant and would benefit little from that policy. It is true that Britain has enjoyed the protection of the USA since the early 1940s, but other nations have also enjoyed the same protection without a 'special relationship'. Britain has also benefited in other bilateral ways, but so have other countries. In Washington, this 'special relationship' hardly even registers – it is very much a British fiction.

CLINGING ON TO POWER

Within nine months of the formation of Churchill's 1951 government, four important members of the Cabinet met to discuss his retirement in the Knightsbridge home of Harry Crookshank, Leader of the House of Commons and Minister of Health (later to become Lord Privy Seal). A similar meeting had occurred in the same house four years earlier, where senior members of the Conservative Party had met for the very same reason.[51]

Churchill had several opportunities to retire: the first was directly prior to the 1945 general election; the next was immediately after his landslide election defeat, and the third came after his 1950 election defeat. At the death of King George VI in 1952 he could have retired but insisted on staying on to oversee the transition, even though he said of the new Queen, the 26-year-old Elizabeth II, 'I do not know her and she is just a child.' In September 1952 he had still not decided when to retire, though in November he said to his niece Clarissa, who had just become Eden's second wife, that he was considering retiring after a visit he wanted to make to the United States. Lord Salisbury, grandson of the former Prime Minister and Commonwealth Secretary in Churchill's government, suggested that Eden should confront Churchill to bring the matter to a head; if no satisfactory response was elicited, the senior ministers, without Eden, should take a judgment on the matter.[52] Instead, in 1952 Churchill reshuffled his Cabinet.

Shortly after Eisenhower became President, Walter Gifford, the retiring American Ambassador to London, told him that, to many, even in the Conservative Party, Churchill was seen as having gone on too long. When Churchill visited New York in January 1953, Eisenhower wrote in his diary:

Much as I held Winston in my personal affection, and much as I admire him for his past accomplishments and leadership, I wish he would turn over the leadership of the British Conservation [*sic*] Party to younger men ... he had developed an almost childlike faith that all of the answers are to be found merely in British–American partnership.[53]

The coronation of Queen Elizabeth II in 1953 was another opportunity to retire, just as Salisbury had done in 1902 on the occasion of the coronation of King Edward VII and Baldwin in 1937 at that of King George VI. This likelihood increased when Churchill had his stroke less than three weeks after the coronation, but Eden, his heir apparent, was in Boston for his operation, and Churchill had this as an excuse not to retire.

Opposition within Churchill's own party was growing irresistibly, and with his 80th birthday approaching in November 1954 it wanted him finally to use this opportunity to retire. If he was to hand over in time to give Eden a good chance to establish himself as Prime Minister before a general election, the timing of the election would be an important factor in determining his retirement. Churchill asked the Chairman of the Party, Lord Woolton, for 'an appreciation of the most suitable month for a General Election' and Woolton replied on 2 April 1954. He said that spring was out because of Easter, Whitsun, the local elections and the budget; summer was out because of the holidays and getting the farmers interested; winter was out because of the weather, holidays and the introduction of the new electoral register. This left autumn, and Woolton favoured October.[54] But Churchill was thinking of 1955, not 1954, and he still had his grand plan to execute. He wrote to Eden on 11 June 1954:

I am increasingly impressed by the crisis and tension which is developing in world affairs and I should be failing in my duty if I cast away my trust at such a juncture or failed to use the influence which I possess in the causes we both have at heart.

Before I can judge the issue I must see what emerges from our talks in Washington, and how they affect the various schemes I have in mind.[55]

In the original draft of this letter he had written 'my' rather than 'our talks in Washington'. He continued:

> It will not I hope extend beyond the autumn . . . I am most anxious to give you the best opportunity to prepare for an election at the end of 1955 and to establish the repute and efficiency of your Administration. I have however to offer wider reasons than this to history and indeed the nation.[56]

On 26 August, in response to another letter from Eden about the election, Churchill would write, 'Of course we must try to make the best plans possible to win the election and to save the world. They are not necessarily opposed.'[57]

Eden wrote to Churchill on 10 August 1954:

> If there isn't enough time for the new Government to make its own name for itself in advance of the general election, then it will have no chance of survival. It will be hard enough anyway. But at least a year, beginning with a Party Conference, seems to be the minimum.[58]

Churchill replied on 24 August:

> I have been oppressed by a series of suggestions that I should retire in your favour. I have done my best to discharge the Commission I hold from the Crown and Parliament, and I am glad to say that I have not missed a single day in control of affairs, in spite of a temporary loss of physical mobility a year ago. Now I have good reports from my doctors, and I do not feel unequal to my burden.
>
> I have no intention of abandoning my post at the present crisis in the world. I feel sure that with my influence I can be of help to the cause of 'peace through strength', on the methods of sustaining which we are so notably agreed. I trust therefore I may count on your loyalty and friendship during this important period, although it will not, as I hoped in my letter to you of June 11, be ended by the autumn.

At another level coming to Party affairs, I have reflected long and deeply on the domestic scene by which we are confronted. The dominant fact is that the changes in the rating valuations are said to make it overwhelmingly desirable to have the election before November, 1955. It does not seem to me that the brief spell which remains till then gives the best chance to the Party or offers a propitious outlook to my successor. Certainly he would court a very heavy responsibility which in fact rests on me. He would have to present in twelve or thirteen months the impression of something new and different which would spread the sense of improvement. But we must ask ourselves whether this is likely in the prevailing circumstances. It is certain that one half of the country, instead of judging the new Government fairly on its merits, will on the contrary make it their target for electioneering abuse and for unfavourable comparisons.

Woolton, whom as Party Chairman I have consulted, tells me that he has already expressed the opinion that such a procedure would be bad electoral tactics. Looking at the scene impartially, as I try to do when I am in a good humour, it seems to me that it might be wiser not to attempt, with the restricted resources available, to conquer the hearts of an audience the majority of whom are hostile Party men. Fag-end Administrations have not usually been triumphant. I can remember Rosebery after Gladstone and A.J.B. [Arthur Balfour] after Salisbury. Both were brushed aside in spite of their ability, experience, and charm . . . the present Government have not got a bad record . . . this is a natural climax, and not a new venture.

As to the election, I ought to bear the responsibility for the past and leave to my successor a fair start and the hope of the future.[59]

In fact Eden's subsequent ministry was not a 'fag-end' government and would not be brushed aside by the electorate, but only by Eden himself over the Suez Crisis. Indeed when Eden held a general election in the summer of 1955 he increased Churchill's modest majority from the 1951 election.

After Eden, the Conservative government would continue under Macmillan, who would increase its majority again in the 1959 election. Only under Alec Douglas-Home would it become a 'fag-end' government, losing power in 1964. The only interpretation of Churchill's statement was that he wished to continue as Prime Minister after the next general election, even though he had accepted the need to retire.

On 27 August Eden had a showdown with Churchill, which he recorded in his diary:

> If I was not fit to stand on my own feet now & choose an administration now, I should probably be less so a year from now. The govt. was not functioning well & this was putting a heavy strain on all the senior ministers. There were able men but there was no co-ordination. Of course he didn't like this & said he had never missed a day since his illness. I said that wasn't the point. There was no co-ordination on home front & Cabinets dragged on far too long. There was much argument about all this which got us nowhere. I said that I would have been glad of the chance to take over a year ago, but it meant less to me now, & would mean much less still next year, if I were still there.[60]

Macmillan would see Churchill on 1 October to add weight to the need for him to go. But he would not. There was at least one person, however, for whom it was an advantage for Churchill to stay on: Rab Butler. Churchill and Butler grew closer, and the more this relationship developed the more it seemed possible that Churchill might see Butler as his heir apparent. Macmillan, on the other hand, who was older than either Butler or Eden, needed a quick Eden ministry if he was to have any chance of becoming Prime Minister himself. Of course, that is precisely what did happen, and Macmillan made sure that Butler would never become Prime Minister.[61]

Just before Christmas 1954 Churchill told the Duke of Edinburgh that he intended to resign in either June or July of the following year. At a meeting at No 10 with Churchill and seven senior Cabinet ministers, Eden stated that such a date was unacceptable, because it was too close to the proposed autumn general election. Churchill replied:

I know you are trying to get rid of me and it is up to me to go to the Queen and hand her my resignation and yours – but I won't do it. But if you feel strongly about it you can force my hand by a sufficiently large number of Ministers handing in their resignations, in which case an Election will be inevitable; but if this happens I shall not be in favour of it and I shall tell the country so.[62]

Butler, Macmillan, Salisbury and Sir Walter Monckton (the Minister of Labour) met with James Stuart, the Scottish Secretary, at his Pont Street home on 28 December, yet were unable to agree on how to proceed.

Churchill, when he had been Home Secretary so many years earlier, had put a chart on his wall to count down the days to the execution of condemned prisoners. He now had such a chart to map out his own last days as Prime Minister. With the friction rising between him and Eden, the chart referred to 'My successor', not 'Anthony Eden'.[63] With pressure continuing to mount inside the Party, retirement at Easter 1955 seemed a possibility. However, in February, with Eden on a trip to India and Iraq, Churchill began to recant on retiring at Easter. Eden became frustrated to the point of incandescence. In Cabinet on 14 March, with Eden, Macmillan, Salisbury, Crookshank and Butler all present, and with even Butler realizing that Churchill could go on no longer, the issue finally exploded. Macmillan recalled:

It looked as if the meeting wd. end without the real issue being dealt with. As so often with our countrymen, it was too awkward & painful for anyone to say anything about it. Then a dramatic moment came when Eden said slowly & without evident emotion 'Does that mean, Prime Minister, that the arrangements you have made with me are at an end?' Eden then blurted out 'I have been Foreign Secretary for 10 years. Am I not to be trusted?' Churchill replied 'All this is very unusual. These matters are not, in my experience, discussed in Cabinets.' There was a long & difficult silence. Salisbury then said 'It is clear that certain plans are known to some members of the Cabinet; would it not be better if they were known to all?' Churchill said 'I cannot assent to such a discussion. I know my duty & will perform it. If any member of the Cabinet dissents his way is open.' After another pause, Butler made a useful intervention saying 'It's not a question of loyalty to you or your leadership, Prime Minister. It's a question of whether an election may become necessary. You have always said that you wd. not lead the party at another election. We must consider all these dates simply from the national interest. In my view another Labour government now wd. be a disaster from which the country might never recover.'[64]

With that it now seemed certain that Churchill would go. However, on 29 March the Soviet Premier, Nikolai Bulganin, appeared to accept the need for a four-power conference, and Churchill at once wanted to stay on. But with the Cabinet now in open revolt, he finally knew he could not go on. Tuesday 5 April 1955 was to be his last Cabinet, and in it he announced that he would be having an audience with the Queen that afternoon and would tender his resignation.

Thus he finally gave up as Prime Minister when it was clear to him that a conference to settle the principal international matters was not to occur. He was forced to retire, on the Cabinet's terms, not his own. He had gone on too long in the job – another error of judgment. By this time he could be hopelessly vague and ineffective, as is clear from some of the recorded speeches he made at the time; his strokes in 1949 and 1953 had hardly helped in this regard. He went at the age of 80: his protestations that Gladstone had formed his last ministry at the age of 82 were to no avail. No prime minister had made it so difficult for their successor to take office.

Churchill only ever faced three general elections as party leader: he lost two of them. The 1945 general election he lost catastrophically: it was the worst defeat for the Conservative Party since 1906. The 1950 general election he lost narrowly. His only victory was in 1951, and then with a very slim majority. It was a poor record.

He continued as Member of Parliament for Woodford until 1964, when his constituency party decided they wanted a younger candidate – Churchill would be 90 that year. He had gone on too long even there. So against his will, he found himself retired from politics, a retirement that would last only a short while until his death in January 1965.

20
CONCLUSION: THE RECKONING

Why did Churchill behave as he did – the irrational, emotional decision-making and vacillation? What drove him to change his mind so readily, to announce policy that had not been discussed or approved by colleagues, to cover his tracks when he had been wrong and deny positions that he had formerly held, to cling on to hobbyhorses contrary to all advice? He was not mad or simple; his misguided decisions were the product of his personality – a mixture of arrogance, emotion, self-indulgence, stubbornness.

Churchill's first major contribution to world events was the calamitous Gallipoli campaign in World War I. This would be the prototype for his strategy in World War II, particularly in respect of the campaigns in Norway, North Africa, the Balkans and Italy, and his desire for one in Sumatra. It has been said that 'insanity is doing the same thing, over and over again, but expecting different results'.[1]

When Churchill first became Prime Minister it was the very qualities that made his judgment so unstable that made him persist in prosecuting World War II at any cost, when the rational policy might have been to make terms with Germany. He said of his role in the war, 'I . . . hope that I sometimes suggested to the lion the right place to use his claws.'[2] Yet, as we have seen, his dispersionist strategy, committing British forces to military operations of no direct strategic importance, his recklessness with Britain's fighter defences in the Battle of France and the Battle of Britain, his failure to understand the vulnerability of armoured warships and to appreciate the resources needed to address the U-boat threat, all cost time and lives.

His strategy sapped available resources from the one campaign where the British did strike effectively at the heart of the enemy in World War II: the strategic bombing campaign. As Albert Speer, Hitler's Armaments Minister, made clear, the air war amounted to a Second Front from 1943 because it took thousands of guns, a hundred thousand men and millions of shells from the Eastern Front. Churchill mounted a botched raid on the French coast at Dieppe in 1942, but then procrastinated over the western

Allies mounting a Second Front in France, costing about a year, during which approximately ten million lives were lost.[3]

Churchill's ability to conduct military strategy was highly defective, as Sir Alan Brooke recorded in his diary on 24 May 1943:

> [Churchill] thinks one thing at one moment and another at another moment. At times the war may be won by bombing and all must be sacrificed to it. At others it becomes essential for us to bleed ourselves dry on the Continent because Russia is doing the same. At others our main effort must be in the Mediterranean, directed against Italy or [the] Balkans alternatively, with sporadic desires to invade Norway and 'roll up the map in the opposite direction to Hitler'! But more often . . . he wants to carry out ALL operations simultaneously irrespective of shortages of shipping![4]

Brooke and the chiefs of staff had to spend much of their valuable time constraining Churchill, as did the Cabinet. Attlee, Deputy Prime Minister in Churchill's wartime government, commented years afterwards, 'I think that it was Balfour who said that what Winston needed was a strong-minded woman secretary to say every now and then "Don't be a bloody fool." We performed that useful function.'[5]

Churchill took much of the credit for the war effort, little acknowledging the role of the staff, as Brooke opined on 20 January 1945:

> It is a strange thing what a vast part the COS takes in the running of the war and how little it is known or its functions appreciated. The average man in the street has never heard of it. Any limelight for it could not fail to slightly diminish the PM's halo! This may perhaps account for the fact that he has never yet given it the slightest word of credit in public![6]

Churchill's policy errors were in no sense confined to wartime. His creation of Iraq and division of Ireland created problems that have lasted to this day. His economic policies before and after World War I were deeply ill conceived, as the greatest economist of the era, John Maynard Keynes, pointed out at the time. The introduction of social reforms, which inhibited the ability of the economy to function in accordance with free market principles, while employing 'classical' macro-economic policy, meant that people were bound to suffer. The economy was thus weakened significantly in the 1920s, with British businesses becoming less competitive and unemployment higher than otherwise would have been the case. This caused the General Strike in 1926, the only national strike Britain has ever endured. The economy was weakened at a crucial time – just prior to the Wall Street Crash and subsequent global Depression in the 1930s. Churchill's economic policies thus caused Britain's economic privations to be more severe than they would have been with more enlightened policies.

Churchill's desire for disarmament in the 1920s weakened national defences just at the time when the threat from the active Nazi movement in Germany was becoming apparent, the limited threat from the Fascist government in Italy from 1922 was palpable, and with the ending of the Anglo-Japanese Alliance in the same year, the threat from Japan was growing. Conversely, if Churchill had been Prime Minister during the 1930s, the public would have interpreted his behaviour as bellicose and aggressive. Britain would not only have been precipitated into war before it was ready, but Churchill and Hitler would have been seen then as aggressive leaders of rival expansionary imperial powers. Thus Churchill and Britain would have been identified as partly to blame for causing World War II. In reality, Neville Chamberlain did Britain the fundamental service of ensuring that all of the blame for the war was to be Hitler's. This was precisely because Chamberlain was genuinely, if ineffectually, searching for peace. Of Chamberlain's mission to Munich in 1938, a German woman commented, 'We feel as long as you are there, the masses in Germany cannot be talked into the belief of English aggression.'[7] In *The Second World War* Churchill wrote of government ministers:

> Their duty is first so to deal with other nations as to avoid strife and war and to eschew aggression in all its forms, whether for nationalistic or ideological objects. But the safety of the State, the lives and freedom of their own fellow-countrymen, make it right and imperative in the last resort, or when a final and definite conviction has been reached, that the use of force should not be excluded.'[8]

Churchill said of his role in World War II, 'It was the nation and the race dwelling all round the globe that had the lion's heart. I had the luck to be called upon to give the roar.'[9] The German philosopher Georg Hegel wrote, in *The Philosophy of Right*, 'The great man of the age is the one who can put into words the will of his age, tell his age what its will is, and accomplish it. What he does is the heart and essence of his age; he actualises his age.'[10] Churchill failed to accomplish the 'will of his age' – others did this – but he did 'put into words the will of his age'; the rhetorical skills were his. However, as the Labour Party politician Aneurin Bevan pointed out, Churchill treated speeches as though they were battles and battles as though they were speeches. His rhetoric inspired the nation, but it was victories that were needed, not rhetoric.

Churchill was the last British Prime Minister to have a serious influence on global events, and his actions during World War II helped to end this influence. His last tired government brought this fact home very clearly. He tried for so long to fan up the last embers of Britain's dominance and to settle the world's major strategic problems, but to no avail. There was a new world order dominated by the USA and the USSR, and they were not interested in either Churchill or in Britain.

Late in life, Churchill became depressed by the fact that he would leave Britain very much worse than he found it. He had been born into the richest and most powerful imperial nation in the world. By the time he died, the wealth had largely gone and the empire was largely going – and with it Britain as a great power. Many factors and many people were responsible for this, and Churchill was one of them. His last book, completed in 1958, *The History of the English Speaking Peoples*, concluded its chronicle before World War I, when Britain was still great – before Churchill had any serious influence.

So why is Churchill remembered so fondly? It is because his speeches were so memorable, and because his pronouncements about Hitler and German re-armament in the 1930s and the failure of appeasement to prevent war appeared to be correct. Churchill became an iconic figure particularly because the British people completely identified him with victory in World War II. The British had a great psychological need to interpret victory as arising from their own efforts and sacrifices – which were of course very great – and so victory was personified in the being of Churchill himself. The fact that victory came later and at higher cost than it could have without him has always been obscured by the very fact of victory itself. The British thought they had won World War II, and Churchill was unquestionably the man who made the principal executive decisions. Once victory had been achieved, how could anyone deny that Churchill was a great man, even though many had denied it before and during the war? The British people needed Churchill to be great, the embodiment of their desires and beliefs. They needed to believe that it was indeed they, the British people, who were responsible for victory.

Within living memory, Britain had been the greatest power on earth, and the British did not believe that this could have appreciably changed by the 1940s. So it seemed natural that they must have won the war, albeit with a little help from others. That the victory was achieved by the USSR and the USA, with help from Britain and many other countries, was not recognized in Britain until many years afterwards. The fact that Britain was no longer the most powerful nation took decades for its people to adjust to. Indeed, the fact that it had only a fraction of the resources necessary to defeat Nazi Germany has hardly been accepted by the British even today.

Those who were too young, or who were born after the war and thus played no role in it, have no efforts and sacrifices needing to be justified through victory. Thus with the passage of time it has become progressively easier to accept that Churchill was not the great heroic figure that previous generations needed to believe he was.

Churchill died on 24 January 1965, 70 years to the very day after his own father's death. He was 90 years and 2 months old. Some time after his grand funeral, two workers from London drove to Bladon in Oxfordshire to erect the huge memorial over his grave. It was pretty hard work. Finally, when it was in position, they stood back to admire their work and one said to the other, 'The bugger'll never get up from under that lot.'[11]

In the deepest of ironies, it was Hitler who made Churchill a historical figure. If it had not been for Hitler, Churchill would never have been recalled as First Lord of the Admiralty in 1939, let alone become Prime Minister. He would have ended his political career in 1929, as Chancellor of the Exchequer – just as his father had. He would have been a minor figure in British political history, and would be largely forgotten today. It is because of Churchill's role in World War II, and because he wrote so much of the history himself, that we remember Churchill, above all else, for Hitler's defeat. Hitler, however, is remembered for himself.

ENDNOTES

Quote on back cover
Enright, p. 81.

Introduction
1 Brendon, p. 19.
2 Clark, Mark., interview for: The World at War, FremantleMedia Limited, 1973.
3 Statistic for deaths in the European theatre for the final year of World War II. Research data provided to the author personally by Dr Duncan Anderson, Head of the Department of War Studies, Royal Military Academy Sandhurst, and his colleagues: Rudiger Overman and Dr Aryk Nusbacher.

Chapter 1. Gallipoli: Churchill's First Defeat
1 Morgan, p. 317.
2 Churchill, Randolph Spencer., Vol. II, p. 517.
3 Marder (1956), p. 450.
4 Massie, p. 778.
5 Ibid., p. 770.
6 Ibid., pp. 782 & 785-786.
7 Charmley (1993), p. 105.
8 Ibid., p. 111.
9 Ibid., pp. 105-6.
10 Ibid., p. 106.
11 Ibid., pp. 106 & 111.
12 Ibid., p. 113.
13 Marder (1965), p. 187.
14 Dugdale, p. 130.
15 Charmley (1993), pp. 112 & 116.
16 Lecture by Sir Martin Gilbert at Churchill College, Cambridge on 26 November 2007.
17 Charmley (1993), p. 118.
18 Ibid., p. 119.
19 Churchill, Sir Winston Spencer. (1923), p. 184.
20 Charmley (1993), pp. 107 & 124.
21 Churchill Archives Centre, Churchill College, Cambridge: CHAR 13/65/1.
22 Ibid., CHAR 13/65/2.
23 Ibid., CHAR 13/65/13.
24 Ibid., CHAR 13/65/70.
25 Ibid.
26 Charmley (1993), pp. 120-1.
27 Ibid., pp. 107 & 124.
28 Churchill Archives Centre, Churchill College, Cambridge: CHAR 13/65/126.
29 Ibid., CHAR 13/65/219.
30 Blake, p. 245.
31 Enright, p. 53.
32 Charmley (1993), pp. 128 & 130-1.
33 McEwen, p. 118.
34 Charmley (1993), pp. 130-2.
35 Ibid., p. 135.
36 Brendon, p. 87.
37 Beaverbrook, p. 127.

Chapter 2. The General Strike and the Depression
1 Churchill, Randolph Spencer., Vol. II, pp. 284-285, 288, 298, 313, 424, 505.
2 Feiling, pp. 130-1.
3 Tim Hatton, 'Unemployment and the labour market in inter-war Britain', in

Floud et al., pp. 381-2.
4 Ibid., p. 381.
5 Lecture by Sir Martin Gilbert at Churchill College, Cambridge on 26 November 2007.
6 Middlemas, et al., p. 303.
7 Churchill Archives Centre, Churchill College, Cambridge: CHAR 18/4/5-7.
8 Mark Thomas, 'The macro-economics of the inter-war years', in Floud et al., p. 333.
9 Ibid., p. 339.
10 Tim Hatton, 'Unemployment and the labour market in inter-war Britain', in Floud et al., p. 360.
11 Mark Thomas, 'The macro-economics of the inter-war years', in Floud et al., p. 340.
12 Tim Hatton, 'Unemployment and the labour market in inter-war Britain', in Floud et al., p. 360.
13 Keynes, p. 17.
14 Ibid., p. 9.
15 Tim Hatton, 'Unemployment and the labour market in inter-war Britain', in Floud et al., p 374.
16 Keynes, pp. 5-6.
17 Ibid., pp. 8-9.
18 Ibid., p. 19.
19 Ibid., p. 17.
20 Ibid., p. 8.
21 Ibid., p. 21.
22 Lecture by Sir Martin Gilbert at Churchill College, Cambridge on 26 November 2007.
23 Enright, p. 151.
24 Martin, pp. 160-1.
25 Brendon, pp. 118-9.

Chapter 3. Disarmament: Weakening Britain's Defence in the 1920s
1 Omissi, p. 20.
2 Gilbert (1971-88), Vol. IV, p. 494.
3 Omissi, p. 21.
4 Ibid., p. 22.
5 Ibid., p. 23.
6 Ibid.
7 Ibid., p. 39.
8 Churchill Archives Centre, Churchill College, Cambridge: CHAR 16/34/20.
9 Ibid., CHAR 16/34/58.
10 Ibid., CHAR 16/34/64.
11 Ibid., CHAR 16/34/67.
12 Ibid., CHAR 17/16/6.
13 Ibid., CHAR 17/15/3.
14 Ibid., CHAR 17/16/22.
15 Ibid., CHAR 17/16/7.
16 Ibid., CHAR 17/16/78.
17 Ibid., CHAR 17/16/131.
18 James, Vol. III, pp. 3100-2.
19 Churchill Archives Centre, Churchill College, Cambridge: CHAR 17/15/169.
20 Ibid., CHAR 17/15/170.
21 Ibid., CHAR 17/15/179.
22 Ibid., CHAR 17/27/34-6.
23 Omissi, p. 39.
24 Gilbert (1971-88), Vol. IV, p 456.
25 Ibid., p. 458.
26 Ibid.
27 Ibid., p. 459.

28 Ibid., p. 463.
29 Ibid., p. 455.
30 Ibid., p. 677.
31 Enright, p. 75.
32 Ibid., p. 23.
33 Ibid., p. 58.
34 Middlemas, et al., p. 323.
35 Ibid., p. 320.
36 Churchill Archives Centre, Churchill College, Cambridge: CHAR 18/4/5-7.
37 Ibid., CHAR 18/32/29.
38 Ibid., CHAR 18/32/41.
39 Ibid., CHAR 18/4/8-9.
40 Ibid., CHAR 18/4/2.
41 Middlemas, et al., p. 336.
42 Churchill Archives Centre, Churchill College, Cambridge: CHAR 18/4/11.
43 Middlemas, et al., p. 326.
44 Chalmers, pp. 403-4.
45 Middlemas, et al., pp. 334-335.
46 Ibid., p. 335.
47 Ibid., p. 336.
48 Ibid., p. 339.

Chapter 4. Churchill under Baldwin: The Wilderness Years
1 Brendon, pp. 119-122.
2 James, Vol. V, p. 5004.
3 Ibid., pp. 4934-5.
4 Ibid., p. 4938.
5 Amery, (diary entry for 9 September 1942), p. 832.
6 Charmley (1993), p. 258.
7 Lecture by Sir Martin Gilbert at Churchill College, Cambridge on 26 November 2007.
8 James, Vol. V, p. 4985.
9 Gilbert (1971-88), Vol. V, Companion Vol. 2, p. 1325.
10 Charmley (1989), p. 55.
11 Middlemas, et al., p. 872.
12 Feiling, p. 278. Middlemas, et al., pp. 910-1.
13 Middlemas, et al., p. 824.
14 Ibid., p. 324.
15 Mowat, p. 475.
16 Young, p. 174.
17 Churchill, Sir Winston Spencer. (1948-54), Vol. I, pp. 66 & 77.
18 Mowat, p. 475.
19 Churchill, Sir Winston Spencer. (1948-54), Vol. I, p. 101.
20 Ibid., p. 93.
21 Ibid., p. 115.
22 Churchill, Sir Winston Spencer. (1947), p. 203.
23 Her Majesty's Stationary Office: CMD 4827; 1935, pp. 4, 6 & 10.
24 Mowat, p. 478.
25 Feiling, pp. 312-3.
26 Charmley (1989), p. 5.
27 Feiling, p. 315.
28 Ibid., pp. 313-4.
29 Churchill, Sir Winston Spencer. (1948-54), Vol. I, pp. 108,110 & 111.
30 Ibid., p. 107.
31 Ibid., p. 109.
32 Ibid.
33 Ibid., pp. 125 & 127.
34 Ibid., p. 189.

35 Ramsden, p. 349.
36 Churchill, Sir Winston Spencer. (1948-54), Vol. I, p. 129.
37 Ibid., pp. 178-9.
38 Williamson, Philip., Christian Conservatives and the Totalitarian Challenge, 1933-1940, The English Historical Review, Vol. 115, No. 462, June 2000, p 618. Gilbert (1971-88), Vol. V, Companion Vol. 3, pp. 290-1.
39 Churchill, Sir Winston Spencer. (1948-54), Vol. I, p. 169.
40 Ibid.
41 Charmley (1993), p. 296.
42 Churchill, Sir Winston Spencer. (1948-54), Vol. I, p. 88.
43 Ibid.
44 Ibid., p. 89.
45 Feiling, pp. 312-3.
46 Churchill, Sir Winston Spencer. (1948-54), Vol. I, pp. 93 & 98.
47 Ibid., pp.147-8.
48 Ibid., p. 148.
49 Ibid.
50 Ibid.
51 Ibid., pp. 151 & 154.
52 Ibid., p. 155.
53 Ibid., p. 152.
54 Brendon, p. 131.
55 Ibid.
56 Ibid.
57 Ibid.
58 Middlemas, et al., p. 1016.
59 Ibid., pp. 993, 999, 1002, 1006-10, 1012-13 & 1016.

Chapter 5. Churchill under Chamberlain: Appeasement
1 Brendon, p. 131.
2 Thorpe, p. 187.
3 Wright, pp. 69-70.
4 James, Vol. VI, pp. 6004-13.
5 Christopher Harvie, 'Alexander Frederick Douglas-Home, Lord Home of the Hirsel' in Eccleshall, p. 330.
6 Churchill, Sir Winston Spencer. (1948-54), Vol. I, p. 255.
7 Feiling, p. 315.
8 Ibid.
9 Ibid., pp. 315-6, 350 & 388.
10 Ibid., p. 318.
11 Ibid., pp. 316 & 387.
12 Ibid., p. 319.
13 Churchill, Sir Winston Spencer. (1948-54), Vol. I, p. 213.
14 Charmley (1989), p. 66. Charmley (1993), p. 335.
15 Feiling, pp. 347 8.
16 Churchill, Sir Winston Spencer. (1948-54), Vol. I, p. 214.
17 Ibid., p. 263.
18 Ibid., p. 214.
19 Charmley (1989), pp. 85 & 117.
20 Churchill, Sir Winston Spencer. (1948-54), Vol. I, p. 214.
21 Carley, passim.
22 Churchill, Sir Winston Spencer. (1948-54), Vol. I, pp. 229-30.
23 Ibid., pp. 225-6.
24 Ibid., p. 283.
25 Ibid., p. 284.
26 Ibid., pp. 283 & 286.
27 Ibid., p. 292.
28 Ibid., p. 294.

29 Ibid., p. 243.
30 Ibid., pp. 244-5.
31 Ibid., p. 245.
32 Ibid., p. 246.
33 Ibid., p. 250.
34 Ibid.
35 Ibid., pp. 263 & 265.
36 Ibid., p. 264.
37 Ibid., p. 271.
38 Feiling, pp. 347-8.
39 Ibid., p. 365.
40 Ibid., p. 364.
41 Ibid., pp. 360-1.
42 Churchill, Sir Winston Spencer. (1948-54), Vol. I, pp. 264-5.
43 Ibid., p. 271.
44 Feiling, p. 413.
45 Churchill, Sir Winston Spencer. (1948-54), Vol. I, pp. 277-8.
46 Ibid., p. 282.
47 Ibid., p. 281.
48 Feiling, p. 413.
49 Ibid., pp. 415-6.
50 Ibid., pp. 416-7.

Chapter 6. Norway: Gallipoli All Over Again
1 Brendon, pp. 135-6.
2 Wegener, p. 26.
3 Brendon, pp. 136-7.
4 Churchill, Sir Winston Spencer. (1948-54), Vol. I, pp. 429-30 & 433.
5 Admiralty papers: 205/2; received by War Cabinet in 1939: War Cabinet paper 57.
6 Cabinet papers: 66/4; received by War Cabinet in 1939: War Cabinet paper 162.
7 Raeder, p. 158.
8 Ibid., p. 163.
9 Ibid., p. 166.
10 Ibid.
11 Ibid., pp. 161-2.
12 Ibid., pp.163-4.
13 Ibid., p. 166.
14 Ibid., p. 167.
15 Feiling, p. 435.
16 Churchill, Sir Winston Spencer. (1948-54), Vol. I, p. 457. Raeder, p. 169.
17 Churchill, Sir Winston Spencer. (1948-54), Vol. I, p. 491.
18 Ibid., p. 470.
19 Ibid., p. 499.
20 Ibid., p. 490.
21 Ibid., pp. 495 & 497-8.
22 Ibid., pp. 508-9.
23 Feiling, p. 437. Mowat, p. 652.
24 Churchill, Sir Winston Spencer. (1940-54), Vol. I, p. 508.
25 Ibid., pp. 505-6.
26 Colville, (diary entry for 25 April 1940), p. 108.
27 Churchill Archives Centre, Churchill College, Cambridge: CHAR 23/2/1.
28 Ibid.
29 Churchill, Sir Winston Spencer. (1948-54), Vol. I, p. 474.
30 Charmley (1993), pp. 385-6 & 391.
31 Churchill, Sir Winston Spencer. (1948-54), Vol. I, p. 510.
32 Ibid., p. 490.
33 Churchill Archives Centre, Churchill College, Cambridge: CHAR 9/139B/161.

34 Churchill, Sir Winston Spencer. (1948-54), Vol. I, pp. 515 & 518.
35 Ibid., pp. 518-9.
36 Ibid., pp. 518-9 & 572.
37 Ibid., pp. 464-5.
38 Ibid., p. 473.
39 Ibid., p. 520.
40 Churchill Archives Centre, Churchill College, Cambridge: CHAR 19/2C/301.
41 Charmley (1993), pp. 387-8.
42 Churchill, Sir Winston Spencer. (1948-54), Vol. I, p. 474. Feiling, p. 437.
43 Feiling, p. 439.
44 Brooke, p. 187.
45 Ibid.
46 Ibid., pp. 189-190.
47 Ibid., p. 191.
48 Kimball (1984), Vol I, p. 494.
49 Ibid., p. 263.
50 Ibid., p. 278.
51 Ibid., p. 321.
52 Churchill, Sir Winston Spencer. (1948-54), Vol. I, p. 500.
53 Ibid., p. 511.
54 Ibid.

Chapter 7. Dunkirk: Churchill's Defeat
1 Gilbert (1971-88), Vol. VI, p. 302.
2 Churchill, Sir Winston Spencer. (1948-54), Vol. I, p. 520.
3 Ibid., pp. 523-4.
4 Brendon, p. 141.
5 Ismay, p. 116.
6 Churchill Archives Centre, Churchill College, Cambridge: CHAR 9/140B/100.
7 Ibid., CHAR 23/1/4.
8 Bond, pp. 27-8.
9 Sebag-Montefiore, pp. 550-1.
10 Keegan, p. 44.
11 Minart, p. 141.
12 Churchill, Sir Winston Spencer. (1948-54), Vol. II, pp. 38-9.
13 Ibid., p. 43.
14 Ibid., pp. 42-3.
15 Ibid., p. 43.
16 Sebag-Montefiore, p. 129.
17 Feiling, p. 448.
18 Royal Air Force official website: history, chapter 3, pp. 178-9.
19 Churchill Archives Centre, Churchill College, Cambridge: CHAR 23/2/1.
20 Churchill, Sir Winston Spencer. (1948-54), Vol. II, pp. 45-6.
21 Ibid., p. 38.
22 Wright, p. 119.
23 Churchill Archives Centre, Churchill College, Cambridge: CHAR 23/2/1.
24 Overy, p. 34.
25 Churchill, Sir Winston Spencer. (1948-54), Vol. II, p. 49.
26 Ibid., p. 52.
27 Ibid., p. 48.
28 Ibid., p. 52.
29 Ibid., p. 54.
30 Ibid., p. 62.
31 Ibid., pp. 74 & 76.
32 Churchill Archives Centre, Churchill College, Cambridge: CHAR 19/2A/97.
33 Churchill, Sir Winston Spencer. (1948-54), Vol. II, p. 91.
34 Ibid., p. 72.
35 Ibid., p. 72.
36 Ibid., p. 65.

37 Churchill Archives Centre, Churchill College, Cambridge: CHAR 23/2/1.
38 Royal Air Force official website: history, chapter 3, p. 99.
39 Churchill, Sir Winston Spencer. (1948-54), Vol. II, p. 84.
40 Brooke, p. 81.
41 Brooke, p. 81. Churchill, Sir Winston Spencer. (1948-54), Vol. II, p. 171.
42 Brooke, p. 82.
43 Churchill Archives Centre, Churchill College, Cambridge: CHAR 9/140A/5-8.
44 Ibid., CHAR 9/140A/10.
45 Ibid., CHAR 9/140A/7.
46 Churchill, Sir Winston Spencer. (1948-54), Vol. II, p. 86.
47 Churchill, Sir Winston Spencer. (1948-54), Vol. IV, pp. 273-4. Keegan, pp. 46-7.
48 Churchill, Sir Winston Spencer. (1948-54), Vol. II, p. 79.
49 Ibid., pp. 172 & 194.
50 Ibid. Vol. III, p. 33.
51 Enright, p. 45.
52 Churchill Archives Centre, Churchill College, Cambridge: CHAR 23/2/1.

Chapter 8. Battle of Britain: Dowding's Victory
1 James, Vol. VI, p. 6238.
2 Deighton, et al., p. 218.
3 Brown, p. 24.
4 Wright, pp. 51, 53 & 55.
5 Ibid., p. 54.
6 Ibid.
7 Royal Air Force official website: history, chapter 3, p. 101.
8 Churchill Archives Centre, Churchill College, Cambridge: CHAR 9/140A/45.
9 Churchill, Sir Winston Spencer. (1948-54), Vol. II, p. 284.
10 Brown, p. 36.
11 Wright, pp. 55-6
12 Middlemas, et al., pp. 781-3.
13 Churchill, Sir Winston Spencer. (1948-54), Vol. I, pp. 120-2.
14 Ibid. Vol. III, p .40.
15 Ibid., pp. 40-1.
16 Royal Air Force official website: history, chapter 3, p. 101.
17 Ibid., p. 104.
18 Churchill Archives Centre, Churchill College, Cambridge: CHAR 9/140A/45.
19 Brown, p. 52.
20 Hastings, Sir Max.: article in the Daily Mail, 26 August 2006.
21 Royal Air Force official website: history, chapter 3, p. 106.
22 Brown, p. 52.
23 Royal Air Force official website: history, chapter 3, p. 106.
24 Deighton, et al., p. 218.
25 Enright, p. 111. Brendon, p. 165.
26 Enright, p. 78.
27 Hill, Rod., from his father's notebooks (Churchill's projectionist): article in the Sunday Times, 18 November 2007.
28 Brendon, p. 153.
29 Royal Air Force official website: history, chapter 3, p. 109.
30 Overy, pp. 34-5.
31 Royal Air Force official website:

history, chapter 3, p. 109.
32 Brown, p. 63.
33 Royal Air Force official website: history, chapter 3, p. 110.
34 Gilbert (1971-88), Vol. VI, p. 785.
35 Churchill, Sir Winston Spencer. (1948-54), Vol. II, p. 297. Royal Air Force official website: history, chapter 3, p. 110.
36 Churchill, Sir Winston Spencer. (1948-54), Vol. II, p. 297.
37 Brown, p. 84.
38 Overy, p. 32.
39 Brown, p. 199.
40 Ibid., p. 200.
41 Bennett, pp. 117-8.
42 Brown, p. 197.
43 Churchill, Sir Winston Spencer. (1948-54), Vol. II, p. 286.

Chapter 9. The War at Sea: Churchill's Battleship Fetish
1 Raeder, p. 227.
2 Woodward, p. 136.
3 Pearce, pp. 212-3.
4 Woodward, p. 135.
5 Thompson, Walter Henry., p. 23.
6 Churchill, Sir Winston Spencer. (1948-54), Vol. I, pp. 385 & 387.
7 Churchill Archives Centre, Churchill College, Cambridge: CHAR 19/6/1.
8 Churchill, Sir Winston Spencer. (1948-54), Vol. I, p. 406.
9 Brendon, p. 137.
10 Churchill, Sir Winston Spencer. (1948-54), Vol. I, pp. 408 & 413-4.
11 Pearce, p. 41.
12 Churchill, Sir Winston Spencer. (1948-54), Vol. I, pp. 408 & 413-4.
13 Pearce, pp. 35 & 37.
14 Raeder, p. 163.
15 Churchill, Sir Winston Spencer. (1948-54), Vol. II, pp. 208-9.
16 Somerville, p. 43.
17 Roskill, pp. 157-8.
18 Churchill, Sir Winston Spencer. (1948-54), Vol. II, pp. 208-9.
19 Pearce, p. 62.
20 Ibid., p. 61.
21 Ibid., pp. 63, 66 & 69.
22 Royal Navy official website: history, Taranto, p. 1.
23 Churchill, Sir Winston Spencer. (1948-54), Vol. I, p. 394.
24 Pearce, p. 105.
25 Royal Navy official website: history, H.M.S. Hood, p. 2.
26 Pearce, p. 113.
27 Ibid., p. 114.
28 Ballard, pp.129-30 & 134.
29 Pearce, p. 124.
30 Ibid., pp. 129-30.
31 Churchill, Sir Winston Spencer. (1948-54), Vol. III, p. 53.
32 Ibid., p. 52.
33 Ibid., p. 550.
34 Pearce, p. 130.
35 Churchill, Sir Winston Spencer. (1948-54), Vol. III, p. 551.
36 Churchill Archives Centre, Churchill College, Cambridge: CHAR 20/36/4.
37 Churchill, Sir Winston Spencer. (1948-54), Vol. IV, pp. 99-100.
38 Pearce, pp. 211 & 222.

39 Churchill, Sir Winston Spencer. (1948-54), Vol. V, p. 245.
40 Brendon, pp. 137 & 157.
41 Edwards, p. 17.
42 Brendon, p. 137. The Naval Memoirs of Admiral J. H. Godfrey, Vol. V, 1939-1942, pp. 111-2, Churchill Archives Centre, Churchill College, Cambridge: GDFY 1/6.
43 Edwards, pp. 201-2.
44 Ibid., pp. 49-50.
45 Ibid., p. 74.
46 Churchill, Sir Winston Spencer. (1948-54), Vol. IV, p. 97.
47 Edwards, pp.101, 140, 188 & 213-4.
48 Churchill, Sir Winston Spencer. (1948-54), Vol. IV, p. 98.
49 Fenby, p. 131.
50 Woodward, pp. 146-152, 176-7 & 185-7.
51 Ibid., pp. 190-3 & 196-9.

Chapter 10. North Africa: Churchill's Dispersionist Strategy Takes Hold
1 Keegan, p. 57.
2 Westphal, General Siegfried. (operations officer under Erwin Rommel), interview for: The World at War, FremantleMedia Limited, 1973.
3 Churchill, Sir Winston Spencer. (1948-54), Vol. III, p. 491.
4 Ibid. Vol. II, p. 369.
5 Keegan, pp. 189 & 196.
6 Churchill, Sir Winston Spencer. (1948-54), Vol. III, p. 9.
7 Ibid., p. 14.
8 Ibid., p. 17.
9 Ibid., p. 16.
10 Ibid., pp. 17-18.
11 Ibid., p. 32.
12 Ibid., p. 59.
13 Ibid., p. 173.
14 Ibid., p. 97.
15 Keegan, p. 79.
16 Churchill, Sir Winston Spencer. (1948-54), Vol. III, p. 181.
17 Ibid., p. 186.
18 Brendon, pp. 180.
19 Churchill, Sir Winston Spencer. (1948-54), Vol. III, p. 212.
20 Ibid., p. 190.
21 Ibid., pp. 73-8.
22 Ibid., pp. 225, 287-8 & 424.
23 Keegan, p. 139.
24 Churchill, Sir Winston Spencer. (1948-54), Vol. III, p. 192.
25 Ibid.
26 Keegan, p. 202.
27 Brendon, p. 155.
28 Churchill, Sir Winston Spencer. (1948-54), Vol. III, pp. 308-310.
29 Keegan, p. 138.
30 Churchill, Sir Winston Spencer. (1948-54), Vol. III, p. 356.
31 Ibid., p. 357.
32 Ibid., pp. 360-1.
33 Ibid., p. 370.
34 Ibid., pp. 482 & 486.
35 Keegan, pp. 204-5.
36 Churchill, Sir Winston Spencer. (1948-54), Vol. IV, pp. 24-6.
37 Ibid., p. 30.
38 Keegan, p. 139.
39 Churchill, Sir Winston Spencer.

(1948-54), Vol. IV, p. 260.
40 Ibid., pp. 261 & 381.
41 Ibid., pp. 342-4.
42 Brendon, p. 174.
43 Churchill, Sir Winston Spencer.
(1948-54), Vol. IV, pp. 352-6.
44 Fenby, p. 131.
45 Churchill, Sir Winston Spencer.
(1948-54), Vol. IV, p. 383.
46 Ibid., pp. 415-420.
47 Ibid., pp. 527, 530-1, 536-8 & 644.
48 Ibid., p. 416.
49 Brendon, p. 179.
50 Sainsbury, pp. 20-1.
51 Ibid.
52 Ibid., p. 22.
53 Ibid., p. 23.
54 Ibid., pp. 24 & 197.
55 Ibid.
56 Ibid., pp. 25-6.
57 Ibid., pp. 26-7.
58 Clark, Mark., pp. 66 & 75.
59 Sainsbury, pp. 28-9.
60 Clark, Mark., p. 54.
61 Ibid., p. 65.
62 Ibid., p. 58.
63 Ibid., p. 74.
64 Ibid., pp. 75-6, 85, 92 & 99.
65 Ibid., p. 61.
66 Charmley (1993), p. 525.
67 Clark, Mark., p. 164.

Chapter 11. The Balkans: Churchill's Obsession
1 Churchill, Sir Winston Spencer.
(1948-54), Vol. III, p. 17.
2 Churchill Archives Centre, Churchill
College, Cambridge: CHAR 20/84/12.
3 Richardson, p. 21.
4 Ibid., pp. 55-6.
5 Churchill Archives Centre, Churchill
College, Cambridge: CHAR 23/10/52.
6 Fenby, p. 267.
7 Gilbert (1971-88), Vol. VI, p. 1043.
8 Churchill, Sir Winston Spencer.
(1948-54), Vol. III, p. 149.
9 Ibid., p. 84.
10 Ibid., p. 63.
11 Ibid., p. 149.
12 Ibid., p. 152.
13 Eden, Anthony., interview for:
The World at War, FremantleMedia
Limited, 1973.
14 Churchill, Sir Winston Spencer.
(1948-54), Vol. III, p. 146.
15 Ibid., p. 152.
16 Ibid., p. 154.
17 Ibid., p. 85.
18 Ibid., p. 89.
19 Ibid., p. 90.
20 Keegan, pp. 189 & 196.
21 Churchill, Sir Winston Spencer.
(1948-54), Vol. III, p. 198.
22 Ibid., p. 223.
23 Ibid., p. 247.
24 Ibid., p. 266.
25 Ibid., p. 259.
26 Brooke, pp. 458-9.
27 Ibid., p. 459.
28 Ibid., pp. 472-3.
29 Ibid., p. 473.
30 Fenby, p. 218.
31 Churchill, Sir Winston Spencer.
(1948-54), Vol. VI, pp. 63-4.

32 Ibid., p. 64.
33 Ibid., p. 65.
34 Ibid., p. 69.
35 Ibid., p. 252.
36 Ibid., pp. 255 & 260.
37 Ibid., p. 482.
38 Ibid., p. 483.
39 Sainsbury, p. 42.
40 Ibid., p. 43.
41 Churchill, Sir Winston Spencer.
(1948-54), Vol. III, p. 27.

Chapter 12. Dieppe: Churchill's Folly
1 Whitaker, pp. 43-4.
2 Eisenhower, David., pp. 84-5. Kelly,
Arthur., "Dieppe" Hamilton This
Month Magazine, October 1989.
3 Thompson, Reginald William., p. 162.
4 Brooke, p. 260.
5 Kimball (1984), Vol. 1, p. 515.
6 Sainsbury, p. 26.
7 Richardson, p. 13.
8 Ibid.
9 Sainsbury, p. 24.
10 National Archives of Canada,
Ottawa: Hughes-Hallett Papers, MG
30 E463.
11 Whitaker, pp. 68-9.
12 Public Record Office: DEFE 2/542.
WO 208/3573 M.I. 14/SIF/26/42,
29 June 1942. Goodspeed, p. 387.
Hamilton, p. 515.
13 Churchill, Sir Winston Spencer.
(1948-54), Vol. IV, p. 444.
14 Whitaker, pp. 192-4 & 9.
15 Ibid., p. 294.
16 Brendon, p. 176.
17 Churchill, Sir Winston Spencer.
(1948-54), Vol. IV, p. 458.
18 Whitaker, p. 45.
19 Ibid., p. 277.
20 Churchill, Sir Winston Spencer.
(1948-54), Vol. IV, p. 467.
21 Liddell Hart Centre for Military
Archives, King's College London: Ismay
II/3/244a & II/3/247/2b.
22 Gilbert (1986), p. 198.
23 Liddell Hart Centre for Military
Archives, King's College London: Ismay
II/3/248 & II/3/251/2a & II/3/261/4a.
24 Ibid. II/3/261/2.
25 Churchill, Sir Winston Spencer.
(1948-54), Vol. IV, p. 458.
26 Whitaker, pp. 282-3.
27 Thompson, Reginald William., p.
203.
28 Churchill, Sir Winston Spencer.
(1948-54), Vol. VI, p. 12.
29 Public Record Office: PREM 3/256.
30 Kennedy, p. 264.

**Chapter 13. The Far East:
Catastrophic Defeat**
1 Churchill Archives Centre, Churchill
College, Cambridge: CHAR 23/9/24.
2 Peter, p. 220.
3 Churchill, Sir Winston Spencer.
(1948-54), Vol. IV, p. 37.
4 Churchill Archives Centre, Churchill
College, Cambridge: CHAR 18/4/10.
5 Keegan, p. 261.
6 Churchill, Sir Winston Spencer.
(1948-54), Vol. III, p. 562.
7 Keegan, p. 261.

8 Churchill Archives Centre, Churchill
College, Cambridge: CHAR 23/9/59.
9 Churchill, Sir Winston Spencer.
(1948-54), Vol. IV, p. 42.
10 Brooke, p. 229.
11 Churchill Archives Centre, Churchill
College, Cambridge: CHAR 20/70/30.
12 Ibid., CHAR 20/70/37.
13 Thompson, Walter Henry., p. 87.
14 Keegan, p. 273.
15 Churchill, Sir Winston Spencer.
(1948-54), Vol. IV, p. 43.
16 Whitaker, p. 279.
17 Churchill, Sir Winston Spencer.
(1948-54), Vol. IV, p. 43.
18 Ibid. Vol. IV, p. 81.
19 Ibid. Vol. V, p. 78.
20 Brooke, p. 401.
21 Ibid., pp. 444-5.
22 Ibid., p. 446.
23 Ibid.
24 Ibid., p. 447.
25 Ibid., p. 456.
26 Ibid., p. 457.
27 Ibid., p. 524.
28 Ibid., p. 529.
29 Ibid., pp. 529-30.
30 Ibid., p. 532.
31 Ibid., p. 533.
32 Ibid., p. 533.
33 Ibid., p. 534.
34 Ibid., p. 550.
35 Ibid., p. xviii.
36 Ibid., pp. 578-9.
37 Peter, p. 186.
38 Slim, p. 523.
39 Ibid., p. 204.
40 Brooke, p. 588.
41 Ibid.
42 Ibid., p. 589.
43 Sainsbury, pp. 47 & 170-1.

**Chapter 14. Italy: The 'Soft
Underbelly' of Europe**
1 Brendon, p. 177.
2 Churchill, Sir Winston Spencer.
(1948-54), Vol. III, p. 489.
3 Churchill Archives Centre, Churchill
College, Cambridge: CHAR 23/10/52.
4 Clark, Mark., p. 13.
5 Charmley (1993), p. 525.
6 Churchill, Sir Winston Spencer.
(1948-54), Vol. IV, p. 590.
7 Brooke, (diary entry for 27 May
1942), p. 261.
8 Sainsbury, pp. 20-1. Charmley (1993),
p. 525.
9 Fenby, p. 169.
10 Brooke, p. 410.
11 Keegan, p. 117. Forty, p. 49.
12 Keegan, p. 117.
13 Clark, Mark., p. 174.
14 Churchill Archives Centre, Churchill
College, Cambridge: CHAR 23/10/60.
15 Ibid., CHAR 23/11/31.
16 Ibid., CHAR 20/159/78-83.
17 Richardson, p. 124.
18 Churchill, Sir Winston Spencer.
(1948-54), Vol. V, p. 85.
19 Clark, Mark., p. 215.
20 Clark, Mark., interview for: The
World at War, FremantleMedia
Limited, 1973.
21 Clark, Mark., p. 244.

22 Brendon, p. 180.
23 Sainsbury, pp. 20-1. Charmley (1993), p. 49.
24 Clark, Mark., p. 272.
25 Ibid., p. 248.
26 Ibid., p. 249.
27 Churchill Archives Centre, Churchill College, Cambridge: CHAR 20/156/66.
28 Clark, Lloyd., p. 272.
29 Brooke, p. 522.
30 Churchill Archives Centre, Churchill College, Cambridge: CHAR 20/173/21.
31 Churchill, Sir Winston Spencer. (1948-54), Vol. VI, p. 51.
32 Ibid., pp. 51-2.
33 Ibid., p. 75.

Chapter 15. The Second Front: Churchill Procrastinates
1 Clark, Mark., p. 57.
2 Brooke, p. 261.
3 Charmley (1993), p. 504.
4 Longmate, p. 217.
5 Kimball (1984), Vol. I, p. 458.
6 State Department, Foreign Relations of the US – FRUS- 1942, III, p. 594.
7 Whitaker, p. 51. Kimball (1984), Vol. I, pp. 436 & 448.
8 Pogue, pp. 319-320.
9 Kimball (1984), Vol. I, p. 459.
10 Ibid., p. 504.
11 Ibid., p. 515.
12 Brooke, p. 275.
13 Kimball (1984), Vol. I, p. 520.
14 Steele, p.160.
15 Sainsbury, pp. 30-1 & 181.
16 Kimball (1984), Vol. I, p. 529.
17 Whitaker, pp. 213-4.
18 Kimball (1984), Vol. I, p. 542.
19 Clark, Mark., p. 36.
20 Ibid., pp. 43-4.
21 Ibid., p. 66.
22 Richardson, p. 13.
23 Brooke, pp. 345-6.
24 Churchill Archives Centre, Churchill College, Cambridge: CHAR 23/10/63.
25 Ibid.
26 Ibid., CHAR 20/84/12.
27 Brooke, pp. 344-5.
28 Kimball (1984), Vol. II, pp. 48-9.
29 Churchill Archives Centre, Churchill College, Cambridge: CHAR 23/10/61.
30 Brooke, pp. 345-6.
31 Charmley (1993), pp. 518-9.
32 Enright, p. 23.
33 Brooke, pp. 347 & 349.
34 Sainsbury, p. 32.
35 Fenby, p. 190.
36 Sainsbury, p. 33.
37 Churchill, Sir Winston Spencer. (1948-54), Vol. V, pp. 134-5.
38 Sainsbury, pp. 45-6.
39 Ibid., p. 46.
40 Brooke, p. 519.
41 Ibid., p. 520.
42 Sainsbury, pp. 53-4.
43 Churchill, Sir Winston Spencer. (1948-54), Vol. V, p. 521.
44 Ibid., pp. 542-3.
45 Eisenhower, General Dwight., p. 269.
46 Churchill, Sir Winston Spencer. (1948-54), Vol. V, p. 543.
47 Ibid. Vol. VI, p. 52.

48 Ibid., p. 58.
49 Ibid., p. 61.
50 Ibid., p. 106.
51 Statistic for deaths in the European theatre for the final year of World War II. Research data provided to the author personally by Dr. Duncan Anderson, Head of the Department of War Studies, Royal Military Academy Sandhurst, and his colleagues: Rudiger Overman and Dr Aryk Nusbacher.
52 Churchill, Sir Winston Spencer. (1948-54), Vol. V, p. 226.

Chapter 16. The Bomber Offensive: The Lost Opportunity
1 Longmate, p. 355.
2 Kennedy, p. 97.
3 Hastings, pp. 53 & 97.
4 Probert, p. 132.
5 Hastings, pp. 97 & 106.
6 Overy, pp. 38-9.
7 Longmate, p. 130.
8 Ibid., p. 355.
9 Longmate, pp. 120-1.
10 Hastings, pp. 118 & 120.
11 Longmate, pp. 123-4.
12 Hastings, p. 121.
13 Ibid., p. 140.
14 Longmate, p. 131.
15 Ibid., pp. 132-3.
16 Hastings, p. 119.
17 Ibid., pp. 232-3.
18 Longmate, pp. 216-7.
19 Ibid., p. 217.
20 Ibid., pp. 223-4 & 226-7.
21 Ibid., p. 229.
22 Ibid., pp. 229 & 231.
23 Churchill, Sir Winston Spencer. (1948-54), Vol. IV, p. 495.
24 Richardson, p. 76.
25 Hastings, p. 107.
26 Ibid., p. 249.
27 Ibid., p. 180.
28 Longmate, pp. 232-4.
29 Ibid., pp. 235-6.
30 Ibid., p. 242.
31 Ibid., p. 243.
32 Ibid., p. 245.
33 Ibid., p. 251.
34 Churchill, Sir Winston Spencer. (1948-54), Vol. I, p. 119.
35 Longmate p. 251.
36 Ibid., pp. 251-2.
37 Hastings, pp. 228-9.
38 Longmate, p. 163.
39 Ibid., p. 252.
40 Hastings, p. 187.
41 Longmate, pp. 256, 261-2, 267 & 269.
42 Speer (1970), p. 284.
43 Hastings, p. 231.
44 Speer (1970), p. 284.
45 Longmate, pp. 280 & 288. Hastings, p. 247.
46 Probert, pp. 318 & 321.
47 Ibid., p. 318.
48 Ibid., p. 321.
49 Hastings, p. 115.
50 Probert, p. 344.
51 Hastings, p. 11.
52 Ibid., p. 245.
53 Ibid., pp. 227-9.
54 Galland, p. 279.

55 Longmate, p. 321.
56 Ibid., p. 322.
57 Webster, p. 252.
58 Longmate, p. 324.
59 Ibid., p. 357.
60 Speer (1976), (diary entry for 12 August 1959), pp. 339-40.
61 Speer, Albert., interview for: The World at War, FremantleMedia Limited, 1973.
62 Longmate, p. 355.
63 Ibid., p. 360.
64 Hastings, p. 118.
65 Ibid.
66 Ibid., p. 11.
67 Longmate, p. 361.
68 Ibid., p. 349.

Chapter 17. The 'Big Two' and the 'Big Three' Conferences
1 Brendon, p. 161.
2 Kimball (1997), p. 15.
3 Fenby, p. 50.
4 Brendon, p. 161.
5 Ibid., p. 162.
6 Fenby, p. 55.
7 Ibid., p. 57.
8 Ibid., p. 58.
9 Ibid., p. 59.
10 Brendon, p. 169.
11 Ibid., p. 170.
12 Sherwood, p. 446.
13 Fenby, p. 96.
14 Ibid., p. 102.
15 Ibid., pp. 101 & 111.
16 Churchill, Sir Winston Spencer. (1948-54), Vol. IV, pp. 297-300.
17 Fenby, p. 127.
18 Wedemeyer, pp. 164-5.
19 Fenby, p. 140.
20 Ibid., pp. 141-5.
21 Gillies, p. 133.
22 Fenby, p. 149.
23 Ibid., p. 164.
24 Ibid., p. 167.
25 Ibid., pp. 169-170.
26 Ibid., pp. 178-9.
27 Kimball (1997), p. 21.
28 Brendon, p. 179.
29 Fenby, p. 188.
30 Brooke, pp. 409-410.
31 Fenby, pp. 194-5.
32 Ibid., p. 197.
33 Ibid., p. 199.
34 Brooke, pp. 450-1.
35 Fenby, pp. 215-6.
36 Sainsbury, p. 46.
37 Fenby, p. 217.
38 Ibid., p. 219.
39 Moran, pp. 131-2.
40 Sainsbury, p. 47.
41 Ibid., p. 51.
42 Ibid., pp. 47-8.
43 Fenby, p. 258.
44 Fenby, pp. 257 & 361. Thorpe, p. 304.
45 Brendon, p.18.
46 Kimball, (1997), p. 21. Brendon, p. 184.
47 Fenby, pp. 265-6.
48 Ibid., p. 267.
49 Brooke, p. 589.
50 Ibid., p. 592.
51 Fenby, p. 311.

52 Ibid., p. 312.
53 Churchill, Sir Winston Spencer. (1948-54), Vol. VI, p. 407.
54 Fenby p. 214.
55 Ambrose, pp. 46 & 79.
56 Fenby, p.322.
57 Enright, p. 25.
58 Brendon, p. 166.
59 Fenby, pp. 322-3.
60 Enright, p. 42.
61 Fenby, pp. 323-4.
62 Ibid., p. 325.
63 Enright, p. 68.
64 Richardson, p. 105.
65 Fenby, p. 351.
66 Churchill Archives Centre, Churchill College, Cambridge: CHAR 23/15/5.
67 Avon Papers, Birmingham University Library, AP 20/1/25.
68 Charmley (1993), pp. 110 & 304.
69 Brendon, p. 183.
70 Avon Papers, Birmingham University Library, AP 20/1/25. Fenby, pp. 193 & 352.
71 Fenby, p. 361.
72 War Cabinet Minutes: 19 & 21 February 1945, Public Record Office: CAB 65/51.
73 Manuscript of broadcast on 30 November 1974; Earl of Home papers, Hirsel, Coldstream.
74 Churchill Archives Centre, Churchill College, Cambridge: CHAR 23/14/19.
75 Enright, p. 88.
76 Thorpe, p. 308.
77 Fenby, p. 410.
78 Moran, pp. 275-6 & 279.
79 Cadogan, p. 765.
80 Churchill, Sir Winston Spencer. (1948-54), Vol. VI, p. 399.
81 Ibid., p. 400.

Chapter 18. General Election Defeat: Into Opposition
1 Charmley (1993), pp. 147 & 150.
2 Thorpe, pp. 302 & 336.
3 Charmley (1993), pp. 637-9.
4 Ibid.
5 Ibid.
6 Knight, p. 58.
7 Charmley (1993), pp. 523-4.
8 Ibid., p. 640.
9 Ibid., p. 645.
10 Enright, p. 67.
11 Charmley (1993), pp. 523-4.
12 Ibid., p. 641.
13 Thorpe, p. 314.
14 Charmley (1993), p. 645.
15 Churchill, Sir Winston Spencer. (1948-54), Vol. VI, p. 530.
16 Charmley (1993), p. 645.
17 Knight, p. 38.
18 Ibid., pp. 37, 77 & 128.
19 Thorpe, pp. 319 & 335.
20 Charmley (1993), p. 646.
21 Enright, p. 21.
22 Charmley (1993), p. 647.
23 Enright, pp. 79 & 151.
24 Thorpe, p. 337.
25 Ibid.
26 Ibid., p. 345.
27 Brendon, p. 202.
28 Hennessy, p. 280.

29 Thorpe, pp. 346-7.
30 Churchill Archives Centre, Churchill College, Cambridge: CHUR 2/18/7-9.
31 Ibid.
32 Ibid.
33 Hennessy, pp. 282-3.
34 Thorpe, p. 308.
35 Enright, p. 18.
36 Churchill Archives Centre, Churchill College, Cambridge: CHUR 2/18/7.
37 Seldon, p. 396.
38 Ibid., p. 397.
39 Thorpe, p. 349.
40 Seldon, p. 39.
41 Thorpe, p. 350.
42 Knight, pp. 58-59. Seldon, pp. 18-19.
43 Seldon, p. 25.
44 Knight, pp. 60 & 128. Seldon, p. 25.

Chapter 19. The Last Tired Government
1 Seldon, pp. 54 & 71.
2 Enright, p. 135.
3 Ferris, pp. 91-3.
4 Thornhill, p. 2.
5 Seldon, pp. 28-29 & 296.
6 Ibid., pp. 28-29 & 94-5 & 102-5.
7 Knight, p. 40.
8 Ibid., p. 60.
9 Ibid., p. 128.
10 Seldon, p. 244.
11 Hennessy, p. 308.
12 Knight, pp. 146-7.
13 Seldon, pp. 296-7.
14 Ibid., pp. 171-2.
15 Told to the author personally by Professor Andrew Gamble.
16 Churchill Archives Centre, Churchill College, Cambridge: CHUR 6/3A/31.
17 Seldon, pp. 355, 364, 369, 370 & 374.
18 Hennessy, p. 290.
19 Knight, p. 169.
20 Ibid.
21 Ibid., p. 170.
22 Hennessy, pp. 283 & 288.
23 Knight, pp. 170-1.
24 Thornhill, p. 2.
25 Ibid., pp. 4 & 5.
26 Public Record Office: FO 800/768 Eg/52/15, 30 January 1952.
27 Thornhill, pp. 55 & 228 (note 56).
28 Public Record Office: FO 371/96985 JE1202/2.
29 Thornhill, p. 92.
30 Ibid., p. 180.
31 Shuckburgh, p. 29.
32 Public Record Office: PREM 11/463 10-11, 23 April 1953.
33 Kyle, p. 464.
34 Public Record Office: FO 371/102761 JE1052/16G, 15 January 1953.
35 Shuckburgh, p. 32.
36 Seldon, p. 397.
37 Ibid., pp. 390-1.
38 Churchill Archives Centre, Churchill College, Cambridge: CHUR 6/3A/112.
39 Seldon, p. 400.
40 Ibid., p. 519 (note 59).
41 Thorpe, p. 395.
42 Seldon, p. 401.
43 Ibid., p. 402.

44 Ibid., p. 403.
45 Ibid., pp. 404-5 & 407.
46 Churchill Archives Centre, Churchill College, Cambridge: CHUR 6/3A/42.
47 Ibid., CHUR 6/3B/176.
48 Ibid., CHUR 6/3A/28.
49 Ibid., CHUR 6/3B/142.
50 Seldon, p. 391.
51 Ibid., p. 38.
52 Ibid., p. 43.
53 Ibid., pp. 390-1.
54 Churchill Archives Centre, Churchill College, Cambridge: CHUR 6/4/87.
55 Ibid., CHUR 6/4/6-7.
56 Ibid., CHUR 6/4/6-7.
57 Ibid., CHUR 6/4/43.
58 Ibid., CHUR 6/4/101.
59 Ibid., CHUR 6/4/20-23.
60 Thorpe, p. 418.
61 Ibid., p. 419.
62 Seldon, p. 51.
63 Thorpe, p. 427.
64 Ibid., pp. 427-9.

Chapter 20. Conclusion: The Reckoning
1 The quote has been attributed variously to Albert Einstein, Benjamin Franklin, the author Rita Mae Brown, and as an old Chinese proverb.
2 Enright, p. 40.
3 Statistic for deaths in the European theatre for the final year of World War II. Research data provided to the author personally by Dr Duncan Anderson, Head of the Department of War Studies, Royal Military Academy Sandhurst, and his colleagues: Rudiger Overman and Dr Aryk Nusbacher.
4 Brooke, pp. 409-410.
5 Thorpe, p. 322.
6 Brooke, p. xxi.
7 Feiling, p. 381.
8 Churchill, Sir Winston Spencer. (1948-54), Vol. I, p 251.
9 Enright, p. 40.
10 Hegel, p. 295.
11 Told to the author personally by Professor Stuart Weir.

BIBLIOGRAPHY

Ambrose, Stephen., *Eisenhower and Berlin, 1945: the Decision to Halt at the Elbe*, New York: W. W. Norton, 1967.

Amery, Leopold., *The Empire at Bay: the Leo Amery Diaries 1929-1945*, London: Hutchinson, 1988.

Ballard, Robert., *The Discovery of the Bismarck*, Toronto: Madison Publishing, 1990.

Beaverbrook, Max., (Max Aitken, Baron), *Men and Power, 1917-1918*, London: Collins, 1956.

Bennett, Air-Vice Marshall Donald., *Pathfinder: a War Autobiography*, London: Muller, 1958.

Blake, Robert., *The Unknown Prime Minister; the Life and Times of Andrew Bonar Law, 1858-1923*, London: Eyre & Spottiswoode, 1955.

Bond, B., *Liddell Hart: A Study in Military Thought*, London: Cassell, 1976.

Brendon, P., *Winston Churchill: a Brief Life*, London: Secker & Warburg, 1984.

Brooke, Alan., (Field Marshall Lord Alanbrooke), *War Diaries 1939-1945*, Danchev, Alex., and Todman, Daniel., Eds., London: Weidenfeld & Nicolson, 2001.

Brown, P., *Honour Restored*, Spellmount, Staplehurst, 2005.

Cadogan, Alexander., *Diaries*, London: Cassell, 1971.

Carley, Michael Jabara., *1939-1945: The Alliance that Never Was and the Coming of World War II*, Chicago, Ill.: Ivan R. Dee, 1999.

Chalmers, William Scott., *The life and Letters of David, Earl Beatty, Admiral of the Fleet, Viscount Borodale of Wexford, Baron Beatty of the North Sea and of Brooksby, P.C., G.C.B., O.M., G.C.V.O., D.S.O., D.C.L., LL. D.*, London: Hodder and Stoughton, 1951.

Charmley, John., *Chamberlain and the Lost Peace*, London: A John Curtis Book: Hodder & Stoughton, 1989.

Churchill: The End of Glory, London: A John Curtis Book: Hodder & Stoughton, 1993.

Churchill, Randolph Spencer., *Winston S Churchill*, London: Heinemann,1966-69.

Churchill, Sir Winston Spencer., *Great Contemporaries*, London: Odhams Press Limited, 1949, c1947.

The Second World War, London: Cassell & Co. Ltd., 1948-1954.

The World Crisis, Vol. II, London: Thornton Butterworth Limited, 1923.

Clark, Lloyd., *Anzio: The Friction of War: Italy and the Battle for Rome 1944*, London: Headline Publishing Group, 2006.

Clark, Lieutenant-General Mark., *Calculated Risk*, London: George G. Harrap & Co. Ltd., 1951.

Colville, Sir John., *The Fringes of Power: Downing Street Diaries, 1939-1955*, London: Hodder & Stoughton, 1985.

Deighton, Len., & Hastings, Sir Max., *Battle of Britain*, Ware: Wordsworth Editions, 1999, c1980.

Dugdale, Blanche., *Arthur James Balfour, First Earl of Balfour by his Niece*, Vol. II, London: Hutchinson, 1936.

Eccleshall, Robert., & Walker, Graham., Eds. *Biographical Dictionary of British Prime Ministers*, London: Routledge, 1998.

Edwards, Captain Bernard., *Dönitz and the Wolf Packs*, London: Arms and Armour Press, 1996.

Eisenhower, David., *Eisenhower at War*, New York: Random House, 1986.

Eisenhower, General Dwight David., *Crusade in Europe*, London: W. Heinemann, 1948.

Enright, Dominique., *The Wicked Wit of Winston Churchill*, London: Michael O'Mara Books Limited, 2001.

Feiling, Sir Keith., *The Life of Neville Chamberlain*, London: Macmillan & Co. Ltd., 1946.

Fenby, Jonathan., *Alliance: The Inside Story of How Roosevelt, Stalin & Churchill Won One War & Began Another*, London: Simon & Schuster, 2006.

Ferris, Paul., *Sir Huge: The Life of Huw Wheldon*, London: Michael Joseph, 1990.

Floud, Roderick., & McCloskey, Donald., Eds. *The Economic History of Britain Since 1700*, Vol. II, second edition, Cambridge: Cambridge University Press, 1994.

Forty, George., *The Armies of George S. Patton*, London: Arms and Armour, 1996.

Galland, Generalleutnant Adolf., *The First and the Last: the German Fighter Force in World War II*, London: Methuen, 1955.

Gilbert, Sir Martin., *Winston S. Churchill*, London: Heinemann, 1971-1988.

Road to Victory: Winston S. Churchill 1941-1945, Toronto: Stoddard, 1986.

Gillies, Donald., *Radical Diplomat, The Life of Archibald Clark Kerr*, London: I.B. Taurus, 1999.

Goodspeed, Major Donald., *Battle Royal: A History of the Royal Regiment of Canada*, Toronto: Royal Regiment of Canada Association, 1962.

Hamilton, Nigel., *Monty: The Making of a General 1887-1942*, London: Coronet Edition, 1984.

Hastings, Sir Max., *Bomber Command*, London: Joseph, 1979.

Hennessy, Peter., *Having It So Good: Britain in the Fifties*, London: Penguin, 2007, c 2006.

Hegel, Georg., *Philosophy of Right*, translated with notes by Knox, Thomas., Oxford: Clarendon Press, 1942.

Ismay, General the Lord Hastings., *The Memoirs of General the Lord Ismay*, London: Heinemann, 1960.

James, Robert Rhodes., Ed. *Winston S. Churchill: his Complete Speeches, 1897-1963*, Chelsea House Publishers in association with R.R. Bowker Company, New York and London, 1974.

Keegan, Sir John., Ed. *Churchill's Generals*, London: Weidenfeld & Nicolson, 1991.

Kennedy, General Sir John., *The Business of War*, London: Hutchinson, 1957.

Keynes, John Maynard., *The Economic Consequences of Mr Churchill*, Stockport: Peveril, 1987, facsimile reprint: London, 1925.

Kimball, Warren., Ed. *Churchill & Roosevelt: The Complete Correspondence*, Princeton University Press, Princeton, New Jersey, 1984.

Forged in War: Churchill, Roosevelt and the Second World War, London: HarperCollins, 1997.

Knight, Nigel., *Governing Britain since 1945*, London: Politicos, 2006.

Kyle, Keith., *Suez*, London: Weidenfeld & Nicolson, 1991.

Longmate, Norman., *The Bombers: the RAF Offensive Against Germany 1939-1945*, London: Hutchinson, 1983.

Martin, Kingsley., *Father Figures*, London: Hutchinson & Co Ltd., 1966.

Marder, Arthur., Ed. *Fear God and Dread Nought: Correspondence of Admiral of the Fleet Lord Fisher*, Vol. II, London: Jonathan Cape, 1956.

From the Dreadnought to Scapa Flow: the Royal Navy in the Fisher era, 1904-1919, Vol. II, London: Oxford University Press, 1965.

Massie, Robert K., *Dreadnought: Britain, Germany and the Coming of the Great War*, London: Pimlico, 1991.

McEwen, John., Ed., *The Riddell Diaries 1908-1923*, London: Athlone, 1986.

Middlemas, Keith., & Barnes, John., *Baldwin: A Biography*, London: Weidenfeld & Nicolson, 1969.

Minart, Jacques., *P. C. Vincennes: Secteur 4*, Vol. II, Paris, 1945.

Moran, Lord Charles., *Winston Churchill: the Struggle for Survival, 1940-1965*, London: Constable, 1966.

Morgan, Ted., *Churchill: Young Man in a Hurry*, New York: Simon and Schuster, 1982.

Mowat, Charles., *Britain between the Wars, 1918-1940*, London: Methuen, 1955.

Omissi, David., *Air Power and Colonial Control: The Royal Air Force, 1919-1939*, Manchester: Manchester University Press, 1990.

Overy, Richard., *The Air War 1939-1945*, London: Europa, 1980.

Pearce, Frank., *Sea War: Great Naval Battles of World War II*, London: Hale, 1990.

Peter, Lawrence., Ed. *Quotations for our Time*, London: Magnum Books, Methuen paperbacks Ltd., 1980.

Pogue, Forrest., *George C. Marshall: Ordeal and Hope, 1939-1942*, New York: Viking, 1966.

Probert, Air Commodore Henry., *Bomber Harris: his Life and Times: the Biography of Marshal of the Royal Air Force, Sir Arthur Harris, the Wartime Chief of Bomber Command*, London: Greenhill, 2001.

Raeder, Großadmiral Erich., *Struggle for the Sea*, London: William Kimber, 1959.

Ramsden, John., *The Age of Balfour and Baldwin 1902-1940*, London: Longman, 1978.

Richardson, Stewart., Ed. *The secret History of World War II: the Ultra-Secret Wartime Letters and Cables of Roosevelt, Stalin and Churchill*, London: W.H. Allen, 1987, c1986.

Roskill, Captain Stephen., *Churchill and the Admirals*, London: Collins, 1977.

Sainsbury, Keith., *Churchill and Roosevelt at War: the War They Fought and the Peace they Hoped to Make*, Basingstoke: Macmillan, 1996.

Sebag-Montefiore, Hugh., *Dunkirk: Fight to the Last Man*, London: Penguin, 2007.

Seldon, Anthony., *Churchill's Indian Summer: the Conservative Government, 1951-55*, London: Hodder and Stoughton, 1981.

Sherwood, Robert., *Roosevelt and Hopkins*, New York: Harpers, 1948.

Shuckburgh, Evelyn., *Descent to Suez: Diaries 1951-56*, London: Weidenfeld & Nicolson, 1986.

Slim, William., (Field Marshall, 1st Viscount), *Defeat into Victory*, London: Cassell, 1956.

Somerville, Vice-Admiral Sir James., *The Somerville Papers*, Publications of the Navy Records Society, Vol. 134, Cambridge University Press, 1996.

Speer, Albert., *Inside the Third Reich*, London: Weidenfeld & Nicolson, 1970.

Spandau: the Secret Diaries, London: Collins, 1976.

Steele, Richard., *The First Offensive, 1942: Roosevelt, Marshall and the Making of American Strategy*, Bloomington: Indiana university Press, 1973.

Thompson, Reginald William., *Dieppe at Dawn; the Story of the Dieppe Raid*, London: Hutchinson, 1956.

Thompson, Walter Henry., *I was Churchill's Shadow*, London: Christopher Johnson, 1951.

Thornhill, Michael., *Road to Suez: the Battle of the Canal Zone*, Stroud: Sutton, 2006.

Thorpe, D. R., *Eden: the Life and Times of Anthony Eden, First Earl of Avon, 1897-1977*, London: Chatto & Windus, 2003.

Webster, Sir Charles., & Frankland, Noble., *The Strategic Air Offensive against Germany*, Vol. 3, HMSO, 1961.

Wedemeyer, Albert., *Wedemeyer Reports!*, New York: Henry Holt, 1958.

Wegener, Vizeadmiral Wolfgang., *The Naval Strategy of the World War*, translated by Holger H. Herwig, Naval Institute Press, Annapolis, Maryland, 1989.

Whitaker, Brigadier General Denis., & Whitaker, Shelagh., *Dieppe: Tragedy to Triumph*, London: Cooper, 1992.

Woodward, David., *The Tirpitz*, London: William Kimber, 1953.

Wright, Robert., *Dowding and the Battle of Britain*, London: MacDonald, 1969.

Young, George Malcolm., *Stanley Baldwin*, London: R. Hart-Davis, 1952.

ACKNOWLEDGMENTS

Professor Stuart Weir and Dr Michael Thornhill provided wonderful help with the book and I can't thank them enough. Also, many thanks to Gavin Fowells for his informal contributions.

I wish to thank everyone at Cambridge who has helped me in my work at the University, but particularly the Master of Darwin College, Professor William Brown, for his unstinting support, and my colleague Dr Kanak Patel, Fellow of Magdalene College, for her exceptional help and support over so many years.

I very much wish to thank the Fellows at Churchill College, who have provided such an agreeable environment in which to undertake research and conduct teaching. The Master, Professor Sir David Wallace; the Senior Tutor, Richard Partington, and Professor David Newbery have been particularly agreeable. I would also very much like to thank my colleague Dr Tiago Cavalcanti for his co-operation in all aspects of my work at the College as well as his help with the book.

The Churchill Archives Centre at Churchill College has been a wonderful source of information and the staff have all been immensely helpful, and I wish to thank them all: the Director, Allen Packwood, and the Archivists – Natalie Adams, Sophie Bridges, Caroline Herbert, Claire Knight, Sarah Lewery, Sandra Marsh, Andrew Riley, Julie Sanderson, Katharine Thomson, Bridget Warrington and Elizabeth Wells.

I wish to give special thanks to Neil Baber at the Publishers for his immense help and support throughout, and to Verity Muir, Sarah Wedlake, Emily Pitcher and Beverley Jollands for their excellent editorial work. Most importantly of all I wish to thank Sally Goodsell, without whom this book would not have been possible.

None of the foregoing are in any way responsible for the content and argument of the book; for all of this, I take full personal responsibility.

Nigel Knight
Cambridge
January 2008

PICTURE CREDITS

Picture credits: Picture researcher: Tehmina Boman tehmina@btconnect.com
1 Churchill/Manchester Mirrorpix; **2** Churchill/Lloyd George Mirrorpix; **3** Admiral Jackie Fisher Popperfoto/Getty Images; **4** British Commission/Cairo Getty Images; **5** Churchill arrives/ Buckingham Palace Mirrorpix; **6** Churchill/budget day Mirrorpix; **7** John Maynard Keynes Bettmann/ CORBIS; **8** Churchill/Baldwin/A Chamberlain Getty Images; **9** Churchill/Baldwin Bettmann/ CORBIS; **10** Churchill/Chamberlain Hulton-Deutsch Collection/CORBIS; **11** Churchill/Bracken Mirrorpix; **12** Marshall Ferdinand Foch Bettmann/CORBIS; **13** Churchill/war cabinet Mirrorpix; **14** Sir Claude Auchinleck Bettmann/CORBIS; **15** Hugh Dowding Getty Images; **16** Lord Cherwell Getty Images; **17** Supreme War Council/Paris Popperfoto/Getty Images; **18** Churchill/Montgomery/ Brooke Bettmann/CORBIS; **19** Churchill/Tito Bettmann/CORBIS; **20** Lord Louis Mountbatten Getty Images; **21** Churchill/Normandy Mirrorpix; **22** Churchill/George Marshall Getty Images; **23** Eisenhower/Clark Time & Life Pictures/Getty Images; **24** Arthur Harris Getty Images; **25** Churchill/ Roosevelt Mirrorpix; **26** Casablanca conference Mirrorpix; **27** Churchill/Roosevelt/Stalin Mirrorpix; **28** Churchill/War leaders Getty Images; **29** 'Big Three' conference/Yalta Mirrorpix; **30** Churchill/ election speech Mirrorpix; **31** Churchill retires/No. 10 Mirrorpix; **32** Churchill/Eden Getty Images; **Front cover** Churchill portrait Mirrorpix; **Back cover** Churchill/War leaders Getty Images.

INDEX